VIOLENCE AND CRIME IN LATIN AMERICA

VIOLENCE AND CRIME
IN LATIN AMERICA

REPRESENTATIONS AND POLITICS

EDITED BY **GEMA SANTAMARÍA**
AND **DAVID CAREY JR.**

PREFACE BY CECILIA MENJÍVAR

EPILOGUE BY DIANE E. DAVIS

University of Oklahoma Press : Norman

Library of Congress Cataloging-in-Publication Data

Names: Santamaría, Gema, 1979– editor. | Carey, David, Jr., 1967– editor.
Title: Violence and crime in Latin America : representations and politics / edited by
   Gema Santamaría and David Carey Jr. ; preface by Cecilia Menjívar.
Description: Norman : University of Oklahoma Press, [2017] | Includes bibliographical
   references and index.
Identifiers: LCCN 2016027829 | ISBN 978-0-8061-5574-6 (pbk. : alk. paper)
Subjects: LCSH: Violence—Latin America. | Crime—Latin America. | Violent
   crimes—Latin America.
Classification: LCC HN110.5.Z9 V58165 2017 | DDC 303.6098—dc23
LC record available at https://lccn.loc.gov/2016027829

Contents

Illustrations

Tables

Preface

Cecilia Menjívar

A recent NBC news report claims that "for more than half a century, Latin America has ruled the world as the most violent place on earth."[1] The statistics on which this claim is based are exceedingly alarming. For several years Honduras had the highest homicide rate in the world, but it was recently replaced by its neighbor El Salvador. About one-third of the murders that took place globally in 2013 were committed in Latin America, a region that contains roughly 8 percent of the world's population. And the United Nations Office on Drugs and Crime's Global Study on Homicide reports that thirteen out of the top twenty countries with the highest murder rates are located in Latin America. Is there something about Latin America that creates such levels of violence? Is it perhaps the region's history, which includes the brutal heritage of the conquest through violence?

There have been several explanations for the images of violence that are associated with Latin America. Given that Latin America is the most socioeconomically unequal region in the world, it has made sense to focus on the strong association between trends of inequality and poverty and violence, even when it is difficult to establish direct causality. It is also conceivable that weak justice systems vulnerable to corruption might be partly responsible for the high rates of violence. Quite plausibly, trends of violence may have roots in the systemic nature of state terror implemented throughout the region in collaboration with U.S. interests since the mid-twentieth century. Or perhaps the Latin American trends of violence, particularly their highly lethal form, are the outcome of a combination of all these deeply intertwined factors.

The present volume sheds light on a critical factor that helps us to make sense of the depictions of violence from Latin America: *perceptions* of crime are just as important as the violent acts themselves in shaping responses to generalized violence. By focusing on representations and on how the public makes sense of violence and crime, the authors in this collection open a window into a crucial piece of the puzzle that has received little attention. Through understanding how violence and crime have been represented and legitimized, how they have been interpreted and justified by those in power, and how they have been resisted or contested, we can begin to understand why crime and violence have persisted through time in so many different corners of Latin America. Equally important, this approach also permits a deeper understanding of why responses to violence have seemed to take similar shape across the region. A particularly insightful contribution of this volume is that it opens up our analytical lens to include the manifold forms of violence that on the surface may not seem linked, and it does so by placing them in a broad historical context. Although the contributions are primarily concerned with physical violence or crime, they do not give primacy to these forms of violence. This general approach helps us to make sense of how present forms of violence have come to be, why some of them persist, and how new ones are created, and, as such, it informs public policy practices that can alter present trends.

The focus on a host of actors who produce representations of crime and violence—beyond the bureaucrats and authorities directly involved in justice systems—helps to unearth the everyday, often naturalized views of violent practices that in turn sustain overall violent structures. It is at this level that representations of violence acquire the power to influence various publics by shaping their views, minds, and responses. Entering the field of representation, public debate, and political discourse allows us to see how Latin Americans perceive, make sense of, and respond to violent practices and crime, as well as how violent practices are routinized and made part of life, a key mechanism for the enduring character of violence in the region. This superb compilation is therefore poised to contribute a fundamental angle to our understandings of violence in Latin America.

The enduring character of multifaceted violence and the representations of such violence in Latin America evoke an array of public

responses. These range from resistance and efforts to quell violent practices to tacit approval of extreme measures that the state may have at
its disposal to subjugate problematic groups. Given the region's recent
history of civil wars, military coups, and state terror, it is puzzling to
see that the public today often seems to favor a return to dictatorship,
military strategies, a general "heavy hand," and even military coups to
combat the violence they are experiencing. To observers, the incongru-
ity between the routine violations of human rights during the brutal
dictatorships of the recent past and the calls by several publics today
for their governments to institute similar militaristic tactics to address
the acute levels of fear and insecurity borders on irrational. How is it
possible that people who suffered the atrocities of dictatorships can long
for a return to that ruthless past? Examining these questions through
the lens of representation, particularly where lines between criminal and
state violence are blurred, may provide some answers.

A major source of sanctioned violence reemerging in Latin America
today comes from the push toward a return to militarization, as experiences and images of past repressive strategies are recast as solutions
to contemporary problems.[2] Representations that blur lines between
the coercive practices of state actors and the violent acts of other groups
are particularly effective. This blurring of lines facilitates normalizing,
erasing, and accepting violent practices and abuses as an answer to current levels of insecurity. Such blurring occurs when violent practices of
state actors and of non-state actors are entwined, such as when vigilante
groups, cartels, narco-traffickers, and gang members use similar military-style operations to reach their objectives, or when members of these
different groups actually collaborate in illicit activities and violent practices. Images of this comingling of forces acquire transformative potential when publics can no longer tell which group is responsible for the
violence, which group is using legal or nonlegal means, or whether the
violence perpetrated is considered legal or illegal. When gang members
dress as soldiers and carry military-type weapons, or when plainclothes
soldiers patrol the streets and engage in unscrupulous activities, the
public consumes images that erase boundaries and normalize violence.
Violence becomes all-encompassing, can come from anyone, is every-
where, and is enduring, and as such it becomes part of life.

But demarcations are also concealed when the actions of different
state agents with presumably different objectives, such as police and

soldiers, become undifferentiated in the public's eyes. Although the police are supposed to protect and serve and soldiers are trained to defend against an enemy of the state, when both rely on similar forms of violence to execute their tasks, the public can no longer discern the responsibilities or objectives of either group. This is the case when military units conduct daily patrols in urban and rural areas, schools, bus stops, tourist centers, and banks. As part of the so-called war on drugs, police forces in countries like Mexico, Brazil, Colombia, and Honduras mix police and army training, and the result is an enforcement agency closer to an army than a police force. To cement images that weaken lines of demarcation between the police and the army in the Honduran case, the uniforms of the new police force resemble soldiers' attire and they carry military-style assault weapons. Images and practices that blur lines become particularly influential in transforming minds and views when they are regularly reproduced for the public through the media. These representations have the potential to engender fear and insecurity today but also to trace an indelible, powerful link to the violence of the past, so that violence becomes perpetual, and in the minds of the people, perhaps unavoidable.

The disproportionate use of force resulting from the commingling of various state enforcement agencies therefore results in a spiral of violence. The muddying of lines generates a sense of all-encompassing violence that often reproduces the prevailing extreme violence of the years of dictatorship and authoritarian regimes in the recent past. Indeed, the joint army-police operations now commonplace in Mexico, Brazil, Honduras, Guatemala, and El Salvador closely resemble the army brutality prior to the democratic transition in these countries. Today, as during the violence of past years, disappearances, tortured bodies, military patrols, kidnappings, and cold-blooded killings in front of family members take place with regularity and impunity. Within this context, new forms of violence have been produced and others have been transformed, such as the killings of women because they are women with governmental impunity.

Furthermore, modalities of violence across the region seem to be converging, as the violence we see in Mexico resembles what El Salvador, Guatemala, and Honduras have been experiencing, and some forms of violence today are similar to those employed by past repressive military regimes in countries such as Chile, Argentina, and Colombia. At the same time, gangs have started to adopt names that fuse presumed sources of violence, as has a faction of a Salvadoran gang that has renamed itself "the Revolutionaries." These images, routinized and entrenched in everyday life, contribute to naturalizing the coercive force of the state such that the public starts to imagine that they live in a state of war and must respond with similar measures. It is in these circumstances that individuals begin to envision that the only way out of the climate of fear and insecurity in which they live is through the expansion of coercive practices by the state into militaristic tactics or through responding to crime and injustice with vigilante violence. Under these conditions the public also begins to accept as justifiable the spillover of state-sanctioned violence beyond the purview of the state to citizens' groups. This is how minds become militarized and violence normalized, allowing a multiplicity of violent practices to take root. This is how perceptions of crime become as important as violent acts in fashioning responses to violence. The chapters that follow shed important light on how this happens.

Notes

1. Mary Murray, "Organized Crime, Gangs Make Latin America Most Violent Region," *NBC News,* April 17, 2014, www.nbcnews.com/news/world/organized-crime-gangs-make-latin-america-most-violent-region-n83026 (accessed November 3, 2014).

2. There is debate about whether countries overwhelmed by violence today, such El Salvador and Honduras, are at war, as some government officials have claimed. Critics have observed that the political violence of the past is qualitatively different from the current violence, even when it is generalized and touches everyone, because the state is no longer engaged in conflict with a specific group identified with a particular ideology. See Roberto Valencia, "Salvador Samayoa: "Mano dura es la que hay ahora, no la de Paco Flores." *El Faro,* www.elfaro.net/es/201604/salanegra/18356/Salvador-Samayoa-"Mano-dura-es-la-que-hay-ahora-no-la-de-Paco-Flores".htm (accessed April 15, 2016).

VIOLENCE AND CRIME IN LATIN AMERICA

Introduction

*The Politics and Publics of Violence
and Crime in Latin America*

David Carey Jr. and Gema Santamaría

Armed with pistols, rifles, and submachine guns, vigilante groups have emerged in at least nine of Mexico's thirty-two states to defend their communities against drug-trafficking organizations. In the southwestern state of Michoacán alone, some twenty thousand people belong to vigilante organizations. Despite their defiance of the state's role as the sole arbiter of security and their illegal use of arms, these groups enjoy the support of local communities, which see them as a necessary and legitimate corrective to the state's incapacity to protect citizens. When in early 2014 President Enrique Peña Nieto dispatched a federal official to strike an agreement with vigilante groups in Michoacán, he too recognized their legitimacy. By attempting to bring them under the army's control, he further blurred the line between state and parastate forces.[1]

In Mexico and other Latin American countries, citizens' distrust in the state's ability to protect them is so entrenched that innovative and risk-taking solutions to crime have been derided even when they have enjoyed some success. For instance, in El Salvador authorities brokered a truce between the two largest criminal gangs, which led to a significant decrease in the number of violent deaths in 2012, but the public rejected the arrangement, calling it a negotiation with murderers. Widely believed to have lessened the killings of established gang members, the truce did not benefit individuals who lived in "red zones" but were not gang members; many continued to be extorted, harassed, and

3

killed.[2] The end of the truce was a blow not only to gang members but also to organizations and practitioners who saw it as a viable alternative to traditionally repressive responses to crime. As these two examples and the essays in this volume demonstrate, perceptions and representations of crime are just as important as violent acts themselves in shaping responses to violence and crime. Different perspectives of the legitimacy and approval of violence, be it acts of vigilantism or gang-related crime, do not necessarily reflect the parameters sanctioned by the state. What is considered criminal can hardly be reduced to unlawful behavior. Hence two practices marked by illegality—vigilantism and gang-related violence—experience starkly different levels of legitimacy.

Shaped by politico-ideological processes and by power relations that exceed the realm of the law, crime and violence are socially constructed categories. The rupture between what is formally illegal and what is considered criminal in everyday interactions between state and non-state actors is a common thread that weaves together the essays in this volume. For instance, while some communities consider witchcraft a crime, authorities seldom punish "magical" powers. By the same token, states often categorize acts such as rape within marriage as a crime even though some communities do not consider it a punishable offense. In turn, police abuse or the incursion of security officials in criminal activities may be ignored or left unpunished, contributing to citizens' distrust in the legal order. Given that lynchings and other forms of vigilantism are perceived as legitimate means to protect citizens, the use of extralegal violence also illustrates this divide.

By providing a multidisciplinary analysis of how different actors and audiences have attempted to normalize, conceal, denounce, and expose violence and crime in Latin America, this volume brings into focus the politics and publics of violence and crime. Whereas "politics" refers to the discourses, conflicts, and policies that violence and crime generate amongst different social and political groups, including criminal organizations or so-called illegal actors, "publics" denotes the multiple audiences that take part in the debates, representations, and meanings of violence and crime. We contend that representations of crime and violence materially impact the production and reproduction of such acts, which in turn carry profound consequences for political and social fabrics of Latin American nations. To cite one example, scholars have demonstrated that fear of crime and actual crime levels can differ significantly.[3] Public and media representations of crime influence levels of fear and insecurity, as do legacies of authoritarian rule and neoliberal policies that have weakened people's trust in each other. Even when perceptions of insecurity are not grounded in reality, they shape people's material and psychological lives and serve to authorize state and nonstate responses to crime that may forge a new reality.[4] So fearful are Mexicans, Guatemalans, Salvadorans, and Peruvians that in a 2010 survey, more than 50 percent of them opined that a military coup was justified to combat increasing levels of crime. Forty percent of Chileans shared that sentiment.[5] That so many people in nations where military dictatorships routinely committed human rights abuses would favor returning to that form of government speaks to citizens' acute levels of insecurity.

Given the seminal role that violence played in the development of authoritarian and democratic governments alike, and of the liberal and neoliberal institutions that sustained them, it is not surprising that the very state institutions (such as the police, military, prisons, schools, and legal systems) that are supposed to instill civilized behaviors among citizens often perpetrate or incubate violence and crime.[6] Since political violence has been part and parcel to Latin American state formation, the line between criminal and state violence has often been blurred. Political and criminal violence frequently have operated, if not in tandem, then on a continuum or in what has been referred to as a "gray zone."[7]

The recent proliferation of drug cartels and their control over or integration into nation-states has done much to polemicize the relationship between criminal and political violence.[8] By working with both government agents and gang members, drug cartels often bring those two groups together. In some parts of Guatemala, Mexico, and Honduras, narco-traffickers have greater control over local politics than government officials do. Their ability to elude justice systems and punishment speaks to the way impunity increases criminal groups' power. Because drug cartels can determine who has access to resources and positions of power in communities where the state has long been more of an idea than an entity, governments may seek to curtail cartels' influence either by offering extralegal protection rackets or by punishing criminal organizations selectively.[9] As Angélica Durán-Martínez, Enrique Desmond Arias, and Kayyonne Marston illustrate in this volume, the existence of illicit networks between criminal organizations and state officials may contribute to the invisibility or silencing of violence in scenarios undergirded by corruption and impunity. In this sense, the politics of violence is constantly shaped by the interaction between criminal actors, governments, and local communities.

Although subject to different interpretations, violence and crime are not free-floating concepts. Their distinct meanings are linked to particular power dynamics that establish and reinforce hierarchies among different forms of abuse.[10] Officials who consider drug-related violence or crimes committed by juvenile gangs as more important than domestic violence or police repression offer but one example of that process. Whether violent or nonviolent, crime is frequently thought about in relation to economic factors such as poverty and inequality. This is equally true for crimes against property as for crimes against people, which are this volume's focus. Violence is usually recognized as a practice informed by political interests or social forms of exclusion and discrimination that may or may not be considered criminal or punishable. The power dynamics that shape notions of criminality, deviance, and danger in Latin America are connected to class, race, gender, sexuality, ethnicity, and political and religious affiliation.[11] Examining violence through those lenses sheds light on what political scientist James Scott calls "domination within domination."[12]

Legally defined as an act or omission constituting an offense that may be prosecuted by the state and punishable by law, crime and criminal acts are often in the eye of the beholder, thus calling for an understanding of their social and cultural underpinnings. Although the contributors herein are primarily concerned with violence, defined as physical acts that intentionally cause bodily harm to another person, they acknowledge that the social, cultural, and symbolic dimension of violence is what "gives violence its power and meaning."[13] Understood as the social and historical construction of meaning, culture constitutes a key analytical foundation for understanding violence and its reproduction. Reading the cultural dimension of violence implies neither aestheticizing nor essentializing violence. This dimension allows us to recognize that illegality alone does not determine which acts are understood as violent or criminal. Their meanings transcend the realm of law and tend to be underpinned by political, ideological, and even individual decisions or trajectories, as David Carey Jr. and Lila Caimari suggest in this volume. Despite its de jure monopoly over the legitimate means of coercion, the state has little control over which public understandings of violence and crime will prevail in a given community. In fact, it may not even control what its own representatives consider criminal or violent, as police agents, judges, and other public officials may develop peculiar and at times disparate law enforcement practices. This volume offers a window into the ways violence and crime have been represented, sanctioned, and resisted in Latin America from the nineteenth to the twenty-first centuries. *Sometimes violence accepted*

Acknowledging that social constructions of crime and violence are contested, negotiated, and resisted, the contributors to this volume go beyond identifying how categories like gender, class, and ethnicity inform representations of violence and crime. Instead, they explore the concrete ways in which these representations translate into actions and behaviors such as the state's use of legal and illegal forms of violence against particular categories of people, and non-state actors' use of vigilantism, homicide, robbery, rape, and other forms of violence. For instance, the authors herein discuss how racialized representations of deviance and crime have reinforced punitive and violent practices that disproportionally target indigenous populations. They also show how marginalized young men have become the ultimate bearers of imaginaries of fear and acts of vigilantism in places as different as Rio de Janeiro, Kingston, and Guatemala. Over time the perceived legitimacy of practices as diverse as lynching, rape, femicide, and extrajudicial violence have led to their reproduction and intensification. Put simply, this volume demonstrates that the field of representation is a fundamental driver of the manifold manifestations of violence and crime in Latin America. *violence → violence → how/when does it stop?*

Attention to representations and perceptions of crime and a concurrent focus on elite discourses does not dismiss questions of responsibility or morality. Never simply the product of abstract forces, violence must be understood within the context of individuals' particular decisions and their moral ramifications. It should also be analyzed in light of the concrete harm it inflicts on people and communities. Faced with a dearth of testimonies or other evidence from perpetrators, the contributors do not claim to understand perpetrators' inner motivations; rather they seek to understand how representations of violence may inform or shape criminal or violent acts. Avoiding essentialist and genetic approaches to violence, the authors explore the processes whereby people develop shared meanings and understandings of the violent phenomena that influence their lives.

Conceptualizing Crime and Violence in Latin America: Implications for Theory and Practice

By analyzing the multiple factors and forces that precipitate crime and violence, *Violence and Crime in Latin America* fills a lacuna in the literature. Scholars have paid surprisingly little attention to how social constructions and representations reproduce certain forms of abuse, repression, and harm, or to the enduring effects of those representations on Latin American political and social fabrics. To address those gaps, the contributors to this volume explore how different forces influence boundaries between legitimate and illegitimate, tolerable and intolerable, and government-sanctioned and unsanctioned forms of violence; they also examine how state and non-state actors deploy violence in ways that shape civil society and political development.

Two approaches to explaining twentieth- and twenty-first-century violence in Latin America have dominated the scholarly literature. One school of thought identifies the transition toward neoliberal economic policies and market-oriented democracies as the main impetus for the recent increase in crime and victimization rates in Latin America. According to these scholars, the economic models and public policies that marginalize people generate increased levels of crime and violence, which in turn spur vigilantism.[14] Articulated mainly by historians and social scientists, a second interpretation stresses state attempts to claim a monopoly over the use of violence. Those works generally argue that past and present levels of violence and crime can be read as direct consequences of Latin American states' failure to maintain the rule of law; in short, weak governments and corrupt institutions are the primary causes of crime and violence. The two interpretations differ, however, in that historians tend to focus on the region's long historical trajectory of violence and state building,[15] whereas social scientists generally stress contemporary faltering judicial systems and ineffective or corrupt state security forces as catalysts of violence and crime.[16]

Arguing that neither a purely economic and structural-level analysis nor a focus on the failure of state institutions fully explains these processes, *Violence and Crime in Latin America* introduces a third explanation to the debate: the tenacity of certain forms of violence among both state and non-state actors needs to be understood with regard to the processes that have led to their de facto legitimation and endurance.

By highlighting the multiple meanings violence has in the public sphere and carefully considering their social, cultural, and symbolic under-pinnings, we question extant explanations of crime and violence. These phenomena cannot be explained merely as a means to attain political or economic goals or as a result of the absence of adequate law enforce-ment. Rather, violence and crime need to be situated at the societal and political levels by entering into the field of representation, public debate, and political discourse. That is where we can analyze how Latin American citizens have sanctioned criminal and violent practices and incorporated them into their social relations, everyday practices, and institutional settings over time and across places.

Different actors' and audiences' representations of violence and crime offer a window into the deeper social and cultural origins that have legit-imated and normalized certain forms of abuse and repression. Under-standing this dimension can prove crucial for practitioners working to curb the spread and reproduction of violence. Mirroring the approaches in the academic literature, violence- and crime-prevention policy ini-tiatives in the region have focused either on strengthening the state's security and justice apparatuses or on implementing economic mea-sures aimed at alleviating the structural drivers of violence and crime. We need to recalibrate these approaches. Inadequate understandings of the cultural and historical patterns of abuse that permeate security forces in Latin America have led to several failed attempts to reform and modernize the security sector. Conversely, the economic approach has resulted in haphazard attempts to alleviate social exclusion and mar-ginality that have tended to overlook the importance of gender, identity, honor, and trust in the production and reproduction of violence. Public officials and nongovernmental organizations need to incorporate the social and cultural dimensions of crime and violence in the design and implementation of public and civil society initiatives.

Recognizing the divide between what is illegal and what is considered criminal has implications not only for theory but also for practice. As illustrated by the Mexican case in our opening paragraph, some com-munities consider vigilante groups, though illegal, a legitimate response to crime, particularly when those groups attempt to create order (albeit in an ad hoc and shifting manner) in otherwise chaotic and insecure societies.[17] In such scenarios, the use of force to punish vigilante groups may further erode the state's legitimacy and propagate violence, which helps to explain why President Peña Nieto chose cooptation in 2014. In a different context, the use of force against criminal groups may be perceived as a legitimate way to tackle crime, even when it leads to extra-judicial killings. Such is the case of El Salvador's *mano dura* (iron fist) antigang policies, which have enjoyed greater support from the general public than alternatives focused on social reinsertion and reintegration. Going beyond formalistic appraisals of crime and violence is thus central to strengthening the design and implementation of prevention and reha-bilitation programs developed by legal and human rights practitioners. It is also relevant for humanitarian and international organizations assisting communities where criminal organizations may be deemed legitimate or may operate as "para-states" or "quasi-states."[18] In those contexts, the implementation of humanitarian assistance may require negotiation and dialogue with illegal armed groups.[19]

Historically and socially contingent, the relationship between vio-lence and crime can be represented visually as a continuum character-ized by two axes: a violence axis that includes noncriminal and criminal forms of violence, and a crime axis wherein crime may be violent or nonviolent (figure 0.1). Not all forms of violence are illegal (some military and police violence enjoy legal status); nor are all crimes violent (corrup-tion and white-collar crime immediately come to mind). Whereas some forms of violence are normalized by social actors or decriminalized by authorities, other forms of violence are defined by law as criminal and punishable. As the essays in this volume illustrate, historical, political, and social (race, class, gender, ethnicity) variables all shape where acts fall on the violence–crime continuum. For example, violence that the state ignores or encourages (covertly or otherwise), such as commu-nity-led lynchings and government-sponsored death squads, is often defined as noncriminal. In contrast, violence considered destabilizing or illegitimate by political and economic elites, such as gang brutality or visible forms of drug-related violence, is understood as criminal. The many forms of violence that fall along this continuum range from honor killings, femicides, and domestic rapes to police killings, gang-related violence, and hate crimes against minorities. In a helpful framework for studying violence, Enrique Desmond Arias and Daniel M. Goldstein use the term "violent pluralism" to capture the interconnected nature and variety of the types of violence that have emerged as central to many Latin Americans' lived experience.[20] Considering the factors that

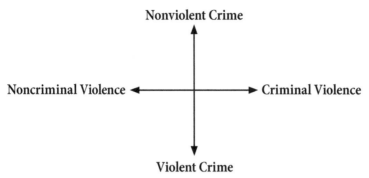

0.1. Axes of crime and violence.

shape violence and crime helps to identify when and how violence tacks between criminal and noncriminal.

Most of the literature regarding violence and crime in Latin America is either specific to a certain type of violence (e.g., insurgent and counterinsurgent, terrorism, vigilantism) or to a country (namely, Mexico, Guatemala, and Colombia because they have experienced significant historical and contemporary violence). To explore different historical and contemporary contexts and types of violence and crime, we examine countries from distinct regions of Latin America and the Caribbean. A number of countries addressed in this volume—namely, Chile, Argentina, Brazil, Guatemala, and Colombia—have experienced military dictatorships. Yet they have taken very different postwar paths. Chile has reestablished a stable democratic government whereas Argentina has suffered regular unrest, though neither nation has suffered the high levels of crime occurring in Brazil and Colombia or the ghastly violence seen in Guatemala. Despite their formal transition to democracy, most countries explored in this volume continue to struggle to maintain the rule of law and guarantee equal access to justice. Under democratic rule, Mexico and Colombia engaged in wars against drug cartels that led to human rights violations, displacement, and *desaparecidos* (disappearances; a euphemism for kidnapping followed by torture and murder).[21] Police forces in countries such as Brazil and Guatemala have been accused of carrying out extralegal killings in the name of security. Moreover, the high approval levels for vigilantism across the region are worrisome. According to a United Nations Development Program (UNDP) Human

Development Report for Latin America, in countries as different as the Dominican Republic, Ecuador, and El Salvador, three out of ten citizens approve of taking justice into their own hands when the state does not punish criminals.[22] Informed by perceptions of violence and crime, such attitudes can be read as an attempt to arrest the disorder, insecurity, and impunity that surround citizens and their communities.[23]

With these distinct national histories of violence and crime as the backdrop, the contributors herein examine such common themes as the inability of legitimacy to guarantee equality; the myriad challenges to the rule of law; the criminalization of certain subjects to further political interests and maintain power; the blurring of legal, illegal, state, and non-state violence; public anxieties about crime; and the fragility of state institutions. They are particularly interested in how those commonalities—related to impunity, corruption, power dynamics, discretionary use of force, and citizens' distrust—play out in different historical periods and national contexts. In order to illustrate the continuities and ruptures between past and present forms of violence in Latin America, the authors deal with a period that stretches from the nineteenth to the twenty-first centuries, encompassing contexts of war and peace, democracy and dictatorships, revolutions and counterrevolutions. To further explore geographies of power as they relate to crime and violence, we have included case studies from rural and urban areas.

Taking Latin America as its site of analysis, this volume addresses dimensions of violence and crime that are both relevant to and connected with trends and challenges identified by historians and social scientists working in different regions across the globe. The rise of punitive and zero tolerance policies, the criminalization of marginalized youth and of ethnic and racial minorities, the securitization of politics and the politicization of security, the rise in insecurity levels, and the apparent increase in the fear of crime are some of the broader global trends of violence and crime highlighted in this volume.

From South Africa to the United Kingdom and the United States, crime and fear of crime have taken center stage in public debates and electoral politics, as well as in citizens' everyday interactions. "Crime looms large in the post–cold war age," assert Jean and John Comaroff.[24] With the advent of new communication technologies and globalization, public imaginaries of crime are transmitted with unprecedented speed, informing an ever-growing economy of (in)security based on privatized forms of policing, gated communities, and expanding prison systems.[25] These contributors' critiques of the racialized character of punitive practices and representations of crime in the region echo scholars' concern about the racial and class biases underpinning crime-control policies and dynamics of imprisonment in the United States.[26] By the same token, the criminalization of youth is equally pressing in Latin America and other regions of the world. Scholars working in Europe, Asia, the United States, and Africa have pointed out the increasing marginalization of youth and their concurrent targeting by zero tolerance measures and crime-control policies administered by prisons, courts, and youth detention centers.[27] *Zero tolerance implications*

Identified as a global phenomenon, vigilantism has attracted the attention of historians and social scientists who have pointed at how different conceptions of justice, deviancy, and danger contribute to legitimating these expressions of violence.[28] Covering a rich geographical and temporal spectrum, from early modern Europe to contemporary India and South Africa, this body of literature confirms this volume's central argument regarding the key role that social constructions of crime and violence play in sanctioning and reproducing violence. It also demonstrates the impact that political elites and state formation processes can have in averting or disapproving these forms of violence, as illustrated by the decline of lynching in the United States and of vigilantism in Western Europe. In contrast, Latin American processes of state building have not generated the necessary social and institutional conditions to delegitimize these practices through the rule of law.

Violence and crime constitute global challenges that cut across multiple regions and countries, regardless of their levels of development or institutional consolidation. Yet, when compared to other parts of the world, Latin America garners disproportionate attention for its violence and crime. Despite significant variations in violence levels between and within countries, the region is often portrayed uniformly as the deadliest region in the world.[29] According to the 2014 Americas Barometer, security has become an increasing concern for Latin American citizens. In 2014, one out of three Latin American respondents considered crime, violence, or insecurity the most pressing challenge in their lives.[30] Latin American citizens report feeling less secure than the citizens of any other region of the world, including sub-Saharan Africa, the Middle East, North Africa, and South Asia.[31] Still, some Latin American countries seem to get more attention than others. For instance, Mexico, Colombia, Brazil, and Guatemala tend to attract greater international news coverage and scholarly attention than Jamaica, El Salvador, and Honduras, despite having comparable or even lower levels of violence.[32]

In addition to facilitating examinations of violence and crime through historical and contemporary lenses, the interdisciplinary approach of this volume is a natural consequence of its analytic scope. The field of representation generally studied by anthropologists is as crucial to our study as are the effects of those representations on the rule of law, social relations, and political institutions studied by political scientists, sociologists, and historians. Whereas historians maintain a keen sense of trajectories, continuities, and change over time, social scientists tend to focus on what is new. Distinct disciplinary approaches, methodologies, and sources allow for unique analyses of crime, violence, and the rule of law in Latin America.

For these reasons, *Violence and Crime in Latin America* brings together historians, anthropologists, political scientists, public policy analysts, sociologists, and urban development scholars. Their collective effort is a reflection of the bottom-up approach that eschews hierarchical frameworks for studying how power and representation function. Instead of focusing solely on national officials, authorities, or criminals (be they powerful drug lords or marginalized murderers), the scholars in this volume shed a bright light on low-level bureaucrats, detectives, beat cops, victims, activists, journalists, and other players whose influences on representations of crime and violence are often difficult to discern. As such, this volume offers an empirically and analytically rich account of the politics and publics behind crime and violence in Latin America. It also provides valuable insights regarding the impact that representations of crime and violence can have for public policy and practice.

To stress our analytical focus, we have organized the chapters thematically instead of by historical period or geographic region. The first of these three interconnected analytical lenses explores extralegal violence and its justifications. Lynching, vigilantism, and extralegal forms of punishment exercised by the state offer a window into how representations of state and non-state violence have shaped civil society and historical trajectories in Mexico, Argentina, and Guatemala. At times subordinate agents—like Buenos Aires beat cops—determined what constituted a crime and who was a criminal. We then turn our attention to the ways criminals have been constructed in order to legitimize state violence and control in Chile, Guatemala, Colombia, Mexico, and Brazil. By examining public and political discourses regarding danger; darkness; criminality; and deviance of gays, indigenous people, and communist bandits, those contributors reveal how defining certain acts and behaviors as illegal affords authorities significant leeway to deploy violence. In the last section, scholars studying Guatemala, Mexico, Brazil, and Jamaica explore the politics of making violence visible by examining the discourses and representations intended either to conceal or to reveal different forms of violence.

Each part is introduced with a brief essay that articulates the context and specifics of the analytic focus, how the contributors approach it, and how the essays relate to one another. Taken as a whole, the essays before you draw upon these three interrelated themes and the central arguments in this introduction to advance and refine our understanding of violence and crime in Latin America.

Notes

1. "Dallying with a Monster: In Failing to Snuff out Vigilantism, Mexico Is Running Big Risks," *The Economist,* March 15, 2014, 36.
2. Cecilia Menjívar, e-mail correspondence to authors, August 12, 2014.
3. Guillermina Seri, *Seguridad: Crime, Police Power, and Democracy in Argentina* (New York: Continuum, 2012); Lucía Dammert, *Fear and Crime in Latin America: Redefining State-Society Relations* (New York: Routledge, 2012); Enrique Desmond Arias and Daniel M. Goldstein, eds., *Violent Democracies in Latin America* (Durham, NC: Duke University Press, 2010); Mark Ungar, *Policing Democracy: Overcoming Obstacles to Citizen Security in Latin America* (Washington, DC: Woodrow Wilson Center Press; Baltimore, MD: Johns Hopkins University Press, 2011).
4. Gabriel Kessler, *El sentimiento de inseguridad: sociología del temor al delito* (Buenos Aires, Siglo XXI, 2009); Rossana Reguillo, "Sociabilidad, inseguridad y miedos: Una trilogía para pensar la ciudad contemporánea," *Alteridades* (México, UAM) 18 (2008): 63–74.
5. Dammert, *Fear and Crime in Latin America.*
6. Deborah Poole, "Introduction: Anthropological Perspectives on Violence and Culture: A View from the Peruvian High Provinces," in *Unruly Order: Violence, Power, and Cultural Identity in the High Provinces of Southern Peru,* ed. Deborah Poole, 1–30 (Boulder, CO: Westview Press, 1994); Carlos Aguirre, *The Criminals of Lima*

and Their Worlds: The Prison Experience, 1850–1935 (Durham, NC: Duke University Press, 2005), 119; Arias and Goldstein, *Violent Democracies in Latin America*; Seri, *Seguridad*; Hugo Fruhling, *Violencia y policía en América Latina* (Quito: FLACSO, 2009); Elena Azaola and Marcelo Bergman, *Delincuencia, marginalidad y desempeño institucional* (México: CIDE, 2003).

7. Javier Auyero, *Routine Politics and Violence in Argentina: The Gray Zone of State Power* (New York: Cambridge University Press, 2007).

8. Luis Jorge Garay Salamanca and Eduardo Salcedo-Albarán, eds., *Narcotráfico, corrupción y estados: cómo las redes ilícitas han reconfigurado las instituciones en Colombia, Guatemala y México* (Mexico City: Debate, 2012).

9. Alan Knight "Narco-Violence and the State in Modern Mexico," in *Violence, Coercion, and State-Making in Twentieth-Century Mexico: The Other Half of the Centaur,* ed. Wil Pansters, 115–34 (Stanford, CA: Stanford University Press, 2012).

10. Jenny Pearce, "Bringing Violence Back Home," in *Global Civil Society 2006/7,* ed. Marlies Glasius, Mary Kaldor, and Helmut Anheier (London: Sage, 2006), 42-61.

11. Pablo Piccato, *City of Suspects: Crime in Mexico City, 1900–1931* (Durham, NC: Duke University Press, 2001); David Carey Jr. and M. Gabriella Torres, "Precursors to Femicide: Guatemalan Women in a Vortex of Violence," *Latin American Research Review* 45, no. 3 (2010): 142–64; Susana Rotker, *Citizens of Fear: Urban Violence in Latin America* (New Brunswick, NJ: Rutgers University Press, 2002); Caroline Moser and Cathy McIlwaine, *Encounters with Violence in Latin America: Urban Poor Perceptions from Colombia and Guatemala* (New York: Routledge, 2004); Greg Grandin and Gilbert Joseph, eds., *A Century of Revolution: Insurgent and Counterinsurgent Violence during Latin America's Long Cold War* (Durham, NC: Duke University Press, 2010); Gabriela Polit Dueñas and María Helena Rueda, eds., *Meanings of Violence in Latin America* (New York: Palgrave Macmillan, 2011).

12. James Scott, *Domination and the Arts of Resistance: Hidden Transcripts* (New Haven, CT: Yale University Press, 1990), 26.

13. Nancy Scheper-Hughes and Philippe Bourgois, "Introduction: Making Sense of Violence," in *Violence in War and Peace: An Anthology* (Oxford: Blackwell, 2004), 1–2.

14. Arias and Goldstein, *Violent Democracies in Latin America;* Auyero, *Routine Politics and Violence in Argentina*; Deborah Levenson, *Adiós Niño: The Gangs of Guatemala City and the Politics of Death* (Durham, NC: Duke University Press, 2013); Angelina Snodgrass Godoy, *Popular Injustice, Violence, Community, and Law in Latin America* (Stanford, CA: Stanford University Press, 2006); Daniel Goldstein, *The Spectacular City: Violence and Performance in Urban Bolivia* (Durham, NC: Duke University Press, 2004).

15. Kees Koonings and Dirk Kruijt, eds., *Armed Actors: Organised Violence and State Failure in Latin America* (London: Zed Books, 2004); Wil Pansters, ed., *Violence, Coercion, and State-Making in Twentieth-Century Mexico: The Other Half of the Centaur* (Stanford, CA: Stanford University Press, 2012).

16. Ungar, *Policing Democracy;* Seri, *Seguridad;* Diane Davis, "Undermining the Rule of Law: Democratization and the Dark Side of Police Reform in Mexico,"

Latin American Politics and Society, 48, no. 1 (2006): 55–86; Lucía Dammert, ed., *Seguridad ciudadana: Experiencias y desafíos* (Valparaíso, Chile: Municipalidad de Valparaíso, Red 14, 2004); Marcelo Bergman and Laurence Whitehead, eds., *Criminality, Public Security, and the Challenge to Democracy in Latin America* (Notre Dame, IN: University of Notre Dame Press, 2009); Kessler, *El sentimiento de inseguridad*; Teresa Pires Do Rio Caldeira, *City of Walls: Crime, Segregation, and Citizenship in São Paulo* (Berkeley: University of California Press, 2001).

17. Daniel M. Goldstein, *Outlawed: Between Security and Rights in a Bolivian City* (Durham, NC: Duke University Press, 2012).

18. Christopher Krupa, "State by Proxy: Privatized Government in the Andes," *Comparative Studies in Society and History,* 52 (2010): 319–50.

19. Elena Lucchi, "Humanitarian Interventions in Situations of Urban Violence," *ALNAP Lessons Paper* (London: ALNAP/ODI, 2013).

20. Arias and Goldstein, *Violent Democracies in Latin America.*

21. Human Rights Watch, "World Report 2015: Mexico," www.hrw.org/world-report/2015/country-chapters/mexico#899ef4 (accessed April 25, 2016).

22. UNDP, "Regional Human Development Report: Citizen Security with a Human Face, Evidence and Proposals for Latin America," 2013, www.undp.org/content/undp/en/home/librarypage/hdr/human-development-report-for-latin-america-2013-2014.html (accessed January 14, 2015).

23. Goldstein, *Outlawed,* chap. 4.; Snodgrass Godoy, *Popular Injustice.*

24. Jean Comaroff and John Comaroff, "Criminal Obsessions, after Foucault: Postcoloniality, Policing, and the Metaphysics of Disorder," *Critical Inquiry* 30, no. 4 (2004): 800–824.

25. Ibid.; David Garland, *The Culture of Control: Crime and Social Order in Contemporary Society* (Chicago: University of Chicago Press, 2001).

26. Loïc Wacquant, "From Slavery to Mass Incarceration: Rethinking the 'Race Question' in the U.S.," *New Left Review* 13 (2002): 41–60; Becky Pettit and Bruce Western, "Mass Imprisonment and the Life Course: Race and Class Inequality in U.S. Incarceration," *American Sociological Review* 69 (2004): 151–69.

27. Sudhir Alladi Venkatesh and Ronald Kassimir, *Youth, Globalization, and the Law* (Stanford, CA: Stanford University Press, 2006); John M. Hagedorn, "The Global Impact of Gangs," *Journal of Contemporary Criminal Justice* 21 (2005): 153–69; Claire Alexander, "Rethinking 'Gangs': Gangs, Youth Violence, and Public Policy," in *Runnymede Report* (London: Runnymede Trust, 2008).

28. William D. Carrigan and Christopher Waldrep, eds., *Swift to Wrath: Lynching in Global Historical Perspective* (Charlottesville and London: University of Virginia Press, 2013); Ann Fuji Lee, "The Puzzle of Extra-Lethal Violence," *Perspectives on Politics* 11, no. 2 (2013): 410–26; Michael Pfeifer, *The Roots of Rough Justice: Origins of American Lynching* (Urbana: University of Illinois Press, 2011); Ivan Evans, *Cultures of Violence: Racial Violence and the Origins of Segregation in South Africa and the American South* (Manchester, UK: Manchester University Press, 2011); Parvis Ghassem-Fachandi, *Pogrom in Gujarat: Hindu Nationalism and Anti-Muslim Violence in India* (Princeton, NJ: Princeton University Press, 2012).

29. United Nations Office on Drugs and Crime (UNODC), *Global Study on Homicide, 2013: Trends, Contexts, Data* (Vienna: UNODC, 2014), www.unodc.org/gsh (accessed October 15, 2015).

30. Elizabeth J. Zechmeister, ed., *The Political Culture of Democracy in the Americas, 2014: Democratic Governance across 10 Years of the Americas Barometer* (Washington, DC: USAID, 2014), 11–12.

31. Jan Sonnenschein, "Latin America scores lowest on security," www.gallup.com/poll/175082/latin-america-scores-lowest-security.aspx (accessed October 20, 2015).

32. David Shirk et al., "Drug Violence in Mexico: Data and Analysis through 2013," *Justice in Mexico Project*, April 2014, 8–9.

PART I
Extralegal Violence and Its Justifications

Despite their negative impact on democracy and human rights, hardline policies and extrajudicial methods to tackle crime are tolerated and even supported by many Latin American citizens. According to a survey published by the 2013–14 UNDP Human Development Report for Latin America, approximately 87 percent of Latin Americans self-reported that they "very much agreed" or "somewhat agreed" that the best way to fight crime was to impose harsher punishments on criminals.[1] Furthermore, an average of 35 percent supported the statement that, on occasion, authorities needed to bend the law or go beyond the law to capture criminals. These attitudes have taken root even in countries with functional democratic systems, stable electoral processes, and thriving civil societies. This apparent paradox is explained by common dysfunctional or disjunctive elements in Latin American democracies, such as corrupt and ineffective security and justice systems, deep social and economic inequalities, and increasing levels of insecurity and violent crime.[2]

Support for extralegal forms of violence is not new in Latin America, nor can it be explained exclusively by looking at the fault lines within the region's transition to electoral and so-called neoliberal democracies. Rather, it is situated within the longer trajectory of state building that has characterized the region and in the ensuing decoupling of legality from legitimacy, and of rule of law from justice. The precolonial period, marked by violent ascensions to and falls from power, was followed by brutal conquest, particularly in countries like Peru and Mexico.

Exploitation and domination under colonial rule gave rise to indigenous revolts, local disturbances, and riots that directly challenged the
colonizers' claim to a monopoly on legitimate violence, most notably
in the Andean region. Far from ushering in a transition to more peaceful and less exploitative societies, the post-independence process of
state-building brought brutal civil wars and internal divisions among
Latin American elites vying for economic and political control of newly
independent nations. Rather than promoting state monopolization of
legitimate violence, as the classical sociological formula of war-making
and state-making would predict, these wars served to weaken the rule of
law by politicizing state institutions, strengthening caudillos and local
power brokers, and reproducing social and political tensions within civil
society.[3] Seeking to hold on to their political and economic privileges,
elites would often scapegoat lower classes and rural populations as prone
to crime and social deviance. As a result, subalterns regarded justice
institutions as biased and unjust.[4]

Revolutions, counterrevolutions, military dictatorships, and unfinished democratic transitions provided fertile ground for the reproduction of both state and non-state forms of extralegal violence throughout
Latin America in the twentieth century.[5] Despite the consolidation of
state-building projects, violence continued to pervade the region's social
and political fabrics as a tool of oppression and liberation. Rather than
correcting the inequalities and social injustices inherited from previous
periods, political elites resorted to violence to eradicate political dissent
and establish social control.[6] In the wake of the Mexican Revolution,
which revealed the divergent social and political forces driving the
country, early twentieth-century Mexican political elites tried to attain
political and national cohesion by modernizing state institutions and
suppressing extralegal violence in both rural and urban areas. As Pablo
Piccato demonstrates, however, the state participated in extralegal forms
of violence such as the *ley fuga* (flight law), in which the killing of criminals was justified by alleged escape attempts. Often perceived as necessary
to bypass obstacles posed by legal due process in dealing with criminals,
the ley fuga was tacitly supported by Mexican officials, journalists, and
average citizens. Just as citizens in various Latin American countries
presently demand the law be bent in order to eliminate drug traffickers,
street gangs, or thieves, constituencies in Mexico authorized and legitimized the use of ley fuga as a means to reassert citizens' sense of security.

Extralegal violence did not emanate only from the state. Ranging from death squads and paramilitary forces to organized vigilantes and lynch mobs,[7] multifaceted expressions of violence reflect the social legacies of decades of impunity, inequality, and injustice. Lynching is perhaps the most dramatic expression of people's distrust in state institutions and willingness to take justice into their own hands. Although lynching gained visibility within the last thirty years in countries like Mexico, Guatemala, and Brazil, Gema Santamaría's chapter on 1930s Mexico demonstrates that the practice has a longer history.[8] She discusses how journalists, citizens, and public officials justified or condemned lynchings based on social constructions of class, gender, ethnicity, and religious affiliation. More than either law or moral judgments, social constructs determined what was legitimate versus illegitimate use of corporal punishment. Santamaría reminds us how justifications of extralegal violence can contribute to perpetuating the practice over time.

Social constructions of gender, class, and ethnicity were also central to the Guatemalan military regime's efforts to control the population by simultaneously heightening citizens' awareness of violence and obscuring its own role in perpetrating it. By portraying himself as the father of the nation, José Efraín Ríos Montt (president in 1982–83) drew upon patriarchal relations and the marginalization of women to craft a narrative that made stable, male-dominated families a cornerstone of good government. So convincing was his discourse that even though the military committed flagrant war crimes during his strong-armed rule and he was found guilty of human rights abuses, people continued to revere him. By relating support for gender-based violence during the civil war (1960–96) to the femicide epidemic that plagues Guatemala today, Gabriela Torres demonstrates how the field of representation offers a window into the deeper social and cultural beliefs that have legitimated certain forms of abuse, repression, and violence.

Revealing how public understandings of violence and crime disparately and even unpredictably shape the state's coercive power, Lila Caimari explores how the Argentine public redefined the police's use of force in ways that compelled law enforcement to change its image. Political, social, and ideological processes inform not only the content of laws but also how laws are enforced by state actors and security forces. Caimari argues that because they had fewer legal constraints, itinerant beat cops enjoyed more power than judges to decide what constituted a crime and who was a criminal. Contesting the notion that use of force by police reflected the politics of the ruling elites, Caimari highlights how society's perceptions of the justifications for police violence were key in both legitimating and limiting the police and their interventions.

The essays in part 1 demonstrate how extralegal violence has been shaped, tolerated, and sanctioned by different publics across distinct historical periods in Latin America. By focusing on how average citizens and marginalized subjects have decided, at different times, to support or participate directly in extrajudicial forms of violence, these studies complicate a top-down understanding of violence by situating it within long-term dynamics of state-society relationships.

Notes

1. UNDP, "Regional Human Development Report: Citizen Security with a Human Face, Evidence and Proposals for Latin America," (2013–14), 182–83, www.undp.org/content/undp/en/home/librarypage/hdr/human-development-report-for-latin-america-2013-2014.html (accessed January 14, 2015).

2. Enrique Desmond Arias and Daniel Goldstein, eds., *Violent Democracies in Latin America* (Durham, NC: Duke University Press, 2010); Teresa Caldeira Pires Do Rio and James Holston, "Democracy and Violence in Brazil," *Comparative Studies in Society and History* 41, no. 4 (1999): 691–729; Angelina Snodgrass Godoy, "When 'Justice' Is Criminal: Lynchings in Contemporary Latin America," *Theory and Society* 33, no. 6 (2004): 621–51.

3. Miguel Angel Centeno, "Centre Did Not Hold: War in Latin America and the Monopolisation of Violence," in *Studies on the Formation of the Nation-State in Latin America*, ed. James Dunkerley (London: Institute of Latin American Studies, 2002), 54–76; Dirk Kruijt and Kees Koonings, "Introduction: Violence and Fear in Latin America," in *Societies of Fear: The Legacy of Civil War, Violence and Terror in Latin America*, ed. Kees Koonings and Dirk Kruijt (New York: Zed Books, 1999), 1–30.

4. Carlos A. Aguirre and Robert Buffington, eds., *Reconstructing Criminality in Latin America* (Wilmington, DE: Scholarly Resources, 2000); Juan Méndez, Guillermo O'Donnell, and Paulo Sergio Pinheiro, eds., *The (Un)Rule of Law and the Underprivileged in Latin America* (Notre Dame, IN.: University of Notre Dame Press, 1999).

5. Greg Gandin and Gilbert M. Joseph, eds., *A Century of Revolution: Insurgent and Counterinsurgent Violence during Latin America's Long Cold War* (Durham, NC: Duke University Press, 2010).

6. Jenny Pearce, "Perverse State Formation and Securitized Democracy in Latin America," *Democratization* 17, no. 2 (2010): 286–306.

7. Martha K. Huggins, ed., *Vigilantism and the State in Modern Latin America: Essays on Extralegal Violence* (New York: Praeger, 1991).

8. Snodgrass Godoy, "When 'Justice' Is Criminal."

1 Ley Fuga as Justice

The Consensus around Extrajudicial Violence
in Twentieth-Century Mexico

Pablo Piccato

In 1933, having been found guilty of murdering China Aznar, a high society lady in Mexico City, Pedro Gallegos was taken by train to the penal colony of Islas Marías in the Pacific Ocean. At some point on the long trip he stood up to retrieve the typewriter he had placed above his seat, and a soldier who was guarding him shot him in the throat. His body was dumped by the tracks, and the official explanation, which few believed, was that he had been shot while trying to escape. A textbook example of the ley fuga (flight law), Gallegos's death was not an unusual occurrence at the time "because," according to a reporter, "guards usually eliminated the most dangerous criminals even though they were sentenced to spend several years in prison."[1] The story even generated a verb: "galleguear," a euphemism for the ley fuga applied to other cases during the 1930s.

The history of the ley fuga helps us understand the interactions between crime, punishment, and politics in modern Mexico. This is a history of public debates over and representations of crime, including a powerful critique of the justice system. The ley fuga was a violent abuse of power that revealed the limitations of the state while recognizing the influence of public opinion. Alan Knight places the ley fuga as part of the "hot, dense, and often dirty undergrowth of local politics" that historians of twentieth-century Mexico tend to overlook. Violence, he suggests, was part of politics at every level, even when the violence was not overtly "political."[2] The ley fuga became a broadly cited reference in public culture, from political struggles to law enforcement. Everard Meade has documented increasing press interest in ley fuga cases in the 1930s, following the abolition of the death penalty.[3]

Another form of critical engagement with justice was lynching, which Gema Santamaría examines in chapter 2. Although lynching should be understood on its own terms—with any analysis starting, as the term indicates, with the emergence of this practice in the United States after the Civil War—the connections with ley fuga are meaningful. The framework David Garland proposed for U.S. lynching is useful here: in Southern towns, lynchings were formalized acts of violence that usually targeted prisoners and often were intended as spectacles, their gruesome results disseminated through postcards. In the case of the Mexican ley fuga, agents of the state, rather than a mob, produced the spectacle, and its results were conveyed through printed images and narratives by journalists.[4] In both cases, these acts reveal political fissures in moments of political transition, at the local and regional levels in the postbellum U.S. South, and in the difficult and uneven consolidation of a national state in 1930s Mexico. Although the following pages might seem to paint a stable picture, this is an artifact of the difficulty of documenting and quantifying ley fuga cases. As I will show, however, its use was probably more significant in moments when, in the eyes of the public, tensions between police and judicial institutions revealed the shortcomings of the state in relation to its obligation to guarantee safety, truth, and justice. Among such moments were the nineteenth-century civil wars, the dictatorial peace of the Porfiriato, and the postrevolutionary decades when the law revealed itself impotent in the face of violence and private appropriation of public resources by the new ruling groups.

Despite their exceptional or disruptive character, it would be erroneous to consider either lynching or ley fuga as examples of the "antipolitical" violence that Hannah Arendt associated with taking justice into one's own hands.[5] Lynching and ley fuga, though illegal, were rarely punished because they expressed tensions between popular moral codes and the written law, and enacted collective sentiments toward transgressors—thus illustrating the distinction between crime and illegality presented in the introduction to this volume. The ley fuga accomplished this through journalistic reporting that justified official extrajudicial violence by referring to the victim's previous crime, just as Southern lynch mobs did while also expressing racism in their selection of victims.

Thus the ley fuga was not merely a demonstration of the weakness of the state: by ironically referring to the legality of executions (it was a *ley*, after all) and giving a central role to state agents, the ley fuga was justified as a complement to state action, increasing the severity of punishment and instilling fear in would-be criminals. The police did reject ley fuga in public statements, but embraced it as a remedy against the legalistic restrictions of procedural codes, which tied their hands in the fight against criminals. The public and civilian authorities tolerated it as a justifiable exercise of power. The ley fuga addressed the limits of the justice system; it demonstrated a deeply rooted contradiction between police institutions and the judiciary that other actors in civil society and government also saw as a weakness of liberal institutions.

The ley fuga, then, was anything but antipolitical. A practice deeply embedded in the rough-and-tumble politics of post-independence Mexico, it provided a key narrative to public debates about crime and violence in Mexico, connecting crime and justice in an ironic and critical way. This is best explained by putting some cases in context. Gallegos was the victim of a long-established practice, but he was also at the center of a case that attracted the attention of the Mexican public for months, with the press characterizing him as a particularly devious criminal who deserved a harsher punishment than was meted out by penal courts. Using this and other examples, I will present a broad outline of the history of the ley fuga and some coordinates for its study in the public sphere. The perception that extrajudicial means are necessary for justice survives today, as Mexican police and armed forces continue to be accused of extrajudicial executions. This chapter, however, will focus on the era up to the middle decades of the twentieth century, when those abuses were not yet framed in terms of human rights violations, but were considered part of regular law enforcement practices.[6]

Since the Porfiriato, journalists, average citizens, and even lawyers had justified the ley fuga as a method to procure justice when official justice was not to be trusted. Although the ley fuga was committed by representatives of the government, most commentators pragmatically recognized the contradiction between it and formal law. They found ways to express favorable views about the ley fuga, usually in conjunction with tacit support for officers who, in dealing with criminals, claimed to be encumbered by the formalities of the law. The ley fuga was simultaneously the object of official condemnation as a violation of the rule of law, and of praise from those who recognized that such rule was impossible to achieve in reality.

These contradictions beg a reconsideration of the relationship between violence and politics inspired by Arendt's observation. As the following pages show, violence was not an irrational byproduct of inequality or culture, but an integral part of politics—if we define politics as a multi-layered realm of life in which shaping policies about public matters of common interest involves a diversity of languages and actors.

The term "ley fuga" seems to have emerged in print during the 1870s, and was probably employed earlier in Spain, as "ley de fugas," in the context of the repression of bandits and later of anarchists and republicans.[7] The first examples of the practice in Mexico for which I could find references date back to the era of civil unrest after independence. They were not called "ley fuga" yet but already consisted of the killing of prisoners on the pretext that they were attempting to flee. The criminologist Julio Guerrero, in *La génesis del crimen en México,* attributed the term to conservative general Anastasio Bustamante, one of the nation's "multitude of little tyrants and murderers" notable for "the art of killing and destroying entire regions." According to Guerrero, the ley fuga was first applied against two rebels who had surrendered on the condition that their lives be spared. "But in spite of the agreement, they were taken out of the capital on the back of mules, their hands and feet tied, surrounded by twenty dragoons."[8] A firm believer in science and the law, Guerrero condemned the practice as a barbarity even worse than lynching.

Yet the practice, according to Guerrero, "has been used by all national authorities from then until not long ago," an indirect reference to the Porfirian regime.[9] At the time Guerrero was writing, however, the ley fuga and its association with lynching were not things of the past. Guerrero himself cited testimony presented throughout the trial of police officer Antonio Villavicencio, in 1898, describing routine use of the ley fuga: "a person would be taken by order of the authority to an uninhabited place at night, and killed by gunshots or stabbing. Noriega [the witness] stated that he had seen more than four hundred indigenous prisoners killed this way in Sonora."[10] Villavicencio had been a participant in the death of Arnulfo Arroyo, a man who attacked Porfirio Díaz during a parade in 1897. While Arroyo was detained at the police station a crowd, which apparently included members of the police, broke into his cell and killed him in an ostensible expression of popular outrage. Liberal journalist Ireneo Paz characterized the attack on Arroyo as "a lesson, as rigorous as it is patriotic, because it reveals the virility of the Mexican people."[11] The police chief who allowed this to happen, Eduardo Velázquez, was nevertheless arrested because Díaz could not condone the violence against his aggressor. Velázquez wrote a note full of regret for disappointing President Díaz, and killed himself at the police station—or perhaps fell victim to a subtler version of the ley fuga. The episode proved that such messy executions could amount to unofficial yet "patriotic" violence, but also that higher authorities would never openly support them.[12]

Though highly publicized, this case merely presented a complicated instance of a routine practice. Francisco Bulnes, an intellectual close to Díaz, wrote that General Bernardo Reyes was the regime's most famous practitioner of the ley fuga: "during the thirty-four years of the Tuxtepec regime about ten thousand individuals must have been killed in order to cleanse the country of bandits . . . the governor who put the greatest effort into this bloody task was undoubtedly General Bernardo Reyes, who for twenty-three years ruled the state of Nuevo León with an iron and bloody hand." Writing in the 1920s, years after the end of the regime and the death of the dictator, Bulnes added that Díaz approved of these methods, describing Reyes and his use of lethal violence as "inspired by Huitzilopochtli."[13] Bulnes was an adversary of Reyes so he might have exaggerated his negative view of extrajudicial murders. In contrast, newspapers during the Porfiriato reported on the execution of suspects at crime scenes without any apparent concern over the illegality of the practice.[14] The unofficial punishment of the killers of a domestic worker in Pachuca in 1897 demonstrated the simple logic of the ley fuga: they were executed in the same place where the body of their victim was found.[15]

President Francisco I. Madero and Vice President José María Pino Suárez were murdered in similar fashion in February 1913, outside the Mexico City penitentiary. Nobody believed that Victoriano Huerta, the general who overthrew Madero, had not ordered the crime, yet the circumstances surrounding it reflected an attempt to justify it. The use of the ley fuga seems to have been less prominent in this period—not for lack of prisoners to execute but because the civil war displaced the established authorities who would have required the ley fuga to skirt legal formalities. In the most famous example from those years, the ley fuga seems to have been used for sport rather than political necessity. According to Martín Luis Guzmán, Villista general Rodolfo Fierro killed prisoners, perhaps even hundreds of them, simply for entertainment. On one occasion, prisoners were told to run toward a wall and try to climb it. If they managed to do so, they would be free, but they had to survive the methodical guns of Fierro, shooting at them as they ran away.[16]

After the revolution, lynching and the ley fuga began to be defended in the context of a state that could not be trusted to protect honor and property. Saydi Núñez Cetina examines the case of Isaac Mendicoa Juárez, a recidivist bandit from the southern suburbs of the Federal District. The use of the ley fuga against him, in 1933, expressed the influence of the press, public frustration over the light sentences imposed, and the ineffectiveness of prisons in rehabilitating criminals.[17] Querido Moheno, a famous Mexican defense lawyer in the 1920s, praised U.S. lynchings as a method to protect the honor of white girls. Representing a young woman accused of killing a politician to avenge her father's murder, he told the judge, in his characteristically melodramatic tone: "I proclaim that all of us have not only the right but also the sacred duty to take justice into our own hands when public authorities deny us the justice we deserve by divine right." He added a rationale that could apply equally to the use of ley fuga in subsequent decades: "only those people who can apply justice themselves, when public authority cannot or would not apply it, have a right to justice." In the context of the consolidation of the postrevolutionary regime, Moheno, a former Porfirista and Huertista, framed his defense of extrajudicial violence as a popular reaction against a new tyrannical state.[18]

Yet there was certain ambiguity about the ley fuga, in terms of both morality and semantics. This, I believe, is the reason why the late Paul Vanderwood is wrong in assuming that the 1938 execution of Juan Castillo Morales, in Tijuana, was an example of the ley fuga: in fact the execution was public, conducted according to regulations, and took place after a military trial. Vanderwood claims that the ley fuga was widely condemned, but cites little evidence other than the popular reaction against the (probably legal) execution of Castillo Morales.[19] The opposite seems to have been true. Multiple examples show that extrajudicial violence against suspects in the interests of justice was condoned in the context of broadly shared skepticism toward penal institutions, yet, unlike the Morales case, the executions were conducted more discreetly.

The clearest expression of this reasoning is found in the crime news from the 1930s. As in the cases of Gallegos, Arroyo, and Mendicoa Juárez, the press created the narratives that shaped public interpretations of the use of the ley fuga. The *nota roja,* as crime news was often called, was the most influential journalistic genre in twentieth-century Mexico. Crime-focused periodicals enjoyed high circulation and financial autonomy, and so were able to engage readers in a critical dialogue with the state, as represented by police officers and judges. Nota roja publications, particularly during the middle decades of the century, appealed to the emotions and critical reasoning of readers, inviting them to become involved in the pursuit and punishment of suspects. Gruesome images were central to this appeal, sometimes including the bodies of ley fuga victims. Editors expected readers to question law enforcement and judicial institutions and seek the truth using the evidence presented in their publication, along with logic, intuition, and experience. In 1934 *La Prensa,* the most popular nota roja newspaper, offered a reward for readers who contributed information leading to the arrest of the main suspect in a triple murder at a barbershop, and a prize to the reader who could explain the true motive of the gruesome crime in no more than one hundred words. Santiago Rodríguez Silva was suspected of killing three women with razor blades and then fleeing the city. He was indeed killed by police detectives while in custody. Calls for swift punishment of suspects, also repeated in nota roja editorial pages, could only be construed as an extension of that involvement.[20]

For readers and editors seeking truth and punishment there was no clear hierarchy between legal and extralegal justice. The sentence was the least important aspect of the judicial process, since many innocent people were behind bars while true criminals fled or served short sentences. The suspect's arrest was more meaningful because it led to prison. What happened there afterwards was uncertain, but could include the ley fuga. Goyo Cárdenas, the famous 1942 serial killer, for example, was the object of multiple public demands for extrajudicial violence. Yet he was sent to a penitentiary and then to La Castañeda mental asylum, where he had an easy life, including excursions that, when discovered, forced his return to the penitentiary. In prison he became a lawyer, married, and had children; on his release in the 1970s he was cited as an example of rehabilitation. As explored by Enrique Desmond Arias and Kayyonne Marston in chapter 11, justifications of police repression and extrajudicial violence are influenced by the degree of visibility of crimes.

The civic engagement fostered by the nota roja did not exclude voicing feelings in favor of the extralegal use of violence against criminals. In a 1932 editorial entitled "Crime and Impunity" *La Prensa* formulated an argument that would remain valid over the following decades: legal penalties were too benign, prisoners escaped, and the "ineptitude and impotence of the police" encouraged criminal activity.[21] In 1934, *La Prensa* columnist Mateo Podan acknowledged the complexity of the argument in favor of the ley fuga. He started by characterizing the ley fuga as a police procedure that was as brutal as criminals themselves. But then, echoing positivist criminologists' views on crime, he proposed that the difference between a law-abiding person and a criminal was greater than that separating the criminal from an ape. In a transparent example of the impact of representations on state practices (see the introduction), these views justified the use of different punishments depending on the criminal's "attributes," thus negating liberal equality before the law. Rather than allowing a criminal to receive the benefit of a jury trial "as if he were a person," it was better to apply the "eye for an eye" rule, "identification and death, nothing more."[22] Echoing Podan's biological argument, a caricature from 1948 presents two apelike prisoners worriedly commenting about application of the ley fuga to a third one (figure 1.1).

La Prensa and other nota roja publications constantly and unsuccessfully editorialized in favor of the death penalty.[23] They also suggested that the extrajudicial execution of suspects or convicts by police was a more satisfactory alternative than the imprisonment dictated by judges. In a famous 1929 case, Luis Romero Carrasco killed an entire family, including their parrot (thus the common expression "mató hasta el perico" used to characterize multiple homicides). After a highly publicized jury trial in which he was sentenced to death, Romero Carrasco had his sentence commuted following the abolition of the death penalty but was killed in 1932, en route to Islas Marías. During the trial, he had refused to speak, much less confess, dozing off at times and exhibiting a rather cynical attitude toward justice. Reporting on Romero Carrasco's death, *La Prensa* commented that the guard's bullets had "freed society, once and for all, from a constant threat." Gallegos, whose death I described at the beginning of this chapter, was still on trial at the time. Unlike Romero Carrasco, he was very eager to speak to reporters and be

1.1. Cartoon depicting la ley fuga. From *La Prensa*, February 28, 1948, p. 8. The first prisoner asks, "Was it a lawful flight?" The other replies, "No. It was a law used with all who fled." *Image courtesy of Sebastián Lerdo de Tejada Library, Mexico City.*

photographed for the newspapers, enjoying brief celebrity. He confessed, then recanted—claiming that another man whom he could not identify had killed Aznar—and in general exasperated investigators with his evasive loquaciousness. Gallegos was shaken when he heard of Romero Carrasco's fate but told a journalist that he did not really expect to be the victim of the ley fuga.[24] He was, however, and <u>many saw it as justice.</u>

The nota roja created the emotional context that made possible the indignation of multitudes waiting for suspects at train stations or outside courthouses. Thereby, these newspapers turned popular responses to crime into news: in the "fascinating and brutal crime" of the barber shop in 1934, *La Prensa* printed photographs of an angry mob outside the crime scene and melodramatic images of grieving relatives during the victims' burial. Editors called for the capture of the "heinous criminal" Rodríguez Silva, echoing Tacubaya neighbors who "demand[ed] the head of the murderer; that he be hanged from a tree; that he receive the ley fuga."[25] *La Prensa* photographs often portrayed crowds of spectators near the crime scene or around the victim's body. Famous photographer Enrique Metinides made these crowds a feature of some of his works, calling them *los mirones* (the onlookers). Their amused stares at the camera resembled those of crowds gathered around lynching victims. The watchful and vengeful public became part of the crime scene and influenced the outcome of investigations. The bodies of victims of ley fuga were portrayed in undignified ways, highlighting the violent circumstances of their death.

Santiago Rodríguez Silva was taken to the crime scene to reenact the events. According to reporters, at one point he found himself alone in a room at the barbershop with two agents, suddenly grabbed one of the many razor blades at hand, and attacked one of the policemen but was gunned down by the other. The medical examiner counted twenty bullet holes in his body.[26] The newspaper printed images of his corpse under a headline that linked his demise with that of Gallegos: "¡Lo galleguearon!" (figure 1.2).[27] The outcome had been a distinct possibility since his capture in León, Guanajuato. During his train trip to Mexico City, Rodríguez Silva denied he would be a victim of the ley fuga because he had cooperated with authorities. But in fact he had not truly collaborated with the police, refusing to give a full confession and arguing that he had killed his victims, all women, in self-defense. After his death, his mother stated to the press that she had expected such an outcome given the gravity of his crime.

The use of the ley fuga continued into the 1940s, but the role of the press in fomenting its use gradually became less prominent. Many cases occurred in the routine of everyday justice. The famous detective Valente Quintana solved a rape in Veracruz, left town, and later learned that the ley fuga had been applied to the suspects.[28] One of the most prominent cases involved the alleged assassins of Senator Mauro Angulo in 1948. When Angulo was coming out of the public baths, as he did every morning, he was shot four times in the head by a man who escaped with

1.2. Photographs of Santiago Rodríguez Silva following his death. *La Prensa*, May 3, 1934, p. 1. "Galleguearon" refers to his death by ley fuga. *Image courtesy of Sebastián Lerdo de Tejada Library, Mexico City.*

an accomplice who was waiting in a Jeep around the corner. This was clearly a political assassination, from the manner of its execution to the response of President Miguel Alemán, who promptly ordered "all police agencies" to participate in the investigation. In an editorial entitled "No hay justicia," *La Prensa* concluded, after its usual advocacy for the death penalty, "In countries like ours, crime becomes a dynastic hierarchy, a political lineage of the darkest and proudest descent."[29] The reference clearly pointed to a family of Veracruzano caciques, the Armentas, as being involved in the crime. Local press in Tlaxcala warned that a failure to act would lead to "*Pistolerismo,* racketeering, swindlers of public ballots, and all antisocial pests seizing power, holding honest people in a reign of terror for many years." *Don Roque,* another local newspaper, reported that Veracruzano cacique Marciano Armenta, the brains behind the operation, was plotting a rebellion against the government.[30]

The result of the case was inevitable: the justice system seemed incapable of preventing the murderers from eventually walking free, as they had done following many other crimes committed in their region. After Armenta and his two alleged accomplices were arrested, authorities received letters and telegrams from their lawyers and relatives protesting their torture and irregular detention. Armenta's lawyer accused the Federal District police chief of ignoring an *amparo* (writ of habeas corpus).[31] Marciano's sister, Elvira Armenta Barradas, presented another amparo and warned that "such extended and unjustified detention makes me think that the goal is to kill my aforementioned brother with the use of the famous Ley Fuga."[32] Sure enough, even though they had not yet been charged, the three men were taken from Mexico City to the state of Veracruz ostensibly in order to assist in the arrest of other accomplices. The motorcade stopped in a lonely and foggy area near Magueyitos, Veracruz, so that the men could relieve themselves. Instead, claimed the police, they ran in different directions, and all three were shot as they disappeared into the fog (figure 1.3).[33] Aware of these tactics, opposition leader Salomón H. Rangel refused to urinate during his transport by government agents from Río Verde to the state capital, San Luis Potosí, after his arrest in 1961: "I told them that if they had orders to kill me they would have to do it inside the car, since I knew the trick of the 'ley fuga' and would not leave the vehicle."[34]

In the press, the episode at Magueyitos meant that justice, if not the law, had been served, although with some rough edges that the establishment of the death penalty could have smoothed out.[35] The afternoon edition of *Excélsior, Últimas Noticias,* always given to more lowbrow and exaggerated rhetoric than the morning edition, claimed that the ley fuga could be understood as a "defensive reaction of society" which involved "the collective subconscious."[36] *La Prensa* described the scene in Magueyitos as the epilogue of "a long career of crimes and professional pistolerismo, where everything had finished and Senator Angulo's blood, among others, had been avenged."[37] It entitled the description of

1.3. "How the assassins were killed. The executioners' version." *La Prensa,* February 24, 1948, p. 1. *Image courtesy of Sebastián Lerdo de Tejada Library, Mexico City.*

events by General Pedro J. Castro, chief of the Federal District's secret service, "The executioner's version."[38]

The use of ley fuga in this case was nevertheless more contentious than in the other cases mentioned previously. In comparison to Gallegos, Romero Carrasco, and Rodríguez Silva, the victims of the ley fuga here were harder for the press to dehumanize, and there were voices, however isolated, raised in their defense. After the killings, relatives of the suspects, including Gloria Flores, wrote to President Alemán acknowledging that they had indeed been executions, intended as a degree of payback for Angulo's death. Yet, invoking the ruthless arithmetic of revenge killings, Flores complained about the unfairness of making three men pay for the death of only one.[39] When news of the Magueyitos shooting reached Mexico City, Attorney General Franco Sodi declared the suspects had been transported without his authorization and suggested that the ley fuga had been applied. After General Castro paid a probably unfriendly visit to his home, Sodi published a letter asserting that he had never doubted Castro's honor.[40] To the press, Castro declared that he was not "un matón" and that the death of the suspects under his direct custody was "very embarrassing" for him, as he was a member of the army with a clean record. He argued that he did not apply the ley fuga because that would contradict his honor as a military man, and also explained that, if he had allowed the cacique Armenta to escape, he would have been suspected of accepting a bribe because of the suspect's wealth; thus he had no choice but to kill him. Yet he also recognized the logic of the ley fuga: facing the dilemma between failing in his assignment to guard the suspects and "avoiding, by any means necessary, that the crime would remain unpunished," he chose the latter.[41]

Castro had public supporters in spite of his flimsy logic. A Veracruzano organization in the capital wrote to Alemán denouncing journalistic attempts to "distort" the circumstances of the death of "the pistoleros Armenta," and praising Castro. Whereas Armenta was the prototype of the cacique pistoleril, Castro was an honorable man who in previous years had helped the state of Veracruz rid itself of criminals.[42] Politicians echoed this view. After the shooting, Castro went directly to Xalapa to notify Governor Adolfo Ruiz Cortines, who would four years later succeed President Alemán, himself a former Veracruz governor.[43] Ruiz Cortines praised Castro to the press, saying "he wholeheartedly agrees with the events and states that he hopes they would be the way to end the era of terror those subjects have imposed on the state, and he also told us public opinion agreed with what had happened."[44] Although authorities never openly claimed responsibility for ordering a ley fuga, the ambivalence of newspaper accounts and their own statements implied that such events were not merely the product of police ineptitude.[45]

The practice continued to be publicly, if not officially, recognized during the fifties. In 1957, police agents gunned down Atalo Herrera Mendoza while transporting him to stand trial in Tuxpan. He had killed two boys, and the people of Poza Rica (where the crime was committed) had come very close to lynching him when he was arrested. His crime produced a "wave of indignation" according to the press.[46] The same year crowds demanded that the murderers of Father Juan Fullana Taberner be handed over to the people "to do justice," or at least that the ley fuga be applied to them.[47] The criminals had killed the priest in a botched robbery, mistakenly believing him to be hiding a large amount of cash designated for a building expansion in the same Mexico City parish. When one of the murderers, wrestler Pancho Valentino, tried to escape from the penitentiary, the chief of guards told him that he could have him killed right then and there without any repercussions. The prisoner fell to his knees begging for mercy and got away with only a beating.[48]

An article in *La Prensa* from 1951 about a different case in Mérida reveals how the ley fuga could now be the object of criticism if the police failed to exercise proper diligence. Describing a botched investigation, the paper opined that state attorney Sauri Peniche was "carrying on his shoulders the ridicule and material responsibility of a warrant and an unjustified arrest, as well as the moral responsibility for the murder of an innocent citizen committed by the agents of the judicial police."[49] In other words, if the ley fuga had been applied against a suspect that public opinion could easily characterize as worthy of such fate, there would be no problem. As opposed to the mob mentality of lynching, the ley fuga could thus be seen as rational and modern.

Even though authorities could not acknowledge using the ley fuga, it was integral to the investigation methods of the Mexican police. The threat of the ley fuga was, along with torture, a tool for extracting confessions from suspects. Confessions, in turn, were the most direct way to get an indictment and bring a case to a rapid judicial conclusion. Police agents often subjected suspects in custody to nonlethal violence. The documents produced by mid-century Mexican authorities do not speak of torture, but some amparos presented by suspects' lawyers and relatives do. Although the police denied using torture, internal documents do recognize the effectiveness of "severe interrogations."[50]

Confessions were essential in a judicial process that was constantly besieged by public skepticism. The murderers' versions of events were considered the most persuasive and legally effective pieces of evidence against them, accounting for the pressures used to extract those confessions and the cost paid by those who, like Gallegos, Rodríguez Silva, and Armenta, refused to make a full confession. The first two were killed after journalists had interviewed them and depicted both as undeniably guilty. In their cases, and many others, the death of the criminal was a fitting end for a trial that had already taken place in the court of public opinion, albeit with information provided in part through judicial means. Ley fuga and confession complemented each other in the pursuit of truth.

A suspect's failure to confess could have dire consequences. Several cases in the Secret Service archives document the death of suspects during investigations. As Martín Luis Guzmán wrote in 1931, "criminals acquired the habit of killing themselves in the cellar of the police head-quarters, and all of them, strangely enough, committed suicide with a 45 caliber automatic handgun."[51] In 1936 *La Prensa* reported the routine: "Two suicides in the police headquarters. Only one of them managed to kill himself immediately. The killer of an alcohol inspector hung himself in his cell. A conman named José Fuentes Núñez tried to slit his throat with a razor blade and is dying."[52] In 1951 *Alarma!* mentioned several other cases of suspicious suicides in the penitentiary.[53]

The ley fuga existed in an area of moral ambiguity ironically alluded to by Guzmán: it seemed to undermine the public search for the truth, as it was predicated on skepticism toward the justice system, yet it also helped the police to obtain confessions by hanging as a threat over suspects' heads; newspapers, in turn, reported it as a validation of the verdict of public opinion. In other words, the ley fuga was intended both to investigate and to punish, state functions that Mexican law had distinctly separated since 1917 by placing all investigations in the hands of the judicial branch, and limiting the role of the police to crime pre-vention and the arrest and transfer of suspects to judicial authorities.[54] Newspapers and magazines like *Alarma!* denounced police abuses, ineptitude, and even criminal complicity; yet, sometimes on the same page, these publications also demanded *mano dura* (zero tolerance) as the proper response to infamous crimes.[55] The critical stance of the nota roja toward the state muddied the distinction between punishment and investigation: violence against suspects solved all problems deriving from a confusing and corrupt set of justice institutions.

Support for the ley fuga was often implicit, as the official line was that such a practice was not acceptable, as established by the law. As with other aspects in the history of crime and justice in twentieth-century Mexico, this contradiction was never openly resolved: support and condemnation coexisted in a field of public discussion where everybody knew that the truth was always uglier than the normative description of the law. Unlike the construction of the truth in North Atlantic societies, wherein the state nationalized reality through science and, in the field of crime, through the investigations conducted and sentences issued by authorities, in Mexico the state was only one among many voices disputing the truth and its consequences.

Endorsements of the ley fuga did not serve any narrow ideological purpose, either in support of or opposition to the government or, more specifically, the death penalty. The critique implied by those opinions was political in a broader sense. It channeled citizen participation in matters of justice through a method considered rough but reliable. In this sense, the ley fuga was not a wellspring of irrational or dehumanizing violence—at least during the middle decades of the last century. It occurred in a small number of cases and, like lynching, remained rare, making its public impact even more effective. Both practices articulated claims for justice by publics that defined themselves as rational in the public sphere yet tolerated extrajudicial violence against transgressors.

Similar impulses for openness and citizen participation expressed through violence are mirrored in more recent manifestations of the search for truth and justice, such as victims' movements and collective demonstrations demanding security.[56] Yet the legacy of transparency that underpinned press debates about justice and the truth is now revealing its ultimate contradiction with the dehumanizing consequences of violence in contemporary Mexico. The use of extrajudicial executions continues to be endorsed, sometimes explicitly, by state authorities and average citizens.[57] Executions of alleged narcos by paramilitary groups are posted on the Internet, now without a need to justify them as attempted escapes or the product of popular rage. In their discourse Michoacán *autodefensas* (vigilante groups) shun brutality and demand state protection, but are effectively taking justice into their own, civilian hands.

This moral ambivalence regarding violent acts and public perceptions echoes the findings of Markus-Michael Müller about relations between the police and contemporary residents of Iztapalapa: the police are not to be trusted, yet their involvement is sought when conflicts cannot be handled by community mechanisms, implying acceptance of a "variety of extralegal practices on the part of the local police forces."[58] As in Central American countries recovering from civil wars, the use of the ley fuga, or of mano dura policies, does not necessarily point to moments of state failure—as foreign critics often assert—but to processes of reconstruction characterized by unmet expectations of justice and lingering social violence.[59]

Today, as in 1932 or 1948, politics cannot be clearly separated from the criminal use of violence, and a consensus in favor of bending the law to achieve swift justice still survives in Mexico. Now, as then, many believe that it is acceptable, perhaps useful, to balance the supremacy of the law with other established, if irregular, practices of violence—as long as they lead to something that resembles order and peace. But the exponential growth in the frequency of these practices today reminds us of Arendt's warning that the effects of violence can only be controlled in the short term: "the danger of violence, even if it moves consciously within a non-extremist framework of short-term goals, will always be that the means overwhelm the end. If goals are not achieved rapidly, the result will be not merely defeat but the introduction of the practice of violence into the whole body politic. The practice of violence, like all action, changes the world, but the most probable change is to a more violent world."[60]

Notes

1. Eduardo Téllez Vargas and José Ramón Garmabella, ¡Reportero de policía! El Güero Téllez (Mexico City: Ediciones Océano, 1982), 27; Jesse Lerner, El impacto de la modernidad: fotografía criminalística en la ciudad de México (Mexico City: Turner-CNCA, INAH–Editorial Océano, 2007), 76–77. This chapter owes a great deal to the comments of Angélica Durán-Martínez, Saydi Núñez Cetina, Benjamin Smith, Mariana Mora, Aída Hernández, Paul Hathazy, Marianne Braig, Markus-Michael Müller, and the editors of this volume. All translations from Spanish are my own.

3. Alan Knight, "Habitus and Homicide: Political Culture in Revolutionary Mexico," in Citizens of the Pyramid: Essays on Mexican Political Culture, edited by Wil G. Pansters (Amsterdam: Thela, 1997), 108, 134.

3. Everard Kidder Meade, "La ley fuga y la tribuna improvisada: Extrajudicial Execution and Public Opinion in Mexico City, 1929–1940" (presentation, Kayden Colloquium, Crime and Punishment in Latin America: Practices and Representations, University of Colorado, Boulder, October 7–8, 2011).

4. David Garland, "Penal Excess and Surplus Meaning: Public Torture Lynchings in Twentieth-Century America," Law and Society Review 39, no. 4 (2005): 793–833.

5. Hannah Arendt, On Violence (New York: Harcourt, Brace, 1969), 64.

6. Human Rights Watch, "Informe Mundial, 2014: Mexico," www.hrw.org/es/world-report/2014/country-chapters/121995 (accessed March 25, 2014).

7. Paul Vanderwood, Juan Soldado: Rapist, Murderer, Martyr, Saint (Durham, NC: Duke University Press, 2004). For the frequency of the term in Spanish-language

books, see Google Books N-gram Viewer, https://books.google.com/ngrams/graph ?content=ley+fuga&year_start=1800&year_end=2000&corpus=21&smoothing =3&share=&direct_url=t1%3B%2Cley%20fuga%3B%2Cco (accessed March 25, 2014). The graph suggests use of the term increased in the early 1880s, late 1910s and early 1920s, 1930s, late 1950s and early 1960s, and decreased steadily since then.

8. Guerrero, *La génesis del crimen en México: estudio de psiquiatría social* (Mexico City: Porrúa, 1977), 241, 240. See Everard Kidder Meade, "Anatomies of Justice and Chaos: Capital Punishment and the Public in Mexico, 1917–1945," PhD diss., University of Chicago, 2005.

9. Guerrero, *La génesis del crimen*, 240.

10. Ibid., 241.

11. Jacinto Barrera Bassols, *El caso Villavicencio: violencia y poder en el porfiriato* (Mexico City: Alfaguara, 1997), 101.

12. Villavicencio continued his sinister career beyond the revolution. Barrera Bassols, *El caso Villavicencio*. On this case, see also Renato González Mello and Ana Laura Cué, "El asesinato de Arnulfo Arroyo," in *Posada y la prensa ilustrada: signos de modernización y resistencias* (Mexico City: Instituto Nacional de Bellas Artes–Museo Nacional de Arte, 1996), 103–19. Claudio Lomnitz, "Mexico's First Lynching: Sovereignty, Criminality, Moral Panic," *Critical Historical Studies* 1, no. 1 (2014): 85–123.

13. Francisco Bulnes, *El verdadero Díaz y la revolución* (Mexico City: Editora Nacional, 1960), 61–63.

14. *La Voz de México*, September 7, 1897, 3. See an exposé of its frequent use in Carlo de Fornaro, *Díaz, Czar of Mexico: An Arraignment by Carlos de Fornaro* (New York City: Carlo de Fornaro, 1909), 87–88.

15. *La Voz de México*, September 7, 1897, 3.

16. Martín Luis Guzmán, "El águila y la serpiente," in *Obras completas* (Mexico City: Fondo de Cultura Económica, 1984), 1:329–38.

17. Saydi Núñez Cetina, "El caso de el 'Tigre del Pedregal: homicidio y justicia en la ciudad de México durante la posrevolución," in *Crimen y justicia en la historia de México: nuevas miradas*, ed. Elisa Speckman Guerra and Salvador Cárdenas Gutiérrez, 315–53 (Mexico City: Suprema Corte de Justicia de la Nación, 2011).

18. Querido Moheno, *Procesos célebres. Rubin: discurso en defensa de la acusada* (Mexico City: Botas, 1925), 177, 187, 168. For similar arguments used in another case, see Pablo Piccato, "The Girl Who Killed a Senator: Femininity and the Public Sphere in Post-Revolutionary Mexico," in *True Stories of Crime in Modern Mexico*, ed. Robert Buffington and Pablo Piccato (Albuquerque: University of New Mexico Press, 2009), 128–53.

19. Vanderwood, *Juan Soldado*, 55, 66.

20. *La Prensa*, April 28, 1934, 3; Pablo Piccato, "Murders of Nota Roja: Truth and Justice in Mexican Crime News," *Past and Present* 223, no. 1 (2014): 195–231.

21. *La Prensa*, March 16, 1932, 5.

22. *La Prensa*, April 28, 1934, 10.

23. Meade, "Anatomies of Justice and Chaos."

24. *La Prensa,* March 19, 1932, 3; Téllez Vargas and Garmabella, *¡Reportero de policía!,* 27; Meade, "La ley fuga y la tribuna improvisada." On Gallegos's celebrity, see José Pérez Moreno, "Crónica del jurado de Carrasco," *El Universal,* August 7, 1929, 2nd sec., 1.

25. *La Prensa,* April 24, 1934; April 25, 1934, 3, 18; April 26, 1934, 3, 6, 18, 21; and April 29, 1934, 30.

26. *La Prensa,* May 4, 1934, 10; Archivo Histórico del Distrito Federal, Sección Jefatura de Policía, Serie Investigación y Seguridad, Servicio Secreto (hereafter AHDF, JP, ISSS), caja 3, exp. 20, N/522/1204.

27. *La Prensa* May 5, 1934, 3, 26.

28. Carlos Isla, *El mejor caso de Valente Quintana. Los "Corta Mechas"* (Mexico City: Fontamara, 2004), 127.

29. *La Prensa,* February 18, 1948, 1–4, 8, 14, 15. The original Spanish reads, "En países como el nuestro, el crimen llega a ser una jerarquía dinástica, una estirpe política de la más sombría y altiva alcurnia."

30. *Don Roque,* December 7, 1947, 1:19, 2; quotation from ibid., February 29, 1948, 1:31, 2; See also April 11, 1948, 1:37, 1.

31. Fernando Novoa to President Miguel Alemán, Federal District, February 21, 1948. Archivo General de la Nación, Mexico (AGN-MEX), MAV, 541/347.

32. AHDF, JP ISSS, caja 4, exp. 30, legajos I–II, 1936, asesinato diputado Manlio Fabio Altamirano, 1 foto, 523, 177 p.

33. *La Prensa,* February 28, 1948, p. 1.

34. Salomón H. Rangel, *Forjando mi destino: apuntes de mi vida* (Mexico City : EPESSA, 1989), 197. I owe this reference to Benjamin Smith.

35. Undated clippings, AHDF, JP, ISSS, caja 10, exp. 65, 1948.

36. Clippings from *Últimas Noticias de Excélsior,* February 27, 1948, AHDF, JP, ISSS, caja 10, exp. 65, 1948.

37. *La Prensa,* February 28, 1948, 10.

38. Ibid., 1, 8.

39. Gloria Flores to President Miguel Alemán, Apizaco, March 10, 1948, AGN-MEX, MAV, 541/347. No response is on file.

40. *La Prensa,* February 29, 1948, 3, 27.

41. *La Prensa,* February 28, 1948, 3.

42. Telegram from José de la Mora, Comité Estatal de la Sociedad Revolucionarios Mártires de Río Blanco, DF, to Miguel Alemán, February 17, 1948, AGN-MEX, MAV, 541/347; *Últimas Noticias de Excélsior,* February 27, 1948, n.p., AHDF, JP, ISSS, caja 10, exp. 65, 1948. For expressions of disapproval against Castro, including an anonymous postcard calling him a murderer, see AHDF, JP, ISSS, caja 10, exp. 65, 1948.

43. *La Prensa,* February 28, 1948, 10.

44. Another agent went days later to survey Veracruzano public opinion and found widespread support. AHDF, JP, ISSS, caja 10, exp. 65, 1948.

45. AHDF, JP, ISSS, caja 10, exp. 65, 1948, asesinato senador Mauro Angulo Hernández. Editorials on ley fuga are "Ojo por ojo y diente por diente" and "El que a hierro mata . . . [a hierro muere]," both in *La Prensa,* April 28, 1934, 10, 18–20.

46. *La Prensa,* March 9, 1957, 12, 33.

47. *La Prensa,* January 12, 1957, 1, 29.

48. Téllez Vargas and Garmabella, *¡Reportero de policía!,* 178.

49. *La Prensa,* May 3, 1951, 42. For a 1970 case see *Alarma!* 361, April 1, 1970, 12.

50. AHDF, JP, ISSS, caja. 11, exp. 75, 1954.

51. Carlos Monsiváis, *Los mil y un velorios: crónica de la nota roja en México.* 2nd ed. (Mexico City: Asociación Nacional del Libro, 2009), 29.

52. *La Prensa,* July 11, 1936, 10.

53. "Sogas siniestras en la penitenciaría," *Alarma!,* May 13, 1953, 21–22, 24.

54. Arturo Villarreal Palo, "Ministerio público y policía de investigación en México: una reforma incompleta," *Letras Jurídicas* 5 (Fall 2007); Diane E. Davis, "Policing and Regime Transition: From Postauthoritarianism to Populism to Neoliberalism." In *Violence, Coercion, and State-Making in Twentieth-Century Mexico: The Other Half of the Centaur,* ed. Wil G. Pansters (Stanford, CA: Stanford University Press, 2012), 68–90.

55. "Son los verdugos de la frontera! Odiosos patrulleros," *Alarma!* 350, 14; "Justicia: ¿cuánto vales?" *Don Roque,* 1:1, February 17, 1946, 4; "Atropellos a granel de la POLICÍA LOCAL," *Don Roque,* 1:7, March 31, 1946, 4; *La Voz de Sinaloa,* July 1, 1963, 1.

56. An example of the successful coupling of justice and publicity can be found in the documentary *Presunto Culpable,* directed by Roberto Hernández and Geoffrey Smith, 2010. On demonstrations for security and calls for direct justice see Buffington and Piccato, introduction to *True Stories of Crime.*

57. See Alan Knight, "Habitus and Homicide," 110. On contemporary violence see Álvaro Delgado, "Asoman los paramilitares," *Proceso,* September 26, 2011, www .proceso.com.mx/?p=282499.

58. Markus-Mikael Müller, "Assessing an Ambivalent Relationship: Policing and the Urban Poor in Mexico City," *Journal of Latin American Studies* 44, no. 2 (2012): 326.

59. I owe this insight to Angélica Durán-Martínez.

60. Arendt, *On Violence,* 80.

2 Legitimating Lynching

Public Opinion and Extralegal Violence in Mexico

Gema Santamaría

Latin America has experienced increased incidences of lynching violence over the last three decades, with Mexico, Guatemala, Ecuador, Bolivia, Brazil, and Venezuela emerging as the most visible and analyzed cases.[1] Lynchings constitute public, gruesome, and highly ritualized forms of collective violence that involve the torture, mutilation, burning, or hanging of the victim in a prominent public space.[2] The persistence of this practice today offers disquieting insights into a region that would otherwise seem well on its way toward sustained political stability and democratic consolidation. In line with the two dominant approaches to violence described in the volume introduction, explanations for lynchings in Latin America have focused either on the pervasive deficiencies in the region's justice and security apparatuses[3] or on the dynamics of social inequality underlying this form of violence.[4]

This chapter brings to the fore a dimension of lynching that has been largely absent from these academic accounts and that lies at the core of this volume's analytical focus: the dimension of representation, public debate, and political discourse. Literature on lynchings in the United States has illuminated the importance of public debates and shifting sensibilities regarding rough forms of justice for their delegitimization and eventual decline during the first decades of the twentieth century.[5] Historical sociologists have furthermore attributed the gradual disappearance of spectacular forms of violence and punishment in Western

Europe to the development of attitudes of restraint and feelings of revulsion toward corporeal and excessive punitive practices, first amongst the elites, then within broader sectors of society.[6] Building on this literature, I seek to elucidate the persistence and apparent legitimacy of lynchings in Latin America by entering the field of representation and discourse.

I analyze the impact that public representations of lynching violence have had in sanctioning and desanctioning this form of violence in Mexico. I do so by examining the diverse and at times contradictory representations of lynchings in the Mexican press during the 1930s, focusing on the state of Puebla.[7] My argument is twofold. First, I argue that lynchings, together with other gruesome and highly visible forms of violence reported at the time in Puebla, were not always considered unacceptable by an economically privileged and politically influential public. Rather, their validity was established on a case-by-case basis and with consideration to the social backgrounds of the victims and perpetrators and the nature of the crime. This logic of representation was also at play in the press coverage of other expressions of violence that, like lynchings, aimed at punishing deviant or criminal behavior, such as the death penalty, the ley fuga (flight law),[8] and extrajudicial killings perpetrated by police, mayors, and other public officials as part of their law enforcement duties.

Second, I claim that representations of lynchings were based, both implicitly and explicitly, on social constructions of class, gender, ethnicity, and religious affiliation. The use of these constructs allowed journalists and their readers to "make sense" of lynchings. By creating a narrative of lynchings in which places, persons, and motivations were characterized according to constructions of ethnicity, religious affiliation, gender, and class, the press established causal relations between these constructs and the occurrence of lynchings. More importantly, these characteristics were usually invoked in order to determine the validity or invalidity of a lynching and hence served to set the boundaries between tolerable and intolerable forms of violence. This argument resonates with the findings of Daniel Núñez, Enrique Desmond Arias, and Kayyonne Marston in this volume, who highlight the centrality of social representations in legitimating extralegal and extrajudicial forms of violence in contemporary Guatemala, Brazil, and Jamaica, respectively.

Locating the Publics of Violence in 1930s Puebla

The 1930s marked a key moment in the consolidation and relative pacification of postrevolutionary Mexico. The 1910 revolution and the Cristero civil war (1926–29) had revealed the multiple and divergent forces driving the country's local and regional politics. Cultural politics, institutional consolidation, and economic development would become central elements in the government's attempts to create a more cohesive and stable political reality at the national level.[9] Although Mexican political elites could hardly aspire to monopolize the use of violence at a national scale, they did see the bureaucratization and disciplining of different forms of violence at the local and regional levels as a necessary step toward the modernization of the countryside and the development of a capitalist economy.[10] In Puebla, the loyalty and discipline of regional caudillos such as Maximino Ávila Camacho would prove instrumental in this regard, as would the strong alliances that local politicians maintained with capitalist elites and the Catholic Church.[11]

Nonetheless, since governing elites controlled violent practices only selectively and in accordance with their economic and political interests, violence was present in Puebla.[12] In particular, press coverage at the time reveals lynchings and other forms of vigilante justice were only partially desanctioned. As in other contexts discussed in this volume (see, for example, David Carey's discussion of so-called indigenous criminality in Guatemala or Robert Alegre's analysis of the criminalization of sodomy in Chile), representations of violence reflected the interplay among political ideologies, power dynamics, and social constructions of crime. Freed from the censorship that characterized press coverage on more political issues, such as electoral politics and party disputes, representations of violence and crime in the media helped to air anxieties regarding the modern, civilized, and respectable character of the state and the nation.

Shaped predominantly by an evolving urban readership that regarded itself as the vanguard of government efforts to modernize the country, public opinion often focused on violence exercised by peasants, indigenous populations, and so-called religious fanatics. Remote indigenous towns were generally regarded as places mired in ignorance, backwardness, and violence. The city of Puebla and its surroundings were also of concern for city dwellers, as car accidents, rapes, and killings by professional criminals demonstrated the dangers brought about by rapid urbanization. By the same token, the press portrayed urban and rural authorities as abusive and corrupt; journalists often accused police officers, mayors, and local judges of being responsible for extrajudicial killings, hangings, shootings, and street brawls. These representations reflected an ongoing distrust of local authorities that contrasted with the generally uncritical press coverage of high-level officials such as the state governor and the president.

Informed by particular conceptions of justice, lynchings constituted illegal responses to apparently criminal activity and thus were at the crossroads of public debates about violence, crime, and justice. In 1930s Puebla, however, not all illegal and violent forms of punishment performed in public spaces fell into the category of *linchamiento* (lynching). "Linchamiento" was reserved for unplanned and relatively spontaneous acts of collective violence. Moreover, it was mostly used in reference to acts of vigilantism performed by non-state actors, even though it was widely acknowledged that state actors operated in a "gray zone,"[13] where legal and illegal forms of violence coexisted on a regular basis.[14] Often written with a *y*, as "lynchamiento," following its English spelling, the word itself reflected the weight that the U.S. history of lynching had within Mexican public understanding of this practice. Similar to what the literature on lynching in the United States has suggested, lynching was recognized as a penal practice.[15] Thus, its legitimacy was usually discussed by comparison with other forms of legal and extralegal punishment. When reporting cases of lynching, journalists and editors alike did not simply describe the events but expressed their opinion as to the motivations and circumstances surrounding each case, justifying or condemning the event based on what they considered just, legitimate, or acceptable uses of violence.

Lynchings as Justice

On July 9, 1933, the newspaper *La Opinión* reported the brutal rape and murder of seven-year-old María Juárez in Cholula, a suburb of the city of Puebla. According to the report, published on the front page under the headline "Unspeakable Crime Committed on the Person of a Little Girl,"[16] two criminals kidnapped María from her house and, after raping her, smashed her skull with a stone and dumped her into a well. News of the crime quickly spread throughout Cholula, causing outrage and indignation and leading to an attempt to lynch the men accused of her murder.

Although the only testimony against the alleged criminals was that of the girl María herself who, before dying, "feebly opened her eyes and muttered" the names of the two men, the newspaper assumed their guilt. The article opened with the statement: "Two inveterate criminals of Cholula, called Manuel González and Ramón Fórtiz, kidnapped seven-year-old María Juárez, abusing her and killing her." The writer then called for an "exemplary punishment" of what was described as the "most monstrous crime known to date," one that obliged "all members of society to clamor and demand a prompt punishment" for the criminals. Even though the authorities prevented the lynching, the unfolding of the case, its press coverage, and its relation to similar cases occurring during the same years make it relevant for my discussion.

The following day, the same newspaper published two articles on María's murder.[17] The first called for the criminals to be made an example of through harsh punishment and reminded readers of the cruelty of the murder, adding new details revealed by the autopsy. The second, an editorial entitled "The Crime in Cholula and the Upturn in Criminality in the State," narrated the case of another girl whose rape and killing resembled that of María Juárez, and whose murderers were set free allegedly due to lack of evidence. The editorial concluded by stating that "as long as justice is not severe enough among this kind of Lombrosian criminals . . . these and other infamous crimes will continue to occur in the state of Puebla."[18] As this quotation illustrates, the newspaper took a clear position regarding the criminals' guilt and the need to punish them "promptly," even though a proper criminal investigation was still pending.

On July 16, one week after María's murder, the newspaper announced the two criminals had "disappeared" from prison, claiming that they most probably had tried to escape, "forcing" the guards to shoot them and "unintentionally" execute them with the ley fuga.[19] Far from criticizing this extrajudicial killing, the newspaper justified it in light of the murderers' cruelty and their alleged attempt to flee the law.

The murder of María Juárez and the extrajudicial killing of her accused murderers resembles the case of "la niña Olga" Camacho in Tijuana, in 1938, and the attempt to lynch Juan Castillo Morales, alias

"Juan Soldado," a Mexican soldier accused of her brutal rape and murder. When Castillo Morales was taken into military custody, a group of people demanding justice for the girl assaulted the fort and attempted to seize and lynch him. The fort was set on fire but the authorities saved Castillo Morales, only to execute him later.[20] The case stimulated lively debates regarding the legitimacy of the death penalty and the validity of extralegal forms of punishment such as the ley fuga and lynchings. The case was so highly publicized that President Cárdenas himself traveled to Tijuana to put an end to the protests and determine, once and for all, what Castillo Morales's punishment ought to be. The local press in Puebla followed the case closely. A few days after the attempted lynching, an editorial under the headline "In This Place, We Do Not Lynch" strongly condemned the mob violence perpetrated against Castillo Morales and attributed the "cannibalistic" incident to Tijuana's proximity to the United States. Denoting the centrality of U.S. lynchings in public representations of the practice, the writer further opined that the people who attempted to lynch Juan Soldado were emulating the type of punishment used in "Yanquilandia against blacks who rape girls, setting fire to them and diabolically dancing around their smoking humanity."[21]

This was not the first time public opinion attempted to differentiate Mexico from the United States and its use of rough forms of justice. During the last decade of the nineteenth century, the attempt to lynch Arnulfo Arroyo, a man accused of assaulting President Porfirio Díaz, was described as an act that stained the honor and "immaculate" sense of justice of the country.[22] Porfirio Díaz himself claimed this was the first recorded lynching in Mexico's history.[23] Interestingly enough, U.S. newspapers echoed this narrative. The *New York Times* stated this was the first time Mexico had witnessed an act of this nature, and the *Washington Post* celebrated the fact that the Mexican government had effectively and fairly tried those responsible for the lynching.[24] This article further complained that in the United States lynchings were committed with impunity: "They do things differently in Mexico . . . and it might be hoped that the officials of the various States will take the lesson to heart and act upon it when the necessity again arises."

Paradoxically, it would be in Mexico and not the United States where this practice would ultimately prove more tenacious. Whereas lynchings significantly declined in the United States during the 1930s, in Mexico they persisted throughout that decade and beyond. Furthermore, the lynching of accused rapists was a practice Mexico and its neighbor had in common. In Puebla, cases of rape against girls and young women from "respectable" families generated public outcries for expeditious and exemplary forms of punishment. For example, on August 5, 1937, a local newspaper reported that the "disgusting rapist" of seven-year-old Refugio Simo was almost killed in an attempted lynching brought on by his vile actions and the "justified popular rage" it generated.[25] On June 24, 1938, in the town of San Martín Tlapala in Atlixco, a newspaper reported that Lorenzo Gómez had been lynched by a mob who "were forced" to carry out such an action because the man had raped two young women.[26] Years earlier, on July 15, 1934, a newspaper reported that Leonor Cruz, daughter of Dr. Marcos Cruz Cázares, had been raped by the "caveman" Fidel López Cortés.[27] The following day, under the headline "He Paid with His Life for the Violation of a Girl," the same newspaper announced the criminal had been shot upon attempting to escape prison and celebrated the steadfast actions of the police in preventing the alleged rapist's flight.[28]

While newspaper reports of rapes and other forms of sexual assault against girls and women were quite common in Puebla during the 1930s, not all of these crimes generated public outrage. Some cases of reported rape were resolved when the offender married the dishonored victim. Press coverage of domestic violence against women by their partners was also frequent. Although the press did not spare its readers any of the gruesome and violent details of the beatings, injuries, or murders perpetrated by men against women, it would rarely if ever demand an end to this form of violence. In some cases, the press did mention attempts organized by women to punish husbands or partners accused of domestic violence. The purported wife beater Dimas Mercado was almost lynched by a group of women on May 4, 1930.[29] In this and other reports, the women were often described as "troublemakers" or as having a "manly" temperament.

Vehicular homicides, especially when the victim was a child, generated similar public outrage and demands to expedite justice. For instance, in the town of Chachapa Eduardo Goya accidentally struck and killed a boy named José Alonso. The accident infuriated those who witnessed it, provoking an attempted lynching of the driver and his passenger.[30] A year earlier, on July 2, 1937, a driver hit and killed eight-year-old Elena Espinosa on her way to school. When they found out about the accident, a group of infuriated women nearly lynched the "savage driver," who had already been involved in a similar incident with another girl.[31] Like rape cases, vehicular homicides did not always generate outrage. Many cases were attributed to the carelessness of pedestrians unfamiliar with the dangers of urban life.

Lynching as Barbarism

In contrast to the approval and justification of lynchings against accused rapists, the lynching of Edgar Kullman was openly condemned as an expression of the backwardness of indigenous people. On April 25, 1930, *La Opinión* reported the brutal death of Kullman, a Norwegian geologist and explorer who had visited the town of Amozoc to study the traditions of the indigenous townsfolk.[32] The report described at length how nearly three hundred "fanatics" beat and wounded Kullman with stones, machetes, and knives, then dragged him by a rope around his neck and threw him into a well.[33] Because the lynching took place on Holy Thursday, the newspaper called the lynching of Kullman a "sacrifice," a "holocaust," and a "Calvary," comparable only to the suffering of Jesus Christ. According to the newspaper, the lynching was motivated by a fantastic myth that attributed the disappearance of various children to a wicked aviator who would abduct them, behead them, and then extract their body fat in order to power his airplane.[34]

A week before the lynching, on April 18, newspapers narrated how recent, mysterious disappearances of several children had caused this absurd story to circulate throughout Puebla's towns.[35] The airplane would supposedly fly every night, terrifying parents, who would run to hide and protect their children whenever they heard the sound of the strange machine.[36] In the same article, the newspaper explained that the fantastic airplane was actually that of renowned pilot Pablo Sidar, who was performing flight tests every night in preparation for attempting the first direct trip from Mexico to Argentina. Sidar's intended flight had raised great expectations in the local press and was celebrated as an exemplar of Mexico's modernity and progress.[37]

Against the backdrop of this story of modernity, the myth of the fantastic airplane powered by children's body fat was portrayed as disgraceful superstition and barbarism. The press urged the authorities to prevent the further propagation of such a fantastic story and to prosecute those responsible for creating a sense of alarm amongst parents.[38]

The lynching of Kullman was attributed to the ignorance of indigenous people and became a source of embarrassment and outrage among the reading public. The press demanded the prompt punishment of perpetrators, including Balbina de la Rosa, alias "La Borrega," responsible for spreading the false rumor that led to Kullman's tragic killing.[39] An editorial published on April 27 lamented the killing as well as the backwardness and superstition that the "natives" had inherited from their "ancestors"; concluding that the perpetrators of this act did not deserve to be treated like rational beings.[40] The outrage generated by Kullman's lynching was so great that more than one year after the event the same newspaper condemned as insufficient the sentence of two years' imprisonment that authorities handed down to the perpetrators, due to lack of evidence to prosecute them for more than the illegal disposal of Kullman's corpse (*inhumación clandestina*).[41] The article announced that the crime would remain unresolved until a "satisfactory public vengeance" had been enacted.

Kullman's death was surely neither the first nor the last to be attributed to the ignorance or backwardness of the perpetrators. The press was very critical of attacks against officials and state bureaucrats who were carrying out the central government's efforts to modernize the countryside, particularly if the attacks were driven by religious beliefs or by what were often described as "acts of fanaticism." The 1930s, particularly the first half of the decade, were characterized by tense and at times violent confrontations between so-called militant Catholics and revolutionaries.[42] Puebla was no exception, even though its ruling elite was more conservative, closer to the church, and hence less enthusiastic about the federal government's secularization campaigns than were their counterparts in Sonora, Guadalajara, and Michoacán.[43]

A national policy that sought to modernize the countryside by promoting the secularization of social life, implementation of agrarian reform, and institution of left-leaning public education, the socialist education project gave rise to local revolt and resistance in support of Catholicism during the second half of the 1930s. Despite adopting a pragmatic version of socialism that avoided iconoclasm or any form of radical anticlericalism,[44] socialist teachers in Puebla were attacked by groups of armed bandits and by spontaneous mobs who considered their actions a threat to communities' material and spiritual well-being.[45] Because the socialist education project was meant to reduce the influence of the church and of local caciques, as well as to acculturate indigenous populations that had traditionally enjoyed a high degree of autonomy, the attacks were more prevalent in indigenous areas characterized by a strong tradition of militant religiosity and cacique leadership.

This wave of violence against socialist public school teachers, known as the Second Cristiada,[46] involved the hanging, mutilation, and killing of approximately one hundred teachers, seventeen of them in Puebla.[47] From 1935 to 1937, reports of teachers being shot, hanged, or wounded with machetes in various towns of Puebla intensified, particularly in the Sierra Norte, a region described in the press as a place where all teachers were "condemned to death."[48] The press strongly opposed the violent assaults and extrajudicial killings of *maestros*. Editorials and news stories urged the government to make examples of those who victimized innocent teachers whose only "mistake" was to lift thousands of indigenous people "out of their ignorance."[49] These articles also echoed the teachers' demands that the federal government give them arms so that they could defend themselves against their attackers.[50]

The press articulated a narrative in which teachers, as bearers of progress and modernity, were pitted against the forces of ignorance and religious fanaticism. A 1936 article reported that yet another teacher had been victimized in Puebla "despite . . . the strong campaign that the federal government has launched in order to transmit the high mission of [socialist education]."[51] A year earlier newspapers had reported on the lynching of three public school teachers in Puebla by a "tumulto de indígenas fanáticos" (a tumult of indigenous fanatics).[52] *Tumulto* suggests disorder and impulsiveness. It resonates with words such as *turba* (crowd) or *chusma* (lower-class mob) both used by the press and government authorities in referring to attacks against state officials. Moreover, the use of *indígenas* to identify the perpetrators is particularly salient considering that this and other attacks were perpetrated not only by indigenous peoples but also by mestizos and people of European descent.[53] The press never used *mestizo* when referring to non-indigenous perpetrators, an omission which confirms that only Indians were racialized in 1930s Puebla.

Similar cases were reported in other Mexican states using similar narratives. In March 1937, a newspaper stated that the maestros of a "cultural mission" in Guanajuato had been attacked by a group of Catholics armed with stones, knives, and pistols, killing thirteen and injuring at least twenty-nine. The priest had "influenced the anger of the believers so that they would fight the official elements . . . otherwise [it would be] inexplicable for them to come out at the end of Mass armed . . . and immediately attack the teachers and those neighbors who had attended."[54] These explanations echoed an official discourse that consistently labeled any type of resistance, whether violent or not, against socialist education as cases of religious fanaticism and popular ignorance. A government official speaking at the 1935 Scientific Congress, for instance, claimed it was difficult to know how effective the "de-fanatization" of the Indian had been since "the Catholic Church has filled a majority of the people's time" and "Indians do not understand the spirit of the constitutional reform" that secularized education.[55]

Although many of the attacks against teachers were performed collectively and in public spaces, the press did not describe all of them as linchamientos. Relatively organized episodes of violence were referred to as acts of banditry carried out by former *cristeros* or by traitors of the revolution. Anti- socialist resistance in Puebla was organized not only by lay Catholics, but also by groups of bandits hired by local caciques to burn schools and assault teachers in order to stop the agrarian reform.[56] For instance, two of the best-known assassins of public school teachers in the state were Enrique "El Tallarín" Ramírez, and Odilón Vega, the "desorejador de maestros." The latter gained his nickname from his reputation for cutting off teachers' ears. In general, Vega and Ramírez led attacks by several armed men against one or two teachers, as well as hangings and mutilations of some victims in visible public spaces, including schools.[57] Because of the relatively organized nature of these attacks, however, the press never referred to them as lynchings but as banditry.

Socialist schoolteachers were not the only public figures lynched during the 1930s. Federal inspectors, tax collectors, soldiers, police officers, and engineers in charge of developing public works fell victim to groups and local communities who opposed and distrusted their presence. On September 26, 1931, engineers Emilio Cuevas and Ignacio Herrera were nearly lynched in the town of Cholula.[58] According to the press, the two engineers were sent by the Public Education Secretariat to clean and repair the prehispanic pyramid located in the town, an important archaeological site on which a Catholic church had been built in colonial times. Catholics considered the church a sanctuary and place of pilgrimage. When the engineers started to repair the site, locals accused them of planning to destroy the church. A mob armed with machetes and pistols surrounded the place intending to lynch the two men. A newspaper report rejoiced that authorities were able to save the engineers from the "ignorance of these locals," who did not understand the economic benefits the site's restoration would bring to their town.

Lynchings as Covert State Violence

Lynchings of and by public officials held a prominent place in Puebla's press coverage. Judges, mayors, and police officers were held directly responsible for instigating and authorizing lynching violence. In these cases, the press would adopt a critical position, emphasizing the abusive and corrupt character of local authorities. Although these lynchings were not described using a narrative of backwardness or ignorance, they were labeled as shameful and unacceptable. The press would often demand the intervention of state and federal authorities in order to restore law and order to towns and communities controlled by drunkard mayors, corrupt police officers, and local politicians who bent the law to serve their own personal agendas. This critical position seems to counter the apparent acceptance of other forms of extrajudicial killings by state agents, such as the ley fuga (as Pablo Piccato analyzes in chapter 1).

On May 24, 1938, the *Diario de Puebla* reported a "bloody disturbance" between residents and police in the town of Axocopan.[59] The incident was initiated by a brawl between Pablo Castillo and Aaron Tufiño, who owned competing transportation companies in the town. After the fight, and taking advantage of the fact that his brother was a local deputy, Castillo mobilized the police (including the chief of the police himself) and led a retaliatory attack. With machetes and axes, the group of policemen assailed Tufiño and his wife, killing him and severely injuring her. Castillo and his accomplices then paraded Tufiño's body through the town, outraging residents and provoking them to attack the police. In reporting on the same event, *La Opinión* stated that the crime had "all the tragic and bloody characteristics of past times, when motivated by the Mexican revolution, there were gangs who organized themselves in order to assault, rob, and carry out personal vendettas."[60]

Despite its collective and public character, the killing of Tufiño at the hands of the police was not referred to as a lynching, most probably due to the participation of official elements. However, earlier that year, another violent incident reported in Cholula and organized by the secretary and president of the *comisariado ejidal* (communal lands board) was described as a lynching.[61] According to the report, the incident followed an attempt by an attorney named Juárez to claim some lands belonging to his client, Tomás Romero. Both the secretary and the president of the comisariado ejidal rejected Romero's claims, and gathered more than three hundred residents armed with sticks who proceeded to lynch Juárez. Another attack described as a *linchamiento* in which local authorities were involved took place in San José Chiapa in August 1930.[62] For "unknown reasons," residents of San José Chiapa under the direction of the secretary of the comisariado ejidal attacked farmer José López, beating him and biting him with such brutality that he nearly lost his right ear. The article concluded by calling for the prompt intervention of the capital's minister of justice to punish San José Chiapa authorities, who instead of protecting the inhabitants, orchestrated several abuses against them.

The press pointed out the conflation between criminal and official elements in these acts, acknowledging the blurred lines between legal and illegal forms of violence. On August 24, 1930, *La Opinión* described an attack ordered by the mayor of Teohiloyocan against six people from a neighboring town.[63] Reportedly the mayor managed to assemble three hundred people armed with stones and pistols by tolling the church bells. The newspaper stated bitterly that this case illustrated the complicity between authorities and criminals in some towns. Only a few days earlier in Santa Isabel Tepetzala, Acajete, a similar case took place wherein five men, including the local judge and the town's mayor, had tortured and hanged two men from a tree. Although the word "lynching" was not used, the report indicates the men were "barbarously tortured" and subjected to "cruel torments."[64]

As Charles Tilly argues, inasmuch as it undermines the legitimacy of the state as the ultimate arbiter of legality, the participation of state authorities in organizing extralegal forms of violence can contribute to the perpetuation and legitimation of such acts.[65] Press coverage of lynchings and other forms of extrajudicial violence organized by state officials in 1930s Puebla illustrates the extent to which the law was bent in order to resolve private vendettas or political disputes. In turn, public distrust and suspicion toward local authorities further deepened the perception that sometimes illegal violence was the only means to attain justice.

Conclusion

Composed mostly of an urban and educated readership, the publics of lynching in 1930s Puebla took diverse and at times contradictory positions regarding the validity of this form of violence. The circumstances of each case, together with the characterization of its victims and perpetrators, delineated the boundaries between legitimate and illegitimate uses of violence. As the analysis of various cases of lynching covered by the local press demonstrates, lynchings and extrajudicial expressions of violence were not always desanctioned by public opinion. In some cases, they were rationalized as a valid response to certain crimes considered excessively offensive or cruel. In other cases, they would be harshly criticized as an expression of perpetrators' ignorance, religious fanaticism, or abuse of political power.

As stated at the beginning of this chapter, the press can both reflect and shape debates about the intricate relations among violence, justice, and the law. Lynchings are located at the crossroads of these three elements. As such, the analysis of this phenomenon needs to account for the impact that shifting sensibilities and public representations of these and other forms of violence have had in their legitimation and potential reproduction.

Notes

I would like to thank Pablo Piccato, David Carey Jr., Andrew Paxman, Angélica Durán-Martínez, and Jeremy Varon for providing valuable comments on previous versions of this chapter.

1. Angelina Snodgrass Godoy, "When 'Justice' Is Criminal: Lynchings in Contemporary Latin America," *Theory and Society* 33, no. 6 (2004): 621–51; Christopher Krupa, "Histories in Red: Ways of Seeing Lynching in Ecuador," *American Ethnologist* 36, no. 1 (2009), 20–39; José Souza Martins, "Lynching—Life by a Thread: Street Justice in Brazil," in *Vigilantism and the State in Modern Latin America: Essays on Extralegal Violence*, ed. Martha K. Huggins (New York: Praeger, 1991), 21–32; Daniel M. Goldstein, *The Spectacular City: Violence and Performance in Urban Bolivia* (Durham, NC: Duke University Press, 2004); Raúl Rodríguez Guillén, "Crisis de autoridad y violencia social: los linchamientos en México," *Polis. Investigación y Análisis Sociopolítico y Psicosocial* 8, no. 2 (2012): 48–49.

2. As the literature on lynching in Latin America indicates, a "linchamiento" may or may not result in the victim's death. Huggins, *Vigilantism and the State in Modern Latin America*, 1–18.

3. Diane E. Davis, "Undermining the Rule of Law: Democratization and the Dark Side of Police Reform in Mexico, *Latin American Politics and Society* 48, no. 1 (2006): 55–86.

4. Antonio Fuentes Díaz, *Linchamientos, fragmentación y respuesta en el México neoliberal* (Puebla: Benemérita Universidad Autónoma de Puebla, 2006); Snodgrass Godoy, "When 'Justice' Is Criminal."

5. Michael Pfeifer, *Rough Justice: Lynching and American Society, 1874–1947* (Urbana: University of Illinois Press, 2004).

6. Norbert Elias, *El proceso de la civilización: investigaciones sociogenéticas y psicogenéticas* (Mexico City: Fondo de Cultura Económica, 2009); Pieter Spierenburg, *The Spectacle of Suffering: Executions and the Evolution of Repression from a Preindustrial Metropolis to the European Experience* (Cambridge: Cambridge University Press, 1984).

7. According to two recent studies, Puebla is amongst the top seven or eight Mexican states, out of a total of thirty-one, with the highest incidence of lynching violence. See Fuentes Díaz, *Linchamientos;* Rodríguez Guillén, "Crisis de autoridad."

8. "Ley fuga" can be defined as the extrajudicial killing of a criminal, allegedly while attempting to escape from custody. See chap. 1 in this volume.

9. Mary K. Vaughan, *Cultural Politics in Revolution: Teachers, Peasants, and Schools in Mexico, 1930–1940* (Tucson: University of Arizona Press, 1997).

10. Alan Knight, "Habitus and Homicide: Political Culture in Revolutionary Mexico." In *Citizens of the Pyramid: Essays on Mexican Political Culture,* ed. Wil G. Pansters, 107–29 (Amsterdam: Thela, 1997).

11. Jesús Márquez, "Oposición contrarrevolucionaria de derecha en Puebla, 1932–1940," in *Religión, política y sociedad, el sinarquismo y la iglesia en México (nueve ensayos),* ed. Rubén Aguilar V. and Guillermo Zermeño P. Mexico City: Universidad Iberoamericana, Departamento de Historia, 1992.

12. Wil G. Pansters, *Política y poder en Puebla. Formación y ocaso del cacicazgo avilacamachista, 1927–1987* (Mexico City: Fondo de Cultura Económica, 1998), 112.

13. For a useful overview of the "gray zones" of state-making and violence in postrevolutionary Mexico see Pansters's introduction to *Violence, Coercion, and State-Making in Twentieth-Century Mexico: The Other Half of the Centaur* (Stanford, CA: Stanford University Press, 2012), 3–42.

14. Gema Santamaría, "Lynching in Twentieth-Century Mexico: Violence, State Formation, and Local Communities in Puebla" (PhD diss., New School for Social Research, 2015). See, in particular, chap. 2.

15. Pfeifer, *Rough Justice,* 6–7; David Garland, "Penal Excess and Surplus Meaning: Public Torture Lynchings in Twentieth-Century America," *Law & Society Review* 39, no. 4 (2005): 793–833.

16. "Crimen sin nombre se cometió en la persona de una niña," *La Opinión,* July 9, 1933.

17. "Hoy seguirán haciéndose diligencias en un crimen," and "El crimen de Cholula y el auge de la criminalidad en el estado," *La Opinión,* July 10, 1933.

18. "Lombrosino" (Lombrosian) is a direct reference to the Italian criminologist Cesare Lombroso, whose ideas about crime and its relation to physical or biological traits were highly influential at the time.

19. "¿Se aplicó la ley fuga a los asesinos de una niña?" *La Opinión,* July 16, 1933.
20. Paul J. Vanderwood, *Juan Soldado: Rapist, Murderer, Martyr, Saint* (Durham, NC: Duke University Press, 2004), 45–47.
21. "Aquí no linchamos," *La Opinión,* February 17, 1938.
22. Claudio Lomnitz, "Mexico's First Lynching: Sovereignty, Criminality, Moral Panic." *Critical Historical Studies* 1, no. 1 (2014): 85–123.
23. Ibid., 106. This was hardly the first lynching in Mexico and, as Lomnitz explains, it was not a lynching at all, as Arroyo was actually executed by police while in custody. Nonetheless, the case serves to illustrate the government's efforts to project an image of Mexico as a place of civility.
24. "Diaz's Assailant Lynched," *New York Times,* September 18, 1897; "A Lesson from Mexico," *Washington Post,* November 25, 1897.
25. "Asqueroso sátiro que estuvo a punto de morir lynchado," *La Opinión,* August 5, 1937.
26. "Lyncharon a un sátiro en Tlapala, ayer," *La Opinión,* June 24, 1938.
27. "Una hija del Dr. Cruz Cázares fue víctima de brutales ultrajes," *La Opinión,* July 15, 1934.
28. "Pagó con su vida el ultraje a una niña," *La Opinión,* July 16, 1934.
29. "Varias mujeres iban a linchar a un cobarde golpeador," *La Opinión,* May 4, 1930.
30. "Un grave motín en Chachapa," *Diario de Puebla,* June 3, 1938.
31. "Iba a ser linchado en Metepec, torpe chofer," *La Opinión,* July 2, 1937.
32. I would like to thank historian Andrew Paxman for sharing information about this case.
33. "La leyenda de los degolladores motiva un horripilante asesinato," *La Opinión,* April 25, 1930.
34. The legend resembles that of the *pishtaco,* a mythical figure of Quechua origin who supposedly beheaded people in order to steal their body fat. The pishtaco is usually imagined as a tall, blond foreigner, as Kullman was. Anthony Oliver-Smith, "The Pishtaco: Institutionalized Fear in Highland Peru," *Journal of American Folklore* 82, no. 326 (1969): 363–68. I thank Marisol López for having referred me to this myth.
35. "Ha despertado temor entre los timoratos una fábula," *La Opinión,* April 18, 1930.
36. The story echoes the myth of the *degollador* (decapitator), which was common among rural folk in central and southern Mexico. Historian Mary K. Vaughan, for instance, described the circulation of similar rumors in 1930s Puebla, which claimed the government was kidnapping children in order to be "sent to the United States and turned into oil for planes." Vaughan, *Cultural Politics in Revolution,* 122.
37. "Pablo Sidar será el primero que vuelo a Buenos Aires," *La Opinión,* April 11, 1930.
38. "Ha despertado temor entre los timoratos una fábula," *La Opinión,* April 18, 1930.
39. "Todo el peso de la ley caerá sobre los asesinos de Van Edgard Kullman," *La Opinión,* April 26, 1930.
40. "A través de la semana," *La Opinión,* April 27, 1930.
41. "Una condena mínima se aplicó a los asesinos del profesor Kullman," *La Opinión,* August 31, 1931.
42. Jean Meyer, "An Idea of Mexico: Catholics in the Revolution," in *The Eagle and the Virgin: Nation and Cultural Revolution in Mexico,* ed. Mary Kay Vaughan and Stephen E. Lewis (London: Duke University Press, 2006), 281–96.

43. Mary K. Vaughan, "El papel político del magisterio socialista de México, 1934–1940: un estudio comparativo de los casos de Puebla y Sonora," in *Memoria del XII Simposio de Historia y Antropología*, vol. 2 (Hermosillo, Mexico: Universidad de Sonora, Departamento de Historia y Antropología, 1988), 175–97.

44. Ibid., 176.

45. Ben Fallaw, *Religion and State Formation in Postrevolutionary Mexico* (Durham, NC: Duke University Press, 2013), 6.

46. Ibid.; Meyer, "Idea of Mexico," 291.

47. David La France, *La revolución mexicana en el estado de Puebla, 1910–1935* (Puebla: Ediciones de Educación y Cultura, 2010), 98.

48. "Todos los maestros rurales están condenados a muerte en la Sierra Norte," *La Opinión*, July 20, 1936.

49. "Dos maestros más fueron plagiados," *La Opinión*, July 29, 1936.

50. "Se autoriza a los maestros rurales para usar armas," *Excélsior*, November 8, 1935.

51. "Fue asaltado un maestro rural cerca de Chilchotla," *La Opinión*, July 11, 1936.

52. "Tres maestros fueron asesinados en Puebla" *El Universal*, November 17, 1935, p. 1.

53. Archivo General de la Nación, Mexico (AGN-MEX), Dirección General de Investigaciones Políticas y Sociales, caja 71, exp. 2; "Los asesinos de maestros muertos por las tropas," *El Universal*, November 19, 1935.

54. "Numerosos muertos y heridos en Ciudad González. Zafarrancho sangriento por causa religiosa," *Excélsior*, March 31, 1936.

55. "No es posible declarar si se ha logrado algo con la desfanatización de indios," *Excélsior*, September 11, 1935.

56. Vaughan, "El papel político," 179.

57. "Otros asesinatos de la banda que manda el criminal Tallarín cometidos ayer," *La Opinión*, March 2, 1938; "Otro maestro es asesinado en la Sierra," *La Opinión*, July 15, 1938; "Otra víctima del grupo de los 'cristeros,'" *La Opinión*, July 18, 1938.

58. "En Cholula iban a ser linchados dos ingenieros por el populacho enfurecido," *La Opinión*, September 26, 1931.

59. "Tremendo zafarrancho en Axocopan," *Diario de Puebla*, May 24, 1938.

60. "Los esbirros del Dip. Castillo cometen un bárbaro crimen en el pueblo de Axocopan," *La Opinión*, May 24, 1938.

61. "Estuvo a punto de ser linchado en Ocoyucan el Lic. J. R. Juárez," *La Opinión*, March 15, 1938.

62. "Las autoridades de San José Chiapa pretendieron linchar a un agricultor," *La Opinión*, May 10, 1930.

63. "Seis personas iban a ser ejecutadas sin formación de causa en Teohiloyocan," *La Opinión*, August 24, 1930.

64. "Prodigiosos crímenes en Santa Isabel Tepetzala," *La Opinión*, August 12, 1930.

65. Charles Tilly, *The Politics of Collective Violence* (Cambridge: Cambridge University Press, 2003), 92.

3 Engendering Violence

Military Leadership through the Moral Crisis of Guatemala's National Family

M. Gabriela Torres

According to General Efraín Ríos Montt, Guatemala's most infamous evangelical military dictator, our Father in the spiritual realm—just like our fathers in the land of the living—demands fear. Ríos Montt, the general who was born again into the Evangelical Christian Church of the Word (El Verbo), openly used evangelical Christian doctrine in 1982–83 in his attempt to restructure Guatemalan society and restore national morality through military force. During Guatemala's Violencia, or civil war, the Guatemalan armed forces and their leaders responded to an insurgency understood to be cemented in a moral crisis of the national family. Forceful leadership—to be manifested as the return of the heavy-handed father—was seen by the armed forces as key to the resolution of the ideological divide in Guatemalan society. Positioning himself as the *pater,* the general based his power to rule on the right and ability of the father to guide the family with a firm hand or iron fist (*mano dura*) in a time of crisis. This act naturalized and extended patriarchal power from the individual familial realm to the broader political sphere.

Ríos Montt's messianic vision was not only popular in Guatemala but also became a cause célèbre within U.S. Christian fundamentalist circles. His mission of strong moral leadership earned him the ideological and financial support of prominent fundamentalist figures like Pat Robertson. International propaganda efforts touted Ríos Montt as a deeply moral figure engaged in a war with a Christian nemesis in the midst of the Cold War. Ignoring the flows of millions of Guatemalan refugees to

Mexico and evidence of assassinations, massacres, and disappearances that have since been defined by the United Nations as acts of genocide, Pat Robertson wrote:

> I knew that only God could sustain this fledgling government. The treasury of Guatemala had been depleted. Communists were attacking villages in the hills. The United States government was refusing to help because of the human rights violations of the previous regime. The world's press—often leftist in orientation—was making Ríos Montt out to be a pietist buffoon. The only recourse was prayer. I enlisted the prayers of tens of thousands of evangelicals across America. We urgently besought the Lord to grant physical safety to Ríos Montt and the blessing of God upon his new government. Little by little the miracle began to unfold. The country was stabilized. Democratic processes, never a reality in Guatemala, began to be put in place. Above all else, the all-pervasive graft and corruption were eliminated along with the terror of death squads.[1]

The miraculous effects of Ríos Montt's promotion of evangelical Protestantism within the counterinsurgency plan are best seen in the "conversion" of approximately a third of primarily rural indigenous Guatemalans from syncretic forms of Catholicism to evangelical Protestantism by the end of La Violencia.[2] Though evangelical Protestant missions had been in Guatemala since the nineteenth century, it was not until the 1980s that indigenous Guatemalans turned to evangelical Protestantism, in part as a way to safeguard their lives in conflict zones.[3] The impact of the same firm-handed leadership extended beyond conversions. Perhaps more significantly, during the time that the Guatemalan armed forces held power—now defined by the United Nations as a period of genocide—more than two hundred thousand people primarily of Maya descent were murdered by the Guatemalan armed forces. The terror in the countryside created by counterinsurgency operations created refugee flows of nearly two million people. During the time that the Guatemalan armed forces held power state-sponsored militaries and paramilitary organizations also orchestrated the systemic disappearance and murder of more than fifty thousand people. The return of the father, key to the reconciliation of the moral state of emergency defined by the Guatemalan armed forces' counterinsurgency doctrine, also morally enabled one of the bloodiest periods in Guatemalan history. Unlike the earlier governments of Ubico, Estrada Cabrera, and Barrios, whose governance also rested on paternal authority, military governments during La Violencia defined paternal authority to justify the brazen and often legal use of force against its own citizens and the rhetorical definition of state-sponsored violent discipline as fitting and righteous governance.

This chapter offers a discourse analysis of Ríos Montt and his regime and argues that power was established through the positioning of the Guatemalan armed forces as the national pater in the midst of a genocide: a self-definition that allowed for the restoration of the natural order of the ideal patriarchal family and demanded the iron fist of the leader. It argues that the mechanisms that support gender inequity can be redeployed to bolster authoritarian forms of power that persist throughout Latin America to the present day. Despite the well-documented charges of mass murder leveled against Ríos Montt in national and international courts, many Guatemalans still revere and respect his violent version of strong-armed rule as the "embodiment of honesty, law and order, and national integrity."[4] Extending beyond Ríos Montt himself, rule with an iron fist was a principal motif of good leadership that ex-president Otto Pérez Molina (2012–15) invoked as the most effective approach to attain national security and the nation's only means of escape from the chaos of crime and violence.[5]

Looking at Ríos Montt's regular Sunday sermons, advertising campaigns, and law-decree legislation during his tenure in power, this chapter demonstrates how culturally shared notions of a strict adherence to gendered duties within the family came to constitute viable forms of political power in Guatemala. Governance with the mano dura of the father conveys a type of power that was born out of a legal state of exception in which military rule flourished in the 1980s. Focusing on the dictator's success in cementing himself as an enduring national pater offers a window into the deeper social and cultural origins that have legitimated and normalized certain forms of abuse and repression. It allows us to trace how violence comes to be represented through the confluence of cultural notions of masculinity, military strategies, religious fervor, and the practice of governance through arbitrary legal exception. The fact that state-sponsored violence and the targeting of indigenous communities also peaked in this period suggests that such representations are not simply rhetorical.[6]

Seeking Refuge from the Father's Ability to Secure Life

I came to the idea that military ideology, law, culture, and religion came together in creating "Ríos Montt, Our Father" in April 1995. In the heat of a Guatemalan refugee camp in Mexico, a young Maya woman explained her flight into exile using a kinship metaphor that haunted me as I read many of Ríos Montt's 1980s Sunday addresses to Guatemalans years later. Sitting in the patio of the standard-issue stick-and-lamina shelter that the United Nations High Commissioner for Refugees had constructed for Guatemalans in the then sparsely settled lowland jungles of the Yucatán peninsula, Marcela provided an enlightening analysis of the role that gender plays through the practice of normative notions of kinship in the reproduction of political and interpersonal power:

> The government said that it saw no reason for us to be doing things—you know, as if we were his children. He is the father of all Guatemalans and we have to respect everything that he says. He made us feel like that. It dominated us a lot. It controlled us a lot so that we couldn't do anything. . . . He did what he wanted with us. He even kicked us out and chased us out of the country. That is what we have thought. It is the same as when our parents fight with us and hit us and hurt us and kick us out of the house. That is what the government did when he kicked us out of the country. Here we have begun to analyze how it was possible for the government to dominate us. The government is a person and we are also people.[7]

Having fled Guatemala a little more than ten years prior to our interview, Marcela understood the ways that power to rule arbitrarily emanated from established gender roles and gendered power disparities. For Marcela, her forced exile was summed up in a clear reference to the mechanics of a typical family spat in which the everyday power of the father, or pater, allows for expulsion from the family to seem simultaneously arbitrary and normative. Marcela defines the "father/government" through his ability to dominate, speak, define, and dissolve. Even the very language suggests gendered power that makes the government a male.

Interestingly, the same notions of the father found in Marcela's account of the gendered power disparities in the Guatemalan family are echoed in General Ríos Montt's own efforts to define the power of the military dictatorship through shared notions of kinship rights and duties. This is particularly striking because Marcela had no knowledge of official government statements, given that she neither spoke Spanish nor was able to read and write before she left Guatemala. In a Sunday sermon in 1982, Ríos Montt himself echoes the same view:

> In order to maintain a nationalist spirit we have to create a conscious sense of nationalism. Nationalism is the fruit of a family's maturity. The family is itself the central focus of the homeland [*patria*]. Families are expressions of love toward Guatemala. Families allow us to transcend the material realm into the spiritual realm of humanity. For our nationalism to be great, you must change yourself for the better so that when you express your ideas and ideals, you are consistently expressing and practicing acts rooted in obedience to moral values. . . . I will tell you why Guatemala is a great nation—because of the excellence of its soul. It is a great nation because you as a man or a woman know and follow your duties as husbands, wives, sons, daughters. Because you show that you fear God in this way you make Guatemala a great and strong nation. . . . Guatemala is a nation that fears God, honors America, and serves as an example to the world.[8]

As David Carey Jr. and I suggest, culturally shared notions of the family in Guatemala are defined by gendered inequity where legally enshrined notions of *potestad marital* (tutelage entitlement of husbands) and *patria potestas* (tutelage entitlement of fathers) through the nineteenth and twentieth centuries have worked to give men legal power over many aspects of their wives and children's behavior and property.[9] The type of kinship relationship both Ríos Montt and Marcela discuss in their accounts is not purely metaphorical. It was enshrined in laws that gave fathers and husbands full disposal of the very bodies of their women and children until the turn of the twenty-first century. The general's speeches, drawing heavily on evangelical doctrine and established notions of masculine power, are perhaps the most blatant, though certainly not the only, examples of how military authority and moral, religious, and nationalist discourses can intersect to create lasting and culturally palatable notions of leadership at a time of crisis. As Carey and Gema Santamaría suggest in the introduction to this volume, violence can indeed come to be represented through gender categories.

The representation of violence through precirculating and palatable social categories makes it simultaneously visible and seemingly a part of culture and invisible as normative gendered practice. Preexisting and accepted gender roles were ideal in Guatemala to both tame and enact a moral crisis managed through violence.

The enactment of a national crisis within the family worked through the idea of the father figure as an omniscient, discerning benefactor. Ríos Montt's regime promoted this notion in ads with well-traveled motifs that infantilized its subjects and capitalized on the idea that militaries fathered the continent. In a full-page advertisement in *Prensa Libre,* a quotation from the military father of the Americas, Simón Bolívar, appeared in bold: "'The poor indigenous peoples are truly in a deplorable state of dejection, I hope to make good for them, first for the good of humanity and second because they have a right to it.—Simón Bolívar.' Making a nation is a question of discipline."[10]

This ad makes the paternalistic nature of national military discipline explicit—particularly as it relates to the military's relationship with indigenous peoples that Marcela so aptly grasped in her comments. Simón Bolívar states that "education" (probably understood in the word's many disciplinary connotations) should be the prime concern of "the paternal love of Congress."[11] The ad positions the wielders of instruction as father figures or saviors of the forgotten and the poor. Ultimately, it portrays the military as the father figure that can make possible some degree of both "progress" and "good" for indigenous peoples.

As the Guatemalan armed forces' slogan—"Making a nation is a question of discipline"—suggests, discipline is not so incongruous with enactment of the gendered role of the father. Both discursively and in effect, men in families and the Guatemalan armed forces in the imagined national family were positioned as paters who were granted full dominance to know and act. In legislation, they held full claim over their subjects' legal personhood. They had the ability to act for and dispose of all those they represented, as they ruthlessly did during the civil war. The discipline of the Guatemalan armed forces was as pervasive as it was particularly targeted at indigenous persons. An analysis by the Commission for Historical Clarification (CEH) points to the state as the agent responsible for 93 percent of all human rights violations and identifies indigenous Guatemalans as 83.33 percent of the identified victims of violence in Guatemala between 1962 and 1992.[12]

To take this analogy further, the Guatemalan armed forces led by Ríos Montt often enacted the role of the father as the provider of life. For example, in a full-page advertisement guised as a Mother's Day greeting, the military government positioned itself as guaranteeing life: "The Guatemalan army greets the Guatemalan Mother this May 10th, offering her the best gift: 'The security of her children.'"[13] In this ad, the military justified its role within the frame of providing for every mother's most basic need: her child's safety. It recasts the military's role in the conflict from aggressors to natural defenders of the family and producers of the essential values of Guatemalan-ness.

Another example of how the military repositioned itself as the author of morality is found in a series of ad campaigns that were sponsored not only to address individual behavior, but to suggest the degree to which the Guatemalan nation and processes of self-governance were meant to be restructured. Many of these ads addressed the reconstitution of the ideal Guatemalan and his or her role in society as a way to promote a rhetorical investment of citizens in a nation-building project.

> THIS GOVERNMENT HAS THE DUTY TO CHANGE. I don't steal. I don't lie. I don't take advantage. Throughout the years, dishonest authorities have taken money, goods, and resources that don't belong to them. Throughout the years, the norm has been that the government and the authorities distort the truth, lie, and do not fulfill their promises. Throughout the years, the authorities have believed that their position gives them rights far and above those of other citizens and that they are not subject to the law. That is stealing, lying, and taking advantage. That should not go on. I don't steal. OUR GOVERNMENT HAS A COMMITMENT TO CHANGE. YOU SHOULD ALSO KEEP YOUR COMMITMENTS. CHANGE.[14]

Ríos Montt's unyielding three-fingered strong hand features in this ad as a form of the benevolent tough love of the father. The logo is a key exemplar of how notions of authority and morality are used to foster gender inequity in wartime. The infamous three-fingered hand attached to the slogan "I don't steal. I don't lie. I don't take advantage" was emblematic of the Ríos Montt regime and the rule of the other military governments throughout the early 1980s. The slogan responded to popular opinion that avidly rejected government corruption in past civilian presidencies. With its blunt assurances this military presidency was discursively distanced in a particularly gendered way. Yet, this ad does not promise unilateral changes on the part of the government; rather, it demands that citizens make a commitment to redefine themselves in the same image as the military: "YOU SHOULD ALSO KEEP YOUR COMMITMENTS. CHANGE." The violent acts of the military state are rhetorically obscured under an ideal transparent, anticorruption authority that, while openly executing those of its citizens deemed enemies, promises not to steal, lie, or abuse its power. The reframing of the state's abuse of power into a problem that should be understood as a shared responsibility for social and governance reforms further distracts from the state's own violent practices.

The leadership this slogan symbolized and the violence it concealed just below the surface endured well past the civil war years. The three-fingered hand reappeared as the symbol of Ríos Montt's political party, the Frente Republicano Guatemalteco (FRG), which touted the slogan "Security, Well-Being, Justice." The populist image that this party logo alluded to contributed to its electoral success in the late 1990s and again in the early 2000s—more than twenty years after the general took power by force. Today staunch Ríos Montt supporters and apologists continue to tout it as the emblem of true, lasting, visionary leadership even as he stands trial for genocide in Guatemala. He might have done "many things," a recent editorial in the Guatemalan press states, glossing over the charges of genocide levied against Ríos Montt, "but he did not lie, cheat, or steal. He led us toward democracy."[15] Genocide is inconsequential. Reflecting on the complexities of his enduring profile in Guatemalan politics, Diane Nelson writes, "He cultivates an image of moral piety as a protestant minister and claims to eschew corruption . . . but for those in the know about Ríos Montt's other, genocidal face, he and his party seem like excellent bamboozlers."[16] The duality of benevolence wrapped up with treachery is for Nelson key to the exercise of power during and after wartime in Guatemala.

Counterinsurgency in the Age of Legal Exception

In addition to the clear rhetorical framing of the military mission as a fatherly responsibility, the armed forces defined the civil war as a national moral crisis in order to justify a comprehensive counterinsurgency operation.[17] Ostensibly, counterinsurgency strategies were designed by the armed forces to deter citizen behavior that put the "nation-state" in jeopardy. In Guatemala—as was the case with other Latin American military dictatorships[18]—the armed forces designed counterinsurgency operations not only to accomplish the destruction of a small armed insurgency, but to ensure that any ideological threats to the military's vision of a nation-state were also destroyed. As then Defense Minister Héctor Gramajo Morales's tactical predecessor, Manuel Benedicto Lucas García, stated reflecting on the massacres of indigenous peoples in the early 1980s: "Without the support of the communities the insurgents could not exist. Because of this, the tactic was to take that support away from them."[19] The military reacted with now well-documented massacres of indigenous communities to rectify both a military and a "cultural" state of emergency.[20] As outlined in the Guatemalan Armed Forces' National Stability Thesis, national security objectives were to be achieved by eliminating all obstacles through the use of "political, economic, psychosocial, and military actions."[21] As part of this plan, periods of "legal exception" were cultivated during Ríos Montt's rule so as to allow greater room for military or disciplinary maneuvers. Paralleling Giorgio Agamben's account of nineteenth-century Italy, Guatemala during the Ríos Montt regime underwent a process by which law-decree "changed from a derogatory and exceptional instrument for normative production to an ordinary source for the production of law" and power was regularly shifted away from congress and concentrated in the leadership of the executive.[22]

Guatemala's legal restructuring, or special exemption, period began with three law-decrees issued on March 24, 1982, that annulled the results of that year's election, dissolved the republic's congress, and suspended the constitution. This set of decrees essentially dissolved all popular representation in government and—mimicking Argentina's Peronist government—established a process through which the military government could use "the legislative faculties to govern through decree."[23] In the Fundamental Statute of Governance, the Guatemalan armed forces defined themselves as sole wielders of executive and legislative powers, including dominion over how the law was created, what constituted a crime against the state, and which persons were executable.[24]

The legal application of iniquitous and arbitrary executions, disappearances, and tortures enabled the counterinsurgency apparatus to ideologically overcome its target population through sanctioned terror. In the Guatemalan context, the juridical order that enabled such terror was built explicitly on the ladino minority vision of Guatemalan society and character. The authority of masculine power within the family to "trace a borderline" between "the normal situation and chaos" was enacted explicitly in the reconstruction of national norms through a rule of law practiced and validated through periods of legal exception.[25] The father's unquestioned authority on issues of morality was particularly useful in legislating the boundaries of licit behavior, as one explicit example from the official public relations organ of the state at the time illustrates:

> When the State, through its authorities, applies measures that guarantee its powers as it guarantees citizen rights, and when the state assumes at the same time a coercive attitude to ensure the rule of the law, it does so because it is the only possible way to defend democratic principles. Lest we fall into that old situation of "the Saracens who, arriving late, were attacked with sticks, and because there were more evil men than there were good men, evil turned out to be good [evil won]." [We say this] because our Guatemalan people are for the most part honest, peace-loving, hardworking people who, above all, are respectful of the rights of others.[26]

In order to enable good to triumph over evil and to best defend democracy, Guatemalans—those that fit within the description of being "for the most part honest, peace-loving, hardworking people"—were asked to suspend their judgment of the state and trust their leader's god-like guiding hand.

Yet the violence inherent in the discipline of the state not only quashed resistance, it also often pushed women to rethink their political participation. Many refugee women inside and outside Guatemala began long careers of activism during the height of Ríos Montt's repression. As a Popular Communities in Resistance activist narrates to Susan Berger, "We've suffered but we've also learned to solve our problems. And something women have learned to do is to stand up for our rights and be proud."[27] The surge of women's organizing, in particular, that has resulted from repression is documented on a more macro scale by Cathy Blacklock, whose work traces the birth of civic activism in Guatemala in the 1990s back to the height of violence during Ríos Montt's regime.[28] The growth in civic organizing during one of the most militarily and legally repressive periods of Guatemala's military regimes demonstrates that illegality alone does not encode social sanction. For immediately practical reasons the growing popular resistance to state repression forced military lawmakers at least to give lip service to more democratic legal practices and, in some instances, even to backtrack from already promulgated laws.

The most contentious period of legal exception saw the enactment of two categories of laws: amnesty laws and the special exemption tribunal law. In designing both sets of laws, military lawmakers attempted to find constitutional foundations for their legal and social re-engineering. Explicitly envisioned within counterinsurgency doctrine, amnesty and special exemption tribunal laws were overt efforts to naturalize counterinsurgent violence within established public legal discourses. While there are doubts as to the overall success of these laws in effecting the legal and social changes they envisioned, they are interesting because of the changes in discursive play they entail and the way in which they expose the processes of the politics of violence.

Power to redress political crimes (defined as acts that threatened the integrity and security of the state) and associated common crimes (acts violating the Guatemalan penal code) traditionally rested with the congress. After the first coup d'état of 1982, this power came to rest in the hands of the head of state. Between May 1982 and August 1983, three sets of amnesty laws were issued: Law-Decrees 33-82, 27-83, and 89-83. Together with the special exemption tribunal laws, amnesty laws served to naturalize counterinsurgent violence by symbolically placing the actions of the military in the realm of "legality" and moral "righteousness." As an article in the government's official bulletin stated: "after having granted a period of amnesty, it is imperative to exercise the right to authority."[29]

Yet, the type of authority that the Guatemalan army sought through amnesty laws rested on the acquisition of a moral justification drawn from the public efforts to reintegrate the country—an effort that seemed to seek national reconciliation. As stated within the text of the first amnesty law, public support of the amnesty meant the reunification of a mythical Guatemalan family:

> Pain, mourning, the destruction of life and goods don't have to mean the deterioration of the nation, and that [outcome] should be avoided with every effort and sacrifice. What better way to do it than to find paths where there will be no more orphans, no more

massacres, no more ungratefulness and violence? Amnesty is the way toward a proper understanding, and the people fully support the governmental conduct that gives a chance to those that have mistakenly chosen a path that destroys human values. Guatemala needs all its children; let there be no more hesitation, let's all take it up with courage so that we can contribute toward an absolute harmony with true dignity and the cloak of law and justice. Such is the explicit purpose of the amnesty decree.[30]

Lack of harmony within the family and dissent within the government are held responsible for the alleged "deterioration of the nation," violence, and imminent destruction of human values. National cohesion—seen as the suppression of dissent and sought through the extension of amnesty to dissenters—was valued by the Guatemalan military in its efforts to rewrite Guatemala's social fabric. As a fair father figure, the state sought to establish national cohesion not only through military violence but also by giving its subjects the legal option to publicly acknowledge their failings and rectify their misguided acts of insurgency of their own accord.

Within the text of the first set of amnesty laws the Guatemalan military carefully delineated the national enemy as one that feeds on exotic philosophies, disregards the country's institutions, and produces political violence. In this effort, it was imperative to identify and promote the image of the enemy as traitors against the nation so as to discursively justify the military's counterinsurgent actions. The preamble of the first set of amnesty laws asserts:

Whereas, it is public knowledge that for many years there have existed in this country personnel and groups dedicated to subversion, who have tried through violent means to capture power in order to cement regimes that feed on exotic philosophies. . . .

Whereas, the Military Government Junta . . . is implementing a politico-juridical structure throughout the Nation that guarantees the path of the country into a regime of constitutional legality . . . [and finally] popular elections.

Whereas, it is imperative that all citizens live without fear of political violence. . . . [it is] necessary to proclaim legal norms that lead to this end—an end that is convenient and in the social interest of public tranquility.[31]

Discursively positioning the players (military and state versus guerrillas) in a moral playing field that naturalized violence against traitors who were legally defined as both criminal and subversive, this text constructs the military junta as the public's savior and as pushing the country onto the path of "constitutional legality." As evidenced by the constant reissuing and extension of amnesty law-decrees throughout the period of legal restructuring, neither the public nor guerrillas actively embraced the military government's extension of amnesty. According to historian Virginia Garrard-Burnett, "as an act of social reconciliation, the amnesty laws were an utter failure" with fewer than 250 people surrendering themselves under the law.[32] In the second set of amnesty law-decrees, it is clear that the armed forces saw reiterating the call for reunification as discursively useful for counterinsurgency and for minimizing the public failure to heed earlier attempts. In the preamble to the second set of amnesty law-decrees, the military government clearly states that its earlier methods had met with success, particularly among those living in the highlands (read as indigenous peoples) who had been tricked into subversion.[33] For Garrard-Burnett, amnesty laws were successful as a moral and counterinsurgent military strategy because they justified military action against those who did not surrender peacefully as outlined by the rule of law.[34]

In 1982, the armed forces leveraged their moral superiority over insurgents unwilling to reconcile with the state to justify counterinsurgency campaigns that killed or disappeared at least eighteen thousand people in that year alone and that militarized the countryside through scorched-earth policies envisioned as part of the "socioeconomic rewards" defined by the National Security and Development Plan.[35] In this case amnesty laws served to complement the image of the nation-in-harmony. As part of its effort to construct an imaginary of peace—based on the public's purportedly unquestioning adherence to military ideologies, the militarization of the rule of law, and a re-envisioning of the ideal Guatemalan—the Guatemalan military tried to overtly incorporate counterinsurgency repression into the letter of the law. Law-Decree 46-82 established the Special Exemption Tribunals on July 1, 1982. Attempting to codify other aspects of military government rule, the Ríos Montt regime established expedited and secret proceedings in specialized courts, run largely under military law, to try and judge so-called subversives. As the preamble to Law-Decree 46-82 suggests, the purpose of establishing these tribunals was to ameliorate the decay in Guatemalan values and way of life and to ensure that subversives would have no hand in changing the nation's institutions:

> Whereas, delinquent groups through subversive activities of an extreme nature have attempted through violent means to change judicial, political, social, and economic institutions of the nation. . . .
>
> Whereas, in order to protect order, peace, and public security it is necessary to promulgate a law that guarantees a fast and exemplary administration of justice when crimes are committed against these values.[36]

The Special Exemption Tribunal and amnesty laws were designed to function together as the two legally sanctioned alternatives open to dissenters: probable death sentence issued in a secret military court, or so-called reintegration through an admission of their sins against the state and nation. Ríos Montt's government tried to bring counterinsurgent violence into the open—to make it lawful. Yet, the processes defined by the Special Exemption Tribunals law violated other contemporary juridical processes and norms by functioning in secrecy, using self-incriminatory evidence, and employing torture to elicit confessions. In practice, it even contradicted its own dictates by ignoring the guaranteed right to effective defense counsel.[37] Nevertheless, according to the CEH,

> It must be recognized that the Special Exemption Tribunals were an attempt at legalizing the prosecution of political opposition in a time when for eighteen years this had taken place through criminal and quasi-state actions. Throughout the whole period, for example, no captured guerrilla leader or person involved in politically related offences had been tried. At any rate, this attempt at legalizing political repression did not mean an end to clandestine procedures that implied arbitrary detentions and torture.[38]

Making the same point, General Gramajo Morales writes, "The [execution] wall was preferable to finding cadavers thrown in the gutters of the road as was unfortunately the case during the previous government."[39] While this process of legitimation may have enabled these tribunals to function within the political climate prevailing in Guatemala, they were utterly rejected by the international community and were a source of much backtracking for the Ríos Montt administration.[40] Reflecting back on the public relations pressures posed by the state's active role in acts of violence, Gramajo Morales writes,

> The international opposition to Guatemala began to be extended to other western bloc countries headed by the United States. These and other countries that were once friendly now kept their distance from Guatemala because of its poor reputation on human rights. . . . This bad reputation developed as a result of political violence, particularly because of the crude methods that were used to face the increasing Marxist-Leninist insurgency. [These methods were] widely divulged to the world press and skillfully presented to public opinion leaders by the international adjunct of the insurgents.[41]

Jennifer Schirmer suggests that the overtness of state-sponsored violence during this period fractured the national economic elite's support for the anticommunist military project led by Ríos Montt. The national economic elite began to see international human rights concerns as damaging to its own business opportunities.[42] Due in large part to the ways that international pressure was brought to bear on the national political landscape, the Special Exemption Tribunals were suspended in 1983 by Law-Decree 93-83 and dismantled on July 18, 1984 (by Law-Decree 74-84), soon after Óscar Humberto Mejía Victores overthrew Ríos Montt's regime in August 1983.[43]

Positioning themselves as the keepers of what they considered to be Guatemalan social values, the armed forces set out both to restrict and to grant the rights of their subjects. Both the gifting of citizens' rights and the denial of equal levels of citizenship to all native-born Guatemalans were based on military leaders' self-perception as fathers, shapers, and guides who functioned above the mundanely political world of their nation. In this sense, the military's role as guarantors of the law was simply a natural extension of the more essential calling to exercise paternal leadership. Yet even the most repressive states, states that actively control the media and micromanage the way violence is represented,[44] often have little control over what public understandings of violence will prevail over time.

Conclusion

In the context of Ecuador, Susana Sawyer notes how notions such as democracy, nation, and family often work to "enframe" social actors into discursively produced imaginations of neutral goals.[45] During the Ríos Montt era the Guatemalan military achieved this type of enframing by legitimating itself and its acts of violence through established notions of paternal love, guidance, and discipline. As expressed in Ríos Montt's regular sermons, government advertising campaigns, and the wording of legislation, the acceptance of gendered roles that gave moral primacy and legitimacy to the male head of household was crucial for the success of this enframing. Adherence to culturally shared notions of one's duties within the family is what, in Ríos Montt's theology, enabled Guatemalans to transcend their current earthly state and show that they feared God. According to this theology, our Father in the spiritual realm, just like our fathers in the land of the living, exerts dominance by defining personhood and its associated abilities to analyze and speak.

Women like Marcela remind us that we need to understand how gender inequities can be magnified through the juxtaposition of military, juridical, and doctrinal discourses. As women activists recognize, the rule of law—which is displaced by constantly renewed states of exception—builds on existing gender inequity that resides in the father's authority to determine and dole out discipline. As the Women's Sector (Sector de Mujeres)—Guatemala's first attempt at a national women's rights association—stated in its submission to the Civil Society Assembly in the wake of the country's peace accords: "The Guatemalan state has always been characterized by its homogeneity, centralization, class orientation, militarism, patriarchy, repression, and ethnocentrism, whose fundamental element has been violence. This characterization of the state is expressed in the patriarchal culture that excludes women from an early age from the educational system, consigning them to menial jobs, or simply to ignorance and being locked up in the home."[46] Naturalizing or framing the counterinsurgent state as a civilizing, lawful, democratizing and, ultimately, familial disciplinary process rests on and reproduces masculine leadership that locates citizens' rights in the male domain. Instead of being conceived as inalienable and constitutionally guaranteed, citizens' rights under Ríos Montt came to be conceived of as bestowed at the discretion of the executive power and its agents. Whereas on its own terms this reframing of citizen rights and subjectivity could be seen as blatantly undemocratic, it was justified as part of a moral masculine, fatherly discourse that presented the survival of the Guatemalan nation as being at stake. Access to power in this case comes to be defined by gendered practices that place the gifting of belonging and personhood as a paternal prerogative.

In his war against insurgents, Ríos Montt carefully and ever so subtly reframed culture in legislation and in his Sunday sermons to imply that the advancement and very survival of the nation rested on the patriarchal authority of the father. Thereby, not only did citizens' rights become discretionary but the degree of citizenship itself was defined and determined by the father's good judgment. This reframing has tangible impacts on women's lives and sheds light on the endurance of gender-based violence in Guatemala today.

— affects gender norms & violence today

Notes

1. Pat Robertson, foreword to Joseph Anfuso and David Sczepanski, *Efraín Ríos Montt: Servant or Dictator? The Real Story of Guatemala's Controversial Born-Again President* (Ventura, CA: Vision House, 1984), ix–x.

2. Linda Green, *Fear as a Way of Life: Mayan Widows in Rural Guatemala* (New York: Columbia University Press, 1999), 150; Victor Perera, *Unfinished Conquest: The Guatemalan Tragedy* (Berkeley: University of California Press, 1993), 89.

3. Green, *Fear as a Way of Life*, 152–53.

4. Virginia Garrard-Burnett, *Terror in the Land of the Holy Spirit: Guatemala under General Efraín Ríos Montt, 1982–1983* (New York: Oxford University Press, 2010), 9.

5. *Prensa Libre*, July 26, 2011, 4.

6. Green, *Fear as a Way of Life*, 32, 67.

7. Marcela, interview with author, April 23, 1995. Last name withheld to protect identity.

8. Ríos Montt, Mensaje Dominical [Sunday Sermon], August 15, 1982, quoted in the *Diario de Centroamérica*, August 17, 1982, 2.

9. David Carey Jr. and M. Gabriela Torres, "Precursors to Femicide: Guatemalan Women in a Vortex of Violence." *Latin American Research Review* 45, no. 3 (2010): 142–64.

10. *Prensa Libre*, July 23, 1983, 30.

11. Ibid., 32.

12. Comisión para el Esclarecimiento Histórico (CEH), "Conclusiones y recomendaciones," in *Memoria del silencio* (Guatemala City: UNOPS, 1999), 4:85.

13. *Prensa Libre*, May 7, 1982, 20.

14. *Prensa Libre*, March 5, 1983, 41. Capitalization in original.

15. César A. García, "En honor a la verdad: el gran ¿pecado? de Ríos Montt fueron sus mensajes morales y de familia," *El Periódico* (Opinion), January 20, 2012.

16. Diane Nelson, *Reckoning: The Ends of War in Guatemala* (Durham, NC: Duke University Press, 2009), 69–70.

17. Garrard-Burnett, *Terror in the Land of the Holy Spirit*, 12.

18. Patricia Marchak, *God's Assassins: State Terrorism in Argentina in the 1970s* (Montreal: McGill-Queen's University Press), 1999.

19. *El Periódico* (Nacionales), May 5, 2000, 4.

20. CEH, "Conclusiones y recomendaciones," 4:82–83.

21. Héctor Alejandro Gramajo Morales, *De la guerra a la guerra: la difícil transición política en Guatemala* (Guatemala City: Fondo de Cultura Editorial, 1995), 7.

22. Giorgio Agamben, *State of Exception*, trans. Kevin Attell (Chicago: University of Chicago Press, 2005), 16.

23. Marchak, *God's Assassins*, 57.

24. Biblioteca del Congreso de la República de Guatemala, Law-Decree 24-82, Estatuto Fundamental de Gobierno, §1.

25. Giorgio Agamben, *Homo Sacer: Sovereign Power and Bare Life*, trans. Daniel Heller-Roazen (Stanford, CA: Stanford University Press, 1998), 19.

26. *Diario de Centro América*, August 16, 1982, 1.

27. Susan A. Berger, *Guatemaltecas: The Women's Movement, 1986–2003* (Austin: University of Texas Press, 2006), 27.

28. Cathy Blacklock, "Democratization and Popular Women's Organizations," in *Journeys of Fear: Refugee Return and National Transformation*, ed. Liisa L. North and Alan Simmons (Montreal: McGill-Queen's Press, 1999), 197.

29. *Diario de Centro América*, July 2, 1982, 1.

30. *Diario de Centro América*, June 29, 1983, 6.

31. Biblioteca del Congreso de la República de Guatemala, Law-Decree 33-82, Ley de Amnistía, §1.

32. Garrard-Burnett, *Terror in the Land of the Holy Spirit*, 70.

33. Biblioteca del Congreso de la República de Guatemala, Law-Decree 27-83, Ley de Amnistía, §1.

34. Garrard-Burnett, *Terror in the Land of the Holy Spirit*, 69–70.

35. Patrick Ball, Paul Kobrak, and Herbert F. Spirer, *Violencia institucional en Guatemala, 1960 a 1996: una reflexión cuantitativa* (Washington, DC: American Association for the Advancement of Science, 1999), 28. Edelberto Torres-Rivas, "Prólogo: la metáfora de una sociedad que se castiga a sí misma," in *Guatemala: causas y orígenes del enfrentamiento armado interno*, ed. CEH (Guatemala City: F & G Editores, 2000), 145.

36. Biblioteca del Congreso de la República de Guatemala, Law-Decree 46-82, Ley de Tribunales Fuero Especial, §1.

37. CEH, "Causas y orígenes del enfrentamiento armado interno," in *Memoria del silencio*, 1:141.

38. Ibid., 139.

39. Gramajo Morales, *De la guerra a la guerra*, 203.

40. *Prensa Libre*, July 19, 1984, 8; Jennifer Schirmer, "Enfoque militar de ley y seguridad," in *Las intimidades del proyecto político militar en Guatemala* (Guatemala City: FLACSO, 1999), 240.

41. Gramajo Morales, *De la guerra a la guerra,* 149.

42. Schirmer, "Enfoque militar de ley y seguridad," 70.

43. *Prensa Libre,* August 9, 1983, 4; August 10, 1983, 6; August 17, 1983, 2; and July 19, 1984, 8.

44. M. Gabriela Torres, "Art and Labor in the Framing of Guatemala's Dead," *Anthropology of Work Review* 35, no. 1 (2014): 14–24.

45. Susana Sawyer, *Crude Chronicles: Indigenous Politics, Multinational Oil, and Neoliberalism in Ecuador* (Durham, NC: Duke University Press, 2004).

46. Sector de Mujeres as quoted in Berger, *Guatemaltecas,* 35.

4 Police Use of Force and Social Consensus in Buenos Aires

Lila Caimari

The People and the Police

Police officers are the only agents of the state with direct coercive power over citizens. Although the use of force accounts for a minimal portion of daily police activities, this potential—the ever-present threat and option to use violence—provides perceptive coherence to a figure whose activities are extraordinarily diverse. What unifies the social image of the police is not what they actually *do* (since even the most cursory examination sends that definition in many directions), but rather what they represent for the citizen with whom they interact. What is distinctive about this interaction is the *possibility* of the use of force—and, more precisely, the use of force against a citizenry that may perceive them as a threat.[1]

As Enrique Desmond Arias and Kayyonne Marston, Gema Santamaría, and Pablo Piccato discuss in this volume, the use of force by police throughout Latin America has often been arbitrary, abusive, and illegal. Even in contexts of relatively low conflict, the exercise of police power raises the critical question of its legitimacy. Whereas police power is outwardly simple and direct, the origin of that power is far from obvious and requires a good deal of symbolic artifice. It is permanently under construction. Relationships with the civilian population are a key concern for all modern police forces, whose power is tempered in an abundance of instructions and codes regarding conduct and behavior.

The use of coercive force is discretionary. The power to arrest—the most obvious manifestation of a power with many incarnations—results from a fragmented and heterogeneous decisional chain, built on countless micro-decisions that are secret, or at least to some degree implicit. Since no police officer enforces the law mechanically (an impossibility, given the gap between theoretical tasks and actual capacities), this modest guardian of order must decide every day which incidents or social groups merit intervention, and how far this intervention will go within the formal or informal framework of the police role.[2]

This essay explores the public relations strategies Buenos Aires police adopted in the context of a deep crisis of consensus in the 1920s and 1930s regarding their right to use force. The findings have broader implications for a question transcending this case: how can police officers act as the guardians of a social order they themselves perceive as unjust while maintaining the respect of individuals who suffer from its injustice? The answer lies within the process of symbolic construction of an idealized police officer, one able to remain connected with those he claims to protect. In this case, the connection between the police and the people was woven using fiction, mass media, and other key elements of popular culture.

In Buenos Aires, social resistance to police use of force has been longstanding throughout the history of the nineteenth and twentieth centuries. Although it is difficult to assess in comparative terms, mass resentment toward, mockery of, and contempt for the police force goes back to the very foundation of the institution, and have survived every attempt at remedy. In his 1885 report, Chief of Police Marcos Paz reflected on this popular animosity and mentioned a problematic attitude that many would echo after him: a stubborn "way of being in relation to authority" on the part of the city population. He complained, "The security agent who looks after the life, property, and honor of persons encounters hostility rather than help or acknowledgment in the general public; therefore, what could be taken care of by a sole policeman requires the presence of many. . . . Contempt always underlies the slightest disorder."[3]

Nowhere was this contempt more eloquent than in popular journalism, where topics such as police corruption were intertwined with discussions of mistreatment of workers, political dissidents, and common citizens. In the 1920s, this discourse migrated from the leftist press to more mainstream mass-market newspapers such as *Crítica,* where the denunciation of police misconduct became an important pillar of the expected content for this daily publication and its tens of thousands (soon to become hundreds of thousands) of readers. The defiance of police authority, mockery of police clumsiness, and exposure of police brutality all underlay the commercial success of *Crítica,* "the voice of the people." Its illustrations, rhetorical style, and interviews all constructed a universe in which the abyss between the people and police was taken as a given.[4]

Upon this substratum lay public hatred of the police force, widely seen as an institution that used intimidation to put down strikes, mistreated and killed workers, or planted false evidence at scenes of conflict. The police force was constructed as the diametrical *other* of working-class identity in turn-of-the-century Buenos Aires. The prevalence of this popular rancor, shared even across different political ideologies, stirred up uneasiness among the higher-ranking police officers who felt responsible for the public image of the institution. These officials were keenly aware of the challenges implicit in police intervention in the "social question," an intervention that required some semblance of social legitimacy. Hence, the issue of public opinion became critical, making the construction of an image of unity between police and society one of the great undertakings of police reforms.

As stated in this volume's introduction, recent public concern about crime has placed the topic of violence and insecurity at the center of scholarly debates about Latin America's past and present. Finding themselves suddenly involved in debates on causes of crime or public policy recommendations, Latin American sociologists and anthropologists are pondering the nature of urban imaginaries of fear. Carrying questionnaires and recording devices, they explore the neighborhoods of large cities, collecting testimonies ranging from physical and mental sensations to causal interpretations of crime and its consequences.[5]

In Buenos Aires, analyses of the various public discourses about fear have yielded certain stable themes. One juxtaposes the "bad cop" of the present against the imagined noble neighborhood watchman of an idyllic past, an important figure in the nostalgia for order on an individual level. In his study on notions of crime and moral order, for instance, Alejandro Isla singles out the *vigilante de la esquina* (corner cop, or beat cop) as implicit in descriptions of what today's police should be.

Negative perceptions of the present, he argues, are conceived as a departure from a normative center that remains resistant. At the heart of the denunciation of the corrupt, violent police officer is the longing for that mythical *vigilante,* very much alive.[6] We know little, however, about the genealogy of this emblematic fixture of the *porteño* neighborhood. This essay is about the genesis of that longest-lived image of the Buenos Aires police, one born in the context of a public opinion crisis at the beginning of the twentieth century.

Crystalized in the 1920s and 1930s, the image of the *porteño vigilante* (Buenos Aires watchman) can be thought of as a local version of the generic community policeman, well known in many cities of the world. In this case, the consolidation of the *vigilante* was linked to a very specific process of settlement of suburban areas that would become the backdrop for new forms of sociability. Meanwhile, the crisis of public opinion transformed the beat cop into a figure of internal consensus, untouched by the tensions dividing the law enforcement institution. This pretechnological and depoliticized policeman maintained a vital connection with society. He preserved the link with the common citizen.

This symbolic construction was not controlled by the upper echelons of the police force, but rather by groups of younger police officers who were peripheral to the decision-making centers of the institution. These young officers were concerned with two fundamental problems: the creation of strong bonds of institutional identity within the ranks and the projection of an image of an efficient, likeable police force. Institutional identity and social legitimacy—these were matters that transcended the kind of professional expertise learned at the police academy. The campaign to achieve them did not depend upon the most commonly accepted indicators of police modernization, such as compiling criminological data or using fingerprinting to identify suspects. Nor did it require better weapons or patrol cars. Rather, it developed in the language of mass culture and strove to construct a popular image of rank-and-file police officers as ethical.

The Triumph of the Street Watchman

The notion of police culture—the aggregate of elements that distinguish a police point of view from that of society at large—has been prominent in explanations of police brutality and police resistance to institutional reform in Latin America. The assumption is that a shared subculture provides meaning and intelligibility to a job that is not easily integrated into a larger symbolic universe. Police work generates thick webs of meaning and casual police talk provides a sense of belonging. Much has been said, for instance, about the importance of machismo, cultural isolation, political conservatism, sense of mission, and glorification of danger as constituent elements of police identity.[7]

The concept of police culture has proven useful for distinguishing police points of view from those of society at large. But simultaneously the notion has contributed to lending this viewpoint an air of the exotic. When we think about historical periods when the separation between police and society was still underdeveloped, or about cases where cultural sensitivity toward the environment is less hermetic—as seems to be the case in Buenos Aires—relying on this category may be inconvenient.[8] Indeed, conceiving of the *porteño* police officer's worldview in less exotic terms opens a window for a critical history of the construction of police identity, one in which this construction arises not only from its divorce from the wider culture, but also from its familiarity with that culture—from a process of selection and resignification of topics that are present in popular literature, tango, and mass media.

The construction of personal bonds within the Policía de la Capital took shape in the 1920s and 1930s, around the notion of a police family, a concept that remains at the center of institutional culture to this day. The police family is a broad community of subjects whose wage concerns and demands to superiors are intertwined with news about births, weddings, parties, and sentimental ups and downs: in other words, a social network.

Founded in August 1922 and intended to remain in publication for a quarter-century, the *Magazine Policial*, a rank-and-file entertainment periodical, was the main player in the construction of the notion of a police family. It followed the miscellaneous style of *Caras y Caretas*, a successful mass-market magazine founded in the nineteenth century by Fray Mocho (a police officer who was well attuned to popular culture and graphic media). With a more populist tone—more *tanguera*, more sensational—*La Gaceta Policial* (1926–31) spoke to the ordinary beat cop and served a similar function as the *Magazine Policial*. Despite their strong resemblance to magazines with much wider circulations, both publications were meant for police consumption only.

The *Magazine* and the *Gaceta* offered a popular and populist way to promote and keep readers abreast of the concerns and interests of this institution-family (especially its lower ranks). Salary issues, personal security, and the promotion system all featured prominently, and always with an eye toward benefiting the police department's most modest agents. Any perceived unfairness toward even the most subordinate street cops by ignorant institutional bureaucrats was strenuously editorialized.[9]

Magazine Policial and *Gaceta Policial* embraced the cause of corporate identity, complementing the more formal recruitment and professionalization strategies employed by the institution's upper echelon. These periodicals' success resulted from the intersection between their involvement in the problems of institution building and the deliberately informal tone that served to reinforce a perception of nonofficial status. The familiarist elements they promoted were formulated in the language of mass culture.

Police cultures, says Robert Reiner, are born not from didactic manuals studied at police academies, but rather from the aggregate mediation of histories transmitted from generation to generation, from everyday jokes, and from practical commonalities.[10] The popular and populist inflection of *Magazine Policial* stemmed from a dense peppering of anecdotes that highlighted the qualities of the street watchman. A diminutive urban hero, the beat cop was seen as the incarnation of the highest professional virtues. He also knew all the juicy anecdotes. The chronicle of his routine was sprinkled with implicit knowledge of wisdom and weakness on the street. The plausibility of this bond of familiarity relied upon a perception of the police officer as a combination of hero and morally vulnerable human being. The reader's tacit understanding was expressed in a chuckle while perusing an account of the all-too-human temptations of the job: illegal lotteries, alcohol, parties. The "Mail" section of the *Magazine* contained a wealth of anecdotes of complicity with the great family.[11]

In the 1930s, these kinds of lighthearted accounts began to give way to the more serious topic of a police mission. Modern technology and formal recruitment policies brought with them a transformation of the street officer, whose image crystallized in the heroic mold. Now cast as a hermetic figure, straitjacketed in a uniform, the police image left little room for vulnerability. With the introduction of the radio and automatic weapons, these devices became prominently displayed signifiers of

strength. Any humorous appreciation for the beat cop's human fallibil-
ity disappeared from public definitions of the police mission. Idealized
street interactions now involved children or old ladies, figures that cast
the policeman's virility into sharp relief, leaving no room for jokes or
human temptation. In this harder pattern of masculinity (closer to the
military model) the policeman was now a step removed from society.
He didn't speak to passersby; rather, he protected them from traffic. He
watched over them. He guaranteed that the violence of the city would not
disrupt the congenial order of the neighborhood. He had now become
an expert in the pursuit and apprehension of criminals.

In order to be persuasive, the image of the heroic policeman needed
a human dimension, one that was sublime rather than humorous. The
construction of the ideal of the heroic policeman was topped off by the
idea of sacrifice (at various levels and often using the language of popular fiction): he was a victim of his calling to public service, neglected by
a state that paid him little and at the mercy of the hardships of the street,
where he passed more hours than anyone else, enduring its relentless
pace and cacophony. Reinforced with technical efficiency, the uniformed
body had its counterpart in the suffering body, the "exposed" body of
the policeman-hero.

The tradition of the Policía de la Capital was to fulfill its mission
stoically, "through the hard nights of torrential rain and the blazing
heat of summer afternoons," observed the director of *Magazine Policial*,
Ramón Cortés Conde, himself a young police officer concerned with
institutional reform.[12] In addition to inclement weather and bewildering
traffic, the police officer was also exposed to the ghosts of the night.
Here is the ancient connection between police praxis and knowledge
of the mysteries of the night, a topic with roots in the colonial figure of
the night watchman, who controls the light sources and confirms the
identities of passersby. The night is the supreme territory of police cognitive authority. As Amy Chazkel demonstrates in chapter 7, nighttime
enables and legitimates police intervention and restrictions in the name
of social order. It is also the locus of camaraderie. Narrated as paternal
sacrifice on behalf of an infant society, this vigilance covered the officer
with a layer of moral superiority. It was a vigil by pastoral police, whose
tutelary power was ever-watchful over their flock, and who knew and
protected both the group and its individuals.[13] Like children who could
sleep in peace "in warm silk sheets" thanks to the watchfulness of their

elders, Buenos Aires rested on the back of the police officer who endured glacial winters, storms, and physical threats in order to watch over this carefree, ungrateful society.

"While the City Sleeps" was the name of a section of *Magazine Policial* devoted to the everyday experiences of the beat cop, who renounced comfort and personal concerns so that others could enjoy the guarantee of domestic order. Soon, similar editorial spaces appeared in other police publications. Written by both high-ranking officials and average officers, the contributions built an anthology of the tragic and picturesque vicissitudes of the job. They fed a shared archive of experiential knowledge about the night shift.

The officer's ultimate mission was to protect citizens from the dangers of urban modernity—from crime, of course, but also from the physical and material violence that loomed at every corner, from noise and speed, from the risks underlying anonymity. This *vigilante,* who owed his name as much to wakefulness (*vigilia*) as to surveillance (*vigilancia*), was more closely related to his colonial ancestor than to his contemporary, the armed and motorized police officer, whom he complemented by opposition. Even if the vigilante was also armed, his weapon was never mentioned.

The "ignored soldier" attained the peak of heroism when he gave up his life for the very society that so disregarded him. As classic ethnographic studies of "police culture" have shown, station house talk about danger plays a major role in police bonding and camaraderie.[14] But in this case, the dominant meaning lies in the tragic dimension of that risk, since police officers "fallen in the line of duty" inject an intense and morally righteous gravity to police identity.

The cult of deceased Buenos Aires police officers developed and expanded during the 1920s and 1930s: the Policía del Capital erected a monument and named surveillance posts after fallen colleagues (who were remembered again in printed institutional histories), while the Panteón Social of the cemetery witnessed a multiplication of rituals. The sacrificial bodies were buried with great pomp in the police mausoleum, built in December 1921. At station houses, small sanctuaries sprang up around the photographs of deceased colleagues. In the mid-thirties, a special section of the cemetery, the "niches of honor" was devoted to those who died in the line of duty.

Our dead: the gallery of martyrs built a moral counterweight to and balm for the popular mockery of the police. *Our dead:* the first-person possessive defined a sense of belonging in contrast with "their" dead. *Our dead* were embraced by an institutional family that constructed itself through the very act of closing ranks around the pain that society refused to acknowledge. Coexistence with an ungrateful public was an essential element of police identity. The constantly mentioned theme of society's indifference toward police sacrifice accelerated the movement of refuge in a community of peer officers. It is present in institutional publications to this day, in the form of poems written by beat cops. The tragedy of sacrifice constitutes a vital element in the symbolization of police work.

The construction of the police officer as public servant had the sentimental intensity of melodrama. Similar elements were used to build fables of reconciliation with the people.

Police Melodramas: the Sentimental Bond Between State and Citizen

During the night watch at a porteño police station, two policemen drink *mate.*

> *Corporal:* Police life is a school of pain!
>
> *Auxiliary:* The police station is where all human calamities converge.
>
> *Corporal:* It's true, Sir. . . .
>
> *Auxiliary:* Tears and intimate dramas, engraved in the books, between traces of black ink. . . . So much pain and misery in such few phrases.
>
> —*Ronda Policial* radio broadcast, September 1938[15]

Between 1934 and 1945 Radio Porteña broadcast *Ronda Policial* (Police Rounds) every day. At its peak, the Radiópolis group—led by Commissioner Ramón Cortés Conde—had programs on eleven radio stations on subjects ranging from life in the old city to great crime cases, secret histories of Buenos Aires, or adventures of the gaucho detective Sergeant Venancio.

Initially produced for police consumption and later scripted for radio, "police melodrama" had a long history inside the institution. It flourished in the 1920s and 1930s as a particular version of commercial melodrama that was enormously popular in literature, radio theater, and the movies. Due to its brevity, simple moral structure, and direct relationship with experience, it was the most frequent genre written by police officer–authors. In the mid-thirties, police melodrama expanded beyond the institution in the form of scripts for radio programs, written by a few officers and civilian collaborators. These productions disseminated the benign image of the night porteño watchman.

The "police melodrama" capitalized on everyday stories of the officer—the one who knew how to *see beneath* the exterior face of the city, understood its characters, and experienced firsthand the drama of the ordinary. In the homelike space of the neighborhood police station, the officer heard numerous stories of the invisible social fabric. The fragmented body of poems, vignettes, and brief anecdotes that constituted police melodrama tended to emphasize the fragility and immobility of its characters: the poor were poor, the rich were rich, and context did not matter. Military coups, the Spanish Civil War, and the world wars all occurred far from the misfortunes of the meek, whom the police officer encountered suspended in time and essentialized in the neighborhood that constituted his stage.

The mild-mannered police officer of these melodramas was represented as the social equal of these characters. His wisdom was a summary of human nature rather than an analysis of the conflicts and tensions underlying social life. Abstraction is foreign to police culture. Its archive of the street is inductive, empirical, and cumulative. It is made up of stories and characters, of a very singular incarnation of political or sociological categories. It was precisely this status of inconspicuous observer of the active school of life that vested the watchman with moral and cognitive authority. The very name of the program, Police Rounds, evoked a world and established a point of view: that of the agent who *walked* the city and narrated its corners as affective spaces marked by concrete references (the corner, the dance salon, the café, specific street names). His concrete knowledge thus complemented more abstract descriptions of police space, represented in blueprints, maps, and construction plans.

The police melodramas published in magazines contained traces of sympathy and familiarity with the cultural universe of the Left, orientations that could even help to cement a certain kind of street credibility inside the institution. But since police knowledge resisted abstraction, it remained radically separate from the point of view of dissident culture.

The stories of street officers were set in the Buenos Aires of the 1920s and 1930s, where upward social mobility was, despite some unevenness, a dominant trend. The neighborhood (el barrio) was the most emblematic product of this process, and the patrolman who watched over it represented the guarantee of an order that was identified with the values of upwardly mobile social groups. Nevertheless, the narratives of the humane officer described a society that was static and dichotomous, an essentially unfair order with asymmetric and irreconcilable poles.

The hero of the police melodrama had distinctive class origins. His moral force stemmed from his otherness in relation to the rich and powerful and his display, anecdote by anecdote, of empathy for the weak. The world of the rich was remote territory, mined with moral hazards, a place that promised little more than humiliation for the police officer forced to travel through it.

With virile disdain, this police officer portrayed the artificial and fundamentally corrupt world in which the privileged lived. "Surrounded by aristocratic palaces," the hero stood on the corner, enduring cold and rain, proudly keeping his chin up.[16] *Gaceta Policial* told stories of the moral bankruptcy of the powerful—their cocaine addictions, their dark financial maneuvers. Evoking an antirevolutionary, antibourgeois, and most of all anti-elitist sensibility, the 1930 anniversary editorial opened with these words: "*Gaceta Policial* is a solid supporter of the social order, as long as it is understood that the powerful are not the only ones in need of protection."[17]

In the imagination of the police, empathy entailed neither closeness with the upper classes nor affinity for organized labor. The territory of intervention of the porteño policeman was not the factory, the union, the barricade, or the workers' union assembly. His stage was the neighborhood street, where the characters victimized by injustice—those who needed his protective arm—walked by. When an anarchist entered the scene, his political condition was immediately absorbed into that world of feelings where the encounter was possible because, ultimately, he was another victim—more idealistic, perhaps more cultivated, but a victim nonetheless. Police melodrama was infused with the emotions of the social diminutive. It was an effort to make state law and human law (understood in intensely sentimental terms) coincide.

The motif of motherly sacrifice recurrent in tango lyrics and mass literature has been a fixture of police narrative to this day. Its leading character is the *mater dolorosa* (suffering mother), who very generously gave up her child. The widowed elderly lady who before her police officer–son's rounds warned him about the dangers of the street was a cornerstone of the great institutional theme of the fallen police officer. It presided over the celebration of *our dead*.

In other respects, the mater dolorosa also figured in the life of the criminal. Police work—a strictly male occupation until the 1940s—was a school of pain where the affective bond was more important than any other criterion, including dictates of the law. Insofar as life found them sharing the same emotions, the suffering of mothers (and fathers) was conceived in terms that connected parents of individuals on both sides of the law.

Another repeated theme in melodramas was the discovery of a virtue in the police that had been invisible or dismissed, hidden under misleading appearances. In his study of the genre, Peter Brook sees melodrama as placing virtue at the center of the scene, as making a spectacle of homage to virtue, both its power and its effects. Melodramas also tell of the invisibility of this quality, which introduces the problem of recognition.[18] What was hindering social perception of police virtue? Perhaps it was the uniform or the intimidating weapons. Definitely it had to do with the deep humility of this public servant who was erroneously feared. The humility of class and calling was contrasted with the frivolous elite characters of the proud metropolis. In this universe of blazing moral clarity, each occupied its assigned place.

Underlying the tale of discovery of police virtue, however, was an ambivalent relationship with the law, in which the emphasis on the human sensibility of the good police officer constructed a form of authority that resided above, or in the interstices of, the law. He was capable of making unnoticed legal accommodations, always based on his human experience and tutelary mission. Here is where the theme of the pact between police and transgressor was born, drawn up in the name of an unwritten moral law that connected these two street-level actors quite apart from their standing in the eyes of the law. (This virtuous pact was the counter-figure of the spurious pact denounced by the popular press as police shenanigans or corruption, a regular feature in *Crítica*'s headlines.)

The authenticity of the pact between the thief and the benign police officer was founded in its power to distinguish between those who committed crime out of evil intent and those who did so out of necessity.

Here is where the issue of police discretion reappeared. The exegesis of the watchman did not respond to press accusations with fables of attachment to legal order. The discretion of the beat cop to determine what was socially fair was not covered up, but rather exalted as demonstrating profound understanding. Police melodramas said that it was not the law, but rather the benign use of discretion that allowed the police officer to decide when to use force and when to forgive. Abuse by police coexisted with the wise discretion of the vigilante de la esquina, who exercised a power that was informed by the landmarks of a just sentimental order.

Police and Social Conflict

If melodrama placed the police officer in a logic of clear moral superiority, his role in social conflict introduced much more resistant ideological and narrative tensions. The coexistence of the watchman as friend of the dispossessed and the police officer as guardian of the status quo (responsible for spying on the dissidents against a clearly unfair order) brought up the obvious question of the moral foundations of the institution's mission. As I have argued, consensus around the repression of protest cannot be explained through class identification. The question about the place of the political enemy in the moral universe of the ideal police officer needs to take into account a fact that is often overlooked: the police role as guarantor of the established order did not in itself create an identity in tune (or in economic alliance or aesthetic fascination) with the upper classes. On the contrary, the evidence points to a marked otherness in relation to tastes and sensibilities of the wealthy, whose interests the police protected as a duty rather than as a calling.

How could surveillance and control of the working classes be legitimized when the class and vital concerns of the working poor were narrated as points of common identity with the universe of the police officer? One clue lies in the religious elements of this imaginary. The influence of Catholic social thought became increasingly apparent in police discourse through the 1920s and 1930s, as the eclectic tolerance of the 1920s gave way to a renaissance of Christian values.

The stigmatization of the political activist might be attributed to this greater ideological context and linked to other examples of polarization in the 1930s, a period when nuances were erased and positions hardened. By then, however, the symbolic construction of the leftwing activist had an endogenous tradition that preceded Catholic anticommunism. The heightened levels of repression during this period were part of a long history of police intervention in the political arena. The elimination of the dissident as an equal has roots in a police culture that is complementary with the context of antiliberal and anticommunist reactions of the 1930s but is also quite compatible with other ideological frames of reference.

Thereby a line was drawn that set artists and writers from the broader cultural field of the Left (whose knowledge might be useful or even enjoyed by metropolitan police officers) apart from leftist agitators who were incompatible with police officers' most fundamental ideals of order. This explains the presence of communist or anarchist authors in police magazines. Another boundary line separated the idiosyncratic details of an individual agitator (whose misadventures might be narrated with sympathy in police anecdotes) from the abstract activist, with whom no association was possible. A third separation occurred between the weak members of society (who deserved a better world and relied on an alliance with the police officer to protect them from harm) and those who pretended to serve their interests by striking and throwing bombs. If the law was not a dominant theme in the police imaginary, order was. One last opposition completed the system: that between criollo familiarity with the point of view of the worker-ally of the police—justly indignant, conservative in his resigned worldview—and the exotic jargon of the worker who had been brainwashed by foreign interests.

This perspective found its most articulate representation in police historiography. Eager to control its institutional memory, the Buenos Aires police had always laboriously reconstructed its past. In the Peronist years (1946–55), when the ideal of a utopian unity between the people and the police permeated official discourse (and the good police force of the present was contrasted with the wicked police force of the past), the question of the prior handling of social conflict became critical. In those years, three officials wrote testimonials of the Semana Trágica (Week of Tragedy), a massacre of workers following a strike in January 1919.[19]

Although these officials were of different political persuasions, all three narratives were marked by Peronist ideals, including greater recognition for the working classes. This orientation opened the door for uncomfortable questions regarding the past alliance of the police institution with the established political and economic powers. Thus, accounts of the Semana Trágica had to be reorganized within the themes of police morality and social identity, which offered guidelines for ideal relationships with the people.

The generic police narrative of the Semana Trágica may be summarized as follows: In January 1919, driven by meager wages and selfish bosses, the workers of the Vassena factory went on strike. The workers' reasonable demands were co-opted and exploited by foreign agitators and an irresponsible leftist press. The real culprits were not the workers but the bosses, agitators, and yellow journalists. The well-meaning majority was dragged along by a small group: "Working people of this country, who are naturally peaceful and traditionally honest, were poorly equipped to distinguish between their necessities and the ambitions of the leaders."[20] Echoing Russian literature—frequently published in *Magazine Policial* as well as many other popular magazines—Officer José Ramón Romariz offered a grim description of the material conditions of "authentic" workers.[21]

Romariz, along with the other two officers who wrote about the Semana Trágica, strove to establish their personal sympathy for even the most politically involved workers. Octavio A. Piñero praised the pioneering initiatives of early twentieth-century socialism. Ramón Cortés Conde emphasized the distinction between professional agitators and "the idealist who dreams of a better humankind." Romariz wrote of his enthusiastic participation in the socialist demonstrations of his youth and his enjoyment of the role of bourgeois-hater.[22] The actors on both sides of the Semana Trágica were just and sincere. The key to the catastrophe was the opposition between false workers and bad bosses. Misguided in their loyalties, the street-level police officers were manipulated by their superiors to align themselves with the status quo, even though everything in their nature and social composition pulled them in the opposite direction (the same direction that had prevailed in Peronism, according to Romariz).

Left exposed in the explosive war between capital and labor were rank-and-file police officers (distinguished from the police force) who were human, scared, confused, and lost in a chaotic landscape of shootings. In certain passages, the patrolmen were portrayed as victims in similar terms as fallen civilians were, all of them trapped in a confusing theater of forces that overwhelmed them. "We, the modest officials and humble agents of the institution didn't count at all in the game of opposing interests," said Romariz.[23] The erasure of the line between repressors and repressed was clear in his description of the disposition of corpses: at the morgue, dead police officers were hastily identified and thrown inside a truck full of dead bodies. Individuals who had opposed each other at the barricades—working-class activists and rank-and-file police officers—were now materially mixed at the crematorium.[24]

Police narratives of the Semana Trágica confirmed that, despite appearances to the contrary, there was a deep connection between the average police officer and the people. Ultimately, the heart of this tale of social conflict lies in the minute experiences of its actors, highlighting their lack of responsibility for having to oppose each other. The average police officer emerged from the Semana Trágica morally intact. The only measure of his heroism was the extent of his sacrifice. His enemies—the unscrupulous upper classes and foreign agitators—were no different from the enemies of the working-class majority. Any repressive initiative led by the institutional hierarchy would have to take into account this distinction between the good and the bad workers, the weak and the strong, the interests of the people and those of the oligarchy. When Peronism redefined communist militants, dissident students, and politicians allied with the rich as the targets of surveillance, it needed only to make official this preexisting symbolic configuration of the relationship between people and police.

Conclusion

Persuading the general public of the justifications for using force to maintain the established order has always been a major challenge for police agencies in the modern era. In order for police interventions to be effective, civilians must be convinced of the fundamental justice of police power—a difficult task, considering the precarious legal foundations of police authority and its obvious use of force. Just as important, police agencies require that rank-and-file police officers—who are recruited mostly from the working classes—also be certain of their right to repress social protest.

The history of the police construction of the figure of the virtuous Buenos Aires neighborhood cop reveals the complexities involved in this task of persuasion. As I have argued, this process began in the lower ranks of the institution, in the context of other demands from rank-and-file officers to their superiors. By the early 1930s, the good vigilante de la esquina was adopted by all institutional organs, and soon crossed over to the commercial media. Countering the widespread notion of a police culture cut off from mainstream culture, I argue that the successful mythology of the vigilante—born in the 1920s and 1930s and alive still to this day—has functioned in conjunction with (rather than separate from) the symbolic universe of popular culture and mass entertainment.

Of course, the ideological success of the vigilante does not translate into widespread acceptance of the Buenos Aires police, whose power is and has always been routinely contested. But current opinion polls show that even the most critical discourses tend to distinguish the "good" neighborhood cop from the counterpart of the abusive, corrupt cop. Moreover, there is ample evidence that this figure has played a key role in the informal mechanisms of identity building within the institution. The notion of a deep bond between rank-and-file police officers and the most vulnerable members of society—routinely reinforced in tales of social sensitivity—has been critical in reconciling even the most traumatic episodes, such as massacres of workers, with notions of social justice. In times of social harmony, the image of the police officer as micromanager of neighborhood conflicts consolidated the notion that good police discretion is often better than impersonal law enforcement.

Notes

This chapter is adapted with permission from Lila Caimari, *Mientras la ciudad duerme. Pistoleros, policías y periodistas en Buenos Aires, 1920–1945* (Buenos Aires: Siglo XXI, 2012), chap. 6.

1. P. A. J. Waddington, *Policing Citizens: Authority and Rights* (New York: Routledge, 1999), 23.

2. Ibid., 15–16; Dominique Monjardet, *Ce que fait la police. Sociologie de la force publique* (Paris: La Découverte, 1996), chap. 2.

3. Paz quoted in Mercedes García Ferrari, *Ladrones conocidos/Sospechosos reservados. Identificación policial en Buenos Aires, 1880–1905* (Buenos Aires: Prometeo, 2010), 39.

4. Lila Caimari, *Apenas un delincuente. Crimen, castigo y cultura en la Argentina, 1880–1955* (Buenos Aires: Siglo XXI, 2004), chap. 6.

5. Lucía Dammert, ed., *Seguridad ciudadana: experiencias y desafíos* (Valparaíso, Chile: Municipalidad de Valparaíso, 2004); Teresa Pires Do Rio Caldeira, *City of Walls: Crime, Segregation and Citizenship in São Paulo* (Berkeley: University of California Press, 2001); Javier Auyero and María Fernanda Berti, *La violencia en los márgenes. Una maestra y un sociólogo en el conurbano bonaerense* (Buenos Aires:

Katz, 2013); Gabriel Kessler, *El sentimiento de inseguridad. Sociología del temor al delito* (Buenos Aires: Siglo XXI, 2009).

6. Alejandro Isla, "La calle, la cárcel y otras rutinas de los ladrones. Tradición y cambio en el mundo del delito," in *Seguridad ciudadana*, ed. Dammert, 59–101.

7. Robert Reiner, *The Politics of the Police* (Oxford: Oxford University Press, 2000), chap. 3; Tom Cockcroft, *Police Culture: Themes and Concepts* (New York: Routledge, 2013).

8. Ruth Stanley, "Conversaciones con policías en Buenos Aires: en busca de la 'cultura policial' como variable explicativa de abusos policiales," in *Estado, violencia y ciudadanía en América Latina*, ed. Stanley, 77–105 (Madrid: Entinema, 2009); Sabina Frederic, "Oficio policial y usos de la fuerza pública: aproximaciones al estudio de la policía de la Provincia de Buenos Aires" in *Un estado con rostro humano. Funcionarios e instituciones estatales en la Argentina desde 1880*, ed. Ernesto Bohoslavsky and Germán Soprano (Buenos Aires: Prometeo, 2010), 281–307.

9. Caimari, *Mientras la ciudad duerme*, chap. 6.

10. Reiner, *Politics of the Police*, 87.

11. "Mentiras policiales," *Magazine Policial*, November 1931; "Buzón," *Magazine Policial*, March 1928.

12. Ramón Cortés Conde, "¡Mientras la ciudad duerme!" *Magazine Policial*, April 1934.

13. Michel Foucault, "'Omnes et singulatim': Vers une critique de la raison politique," in *Dits et écrits II, 1976–1988* (Paris: Quarto Gallimard, 2001), 953–80.

14. Reiner, *Politics of the Police*, 87.

15. "Lo que se transmite por Ronda Policial," *Radiópolis: Magazine Policial*, September 1938.

16. Oficial Thermidor, "El agente de policía," *Magazine Policial*, December 1924, 9.

17. *Gaceta Policial*, May 31, 1930, 7; "Los agentes financieros. La alta sociedad en sus diversas actividades," *Gaceta Policial*, May 1, 1926, 2; "Quiso matarlo porque no la dejó que comprara cocaína," *Gaceta Policial*, August 20, 1927, 9.

18. Peter Brooks, *The Melodramatic Imagination: Balzac, Henry James, Melodrama, and the Mode of Excess* (New Haven, CT: Yale University Press, 1995 [1976]), 27.

19. Julio Godio, *La Semana Trágica de enero 1919* (Buenos Aires, Hyspamérica, 1985). The two published police accounts of this historical landmark are José Ramón Romariz, *La Semana Trágica. Antecedentes sociales, económicos y políticos: episodios y relatos históricos de los sucesos sangrientos de enero del año 1919* (Buenos Aires: Editorial Hemisferio, 1952); and Octavio A. Piñero, *Los orígenes y la trágica semana de enero de 1919* (Buenos Aires: s/ed, 1956). The third account, by Ramón Cortés Conde, was never published due to his death in 1946. Several chapters were published, however, by *Magazine Policial*.

20. Cortés Conde, "La Semana Trágica," unpublished manuscript in possession of Sonia Cortés Conde, 6.

21. Romariz, *La Semana Trágica*, 37.

22. Ibid., 60.

23. Ibid., 91.

24. Ibid., 154.

PART II
Constructing Crime

Exploring the multiple audiences that take part in the debates, representations, and meanings of crime—and the myriad factors beyond
the realm of law and legality that shape portrayals of crime and criminals—the essays in this section demonstrate that illegality alone does
not determine which behaviors are defined as criminal nor which social
groups are associated with crime. As much as legislators and intellectuals wanted to dictate proper comportment and reify national culture
through laws and discourse, crime and violence were negotiated concepts
that were as likely to be shaped by the officials charged with enforcing
the law as by the litigants and perpetrators who were targets of it. The
burgeoning historiography of crime and punishment in Latin America
has demonstrated how through their interpretations of the law, judges
shaped the fates, if not necessarily the identification, of criminals.[1] Political, social, and ideological processes inform not only the law but also
the definitions of crime and portrayals of criminals and security forces.

By the late nineteenth and early twentieth centuries, positivist criminology and other forces associated with modernization encouraged
Latin American intellectuals and authorities to reconceptualize crime
and recast populations on the margins of modernization as criminals. To
those ends, Latin American elites deployed science to justify eugenic policies and practices.[2] Courts throughout Latin America turned to doctors to
confirm such sexual crimes as rape. Often medical professionals' opinions
trumped the testimonies of witnesses and even victims. As Robert Alegre

points out in his exploration of how Chilean law, magistrates, and authorities criminalized sodomy because it "hindered modernization," sexuality was fodder for nation-builders' notions of progress and order. Similar to the way those reforms defined sexually active gay men as potential criminals, in nations like Mexico and Argentina positivist criminology altered the relationship between the state and the working class by redefining the latter's rights and criminalizing their everyday practices.[3] Criminal sociologists in revolutionary Mexico regularly identified penury as a contributor to crime.[4] In addition to class and sexuality, race and gender figured prominently in proscriptions and prohibitions that expanded notions of criminality.

Throughout Latin America and especially in places with significant indigenous populations, nation-builders portrayed those indigenous people as criminals.[5] David Carey Jr. reveals that modern police practices often countervailed and even disproved the racist strains of Latin American understandings of criminality. Criminal statistics in Guatemala reveal that the police arrested more nonindigenous than indigenous Guatemalans for crimes associated with Indians' alleged degeneracy. Even when police forces tailored their practices to adhere to discourses of crime, race, and class, racist rhetoric often rang hollow in the line of duty.

Focusing on the field of representation, Amy Chazkel reveals how nineteenth- and early twentieth-century Brazilian authorities sought to establish control over people's lives after dark. Purportedly seeking to make crime and criminal elements visible in an era before electric lighting, the state socially and legally constructed nighttime as a lawless period that demanded curfews and other state interventions to maintain public peace and social order. In short, they crafted noxious notions of nighttime to evoke fear of crime and violence. That discourse facilitated the arbitrary and often violent treatment of an already vulnerable population: poor and black people in the city's public spaces, on whose shoulders rested the burden of proving that they deserved the rights of full freedom of movement and assembly granted to privileged urban residents. This underclass learned about such abstract notions as justice and power through their everyday encounters with the violent and coercive power of the state; from those concrete experiences, they also gleaned how to assess risk and assign meaning. In Chazkel's account, race and class emerge as fundamental drivers of how notions of nighttime and such restrictive legislation as curfews developed. Even as many welcomed the close surveillance of slaves and their companions at night, elites wanted to retain the freedom to circulate after dark. To do so, they had to parse the discourse that portrayed nighttime as dangerous. Like other forces that shaped violence and crime, the field of representation seldom enjoyed hegemony.

Political contexts too helped to determine definitions of crime and criminals. The dictatorship of Jorge Ubico Castañeda (1931–44) was the catalyst for Guatemala's concerted turn toward positivist criminology. On the other end of the political spectrum, Chilean legislators turned gay sex into a crime during that nation's burgeoning democracy. In government structures that ranged from dictatorship (in Guatemala) and one-party rule (in Mexico) to democracy under fire (in Colombia during the early years of the civil war), where political elites held on to power tightly, dissent became a punishable act. As Luis Herrán Ávila charts in Mexico and Colombia, the Cold War elevated concerns about internal unrest and political opposition; many Latin American leaders came to see communism as a crime and communist sympathizers as criminals. More to the point, as authorities deployed the term "communist" to label any act or person that disrupted social peace and order, they not only emboldened their purview to define who was a criminal, they also legitimized their (and civil society's) use of force to suppress any alleged communist threat. In those settings, the difference between intellectuals and agitators was determined more by their opinions than by their actions. Even in the absence of violence, as Herrán Ávila demonstrates with the case of Mexico from the 1940s to the 1960s, the state used laws and discourse about communist threats to justify its own and civil society's use of violence. The Cold War had profound effects on notions of crime and violence.

Taken as a whole, the essays in "Constructing Crime" demonstrate how power relations and politico-ideological processes that transcend the realm of law contribute to the social construction of crime, danger, and violence. In turn, the authors also explore the myriad publics and politics that shape how and why groups and individuals become portrayed as criminals (or not). These granular studies of Chile, Guatemala, Brazil, Colombia, and Mexico remind us that notions of crime and criminals are historically and culturally contingent processes that vary by place.

Notes

1. Carlos A. Aguirre and Robert Buffington, eds., *Reconstructing Criminality in Latin America* (Wilmington, DE: Scholarly Resources, 2000); Ricardo D. Salvatore, Carlos Aguirre, and Gilbert Joseph, eds., *Crime and Punishment in Latin America: Law and Society since Late Colonial Times* (Durham, NC: Duke University Press, 2001); Robert Buffington and Pablo Piccato, *True Stories of Crime in Modern Mexico* (Albuquerque: University of New Mexico Press, 2009).

2. Nancy Stephan, *"The Hour of Eugenics": Race, Gender, and Nation in Latin America* (Ithaca, NY: Cornell University Press, 1991), 41.

3. Pablo Piccato, *City of Suspects: Crime in Mexico City, 1900–1931* (Durham, NC: Duke University Press, 2001), 212; Lila Caimari, "Remembering Freedom: Life as Seen from the Prison Cell," in *Crime and Punishment in Latin America,* ed. Salvatore, Aguirre, and Joseph, 391–92.

4. Robert Buffington, *"Los Jotos*: Contested Visions of Homosexuality in Modern Mexico," in *Sex and Sexuality in Latin America,* ed. Daniel Balderston and Donna J. Guy (New York: New York University Press, 1997), 123; Piccato, *City of Suspects,* 3; Elisa Speckman Guerra, "'I Was a Man of Pleasure, I Can't Deny It': Histories of José de Jesús Negrete, aka 'The Tiger of Santa Julia,'" in *True Stories of Crime in Modern Mexico,* ed. Buffington and Piccato, 75.

5. Benjamin Orlove, "The Dead Policemen Speak: Power, Fear, and Narrative in the 1931 Molloccahua Killings (Cusco)," in *Unruly Order: Violence, Power, and Cultural Identity in the High Provinces of Southern Peru,* ed. Deborah Poole, 63–95 (Boulder, CO: Westview Press, 1994); Jim Handy, "Chicken Thieves, Witches, and Judges: Vigilante Justice and Customary Law in Guatemala," *Journal of Latin American Studies* 36 (2004): 553.

5 Sodomitic Violence in Chile

*Medical Knowledge and the
Ambivalent Application of Law*

Robert F. Alegre

On November 10, 1919, police arrested Eduardo Trujillo Aránguiz, a twenty-six-year-old electrician from the northern city of Antofagasta, and charged him with the crime of sodomy.[1] According to the authorities, Trujillo Aránguiz had sodomized Carlos Riquelme Valenzuela, a minor, that morning. Gonzálo Cooper, Riquelme Valenzuela's uncle and guardian, testified that he was awakened early in the morning by his nephew's screams. He leaped to his feet, left his room, and saw Carlos approaching him with his pants down and a kerchief in his mouth. Carlos Riquelme Valenzuela explained to his uncle that when he woke up that morning and got ready to go to work, an employee from a nearby cantina grabbed him, struck him, and muzzled him with the kerchief. He then sodomized the boy and fell asleep. When police arrived on the scene, they went to see Trujillo and noted that his zipper was undone, exposing his penis.

Trujillo Aránguiz was one of countless men prosecuted for committing the act of sodomy as defined by article 365 of the Chilean Penal Code (1874), which identified sodomy as an unlawful act. From the beginning of the Chilean Republic in 1818 until 1874, there had been no laws regarding sodomy. No longer an agent of the crown, the Catholic Church did not persecute sodomites during this time.[2] When Chilean legislators outlawed sodomy in 1874, they followed a hemispheric trend among newly independent nations of outlawing what authorities considered scandalous behaviors, from prostitution to sodomy.[3] These practices, legislators feared, undermined social mores that buttressed civilization. In Chile, someone convicted of sodomy could serve up to three years in prison.

Unlike its Argentine counterpart of the late nineteenth century, the Chilean Penal Code did not distinguish between consensual sodomy and rape. Whereas the Argentine code applied exclusively to acts committed against legal minors, the Chilean code was remarkably inclusive, criminalizing violent acts (or nonconsensual acts) against minors and adults along with consensual sodomy between adults.[4] In short, over the course of the late nineteenth and early twentieth centuries, the Chilean state came to produce a monolithic, reductionist understanding of sodomy, designating consensual sodomy and violent anal penetration as commensurate criminal acts. The act did not have to be violent to be taken before the court; violent or not, it was a crime. The law in the abstract did not differentiate between pedophilia, rape, and consensual sex.

However, in practice, sodomy came to be represented as an act of violence between individuals. The government entrusted the police and the courts to discern what signs—behaviors, stains on clothing, bodily distortions—marked a person as a sodomite or as a victim of sodomy. Police decided what behaviors or acts warranted arrest for sodomy, and judges ruled whether the evidence proved that the act had occurred. Victims, defendants, prosecutors, judges, and witnesses constituted the publics associated with sodomy's prosecution; the courts provided a forum for these individuals to, as the authors put it in the introduction to this volume, take part in "debates, representations, and meanings of these practices." In the process, the courts constructed sodomy as a legible act and the sodomite as a discernable personage.

In this chapter I argue that the Chilean juridical system applied the law ambivalently; judges were more likely to convict a defendant if a violent crime took place, and very rarely did they convict those engaged in consensual anal sex. Even so, many alleged perpetrators of violent acts escaped prosecution for lack of evidence or because of the evidence's unreliable nature. This ambivalent application of the law, ironically, took place during a moment when the courts sought to diminish speculation, ambiguities, and intuition in the application of justice by calling upon the positivistic knowledge offered by science and medicine. More concretely, the courts relied on the emerging field of medicine to legitimate evidence of violence found at the scene of an alleged crime—a loose anus or a bloody towel represented violence. Doctors came to declare whether scientific proof existed that a violent crime had taken place. These representations came to define the material world of sex and crime. Marks on the body became material evidence of acts against civilization and, as such, a mighty threat to the new nation.

In the colonial era, an alleged sodomite was also subject to a juridical system, but no authoritative institution existed outside the church or government to legitimize evidence. In the colonial period, the sodomite came under the jurisdiction of ecclesiastical courts, which condemned the act as a sin against nature, and, therefore, a threat to social stability and an affront to Catholic morals. In the modern period, Chilean jurisprudence secularized the censure of sodomy while maintaining the view that the act undermined the moral order and the social good.[5] Secular courts were unconcerned about the status of the defendant as a sinner; they focused on condemning him as a criminal. If in colonial courts ecclesiastical authorities determined whether a defendant would be designated a sodomite, in the modern period judges, aided principally by doctors, would come to determine what counted as sodomy and who would be condemned as a sodomite.

As the medical profession and sciences expanded in the late nineteenth century, they became instrumental in determining whether a person had been anally penetrated—regardless of whether the act had been consensual or not.[6] Thereby, as in Europe, in Chile sexuality became, in Foucault's idiomatic rendering, "a medical and medicalizable object, one had to try to detect it—as a lesion, a dysfunction, or a symptom—in the depths of the organism or on the surface of the skin."[7] In this context, the medical examiner constituted one of the publics who issued discourses regarding sodomy. He provided what appeared to be a judgment free of the ethical or moral concerns of secular or religious authorities. Based on scientific requirements and distinguished by the doctor's impartiality, medical reports became authoritative proof in a court of law.[8] These medical reports and other doctors' statements regarding sodomy and the bodies of the victim and defendant comprised important elements in the politics of sodomy. Moreover, if marks on the alleged victims' bodies became representations of sodomy, the sodomite himself came to represent a peril to the national cause.

The cases under review came before the courts between 1919 and 1956, a period of rapid urbanization and dizzying social change.[9] The Parliamentary period (1890–1920) witnessed an influx of foreign investment in the nitrate industry and a concomitant growth of the industrial working class, especially in sectors linked to nitrate production and the export sector generally.[10] Not only did the northern cities near the nitrate nexus, such as Antofagasta, grow considerably, but the populations of the centrally located capital of Santiago and even of the southern city of Concepción expanded as well. The emergence of the working class brought labor conflict and consequent attempts by the state to contain popular discontent.[11] The working class also came to occupy spaces where police arrested individuals for the crime of sodomy. To be sure, every case under review involved lower-class individuals as both alleged victims and defendants.

When Lieutenant Carlos Ibáñez del Campo came to power in 1927, he sought to bring order through paternalistic policies and autocratic rule. He delivered measures aimed at addressing the plight of the urban populations, from new labor laws to educational reforms. Most important for my study, his administration founded the *carabineros,* Chile's first modern police force. These agents of the state came to enforce laws against sodomy in streets, bars, houses, and beyond. Carabineros joined judges, lawyers, doctors, witnesses, and sodomites in forming the publics associated with defining sodomy and locating sodomites in modern Chile. In efforts to contain the spread of the practice of sodomy, the state entrusted carabineros with preserving the moral and social order.

Establishing the Evidence of Violence

While the Chilean Penal Code marked the first instance of outlawing sodomy in the Chilean Republic, it was not the first time the act had been outlawed in the region.[12] For the duration of the colonial period, the Spanish government along with the Catholic Church prosecuted those suspected of sodomy under the Siete Partidas (Seven-Part Code), a legal code applicable to the entire Spanish Empire.[13] With the fall of the empire in the first quarter of the nineteenth century, revolutionaries throughout Latin America set out to construct new nation-states based on the principles of liberalism. Liberal laws derived from democratic governance would come to supplant Christian edicts (weakly) enforced by a faraway crown. In Chile, this liberal spirit became codified in the penal code more than fifty years after its break from the Spanish Empire.

In 1919 Trujillo Aránguiz was prosecuted for what in the colonial era the church had considered a sin against God. By the turn of the twentieth century, sodomy had become a crime against nature and an uncivilized act.[14] With the intellectual and political elite viewing sodomy as a practice that hindered the modernization of Chile, sodomy took on social implications. In an example of one of the central themes in this volume, the courts provided a privileged space for the articulation of what we can call a "politics of sodomy"—a space where experts, defendants, and witnesses together hashed out what constituted sodomy. They came to assess representations—or evidence—that signaled an act of sodomy had taken place, and these representations in turn had material effects— the arrest of individuals followed by a trial and a public discussion of the representations based the experts' assessments.

With secular courts in charge of prosecuting sodomites, establishing the legitimacy of evidence was key to garnering a conviction. Hence, it was of enormous significance for the court to decide whose opinion to trust. It was in this context that courts turned to the medical profession, as well as to societal commonsense, to determine if a crime had been committed. The documents reveal that certain voices, or publics, held more power than others and that some were deemed entirely inadmissible. A child's testimony, for example, held no weight; it was common for judges to throw out cases in which a child witness provided the key piece of evidence. The indigent, the illiterate, the unschooled, and women in general could testify, but judges were given a great deal of discretion in determining how heavily to weigh their testimony. Defense attorneys often contested testimony based on the socioeconomic status of the witness. Since the overwhelming majority of the cases involved working-class individuals without social or cultural capital, courts turned to doctors and medical exams to confirm or discredit witness testimonies. Hence, authorities created a hierarchy among the publics entwined in the debates, or politics, regarding sodomy; those at the bottom of the socioeconomic ladder were regarded with suspicion and the courts more readily disregarded their testimonies.

In order to discern whether Trujillo Aránguiz had violated the minor Riquelme Valenzuela, the court ordered the latter to undergo a medical exam, a practice that became routine in sodomy cases. Not only did the exam indicate that Riquelme Valenzuela had been sodomized, but the doctor claimed that this was not the first time. The case seemed to present elements of what at the time had been framed as dangers to civilization. Not only was an "indecorous and unnatural act" committed, it was enacted on a child, thereby supposedly perverting a member of the next generation.

The case was dismissed because the child's testimony was inadmissible in court. Children (defined as anyone under the age of seventeen in Chilean law) had no juridical personality, and therefore could not be convicted for sodomy or testify in any cases. The child's lack of status in the courts helps explain why those prosecuted for sodomy often invoked their young age, or their ignorance that the act was socially taboo and illegal. Like an uncorrupted child, they lacked the worldly sophistication to understand what constituted sodomy. The courts, in other words, included children in the publics of sodomy, but only as victims or silent audiences, while they forbade children entirely from engaging the politics of sodomy. The ambivalent application of the law in this case was due to a juridical view of children and childhood that precluded lending weight to their testimony. A child's testimony could not be trusted.

For a myriad of reasons, those accused of committing sodomy were not normally convicted unless evidence of rape existed. The forty-three cases that I have reviewed, dating from the 1910s to the 1950s, typically involved two adult men accused of committing sodomy, with no violence against adults or children. In each case, a private act became public knowledge, and in the process the act itself—how it was executed, what it meant to those engaged in it, and even if it actually occurred—appeared ambiguous and even benign. And perhaps that is why these cases were so often dismissed. Nine cases, however, represented episodes of extraordinary violence.

The case of Carlos Luna offers an instance in which an act of rape, with all the violence the term evokes, was treated as an act of sodomy, no different than if there had been no force or struggle involved. Luna, who was arrested for having engaged in sodomy, claimed that he was drunk when the act occurred and, to further distance himself from any culpability, he maintained that he did not even know the meaning of sodomy. He admitted to approaching Santiago Albuquerque on December 26, 1925, along the train tracks. He then proceeded to beat up Albuquerque and violate him anally. He knew that it was wrong to beat someone, but did not realize that anal rape was any different than striking someone's face, for example. Luna's case was thrown out, and he walked away without being sentenced. It is unclear why the court released Luna, but it appears that the judge concluded that, as a minor, he was too young to convict of sodomy.[15] This ambivalent conclusion to the case appears to have been more the norm than an exception.

Luna's case exhibits a strategy often used by defendants. In case after case, men who were accused of sodomy distanced themselves from the act by claiming that they were inebriated; when confronted with evidence, they often explained that it was an act of violence, not of sex. Although the law did not distinguish between consensual sodomy and forced anal penetration, the courts were unlikely to convict men engaged in consensual sex. By admitting to an act of violence, defendants in fact exposed themselves to prosecution. It is unclear if men used this strategy in order to avoid a stigma associated with same-sex desire, or if they believed that they would receive a lighter sentence if the judge chalked up the act to a lapse in judgment due to alcohol consumption.

As stated earlier, although the law classified both anal rape and consensual sex as sodomy, courts were far less likely to prosecute cases of consensual sex. Therefore, we can posit that there existed a formal and an informal understanding of what constituted the crime of sodomy. It appears that nonconsent, and especially violence, played a decisive factor in a conviction. It is also likely that violent cases came before the court more often simply because consensual sodomy would be far less likely to be witnessed. The act would have to have taken place in public for people to witness it and alert the authorities. Even so, the courts frequently dismissed cases where consensual sodomy was presented to them. Clearly, while sodomy as a practice constituted a social taboo and violation of the law regardless of whether it was violent or not, judges often applied a much more narrow definition of the law, revealing an ambivalence, a reluctance to apply the letter of the law to acts of consensual sex. State and non-state actors came to understand this pliable definition of sodomy. If he knew that it made him more likely to be convicted, Luna's admission that he violently sodomized the victim is remarkable. Perhaps he chose admitting to a crime over confessing to the social taboo of consensual sodomy.

The Child Victim

Violence against children especially caught the attention of police and courts. On September 12, 1956, Benjamín Leiva Sepúlveda, an illiterate rural worker, filed charges with the police against José Miguel Lazo for raping his nine-year-old stepson Marcos Salinas Aliste.[16] According to Sepúlveda, Lazo had followed Marcos to a field near his house and proceeded to pull down his pants and rape him. The defendant lived on the same farm as the child and his uncle, and would regularly see the boy picking up the morning milk.

Almost on cue, Lazo claimed that he was too inebriated to be convicted of a crime. He admitted to threatening a man on horseback with a knife, but could not remember all of the details due to alcohol consumption. Of one thing he was certain: he did not engage in an act of sodomy with Salinas Aliste. When the medical report indicated that the boy had clearly been sodomized, the defendant repeated his denial.

In this moment of the documentary record, we find that the courts and working-class Chileans—two publics that would determine how Chileans understood sodomy—viewed the medical profession differently. For the courts, medical exams produced accurate, scientifically backed assessments, or knowledge, of behaviors and acts. Doctors judged whether an act of violence had occurred by affirming that certain signs on the body or on an individual's clothes indicated as much. Defendants such as Lazo (as well as witnesses) did not recognize medical knowledge as superior, or more authoritative, than their testimonies; they did not accept that their words held less power than the doctor's gaze. Instead of addressing the doctor's report and suggesting someone else had sodomized the victim, Lazo ignored it, certain that his words would be considered valid on their own.

Unlike the Riquelme Valenzuela case, in which the primary testimony came from a child, the primary testimony against Lazo came from the twenty-year-old Inés Contreras Espinoza. She explained how she came to be embroiled in the case: "I was cleaning wheat and there was the minor whose name I do not know. He told me that the previous Friday he went to get wool and came upon 'El Carrera' in a field. The guy said, 'Lend me your ass' (*Préstame tu poto*)." In exchange for having sex with the man, the boy received two pesos. The boy explained to Contreras Espinoza that he lost the pesos. It was Contreras Espinoza who told the boy's stepfather what had occurred. Despite the violent nature of the crime, the medical report, and the testimony from an adult, it is unclear whether the court convicted Lazo. The case file ends with Contreras Espinoza's testimony.

The role that money played in these cases is important. After initially admitting that he had paid the child for sex, Lazo backtracked claiming he simply had sex with the boy. Either way, he distanced himself from the violence associated with the alleged crime. While it was true that the law in the abstract did not differentiate between consensual sex among men and the rape of a child, the courts were notably perturbed when a man anally penetrated a boy, an act that evoked scenes of unspeakable violence. By paying the child, or by saying that he did when questioned by authorities, Lazo and other men sought to transform an act of violence into an act of exchange.

Unlike the preceding cases, the case against Marcos Círico Guerrero resulted in a conviction. On April 10, 1927, police in Antofagasta charged twenty-six-year-old Círico Guerrero with sodomizing the minor Ernesto Contreras. Two elements of the case stand in contrast with the previous cases. First, the police (and the doctor) had found abundant convincing material evidence. Second, the defendant confessed to the crime. Despite his best efforts to retract his confession and talk his way out of prosecution, the defendant's retraction bore little weight against his initial confession combined with the strength of the physical evidence.

No one denied that an act of violence had occurred. Círico Guerrero conceded that an act of aggression took place but denied he was the perpetrator; rather, he claimed he provided the boy empathy and comfort. On the morning in question, Contreras, who was crying because another boy had hit him, entered the defendant's room to pick up clothes for his mother to launder. It was this other boy, who remained nameless in the documentary record, who was to blame for the violent act. However, the defendant's own testimony on the day that he was arrested betrayed his explanation.

At the scene of the crime, police found a bloody towel on the defendant's bedroom floor. When the police on the scene pressed him, Círico Guerrero confessed to having closed the door behind the boy when he entered the room, and then proceeding to rape him. Police concluded that the defendant bloodied the towel by wiping his penis and the boy's anus after sodomizing Contreras. When he was done, Círico Guerrero gave the boy five pesos in exchange for his silence. He began walking Contreras home but left when he saw the boy's mother.

By the time the defendant arrived at the police station, his story had changed dramatically. He now explained that he confessed to officers because they roughed him up. In order to stop the thumping, he admitted to having sodomized the boy. He went on to explain that the towel had been stained when he wiped his bloody nose, and that police used their imagination when they said he used it to clean his penis and the boy's anus. Círico Guerrero now wanted the judge to punish the officers who arrested him.

To the defendant's dismay, the medical exam—while not finding evidence of rape on the man's penis—documented signs of rape apparent on the boy's body. Lesions on the boy's anus, along with traces of the lubricant Mentholatum, proved that the boy had been anally penetrated. His bloody underwear came to represent rape, suggesting that the act had been violent. Unlike the cases above, in which defendants walked away without jail time, the judge convicted Círico Guerrero to two years in jail.[17]

Círico Guerrero's confession was a unique variable in this case. The confession had a longstanding status in both secular and ecclesiastical courts. However, by the late nineteenth century the status of the confession changed. Whereas in the past a confession had stood on its own as the transparent truth of the confessor, by the late nineteenth century the confession became bound to scientific discourses—the "truth" of the confession became both the product and subject of scientific practices. In other words, the confession became subject to scientific scrutiny insofar as criminology established standards and procedures for extracting or inducing confessions.[18] The confession simply confirmed what the representations—that is, lubricant on the anus and blood on the towel— suggested.

In the case of Círico Guerrero, the man's confession was validated only after the doctor examined the boy's body. Once scientific evidence affirmed the events described in the confession, there was no turning back for the confessor. He could not recant his words. His words attained the status of truth when affirmed by the medical exam. In this way, Chilean courts and the scientific community introduced new, modern procedures for establishing evidence as legitimate or, put another way, for affirming the truth of a representation on the body or in the form of an object. Whereas in other contexts, Círico Guerrero could have been labeled a rapist, a child abuser, or a violent sexual deviant, in turn-of-the-century Chilean courts he was named a sodomite.

Of Violence and Pain

Scientific knowledge proved critical in determining whether a defendant had executed an act of violence on an alleged victim. In this regard, Chilean jurisprudence followed a hemispheric if not global trend that relied on, and privileged, the physical and social sciences in assessing evidence of sodomy. As historian Martin Nesvig points out, "Criminologists and social thinkers rendered homosexuality both a personal sin and a social vice and contagion."[19] Clearly, this opinion constituted a politics of sodomy. Courts elicited doctors' reports to judge whether a defendant had participated in this "vice and contagion," evidence that in Chile at the time homosexuality was becoming medicalized, as it was elsewhere in Latin America.[20]

The hospital exam became a key discourse in the medicalization of sodomy in Chile, and was instrumental in determining the guilt or innocence of a defendant, as evidenced in the case against fifteen-year-old Bolivian Navier Quiper. On December 6, 1926, Chilean police arrested Quiper for the rape of five-year-old Dagaberto Gallorde. Unlike in most cases, the accused did not deny the accusation. The hospital exam found that the boy had an irritated anus that was most likely the result of having been sodomized. (Once again, the anus came to represent an act of violence.) The suspect's mother pleaded with the judge for leniency, asserting that her son was demented and under sixteen years of age. That her son raped the boy because the boy refused to share his toothbrush underscored the severity of his mental impairment. In short, his youth and his cognitive limitations should be heavily weighed in determining the teenager's punishment.

In most sodomy cases, doctors focused exclusively on determining whether an individual had been sodomized. This always included an examination of the victim's genitalia and anus; in some cases, doctors also examined the penis of the accused, but those exams proved much less conclusive. While in this case doctors had examined the victim's body, the verdict hinged on a different sort of medical determination: the doctor was tasked with determining the age of the defendant, since Quiper's mother could not produce a birth certificate for her son.

The defendant admitted to committing the violent act. He explained that he had taken the boy to a dark room and made him drop his pants before doing the "dirty deed" (*cochinada*) on the floor. As he penetrated the boy, the victim screamed.[21] If pain, as literary critic Elaine Scarry stresses in her classic study on the subject, is beyond words, or incapable of being represented through language, then the boy's scream evoked pain's most basic characteristic.[22] The scream itself alluded to a pain the boy lacked words to describe. The scream proved the violent character of the act, the cochinada.

A scream also served as a sign, or representation, of violence in the case of José Collazo Cides, a twenty-four-old man accused of raping eight-year-old Carlos Guillermo Araya Aracena.[23] On November 4, 1933, at eleven in the morning Collazo approached the boy in front of his house, sliding a finger in his anus. According to the boy's mother, Collazo threatened to beat the boy if he screamed, which he nonetheless did. When the medical exam revealed that either a penis or a finger could have caused the lesion on the boy's anus, the scientific legitimacy, or "truth," of the exam affirmed the mother's testimony; the representation could now be affirmed by filing a case of sodomy. Clearly, an act of violence had occurred. In both of these cases, a scream, as a representation of the pain that an unspeakable act of violence induced, conveyed the severity of the crime. The scream marked the separation between consensual sodomy and rape, a distance and ambivalence that the Chilean legal code did not acknowledge but that citizens and judges recognized.

Sex Between Men

Not all cases were as unambiguous as those involving acts of violence between a man and a boy. Some cases, especially those in which all the actors involved were adults, could have been instances of consensual sex. For example, on July 10, 1933, Carlos Alberto Ferrera, a twenty-one-year-old waiter with no previous police record, was accused of committing the crime of sodomy with José Rojas Araya, a low-ranking soldier.[24] While Ferrera claimed that he and Rojas were simply friends who did nothing wrong, Rojas claimed not to know Ferrera. Why, then, were they together in the dark outside the El Merítimo watering hole? Ferrera stated they were just having drinks, but the court turned to doctors to determine the truth.

After a thorough exam, the doctor concluded there was evidence of "degeneracy," because an act of sodomy had clearly been committed. Ferrera's anus, he explained, was loose. The use of the word "degeneracy" is important. Whereas cases involving men and children elicited plenty of condemnation, and even resulted in jail sentences, defendants were not regarded as degenerates, and the crime was not described as a sign of degeneracy. However deplorable the rape of a child might have been, it was an act of pure violence, not of sex. The defendant was a sodomite, a violent individual, but not a degenerate. Doctors reserved the pejorative status of degenerate for those who engaged in sexually immoral and indecent behavior.

With Ferrera and Rojas in danger of being labeled degenerates, Rojas did what defendants, especially men accused of having unnatural sex, often did: he claimed that he was too drunk to remember what had occurred. He refused to admit knowing Ferrera. The problem with this defense was that his army superior, attempting to protect Rojas, testified that Rojas was an excellent soldier—so excellent, in fact, that he did not even drink alcohol because of health problems.

Further probing revealed that Ferrera had in fact been sodomized, but that the act had been voluntary. Ferrera confessed that two soldiers kept watch as Rojas sodomized him. These soldiers, presumably Rojas's friends, were entrusted to block passersby from witnessing the act. When the police arrived, the soldiers keeping watch had fled, leaving Rojas penetrating Ferrera in full view of everyone who passed by. It was unclear, according to the medical exam, if an act of violence had occurred or if the two had engaged in consensual sex. Although he did not admit to committing an act of sodomy, by describing Rojas as his friend Ferrara suggested that no violence had occurred between the men. His statement made it clear that he did not feel violated.

If the court had followed the letter of the law, Rojas and Ferrera should have been convicted of the crime of sodomy, but they were exonerated. By providing physical evidence that Ferrara had been penetrated, the medical exam confirmed what police testified to witnessing. Moreover, the doctor described the act as one of "degeneracy," alluding to the socially unacceptable act of consensual sex between men.

While it is impossible to determine exactly why Ferrara and Rojas were let go, a review of the cases I have found in the Chilean National Archive suggests that courts expressed ambivalence in applying the law against sodomy, especially in cases of consensual sex between adult men, where courts exercised leniency. Of the forty-three cases I reviewed, no one who engaged in consensual sodomy was jailed. As the preceding cases reveal, even defendants who committed violent anal penetration or rape could be acquitted based on the nature of the evidence. In short, the courts exercised a great deal of discretion over who was convicted, and judges were much more flexible in their determinations than the Chilean legal code would suggest.

Conclusion

During the late nineteenth century, Chile underwent a process of modernization and urbanization similar to that experienced by countries throughout the hemisphere, especially those that had been subject to Spanish colonial rule. Politicians, intellectuals, and the general public grappled with what it meant to be an independent nation. With the new constitution, liberal law supplanted ecclesiastical edicts. The act of sodomy, which in the colonial era had been denounced as a sin and an unnatural act, came to be defined by the secular state as a threat to civilization. These legal changes took place as economic development led to urbanization and labor changes led to increased proletarianization. It was precisely in spaces where working-class men lived and worked that police arrested men for the crime of sodomy.

The modernization of medicine proved critical to the ambivalent application of the law against sodomy. The Chilean courts provided a forum for medical knowledge to establish its social and cultural legitimacy as authoritative. Conversely, the medical sciences conferred scientific validity on subjective evidence, representing sodomy in terms such as bloody underwear or towels or irritated anuses. In these cases, doctors became the supposed independent, impartial arbitrators of physical evidence. Defendants' words lacked the social and cultural power of doctors' modern training in the sciences.

While Chilean law did not recognize a difference between violent anal penetration and consensual sodomy, as Argentine law did, Chilean judges did in practice recognize this distinction, as evidenced in their ambivalent application of the law. Perpetrators of violent anal rape were much more likely to be prosecuted for the crime of sodomy than those engaged in consensual sex. It is unclear if judges were reflecting a broader understanding among the Chilean public—whether there was a tacit public understanding that a hierarchy existed among sodomitic acts, with rape being particularly egregious. These publics, especially those interested in engaging in consensual sodomy, relied on the courts to mark the boundaries between the criminal and the merely degenerate.

Notes

1. Archivo General de la Nación (hereafter AGN-CHI), Ramo Judicial, Antofagasta, caja 31572, exp. 7.

2. In fact, the church persecuted very few sodomites after 1700. There is a dearth of scholarship on sodomy in the New World from 1700 until 1870. See Martin A. Nesvig, "The Complicated Terrain of Latin American Homosexuality," *Hispanic American Historical Review* 81, nos. 3–4 (2001): 689–723.

3. Donna Guy, *Sex and Danger in Buenos Aires: Prostitution, Family, and Nation in Argentina* (Lincoln: University of Nebraska Press, 1991).

4. Cristian Berco, "Silencing the Unmentionable: Non-Reproductive Sex and the Creation of a Civilized Argentina," *Americas* 58, no. 3 (2002): 419–41.

5. Carolina González Undurraga, "La sexualidad como representación y las representaciones de la sexualidad: la construcción del sodomita en Chile, 1880–1910," in *Del nuevo al viejo mundo: mentalidades y representaciones desde América*, ed. Alejandra Araya Espinoza, Azun Candina Polomer, and Celia Cussen (Santiago, Chile: Fondo de Publicaciones Americanistas–Facultad de Filosofía y Humanidades de la Universidad de Chile, 2007), 184–99.

6. Carolina González U., "Entre 'sodomitas' y 'hombres dignos, trabajadores y honrados.' Masculinidades y sexualidades en causas criminales por sodomía (Chile a fines del siglo XIX)," MA thesis, Universidad de Chile, 2004.

7. Michel Foucault, *The History of Sexuality*, 3 vols. (New York: Vintage Books, 1988–90), 1:44.

8. Guy, *Sex and Danger in Buenos Aires*, esp. 77–105.

9. Harold Blakemore, "From the War of the Pacific to 1930," in *Chile since Independence*, ed. Leslie Bethell (New York: Cambridge University Press, 1993), 33–85.

10. Charles Bergquist, *Labor in Latin America: Comparative Essays on Chile, Argentina, Venezuela, and Colombia* (Stanford, CA: Stanford University Press, 1986).

11. Julio Pinto V., *Desgarros y utopías en la pampa salitrera: la consolidación de la identidad obrera en tiempos de la cuestión social (1890–1923)* (Santiago, Chile: LOM Ediciones, 2007); Manuel Vicuña, *La belle époque chilena: alta sociedad y mujeres de elite en el cambio de siglo* (Santiago: Editorial Sudamericana, 2001).

12. Peter Sigal, "Queer Nahuatl: Sahagún's Faggots and Sodomites, Lesbians and Hermaphrodites," *Ethnohistory* 54, no. 1 (2007), 9–34; Zeb Tortorici, "'Heran todos putos': Sodomitical Subcultures and Disordered Desire in Early Colonial Mexico," *Ethnohistory* 54, no. 1 (2007), 35–67.

13. Ann Twinam, *Public Lives, Private Secrets: Gender, Honor, Sexuality, and Illegiti-macy in Colonial Spanish America* (Stanford, CA: Stanford University Press, 1999).

14. Nesvig, "Complicated Terrain of Latin American Homosexuality."

15. AGN-CHI, Ramo Judicial, Talca, caja 362, exp. 6.

16. AGN-CHI, Ramo Judicial, San Felipe, caja 2081, exp. 11.

17. AGN-CHI, Ramo Judicial, Antofagasta, caja 31583, exp. 1.

18. Foucault, *History of Sexuality,* 65.

19. Nesvig, "Complicated Terrain of Latin American Homosexuality," 714.

20. Jorge Salessi, *Médicos, maleantes y maricas: higiene, criminología y homosexualidad de la construcción de la nación argentina, Buenos Aires, 1871–1914* (Rosario, Argen-tina: B. Viterbo, 1995); James N. Green, *Beyond Carnival: Male Homosexuality in Twentieth-Century Brazil* (Chicago: University of Chicago Press, 1999).

21. AGN-CHI, Judicial, Antofagasta, caja 31585, exp. 1.

22. Elaine Scarry, *The Body in Pain: The Making and Unmaking of the World* (New York: Oxford University Press, 1985).

23. AGN, Judicial, Antofagasta, caja 31640, exp. 1.

24. AGN, Judicial, Antofagasta, caja 31641, exp. 1.

6 Debunking Indigenous Criminality

Discourse, Statistics, and the Ethnicity of Crime in Guatemala

David Carey Jr.

As the contributors to this volume so convincingly argue, discourses of violence and crime have profound consequences for how people assess their own security and for the political and social fabrics of nations. At times the same authorities who articulate discourses of crime espouse countervailing rhetoric about the very populations they seek to criminalize. Further complicating public perceptions of crime and violence, modern police techniques could disprove racist rhetoric. Those instances offer an opportunity to explore the influence of discourse and its effect on behavior, particularly police practices.

Without abandoning the use of force to maintain order or deal with dissidents in Guatemala, the dictatorship of General Jorge Ubico Castañeda (1931–44) deployed criminology and modern police techniques (fingerprinting, basic forensic evidence, record-keeping) to professionalize the police force and buttress its battle against crime. Late nineteenth- and early twentieth-century Guatemalan elite discourse that characterized *indígenas* (indigenous people) as lazy, drunk wards of the state prone to crime dovetailed nicely with the rhetoric of positivist criminology's advocates. The director of the National Police, Brigadier Roderico Anzueto Valencia (1932–36) was convinced that the criminal underworld was formed of the "unemployed, beggars, and vice-ridden"—descriptions that elites frequently associated with *indios* (Indians).[1] According to Anzueto, there was an "urgent need for police action . . . where the indigenous element predominates."[2] The discursive and social constructs of indigenous people as criminals reproduced social, economic, and political exclusions that limited their mobility and curtailed their rights.

Double Standard

Even as authorities criminalized indigenous traditions and livelihoods, Ubico and the Guatemalan state celebrated indigenous people's cultural markers and knowledge. Though the target audience was foreign (mainly tourists and dignitaries), when Ubico showcased the nation's indigenous peoples in such public venues as military parades and national fairs, his message shaped Guatemalans' perspectives in ways that contradicted images of indigenous criminality. Hailed as a modern policing tool and deployed to help states advance their own version of society,[3] statistics too countered authorities' narratives of indios' proclivity to crime. Empirical evidence gained through scientific methodology and improved investigation techniques disproved public discourse about the amoral and criminal inclinations of the indigenous population. From the moment the National Police began keeping statistics on race and crime, they arrested more ladinos (non-indigenous people) than indígenas (see table 6.1). Considering that ladinos comprised between 35 percent (in 1921) and 44 percent (in 1940) of the population, proportionally ladinos were arrested at a far greater rate than indios.[4] Modern police practices disproved the biological causality that criminologists like Cesare Lombroso (1835–1909) advanced. In light of the much higher rate of literacy among ladinos and the middle and upper classes than among indígenas and the poor and working classes, criminal data on literacy similarly upset criminological theories about class and crime. The statistics of statecraft could threaten as well as buttress political, racial, and class hegemony.

That racialized representations of crime, which disproportionately targeted indigenous peoples, failed to produce evidence of indigenous criminality is not surprising. More surprising is the limited ability of criminal discourse to shape the practice of authorities charged with implementing it, particularly among a ladino officer corps that, informed by racism, were predisposed to denigrate if not criminalize indigenous populations. As Lila Caimari points out in chapter 4, police officers had the power to decide when, how, and with whom to intervene. She argues the development of an efficacious, united, and legitimate police force in early twentieth-century Buenos Aires "did not depend upon the compiling of criminal data" but rather on discourse and the construction of a

Table 6.1

Crimes by race and literacy status, Guatemala, 1933–1945

	Ladinos	Indios	Literate	Illiterate	Total, Ladino and Indio
1933	19,069	15,210	—	—	34,279
1934*	19,240	12,999	17,773	14,666	32,239
1935	17,976	15,213	16,243	16,946	33,189
1936*	23,388	15,043	18,735	19,686	38,431
1937	21,330	12,713	15,781	18,262	34,043
1938*	18,381	10,975	15,690	15,376	29,356
1939	21,774	15,058	20,163	17,669	36,832
1940	25,102	14,412	23,346	16,168	39,514
1941*	23,974	15,596	21,624	18,647	39,570
1942	27,022	16,243	23,985	19,280	43,265
1943	31,040	15,606	27,491	19,155	46,646
1944	26,321	13,922	25,024	15,219	40,243
1945	23,122	9,664	20,931	11,855	32,786
Total	297,739	182,654	246,786	202,929	480,393

Source: *Memoria de los trabajos realizados por la dirección general de la Policía Nacional* (Guatemala City: Tipografía Nacional, 1933–1945).

*For some years the totals of ladinos and indios do not add up to the total number of crimes, an indication that in some cases, local authorities did not or could not identify perpetrators by ethnicity.

moral image for the rank-and-file police officer. Although recordkeeping was critical to the capacity of the Guatemalan police (and covert security forces) to track and eliminate enemies of the state, if criminal data influenced rank-and-file officers, it may have done so in ways that contravened public prejudices.

Even without access to criminal statistics that contested the relationship between crime and race, indigenous litigants challenged assumptions about indigenous criminality. As the French philosopher and historian Michel Foucault argues, "Discourse can be both an instrument and an effect of power, but also a hindrance, a stumbling-block, a point of resistance and a starting point to an opposing strategy. Discourse transmits and produces power; it reinforces it, but also undermines and

[handwritten: ~allows truth to come under question]

exposes it, renders it fragile and makes it possible to thwart."[5] Subject to interpretation and appropriation, discourse has a capillary quality and thus seldom moves in one direction even when introduced with a specific purpose (such as to criminalize a particular population).

Even though citizens often considered its coercion legitimate, the state had little control over how populations defined crime and illegality. Authorities regularly incarcerated indigenous moonshiners, for example, but few indigenous people considered bootlegging a crime. Similarly, criminalizing such aspects of indigenous merchants' and vendors' trades as the location and organization of markets did little to dissuade those activities.[6] Since the meanings of crime exceed the realm of law, illegality alone does not determine which acts are defined as criminal. As indigenous people prodded the state to revisit its discourse on indigenous criminality by introducing questions of poverty, they demonstrated how particular populations and the public more broadly contested, negotiated, and resisted authorities' social constructions of crime.

Of the multiple audiences that participated in the debates, representations, and meanings of what constituted punishable criminal and violent acts, the Guatemalan National Police and its mouthpiece *La Gaceta: Revista de Policía y Variedades* were among those most closely associated with acting upon and implementing the ideas emerging from these debates. That is, violence and crime were not abstract notions but real threats that the National Police were charged with eradicating. As such, in many ways, the National Police helped to set the stage for the contested discourses, policies, and practices that violence and crime generated.

Concern that violence would disrupt the social order undergirded Ubico's promise to rule with an iron fist. Deployed by the Ubico administration, attempts to manufacture fear and ultimately terror became more pronounced and diabolical during Guatemala's thirty-six-year civil war (1960–96).[7] Widespread violence seldom (if ever) materialized during the Ubico regime, but the threat of it lurked in the background of Guatemalans' complicity with his tyrannical rule and authorities' criminalization of certain types of people and their customs.

Some Guatemalan authorities and elites argued that modernizing the nation and marginalizing indios were mutually dependent efforts. Proponents such as Anzueto asserted that modern policing techniques and profiling made the country safer and more civilized. Modernization

[handwritten margin notes: don't see their own actions as criminal; actions made criminal simply to criminalize news]

and marginalization marched in lockstep. Yet even as public discourse about indigenous depravities informed authorities' criminalization of indigenous practices, criminal data from the Ubico period turned those assumptions on their head and suggested ladinos were more inclined toward crime, drunkenness, and vagabondage than indígenas were.

Constructing Criminals

Throughout Latin America, elites deployed science and positivism to uphold racial hierarchies. As historian Nancy Stephan has pointed out, many Latin Americans "embraced science as a form of progressive knowledge . . . and as a means of establishing a new form of cultural power."[8] Emerging in Europe and the United States in the last decades of the nineteenth century, positivist criminology quickly caught on in Mexico, Argentina, Peru, and Brazil, where it provided elites with a means of reinforcing their power and privileges.[9] Positivist criminology's most influential figure, Cesare Lombroso, used physiognomy to discern criminality. Delinquents were born with mental and physical deficiencies that predisposed them to crime, and could be identified by these qualities, he reasoned. As positivist criminology developed, race remained central to it. Italian criminologist and student of Lombroso Enrico Ferri (1856–1929) softened biological determinism by arguing that criminals were not equally inclined toward crime, some committed transgressions only under certain circumstances. By reinforcing signs of social difference and lending scientific credence to the idea that criminals were a certain type of human being, criminology's classifications reinforced racism and marginalized subalterns.[10] As Latin American authorities and elites used positivist criminology to envision more specific criminalities based on gender, class, and race, Latin American nations with large rural indigenous populations deployed it as a tool to control them.[11]

Much of the groundwork for associating crime with indigenous culture had been laid by intellectuals who portrayed indios as degenerate because of their adherence to their ancestral languages, customs, and traditions. Historian Pablo Piccato points out, "Positivist theories about the shapes of criminals' heads and the determining influence of their family backgrounds fit nicely with old views of Indians and the urban plebes as backward and inferior."[12] As in Peru, where the police and courts framed crimes committed by indigenous peoples as evidence of their tendency toward crime, cultural descriptions became part of criminal profiles in Guatemala.[13] In thinly veiled descriptions of indigenous customs, traditions, and livelihoods, the police identified midwives, *buhoneros* (peddlers), *curanderos* (shamans), *brujos* (witches), and market vendors as suspects.[14] To broaden the margins of criminality, the state associated illegality with the lower strata's conditions of existence.[15]

Lombroso's argument that human evolution was subject to atavism, in that those inclined toward crime resembled Neanderthals who were better suited for the stone age than modern society, resonated with Guatemalan intellectuals' perspectives of indígenas. At the turn of the twentieth century, Guatemalan historian Antonio Batres Jáuregui argued that indigenous people "live more backwards now than they did in the first centuries . . . even today . . . they are regressing and have lost their spirit to move forward."[16] Similarly atavistic assumptions about indígenas abounded in Guatemala. A half century later, legislators considered "the Indian . . . a pariah stuck in the cultural formulas of a thousand years ago."[17] Positivist criminology and Guatemalan prejudices contained mutually reinforcing notions about racial inferiority, which encouraged authorities to deploy modern policing techniques in ways that highlighted race as a factor in crime. Anzueto celebrated the role of "all the data that allow [us] to form conclusions and scientific concepts with regard to . . . the racial condition of delinquents."[18] Those ideologies, however, only gradually and intermittently influenced police practice.

Founded in 1881, the Guatemalan police came to criminology and modern police practices slowly. Concentrating his efforts on professionalizing the military, President Justo Rufino Barrios (1873–85) largely ignored the National Police.[19] Except for initiating the use of telephones, the dictator Manuel Estrada Cabrera (1898–1920) similarly did little to modernize the police and other security forces that were so vital to his rule.[20] Despite his rhetoric about progress, he largely ignored the potential of such scientific methods as fingerprinting. Even though the new director of the National Police, appointed in 1899, had been trained in Washington, DC, and organized "even the tiniest details" of his force according the U.S. model, criminology held little sway.[21] Informed by a long tradition of caudillo rule, Estrada Cabrera encouraged his agents to demonstrate their loyalty and usefulness by carrying out his explicit orders rather than experimenting with criminological methods.[22]

6.1. "The Director General of the National Police, Brigadier C. Roderico Anzueto, in his office." *La Gaceta*, June 30, 1936. *Image courtesy of Hemeroteca Nacional de Guatemala.*

In the transition from Estrada Cabrera's to Ubico's rule, professionalizing the police became part of a larger program of modernization aimed at extending the state's control and imposing its vision of an enlightened nation. The National Police pursued some aspects of modern policing in the 1920s,[23] but not until the 1930s, during Ubico's regime, did they implement new techniques in earnest. Informed by typed reports that closely tracked the movements and lives of enemies of the state, the secret police disposed of political rivals with remarkable keenness and precision.[24] In his first annual address as the director of the National Police in 1932, Anzueto distinguished his leadership and officer corps from those of his predecessors by highlighting what he called a "turn toward scientific police."[25] Placing this approach firmly within the "positivist criminal school,"[26] Anzueto had his agents take classes to learn about the latest criminological methods, "legal medicine, urgent surgery, constitutional rights, penal procedures, identification, etc."[27] As his list suggests, Anzueto was as concerned about instilling modern police practices as advancing race-based understandings of criminality informed by positivist criminology. Above all, Anzueto emphasized "scientific knowledge in the distinct means of investigation."[28]

Although modern science offered the most obvious signs of progress, Anzueto was quick to acknowledge the support of Ubico whose "constant concern for the improvement and exaltation" of the police force allowed it "to perfect" much of its administration, especially the "technical preparation of personnel who could make use of scientific progress and take advantage of the modern systems of identification and investigation, utilizing such aids as photography, chemicals, [and] ultraviolet rays."[29] Seated at his desk with telephones and other technological trappings of modernization in the background, Anzueto evokes an image of an informed, knowledgeable, and organized leader (figure 6.1). He proudly observed that positivist criminology and forensic methods have "banish[ed] the empirical or ignorant Agent."[30] The two photographs of Ubico on the wall suggest he also astutely portrayed his loyalties.

Anzueto was confident that police work was becoming more efficacious through a scientific approach to crime. According to one historian, the police system had become so efficient, it had to dispatch only one officer to make arrests.[31] By studying fingerprints, palm prints, footprints, and other evidence at crime scenes, agents were developing "policisociological [*policisociologicos*] reports" about crimes and criminals that helped judges to convict suspects.[32] Despite the problematic findings from data, *Gaceta* journalists praised "the irrefutable eloquence of statistics" that Anzueto used to proclaim his success.[33] An advocate of using records to police and control the populace, Ubico also used statistics to prove his administration was effective against crime.[34]

Within a few years, this methodology was bearing fruit. Anzueto deployed statistics to attract media attention. When he sent crime data to a newspaper in New York, his force and the Ubico government earned the editors' (paternalistic) respect. The numbers legitimated Ubico's rule and Anzueto's leadership. Focusing their observations on the nearly 50 percent decrease in homicides from 1933 to 1934, the editors noted, "This reveals . . . that order has planted its magnificence in the small Central American Republic since President General Jorge Ubico assumed power."[35] Praising the "honorable administration that is interested in the wellbeing of its associates," they held up Guatemala as a model for other Spanish-speaking nations.[36] If the quotations were accurate (Anzueto failed to cite the article, let alone identify the newspaper), they were a manifestation of what Ubico hoped to achieve: the respect of such industrialized nations as the United States. At home, Kaqchikel-Maya oral histories suggest Ubico effectively communicated that his strong-arm rule reduced violent crime. So confident were Mayas in their safety during Ubico's rule that they slept with their doors open; some did not even have doors on their homes.[37] The diminution of violent crime (real or imagined) legitimated Ubico's rule in the eyes of foreigners and Guatemalans alike.

Whether the praise bred complacency or the timing was coincidental is unclear, but homicides spiked in the years immediately following this media attention, reaching a high of 130 in 1936 (compared to only 21 in 1932). Ironically, the emphasis on statistics and more efficacious police work gave the impression that crime was increasing, particularly from 1935 to 1937, toward the end of and immediately after Anzueto's directorship.[38] The data indicating a growth in violent crime may have served to justify Ubico's turn toward totalitarianism and the redoubled efforts of the National Police to implement scientific police work. Although Ubico's history of altering statistics makes analyzing them precarious, his administration seemed to turn its attention again to prosecuting crime (or at least reporting it) in 1942 and 1943.[39] Anzueto's successors suggested the increased arrests were an indication of success, but the effects of modern policing were complicated.

Racializing Crime

In Guatemala, race was identified by culture not blood, which precluded linking criminal tendencies with biological traits, as positivist criminologists sought to do. Reluctant to acknowledge *mestizaje* (interracial mixing, miscegenation), Guatemalans turned to such cultural characteristics as dress, language, traditions, customs, and footwear (or lack thereof) to identify race and avoid recognizing racial mixing among the population. The term *mestizo* seldom entered the early twentieth-century Guatemalan vernacular; people were some variation of indio or indígena, ladino, or creole (pure-blooded Spaniard). Consequently, the police glossed over the relationship between biology and race in their explanations of criminality. Unlike many of their counterparts elsewhere in the Americas, the Guatemalan police refrained from developing criminal identities based on phenotype or identifying race in mug shots. Even as Anzueto acknowledged "the *grandes cultores* of modern criminology," the Guatemalan police developed their own brand of cultural, not biological, determinism to identify criminals (figure 6.2).[40]

Just as in places like Mexico and Argentina where positivist criminology altered the relationship between the state and the working class by redefining their rights and criminalizing their everyday practices, a similar process altered the relationship between indigenous people and authorities in Guatemala.[41] By associating Maya culture, and even its very essence, with crime, Guatemalan authorities hit upon a hot topic in the field of criminology: whether biology or culture (which could also be described as the influence of the environment) offered a better explanation of crime. Yet unlike their counterparts in Mexico and Argentina, they did not refer to biology-versus-culture debates or to such theorists as Gabriel Tarde (1843–1904), who criticized Lombroso's notion of atavistic criminals.

In the sense that Guatemalan notions of criminality stigmatized traits inherent to an individual, the shift from biological to cultural determinism was not radical. The adaptation of criminality to the prevalent racial discourse in Guatemala facilitated authorities' efforts to redefine crimes along cultural lines. By defining as crimes what it knew to be everyday cultural practices, the state illegitimatized and criminalized activities that departed from what it considered modern.[42] Although police efforts to turn supposed delinquents into disciplined workers were most evident in the anti-vagrancy campaign, they extended into other areas of modernization, such as public health and trade, to justify interventions aimed at controlling the lives of the working class, poor, and indígenas.[43]

Public health reforms aimed at combatting what authorities considered problematic indigenous healthcare practices and lifestyles added an air of legitimacy to Guatemalan authorities' efforts to associate indigenous traits with crime. By the early twentieth century, healthcare personnel and authorities were accusing indios of being propagators of disease. After smallpox ravaged the predominantly Kaqchikel community of Nahuala, killing 959 people in 1926, the police conjured atavistic images, insisting "epidemics . . . found their development in the indigenous class that is accustomed to living without any foresight."[44]

To expand its reach beyond major cities, the National Police founded the Rural Police in 1932. Because one goal was to "maintain order" by increasing police access to indígenas and fugitives, officers established a permanent presence in some regions to facilitate their travel to others.[45]

6.2. Mug shots of criminals in *La Gaceta,* June 8, 1941. Despite Guatemala's reluctance to recognize mestizaje, racial miscegenation was common. As these photos suggest, making racial distinctions based on phenotype could be difficult. Perhaps for that reason, the National Police preferred to use cultural markers (such as the woman's *traje* [traditional indigenous clothing] in the sixth mug shot) rather than biological indicators in their pursuit of positivist criminology's racial assertions. *Image courtesy of Hemeroteca Nacional de Guatemala.*

"In Quetzaltenango where the indigenous population habitually fills the streets," the police set up sentry huts.[46] Although indígenas in the highlands immediately felt the effect of these control forces, modern forensic methods remained largely confined to the capital; not until 1939 did Guatemala City police begin to train their rural counterparts in fingerprinting and other means of identifying criminals.[47] Even then, evidence of modern police techniques in rural areas seldom appears in the judicial record before 1944. In contrast to the situation in Mexico and Argentina, scientific policing in Guatemala was primarily confined to the capital.[48]

The Law of Statistics

Even as Guatemalan authorities defined crimes in ways that associated indigenous culture and communities with transgressions, the scientific tools those authorities used to spur their battle against crime produced results that disproved their racial rhetoric. Unlike in nineteenth- and early twentieth-century Lima, Peru, where historian Carlos Aguirre asserts the "research guided by the 'science of the criminal' was . . . wanting, turning the doctrinal debate over crime and punishment into a usually vacuous exercise,"[49] in Guatemala, the debate remained vacuous even when statistics offered data that could have informed it. When modern policing demonstrated that race-based understandings of criminality were unsubstantiated, authorities avoided introducing such findings into national conversations. Two examples demonstrate how statistics revealed the spurious nature of the discourse on indigenous criminality.

Although intellectuals and elites associated alcoholism with indios, the statistics generated as part of Guatemala's scientific policing reveal that police arrested more ladinos than indígenas for public inebriation and other crimes closely associated with alcohol use, such as "scandalous behavior."[50] Excepting 1934, for the first few years data were collected on race and crime, police arrested more indígenas than ladinos for public intoxication. Beginning in 1937, however, that trend shifted dramatically, as table 6.2 demonstrates. In 1943, nearly 70 percent of those arrested for public inebriation were ladinos. Despite their minority status, ladinos were drawing authorities' attention to their drunkenness at a far greater rate than indios were.[51] Given that arrests for public inebriation far outnumbered those for any other crime from 1900 to 1944, overall, the police were steadily arresting ladinos. (There were 145,453 inebriation-related arrests—165,913 if you add the 20,460 people arrested for scandalous behavior—as compared to 46,460 arrests for fighting, the next most frequently reported crime, a statistic that suggests violence was a common characteristic of crime throughout the first half of the twentieth century.) This trend continued into the democratic rule of Juan José Arévalo Bermejo (1945–51). In San Miguel Dueñas, for example, where 68 percent of the population was indigenous according to the 1940 census, authorities arrested three times more ladinos than indios in March 1948.[52]

Similarly, having defined indios as idle, lazy, and unproductive, authorities focused much of their energy on enforcing vagrancy laws. The data for 1899 and 1900, when vagrancy was the second most prosecuted crime, suggest Estrada Cabrera took this charge seriously. Lázaro Chacón González's administration (1926–30) was equally vigilant, as the arrest of 2,488 vagrants in 1929 indicates. Oral histories and archival records similarly bear out Ubico's commitment to this campaign. Hailed by many Mayas for abolishing debt peonage in 1934, Ubico established the Ley Contra la Vagancia (Vagrancy Law) in its stead to address labor shortages in the agricultural export economy. By requiring workers to carry cédulas de vecindad that verified their labor, the law made workers beholden to landowners and foremen (for their signatures) and created a new class of criminals: men (the law did not apply to women) who had not worked the requisite number of days.[53]

Echoing Foucault's argument for Europe, the goal of vagrancy laws in Guatemala was to turn offenders into disciplined workers.[54] Indigenous farmers who produced enough to support themselves and their families without resorting to wage labor defied the state's efforts to integrate them economically, if not socially. But few of them owned enough land to be exempted from the Vagrancy Law.[55] Once police began collecting data on race, their statistics indicated assumptions about indigenous sloth were misdirected. Despite ladinos' minority status and the law's bias against poor indigenous men, police arrested more ladinos than indígenas for vagrancy from 1933 to 1943. Most dramatically, the police arrested more than twice as many ladinos as indígenas (5,655 and 2,730, respectively) between 1933 and 1939.[56]

At first glance, the statistics may appear to reflect an urban bias for Guatemala City where ladinos outnumbered indígenas and where enforcement (aided by modern police techniques) may have been more rigorous than in rural areas, but the data did include rural areas where

Table 6.2
Arrests for public inebriation by ethnicity in Guatemala, 1933–1944

Year	Total	Maya	% of total*	Ladino	% of total*
1933	6,905	4,012	58.1	2,893	41.9
1934	6,974	3,250	46.6	3,724	53.4
1935	7,697	3,992	51.9	3,705	48.1
1936	8,970	4,713	52.5	4,257	47.5
1937	7,835	3,580	45.7	4,255	54.3
1938	4,105	1,636	39.8	2,469	60.2
1939	4,196	1,695	40.4	2,501	59.6
1940	5,018	1,929	38.4	3,089	61.6
1941*	5,975	2,523	42.0	3,442	58.0
1942	7,164	2,595	36.2	4,569	63.8
1943	9,055	2,910	32.0	6,145	68.0
1944	7,502	2,991	40.0	4,511	60.1
Total	81,396	35,826	44.0	45,560	56.0

Source: *Memoria de los trabajos realizados por la dirección general de la Policía Nacional* (Guatemala City: Tipografía Nacional, 1933–1944).

* Since the totals of ladinos and indios do not add up to the total number of crimes in 1941, I rounded percentages off to the whole number.

indígenas outnumbered ladinos. If criminal records from Chimaltenango are any indication, rural authorities did not refrain from arresting indígenas.[57] Other studies have revealed that twentieth-century law enforcement was more lax in ladino than indigenous areas.[58]

Even as criminal data disproved disparaging descriptions of indigenous people, racial rhetoric continued unabated. Setting aside for a moment the empirical and interpretive pitfalls associated with Guatemalan government statistics, National Police directors ignored arrest figures in their annual reports, thereby shaping social constructions of race and crime. In contrast to their international dissemination of homicide data, neither Anzueto nor Ubico publicized statistics that tracked crime and race. Although as Peter Andreas and Kelly Greenhill argue, "Numbers are not dependent on their creators to be perpetuated and legitimated,"[59] creators can limit debate by not disseminating statistics. Data that did not substantiate discourse could be buried in dense annual reports. According to National Police statistics, more ladinos than indígenas fit the derogatory descriptions associated with the term indio. In an indication that the omission of statistics can shape discourse as much as their inclusion, suppressing those data facilitated rhetoric, policing, and behavior that prejudiced indígenas. As much as positivist criminology's racial tenets resonated with Guatemalan understandings of criminality, modern police techniques still often ensnared more ladinos than indígenas.

Countervailing Criminality

Although their courtroom testimonies betray no knowledge of the aforementioned statistics, indigenous litigants crafted narratives that countered discourses of indigenous criminality. Faced with racial profiling throughout the first half of the twentieth century, some indigenous litigants shrewdly associated their behavior with ladinos to exculpate themselves. Arrested for producing *aguardiente* (moonshine), the forty-five-year-old indigenous day laborer Agustín Muj claimed he was unaware it was a crime, explaining, "Since I saw ladinos doing it, I thought I would make a little."[60] In a nation that advanced ladino behavior as the model of citizenship, civilization, and the rule of law, who was he, a simple Indian, to suspect that following the example of a ladino would put him in trouble with the law? Such evidence of perpetrators' self-representation suggests how targets of criminal discourse deployed it and its corollaries.

Crime and violence were in the eye of the beholder. Refuting associations of crime and race, some indigenous litigants, most notably female bootleggers, attributed their crimes to poverty and other social injustices. In order to survive, they had little choice but to violate alcohol, marketplace, and other laws, they claimed. Whereas intellectuals and state agents asserted that indigenous backwardness and culture explained their failures, indigenous litigants emphasized their diligence and adaptability in ways that negated notions of indigenous criminality.[61]

Just as positivist criminology provided representatives of the state with opportunities to create certain types of citizens and subjects, suspects and defendants influenced interpretations of the law, their identities, and the nation with their comments about constructions of race, gender, class, crime, and violence. Indígenas had to tread carefully in a criminal justice system whose representatives were oftentimes biased against them. Despite their vulnerable positions, they refused to allow Guatemalan authorities to define indigenous people, customs, or practices as inherently criminal or violent. If statistics and police behavior are any indication, more than a few ladino officers agreed with them.

While few rural indígenas claimed that race or class determined criminal conduct, some Mayas portrayed ladinos as criminals; others associated political power with criminality. "The Ubico period was a criminal dictatorship. . . . Those were times when they began to make the roads merely with picks. . . . Earning a piece of paper [not money]. Ah yes, it was tough! That General Ubico was . . . a criminal," complained one Ch'orti'-Maya man.[62] The specificity of that portrayal stands in stark contrast to Guatemalan elites' and authorities' broad depictions of indigenous criminality.

Despite the detrimental effects of criminological reforms, indígenas took advantage of modernizing discourse that regarded some aspects of indigenous culture as a source of national pride. Historian Greg Grandin posits, "If the process of capitalist modernization entails disruption of traditional practices and the placing of all social relations in a state of perpetual flux, then modernity, or at least one aspect of it, entails the desire to generate new myths and traditions that will lend meaning to that flux."[63] In Guatemala, those new myths were not devoid of indigenous traditions. At the same time the National Police cloaked the criminalization of indigenous livelihoods and customs in the discourse of science and modernization, Ubico celebrated indígenas in national fairs, visited them in their villages, and allowed them to wear their *traje* (traditional indigenous clothing) in the military (figure 6.3).

One of the clearest manifestations of Ubico's endorsement of the potential symbiosis between indigenous traditions and Guatemalan modernity could be seen at the national fairs (figure 6.4). To attract international investment and travelers, the government hosted a national fair each November that showcased Guatemala's industrial and technological development alongside an "Indigenous Village" with indígenas performing their quotidian tasks. Although many tried to avoid compulsory labor at the national fairs, some Kaqchikel emphasized the potential benefits of such exposure, including access to new markets.[64]

The national fairs also portrayed Guatemala as a nation that adhered to Latin American liberal dictators' mantra of order and progress. Implicit in this social pact was the assertion that national stability and

ALBUM DE LA GACETA   EN TIERRAS DEL OCCIDENTE DEL PAIS

EXPEDICIÓN ADMINISTRATIVA PRESIDENCIAL.—Diversos aspectos del recibimiento que se hiciera al Presidente de la República a su paso por la ciudad de Sololá y poblado de Chichicastenango. En el centro la nueva figura guerrera de un indígena de Nahualá que antes supiera sólo del machete y del arado; hoy, también, es un ciudadano que disciplinadamente forma parte de la guardia de las instituciones del país.

6.3. Indígenas in traje in the Guatemalan military. The caption reads in part, "An indígena from Nahualá who previously only knew the machete and plow; today is also a citizen who with discipline forms part of the nation's security force." *La Gaceta*, November 10, 1940. *Image courtesy of The Latin American Library, Tulane University.*

economic development were contingent upon containing violence. To that end, early twentieth-century Guatemalan dictatorships ignored such low-visibility transgressions as gender-based violence and concentrated on eradicating more sensational violence such as uprisings and homicides. Though gender-based violence and political violence are distinct phenomena, the state had a vested interest in channeling men's violence toward women and away from the state to avoid disrupting public order.[65]

Unlike his predecessors and many of his contemporaries, Ubico agreed with indígenas who argued that tradition was not necessarily opposed to modernity or capitalism. Putting those perspectives into practice in military parades, national fairs, and other venues countervailed discourses of indigenous criminality. The effect may have tempered police officers' penchant for identifying indígenas as criminals. The aforementioned statistics demonstrating that indígenas were committing (or at least arrested for) fewer crimes also imply that the deployment of notions of indigenous criminality was mostly discursive—reflected in the portrayal

ADMINISTRACION UBICO

NOVIEMBRE DE 1936.—CIUDAD DE GUATEMALA

Aspecto general de las construcciones en el campo de la Feria.

6.4. The National Fairgrounds, Guatemala, 1936. *La Gaceta*, February 14, 1937. *Image courtesy of Hemeroteca Nacional de Guatemala.*

rather than the policing of crime. *La Gaceta* circulated discourses of criminality that police officers did (or could) not necessarily act upon. If, as Caimari argues in chapter 4 with regard to the Buenos Aires police, officers operated "in the interstices of the law" and thus made "imperceptible legal accommodations" based on their "human experience and tutelary mission," then perhaps Guatemalan officers too made accommodations for indigenous people when they considered the racism and poverty that marked their lives. In chapter 9, Daniel Núñez persuasively argues that contemporary police in eastern Guatemala made decisions on which vigilante killings to report based on their perceptions of (and relationships with) the perpetrators and victims. Their predecessors may have responded similarly in their pursuit of crime. Although the early twentieth-century judicial record sheds little light on rank-and-file officers' considerations and calculations, their counterparts in the courts frequently reduced the sentences, fines, and court fees of indigenous defendants because of their "evident poverty."[66] While we know much about judicial officials' legal accommodations, those of police officers beg further research.

Conclusion

Grounded in their readings of such Marxist theorists as Antonio Gramsci, Latin American historians who study hegemony have noted that states that use cooptation instead of coercion have garnered support for their programs even among marginalized populations steeped in resistance.[67] Many indigenous military conscripts, and even some national fair Indigenous Village participants, were buoyed by Ubico's valuation of their culture and traditions in national venues. That message may have shaped the practices of ladino officers, particularly since the discourse of indigenous criminality rang hollow in the face of their daily police work. The statistics that were a crucial component of modern policing demonstrated that crimes associated with indígenas were in fact more often committed by ladinos.

Guatemalan authorities' use of statistics demonstrates the (lack of) relationship between numbers and narratives. Falling homicide rates supported Guatemalan authorities' commitment to modernizing national policing personnel and practices. When data contradicted the discursive relationship between crime and race, however, National Police reports muted those differential crime rates by ethnicity by burying them in tables with copious data. Like other Latin American states, the Guatemalan government deployed statistics that justified its political objectives and ignored those that disproved its discourse.

More broadly, the state implementation of modern police practices undermined its use of racism (and notions of indigenous criminality) as an instrument of social control. Approached as symbiotic forces by many authorities, modern policing and criminological discourse were linked in unexpected ways. Racialized representations of crime did not over-determine how indigenous people understood their actions or apparently even how many police officers behaved. Evident in Guatemala, the paradox of modern police methods challenging criminological discourse was likely true in other countries as well. That complex relationship begs for further research.

Notes

I want to thank Steve Hughes, Gema Santamaría, Pablo Piccato, Angélica Durán-Martínez, and the two anonymous reviewers for the University of Oklahoma Press for their critiques and comments on earlier drafts of this essay.

1. *Memoria de los trabajos realizados por la dirección general de la Policía Nacional durante el año de 1932* (Guatemala City: Tipografía Nacional, 1933) (hereafter *MPN*), 6; David Carey Jr., "Drunks and Dictators: Inebriation's Gendered, Ethnic, and Class Components in Guatemala, 1898–1944," in *Alcohol in Latin America: A Social and Cultural History,* ed. Gretchen Pierce and Áurea Toxqui (Tucson: University of Arizona Press, 2014), 131–57. "Indio" is a derogatory term informed by nonindigenous Guatemalans' perceptions of indigenous people as dirty, ignorant, lazy, and retrograde. In the United States a similar racial discourse associating African Americans with crime has deep historical roots. See Ta-Nehisi Coates, "The Black Family in the Age of Mass Incarceration," *The Atlantic,* October 2015, 60–84.

2. *MPN, 1932,* 40–41.

3. Alain Desrosieres, *The Politics of Large Numbers: A History of Statistical Reasoning* (Cambridge, MA: Harvard University Press, 1998); James C. Scott, *Seeing Like a State: How Certain Schemes to Improve the Human Condition Have Failed* (New Haven, CT: Yale University Press, 1998).

4. Dirección General de Estadística (hereafter DGE), *Censo de la República de Guatemala, 1921* (Guatemala City: Talleres Gutenburg, 1924); DGE, "Quinto censo general de población levantado el 7 de abril de 1940" (Guatemala, June 1942), 214.

5. Michel Foucault, *The History of Sexuality,* trans. Robert Hurley, 3 vols. (New York: Vintage Books, 1978–90), 1:101.

6. David Carey Jr., *I Ask for Justice: Maya Women, Dictators, and Crime in Guatemala, 1898–1944* (Austin: University of Texas Press, 2013), 101–17.

7. Kirsten Weld, *Paper Cadavers: The Archives of Dictatorship in Guatemala* (Durham, NC: Duke University Press, 2014) 102–3.

8. Nancy Stephan, *"The Hour of Eugenics": Race, Gender, and Nation in Latin America* (Ithaca, NY: Cornell University Press, 1991), 41.

9. Pablo Piccato, *City of Suspects: Crime in Mexico City, 1900–1931* (Durham, NC: Duke University Press, 2001), 8, 50, 58; Robert M. Buffington, *Criminal and Citizen in Modern Mexico* (Lincoln: University of Nebraska Press, 2000); Paul J. Vanderwood, *Disorder and Progress: Bandits, Police, and Mexican Development* (Wilmington, DE: Scholarly Resources, 1992); Lyman L. Johnson, ed., *The Problem of Order in Changing Societies: Essays in Crime and Policing in Argentina and Uruguay, 1750–1919* (Albuquerque: University of New Mexico Press, 1990); Donna Guy, *Sex and Danger in Buenos Aires: Prostitution, Family, and Nation in Argentina* (Lincoln: University of Nebraska Press, 1991); Thomas Holloway, *Policing Rio de Janeiro: Repression and Resistance in a Nineteenth-Century City* (Stanford, CA: Stanford University Press, 1993).

10. Piccato, *City of Suspects,* 58, 64, 71, 163, 257 n. 4; Buffington, *Criminal and Citizen in Modern Mexico;* Elisa Speckman Guerra, "'I Was a Man of Pleasure, I Can't Deny

It': Histories of José de Jesús Negrete, aka 'The Tiger of Santa Julia,'" in *True Stories of Crime in Modern Mexico*, ed. Robert Buffington and Pablo Piccato (Albuquerque: University of New Mexico Press, 2009), 72–75; David Garland, "Of Crimes and Criminals: The Development of Criminology in Britain," in *The Oxford Handbook of Criminology*, ed. Mike Maguire, Rod Morgan, and Robert Reiner (New York: Clarendon Press, 1994), 17–68; Alessandro Baratta, *Criminología crítica y crítica del derecho penal* (Mexico City: Siglo XXI, 1991); Rosa del Olmo, *América Latina y su criminología* (Mexico City: Siglo XXI, 1981).

11. Robert Buffington, "Introduction: Conceptualizing Criminality in Latin America," in *Reconstructing Criminality in Latin America*, ed. Carlos A. Aguirre and Robert Buffington (Wilmington, DE: Scholarly Resources, 2000), xvi; Lila Caimari, "Remembering Freedom: Life as Seen from the Prison Cell," in *Crime and Punishment in Latin America*, ed. Ricardo D. Salvatore, Carlos Aguirre, and Gilbert M. Joseph (Durham, NC: Duke University Press, 2001), 391, 399; Brooke Larson, *Trials of Nation Making: Liberalism, Race, and Ethnicity in the Andes, 1810–1910* (Cambridge: Cambridge University Press, 2004), 63.

12. Pablo Piccato, "'Such a Strong Need': Sexuality and Violence in Belem Prison," in *Gender, Sexuality, and Power in Latin America since Independence*, ed. William E. French and Katherine Elaine Bliss (Lanham, MD: Rowman & Littlefield, 2007), 89.

13. Carlos Aguirre, *The Criminals of Lima and Their Worlds: The Prison Experience, 1850–1935* (Durham, NC: Duke University Press, 2005); Benjamin Orlove, "The Dead Policemen Speak: Power, Fear, and Narrative in the 1931 Molloccahua Killings (Cusco)," in *Unruly Order: Violence, Power, and Cultural Identity in the High Provinces of Southern Peru*, ed. Deborah Poole (Boulder, CO: Westview Press, 1994); Jim Handy, "Chicken Thieves, Witches, and Judges: Vigilante Justice and Customary Law in Guatemala," *Journal of Latin American Studies* 36 (2004): 553.

14. *MPN*, 1938, 40; Piccato, *City of Suspects*, 3; Carey, *I Ask for Justice*, 90–117.

15. Michel Foucault, *Discipline and Punish: The Birth of the Prison*, 2nd ed. (New York: Vintage Books, 1995), 83.

16. Antonio Batres Jáuregui, *Los indios, su historia y su civilización* (Guatemala City: Tipografía La Unión, 1894), III–XII.

17. Clemente Marroquín Rojas, *Crónicas de la Constituyente del 1945* (Guatemala City: Tipografía Nacional, 1970), 113.

18. *MPN*, 1932, 8.

19. *La Gaceta: Revista de Policía y Variedades* (hereafter *La Gaceta*) July 19, 1935, 450.

20. Catherine Rendon, "El Gobierno de Manuel Estrada Cabrera," in *Historia general de Guatemala*, ed. Jorge Luján Muñoz, vol. 5, *Época contemporánea: 1898–1944*, ed. J. Daniel Contreras R. (Guatemala City: Asociación de Amigos del País, Fundación para la Cultura y el Desarrollo, 1996), 20.

21. *Memoria de la Dirección General de Policía Nacional, presentada al Ministro de Gobernación y Justicia, correspondiente al año de 1899* (Guatemala City: Tipografía Nacional, 1900), 3; Rendon, "El Gobierno de Manuel Estrada Cabrera," 20.

22. Ralph Lee Woodward Jr., *Rafael Carrera and the Emergence of the Republic of Guatemala, 1821–1871* (Athens: University of Georgia Press, 1993).

23. For example, the police cautiously began to use fingerprints to determine the identity of criminals in the 1920s; see *Memoria del cuerpo de policía de la república rendida al ministerio de gobernación y justicia, correspondiente a los años 1922 y 1923* (Guatemala City: Tipografía Nacional, 1924).

24. Archivo Municipal de Sololá (AMS), "Libro de actas de sesiones municipales del 1-10-35 al 10-6-43," November 11, 1936, July 12, 1939; Rachel Sieder, "'Paz, progreso, justicia y honradez': Law and Citizenship in Alta Verapaz during the Regime of Jorge Ubico," *Bulletin of Latin American Research* 19 (2000), 295–96; Weld, *Paper Cadavers*, 87, 99.

25. *MPN*, 1932, 7.

26. Ibid., 7.

27. *MPN*, 1933, 7.

28. *MPN*, 1932.

29. *MPN*, 1933, 8.

30. Ibid., 8.

31. Kenneth Grieb, "El Gobierno de Jorge Ubico," in *Historia General de Guatemala*.

32. *MPN*, 1932, 24.

33. As early as 1932, for example, the police claimed they captured the majority of criminals. From 1932 to 1934, the force cut crime in half; the crime rate dropped again in 1935, according to police data. See *MPN*, 1932, 24–26; *MPN*, 1934, 35; *MPN*, 1935, 129; *La Gaceta*, July 19, 1935.

34. Sieder, "'Paz, progreso, justicia y honradez,'" 295–96; Weld, *Paper Cadavers*, 54, 87.

35. *MPN*, 1935, 31.

36. Ibid., 31.

37. David Carey Jr., *Our Elders Teach Us: Maya-Kaqchikel Historical Perspectives. Xkib'ij kan qate' qatata'* (Tuscaloosa: University of Alabama Press, 2001), 206–11.

38. Carey, *I Ask for Justice*, appendix 3, 244–47.

39. Since Ubico altered data from the 1940 census, its statistics (and other statistics compiled during his regime) are unreliable. Official statistics are often highly problematic and "mythical," yet they are seldom met with much public scrutiny. See Peter Andreas, "The Politics of Measuring Illicit Flows and Policy Effectiveness," in *Sex, Drugs, and Body Counts: The Politics of Numbers in Global Crime and Conflict*, ed. Peter Andreas and Kelly M. Greenhill, 23–45 (Ithaca, NY: Cornell University Press, 2010).

40. *MPN*, 1935, 44. Of course, dismissing racial fusion does not necessitate denigrating indigenes. In the Andes, for example, some politicians and intellectuals adhered to a binary ethnic hierarchy and celebrated the civilized, pious, and diligent "authentic Indian"; see Larson, *Trials of Nation Making*, esp. 66.

41. Piccato, *City of Suspects*, 212; Caimari, "Remembering Freedom," 391–92.

42. Gilbert M. Joseph, "On the Trail of Latin American Bandits: A Reexamination of Peasant Resistance," *Latin American Research Review* 25, no. 3 (1990), 25; Piccato, *City of Suspects*, 2–3.

43. *MPN*, 1938, 40; Piccato, *City of Suspects*, 20, 29; Carey, *I Ask for Justice*.

44. *MPN*, 1926, 114.

45. *MPN, 1932*, 40–41; *La Gaceta*, July 19, 1935.
46. *MPN, 1934*, 36.
47. *MPN, 1939*, 95.
48. Guy, *Sex and Danger*; Piccato, *City of Suspects*; Buffington, *Criminal and Citizen*; Caimari, "Remembering Freedom." See also Ricardo D. Salvatore, Carlos Aguirre, and Gilbert M. Joseph, eds., *Crime and Punishment in Latin America: Law and Society since Late Colonial Times* (Durham, NC: Duke University Press, 2001), especially the essays by Pablo Piccato, Donna J. Guy, and Cristina Rivera-Garza.
49. Carlos Aguirre, *Criminals of Lima*, 219.
50. Carey, "Drunks and Dictators."
51. DGE, *Censo de la República de Guatemala, 1921*; DGE, "Quinto censo general de población levantado el 7 de abril de 1940," 214.
52. Loyola–Notre Dame Library, Special Collections, Guatemala Collection, Box 23, Estadística, Dirección General de Estadística, Estadística de Faltas, San Miguel Dueñas, Marzo 1948; DGE, "Quinto censo general de población levantado el 7 de abril de 1940," 218.
53. Grieb, "El gobierno de Jorge Ubico," 46; Carey, *Our Elders Teach Us*, 203–6.
54. Foucault, *Discipline and Punish*, 291; Caimari, "Remembering Freedom," 391.
55. David McCreery, *Rural Guatemala, 1760–1940* (Stanford, CA: Stanford University Press, 1994), 304, 316–18.
56. *MPN, 1933–45*.
57. Carey, *I Ask for Justice*.
58. Virginia Garrard-Burnett, "Indians Are Drunks, Drunks Are Indians: Alcohol and Indigenismo in Guatemala, 1890–1940," *Bulletin of Latin American Research* 19, no. 3 (2000), 354.
59. Andreas and Greenhill, "Introduction: The Politics of Numbers," in *Sex, Drugs, and Body Counts*, 3. Unfortunately, the Guatemalan National Police annual reports do not elaborate on the methodologies used to compile statistics.
60. Archivo General de Centro América (hereafter AGCA), Índice 116, Chimaltenango 1900, leg. G, exp. 75.
61. Carey, *I Ask for Justice*.
62. Brent E. Metz, *Chorti-Maya Survival in Eastern Guatemala: Indigeneity in Transition* (Albuquerque: University of New Mexico Press, 2006), 60.
63. Greg Grandin, *The Blood of Guatemala: A History of Race and Nation* (Durham, NC: Duke University Press, 2000), 165.
64. Ix'aj, oral history interview by author, February 9, 1998, San Juan Comalapa, Guatemala; AGCA, Jefe Político, Sacatepéquez, carta de intendente municipal de San Antonio Aguas Calientes al Jefe Político, November 15, 1941; Walter E. Little, "A Visual Political Economy of Maya Representations in Guatemala, 1931–1944," *Ethnohistory* 55, no. 4 (2008): 633–63. Due to the continued political volatility of Guatemala and recurrent human rights abuses, I have preserved the anonymity of oral history sources. I use pseudonyms that derive from the Maya calendar. Female interviewees can be recognized by the "Ix" prefix to their one-word names. The interview was conducted in Kaqchikel.

65. Carey, *I Ask for Justice.*
66. Ibid.
67. Tanja Christiansen, *Disobedience, Slander, Seduction, and Assault: Women and Men in Cajamarca, Peru, 1862–1900* (Austin: University of Texas Press 2004); Florencia E. Mallon, *Peasant and Nation: The Making of Postcolonial Mexico and Peru* (Berkeley: University of California Press, 1995); William H. Beezley, Cheryl E. Martin, and William E. French, eds., *Rituals of Rule, Rituals of Resistance: Public Celebrations and Popular Culture in Mexico* (Wilmington, DE: Scholarly Resources, 1994); Gilbert M. Joseph and Daniel Nugent, eds., *Everyday Forms of State Formation: Revolution and the Negotiation of Rule in Modern Mexico* (Durham, NC: Duke University Press, 1994); Buffington, "Introduction," xvi.

7 The Invention of Night

Visibility and Violence after Dark in Rio de Janeiro

Amy Chazkel

In 1933, just as the last gasworks in Rio de Janeiro, then the capital of Brazil, were being closed down, a striking image appeared on the front cover of the magazine *Light*. Published by the Rio de Janeiro Tramway Light and Power Company Limited, the public utility known as "Light," the magazine was intended to educate residents of Rio de Janeiro in the mysteries of modern technology (such as telephone etiquette), to promote the use of electricity, and to provide much-needed positive spin for this foreign company nicknamed the "Canadian Octopus" for its prodigious, neo-imperialistic reach into all aspects of Brazilian urban public life. The image showed a cluster of shoeless, brown-skinned, rag-clad children gathering around and even climbing up a lamppost. Beside these children a man, clearly identifiable to readers as enslaved within the context of the familiar street scene, held up a long pole to the glass lantern at the top of the lamppost.

This daily ritual of the lighting and extinguishing of the public gas lanterns was first done largely by enslaved laborers. Over the course of the nineteenth century it gradually became wage work, until abolition finally came in 1888, and by 1933 the lamplighter had become extinct altogether. Yet the image of the lamplighter still appeared repeatedly in popular iconography, most often as a barefoot and bedraggled slave, a nocturnal worker who symbolized pre-abolition Rio's backwardness. These popular images made much of the lamplighter's disappearance: the enslaved lamplighter was now replaced by the electrical technician, depicted on the cover of a different edition of the same magazine as a decidedly white figure smilingly carrying out his repair and maintenance work during daylight hours.[1]

Despite their racial content (and in the case of *Light,* their propagandistic intent), these images may seem to be rather self-evident and uncontroversial evidence of the gradual illumination of the city's public spaces as a crucial part of the Brazilian capital city's forward march of modernization. The desire to illuminate the city makes eminent sense; after all, we humans are naturally diurnal creatures. We see best in the day, and the darkness that engulfed the city each night was full of inherent dangers. Yet it is crucial to bear in mind that nighttime is a social category that has its own logic, which developed separately from the history of public illumination. Independent of the technological progress that cast increasingly bright light on Rio's public spaces in the century after Brazilian independence, the nighttime simultaneously came to designate a time of such danger to society as to justify the imposition, in effect, of a nightly state of emergency.

In nineteenth-century Rio de Janeiro, the busiest slaving port in the South Atlantic, the ability to see one's way through the city streets—and, perhaps above all, to identify passersby—took on special meaning in a society run by the labor of enslaved workers and filled with an ever-growing population of freedpersons constantly suspected of colluding with slaves or being fugitives themselves. At night, the municipal government oversaw public illumination to meet the local population's shared need for safe passage after dark, providing the city's first truly public service apart from (but linked to) policing. By the 1840s, public authorities had come to take for granted that lighting the city streets was a—or perhaps the most—crucial element in maintaining the fragile social peace in Brazil's capital city.

Those who operated the levers of criminal law relied on human sight not just to garner evidence and patrol the streets but also to justify a nightly suspension of rights. In early and mid-nineteenth-century Rio, each evening the setting sun triggered a legal regime distinct from that which prevailed in daylight. From the earliest years after independence through much of the nineteenth century, legal codes and law enforcement officials in Brazil invoked the inability to "see a man's face" after dark as a rationale to impose dramatic restrictions on public rights and freedoms, and to differentiate between persons who were ostensibly equal before the law. Indeed, during most of the period of monarchical rule in post-independence Brazil called the Empire (1822–89), Rio de Janeiro was under a selective curfew that criminalized being outdoors at night. The night, a site of potential racial confusion, became a space where the already shaky civil rights of Rio's population of color virtually disappeared.

Even as authorities aggressively sought to extinguish the difference between day and night by installing lanterns to illuminate the city streets, thus allowing the beginnings of the twenty-four-hour cycle of work and commerce, the same authorities persistently sought to preserve the legal difference between day and night. Considering how the law apprehends the daily cycle of darkness and light, I trace the policing practices developed in a postcolonial city largely run by the labor of enslaved persons and free persons of ambiguous legal status. The social construction of night created the conditions that "produced a certain type of harm," to quote the introduction to this volume. It normalized the selective curfew and nurtured the politics that made state violence both possible and invisible day and night.

More than a half century of reflection on the history and sociology of violence has yielded schemes for categorizing its varied manifestations. Above all, scholars have shown that violence persistently evades definition but demands our keen understanding in a world "that mistakes peace for a lack of war and defines nonviolence as nonphysical," to borrow from Deborah Levenson's reflection on the recent history of Guatemala.[2] As Lila Caimari illustrates in chapter 4, analyzing the establishment of the structure in which acts of violence take place is crucial to fathoming how violence functions in society. Police authority to compel citizens to abide by rules, as Caimari points out, results from "a good deal of symbolic artifice." The sociolegal construction of nighttime, like the history of race and racism itself, illustrates eloquently how vaulting acts of artifice come to be taken as biological truths, with powerful material consequences.

Representation fuels violence by establishing the scene in which it might happen—the city streets after dark—and constructing this place and time as a natural space of exception to established rights. Policing the streets of the Brazilian capital after dark occurred under a pretext that was as omnipresent in the criminal jurisprudence as it was absent from the records of the actual interactions between the police and the

i.e. darker
skin more
hidden & more
criminal

people of the city: that danger reigned after nightfall because of the impossibility of discerning a person's face. Even in an epoch before mass media dispersed images of people committing acts of aggression against each other, violence could become a "communicating tool," as Angélica Durán-Martínez notes in chapter 10. In a newly independent Brazil struggling to forge citizens from former subjects, the differential treatment of people based on class, and especially race, contradicted the nation's liberal constitutional principles but responded to perceived realities and became an entrenched means of maintaining order. Paying special attention to the after-dark state of exception allows a new understanding of the sociolegal mechanics of the everyday violence that radiated through a system of captive labor even as the society sought to define itself as a country of laws.[3]

Darkness, Visibility, and the Law in Nineteenth-Century Rio de Janeiro

Premodern forms of illumination were costly, weak, and entirely dependent on private initiative. When the Portuguese moved Brazil's viceregal capital from Salvador da Bahia to Rio in 1763, public lighting existed nowhere in Brazil. Candelabras or whale oil lanterns hung in front of religious buildings shed the only glimmers of light after the sun set. Church devotees lit wax candles in private niches and altars recessed in walls at some street corners or on building facades, where they could pray by candlelight until the night watchmen made their rounds. City residents who needed to walk around at night would rely on moonlight and their own lanterns as they faced the perils of Rio's twisting, dark, narrow streets. As part of city improvements made from 1790 to 1801, Rio's municipal government introduced public illumination. One hundred whale oil lanterns were installed at public cost in the central area, four on busier and two on quieter streets. Suspended by iron hardware, these smelly lanterns were lit except when the full moon obviated their weak light. In the early 1850s, the city signed a concession with a private company to install gas streetlights in specified areas of the city's center.[4] Even as Rio gradually accumulated more public lanterns, throughout the first decades after independence administrative correspondence between the police forces and the municipal government repeatedly cited public lighting as a matter of the gravest importance for public safety and tranquility. Rio's police, government authorities, and residents debated the precise number and location of lanterns, who would fund and take responsibility for their installation, and how swiftly and efficiently they would be installed, but the desire to light the city streets seems to have generated little controversy. It also seems clear that public illumination had become, at least by the 1840s, a matter for the police.[5]

In early nineteenth-century Rio, nighttime policing and restrictions on movement after dark derived from the Portuguese legal tradition of (often conscripted) night watchmen. Its history is, however, inseparable from the prevalence of enslaved persons, estimated to have numbered 36,182 in 1821, fully 46 percent of the city's population of 79,321.[6] The number of slave ships entering Rio between 1809, after the arrival of the Portuguese royal family and the consequent opening of the ports to international commerce, and by 1825 had increased more than ever before, by 143 percent.[7] The post-independence 1824 constitution explicitly upheld masters' property rights and neither conferred any rights or legal personhood on Brazil's slaves nor provided any explicit rules for controlling and governing enslaved persons. Brazil never adopted a legal code specific to slaves. The legislative chambers of individual Brazilian cities passed municipal ordinances touching on the daily work and circulation of enslaved residents but these never amounted to a thoroughgoing system of regulation or a means of limiting the power of masters over slaves. It fell to a delicate and always shifting balance of proprietary private jurisdiction and criminal law to control enslaved persons; the nomenclature "slave people," used in the country's otherwise quite liberal Criminal Code of 1830 (and Code of Criminal Procedure in 1832), embodied their paradoxical status as both human beings subject to criminal interdictions and chattel with no legal personhood.[8]

The municipal chamber that passed and enforced city regulations, the police, and individual slave owners worked together, though often at cross-purposes, to control slaves in the city's public spaces. Brazil was also home to the continent's largest population of free persons of color, whose quotidian public lives the Rio police zealously oversaw.[9] The ancient distinction between day and night made its way into post-independence policing and judicial practice as one such means of control. Curfew violation was among the relatively minor crimes that preoccupied the police but were absent from the 1830 code. Walking about the city after the dark fell within an expansive category of activities, like gambling and the

Afro-Brazilian martial art called *capoeira*, whose oversight was left to a combination of local regulation under city ordinances and police regulations on the one hand, and a customary mandate to preserve "order and public tranquility" on the other.[10]

Not surprisingly the issue of "public tranquility" arose constantly in Rio, a city reeling from a decade and a half of political and demographic changes, and where roughly half the residents were enslaved. Reading the river of documents that flowed daily down the police hierarchy, one gets a sense of the breadth of the public order fears that this institution, itself very much in formation and in flux, confronted. The dominant but by no means only concern was enslaved persons subject to public jurisdiction as they circulated through the city during their daily labor. Soon after taking his post as Rio's sixth police chief (*intendente*), the Lisbon-born aristocrat and jurist Francisco Alberto Teixeira de Aragão wrote to colleagues in Rio de Janeiro and other Brazilian cities to decry the dangers of "illicit societies," of the ubiquitous foreigners wandering about the streets without any documentation, and of general threats to the safety and tranquility of law-abiding residents.[11] Aragão was an especially forceful leader who introduced a number of measures to professionalize and expand the power of Rio's police. Under his direction the Imperial Court of Rio de Janeiro developed an organized, centralized, and round-the-clock police force.[12]

One of the major issues that Aragão confronted in his first months as intendente was a raging public debate about the forced recruitment of slaves for public works projects and the desperate need for more laborers to keep up with the capital city's expanding infrastructure needs. "Slaves for hire" doing work ordered by their masters were routinely snatched off the streets and put to work constructing fortifications for the city. Slave owners as well as some police officials expressed horror at the infringement of property rights, while other municipal officials wrung their hands wondering how the city's many unfinished infrastructure projects would ever be completed without more workers to carry them out. The official reports and other correspondence on this matter coming from the desk of Aragão himself reached something of a fever pitch in the final months of 1824.[13]

Immediately on the heels of this controversy, Aragão issued new policing regulations in the form of an administrative order (as opposed to legislative act) with the force of law. This 1825 edict, the police chief's most famous act, was essentially a stop-and-frisk law; anyone, whether enslaved or free, who encountered a law enforcement official had to submit to questioning. Failure to do so automatically constituted a criminal act of resistance, and the person would be subject to "whatever violent methods the circumstances require." The central provision in the 1825 edict established what soon came to be known as the "Toque de Aragão" (Aragão's Curfew) a curfew of 10 P.M. in summer and 9 P.M. in winter. Patrols could search anyone out after curfew "for illegal weapons or instruments that could be used in a crime." The bells of the São Francisco de Paula church and the São Bento convent were to ring for a half hour to announce the commencement of curfew so that no one could claim to have lost track of time.[14] When the police noticed a few months later that some shop owners and tavern keepers defiantly opened their establishments in the still-dark hours just before dawn, Aragão published an additional edict reinforcing the requirement that the city shut down altogether between the tolling of the evening church bells and the cannon shot that announced the start of the next day at dawn.[15]

The boundaries of the night were announced by loud sounds, but it was the sense of sight that was at stake in criminalizing nocturnal public life for some of the city's residents.[16] Legal codes and jurisprudence generally define the night as the time between sundown and sunrise, but the moment when it goes into effect and exactly what should change at nightfall have always been the subject of some controversy. In the English common law tradition, cited in Portuguese and Brazilian jurisprudence, "night" is defined as not beginning "until after dusk and ceasing when there is daylight enough to discern a man's countenance."[17] Visigothic and Iberian medieval law, sources for Iberian legal tradition, further distinguished some types of crimes that were more severely punished, and often even fell under a separate jurisdiction, if committed after sunset rather than during the day.[18] Nocturnal crimes were worse than diurnal ones not simply because they took place at night, but rather because the perpetrator purposely sought out the cover of darkness.

The Philippine Ordinances, the legal code compiled by the king of Portugal in the sixteenth century, held force in Portugal and in Brazil until the passage of the first national Criminal Code in 1830. The Ordinances give much consideration to the importance of nightfall, indicating how long and at precisely what time the customary *sino de recolher* (literally, "shutting-in signal") should ring.[19] Woven prodigiously throughout this body of Portuguese law is a reliance on visual perception to uphold social order, a theme that took on special meaning and was felt with the greatest force in the racially and ethnically diverse overseas colonies. As the historian Sílvia Hunold Lara's research demonstrates, the documents that the Portuguese crown issued to establish norms for the overseas empire made specific reference to sumptuary restrictions on fabrics and other aspects of outward display, to the skin color of colonial subjects, and to controls on the costume and outward appearance of "blacks and mulattos in the Conquistas," whether enslaved or free, to maintain everyone in their place in the social order.[20] The ability to uphold the social hierarchy depended on being able visually to identify and recognize individuals in the city's public spaces. The way authorities and city residents perceived a person in public had real material and often immediate consequences; appearing in public subjected one's skin color and legal status (that is, enslaved or free)—crucial aspects of each individual that determined his or her legal treatment but were never completely clear, even in daylight—to evaluation.

In Rio's first postcolonial century, the time when one could "no longer discern a man's countenance" was precisely when police patrols acquired enhanced power to arrest and harass people. Aragão's curfew was part of a trend in policing that granted greater discretion to the patrols on the street to handle the most common offenses (such as vagrancy and curfew violation); effectively, law enforcement personnel assumed the roles of policeman, judge, and jury, all at once. The order to enforce this new curfew cautioned that it should not be abused "nor be applied to well-known persons of integrity"; it was overtly intended to be applied selectively, in accordance with the class and racial inequalities of the day. José Vieira Fazenda, in his nostalgic account of the Toque de Aragão, writes, "it was the signal to run, or to go shut yourself indoors, and the little black boy walking around in the street any time after [the church bells], without written permission from his master, would be thrown in jail or into the slave dungeon and would get a beating."[21]

The Aragão edict showed how night could collapse the difference between slaves and the free poor; the new legal regime that nightfall triggered could widen that difference in other ways as well. After curfew, it became illegal to whistle in the streets or do anything that could be construed as a signal. This prohibition applied "to blacks and men of color any time after dark, even if prior to the curfew." A slave violating curfew "in any store, tavern, bar, or gambling house" was sent to the infamous Calabouço slave dungeon and whipped; free persons paid a fine.[22]

The Toque de Aragão facilitated the maintenance of public order by taking to an extreme the existing disregard for the public life and culture of the city's poorer classes and residents of African descent, and by explicitly condoning the use of any means necessary to force compliance. The curfew applied a blanket prohibition on any type of activity in Rio's public spaces after nightfall, with no consideration for either public culture or commerce. Even before the new curfew regulations, slaves generally were not permitted to congregate socially in shops, taverns, gambling houses, or public places at any time of day.[23] The edict targeted not just individuals but also businesses where people gathered after hours, suggesting, again, that the kind of people who would be subject to this curfew patronized places like taverns, despite the extreme darkness and supposedly inhospitable streets. According to the historian Thomas Holloway, "Aragão's instructions, centering on the curfew and on the sites of public entertainment and social interaction for both slaves and the nonslave lower classes, *put the civil rights provisions of the constitution in a more realistic context.* 'The law will be the same for all' turned out to be a high-minded statement of principle that had little to do with life on the streets." While the inequality derived from slaves' status as property instead of legal persons, free blacks and the poor in general encountered the same problem. "Persons of 'integrity' were spared the restrictions of the curfew" and the indignity of physical aggression by police patrols.[24]

When the Toque de Aragão was put into place, it ostensibly allowed for daily activities and commerce to occur as they had before in this growing port city. Yet the curfew did more than curtail people's movements after dark; it literally transformed material life. Sandra Lauderdale Graham explains that "slaves carried written notes from their masters to explain their presence, and *cortiços* (the collective slums of the poor) locked their gates against runaway slaves, unruly intruders, and to keep their own tenants inside. The tools an artisan casually carried during daytime working hours became arms after the evening ringing of the 'Ave Maria' and were forbidden."[25] The mention of working hours is important here; the curfew aimed to impose rules without harming the urban economy.

Arrests for curfew violations and other infractions made more serious because they happened after dark are scattered throughout the daily police logs from the curfew period. The smattering of cases that survive in the archive provide anecdotal evidence of the conditions under which police stopped and detained individuals found on the streets after dark, and offer hints about Rio's after-hours social world. Cumulatively, these arrests also highlight how the practice of enforcing the curfew shaped the social construction of night. An 1829 communiqué sent to the inspectors in the Naval Arsenal indicated that seven "sailors" were "walking about fomenting disorder on the streets after hours" and, in the name of "public tranquility," should be sent to perform service aboard warships "or whatever type of service" his interlocutor judged appropriate.[26] Four years later, in 1833, a criminal judge in the São José neighborhood of Rio reported to the police that "the black man João Braga, who claims to be a freed slave and Spanish," was arrested "for having been found at one o'clock at night by a foot patrolman."[27]

The archival record reveals little about the nature of interactions between police and the people they arrested for curfew breaking; police daily activity logs registered these arrests in the most concise terms, with little narration or description. The arresting officers may not always have deployed physical force against those they stopped in the streets— although Aragão's edict explicitly gave them license to do so. Yet the establishment of the nighttime as a zone of normalized violations of civil and political rights created the structural possibility for state violence (and impunity) to become normalized.

In sum, Aragão's curfew initiated an unbroken period of fifty-three years during which nighttime triggered a state of exception. Subsequent regulations altered or refined the 1825 law. A new curfew was ordered in 1831 in response to a perceived crime wave and general breakdown of public order; now the nightly, selective shutting in would take place at sunset (around 6:30 P.M.) rather than 9 or 10 P.M., and only slaves and sailors were subject to it, "not other free persons"; of 224 persons arrested from late May to early June 1831 in Rio, 34 were tried for curfew violation (14 sailors and 20 slaves)—compared to 35 for vagrancy and 25 for weapons possession, the other most common categories. Despite police vigilance, however, free people of color and others who would have been subject to the curfew often attended public events. These included both nighttime social and drumming events, where large numbers of people gathered, and smaller gatherings in public squares. If these events became too big or unruly or occurred after curfew, military police arrived to disperse the crowd and, in accordance with the January 1825 edict, arrest anyone who resisted or objected. In 1833, one tavern was closed down when a military police patrol found "the place bustling at 2 A.M.," long after the 10 P.M. curfew. New policing guidelines issued in 1858 to professionalize the police force and make it more efficient reinforced the authority to shut down taverns and small bars (*botequins*) at 10 P.M. and reaffirmed that any person found on the street after curfew could be presumed to be a criminal.[28]

The Curfew and Its Long Shadow

By the 1870s, the curfew had lost its effectiveness. It is never clear what a dip in arrests really signifies, but in this case the decrease in arrests for curfew violations suggests a lassitude in enforcing the nightly lockdown rather than a decrease in nighttime activity. The strict curfew, it seems, had begun to soften. In July 1873, the military police commander reiterated the order that all businesses close at 10 P.M. When a public outcry ensued, municipal authorities relaxed the rule a bit: the 10 P.M. closing time would still apply to "taverns, houses where alcoholic beverages or beer are sold, boarding houses, and similar establishments that might serve as meeting places of drunks, vagrants, and ruffians." But the city's new, European-style kiosks, confectionaries, and hotels could stay open until 1 A.M. As public life became more commercialized, the differential application of the curfew law did as well. Notably, if a business was now exempt from the 10 P.M. curfew, then its customers were too. During those three hours from 10 P.M. to 1 A.M., it was entirely up to police discretion whether to arrest someone for violating curfew. In 1878, Rio's city council allowed all legitimate businesses to stay open until 1 A.M., and later the same year the Toque de Aragão was at last formally lifted.[29]

Interestingly, just as the long, unbroken period of curfew was ending, Rio de Janeiro began to instate a private night-watch system to augment its regular, publicly employed civilian police force and the military police. This nocturnal guard was initially unarmed but gradually acquired weapons, technically breaking the law. They patrolled after dark and carried on the tradition of arbitrary policing in the empire. No longer under curfew for the most part, the city now controlled its nighttime commerce through the selective granting of licenses to operate. Businesses that were not favored with a license or could not afford licensing fees had to close early, which some did, or operate illicitly, oftentimes paying off the police.[30]

From the 1880s on, changes in the built environment and urban culture attenuated the legal and political importance of nightfall. Yet there are surprisingly far-reaching continuities from the earlier period when sunset predictably triggered an explicit state of exception to the rule of law. Public illumination expanded dramatically in the late nineteenth century, with gas lanterns reaching the suburban outskirts of the city, which then still used whale oil, beginning in 1877. An 1879 law started the process of bringing recently invented electrical lighting to Rio de Janeiro. In 1933, electrical lights replaced the last gas lanterns still illuminating some of the working-class suburbs, thus ending the nearly eighty-year career of the lamplighter, the popular figure with whom this chapter began.

Rio's residents had already started to enter the streets for entertainment and sociability after dark well before the lifting of the curfew in 1878. Commercialized nighttime entertainment began on a small scale in the 1860s as the wealthy took to the gas-lit streets. For example, an 1868 issue of A Vida Fluminense (a fashionable illustrated magazine from the late empire) has an illustration showing well-heeled people watching the bay at night; the caption explains that "from now on, the regattas will begin at midnight for greater public enjoyment."[31] In the following decades, a widening swath of residents of Rio de Janeiro and other Brazilian cities regularly partook of nighttime leisure.[32]

Tellingly, it was not the gradual introduction of artificial light that mitigated the imposition of states of siege and curfews. The more obvious and familiar story of technological progress does indeed appear here in terms of both public finance and the capacity to produce brighter, cheaper, and less malodorous forms of light to illuminate the city's public spaces. Yet, the juridical apparatus that developed to define the night as dangerous did not keep step with the rhythm of technological change. Instead, the municipal and national governments continued to impose curfews at moments of political conflict or perceived social chaos. Curfews were meant to curtail freedom of movement to the degree possible while still allowing the city to do what it was supposed to do: distribute export commodities from the hinterland to the port and provision the workers who ran these industries. A commercial center as active as

Rio that depended on captive labor fulfilled its economic purpose in this manner; daytime freedom of movement and nighttime lockdown worked together.

Aragão's edict and similar regulations that followed it made a great deal of sense during the conflict over the recruitment of "other people's slaves" to labor in public works and the desperate need for more hands to build, fix, and run the capital city. It was this context, combined with the horror of any type of "agglomeration" of the masses in Rio's public spaces, that produced curfew laws.

Revoking these rules also made a great deal of sense once the city's commercial life became organized around public entertainment requiring free circulation in the streets after dark, and once free labor replaced enslaved labor. In this context anti-vagrancy laws took the place of curfew laws as the broad category police used most frequently to arrest socioeconomically vulnerable persons identified as being in the wrong place at the wrong time. As a misdemeanor that prohibited unemployment irrespective of the time of day, vagrancy was tailored to fit non-enslaved workers caught in the act of doing nothing in an industrializing city that could not shut down after sunset. In other words, the Aragão edict was not just a relic of a premodern age that disappeared with the advance of technology and modernity. The church bells no longer tolled to signal curfew by the century's end, but the normalized suspension of rules after nightfall remained.

During the First Republic in the decades just after repeal of the Toque de Aragão, the government repeatedly invoked its emergency powers, placing state security above individual rights and juridical norms in the wake of labor unrest. In 1917, as social upheaval rippled through São Paulo, Santos, Rio, and other cities, the federal government used the pretext of Brazil's formal entrance into World War I to place the Federal District under this provisional emergency political-legal regime. Such states of siege and selective curtailment of freedom of movement after dark recurred throughout the twentieth century.

Conclusion: Everyday Violence and the Politics of Nightfall

How can we consider Rio's modernization and the rise of its nightlife alongside the cyclical imposition of states of siege and curfews that targeted the nighttime as fraught with dangerous possibilities throughout much of the twentieth century? Returning to the early nineteenth century and tracing how criminal law constructed nighttime can free us of the superficial obviousness that having more people on the streets at night should present new dangers for law enforcement. This history can also challenge the naturalized idea that nightfall poses a public security threat that is a simple function of biological rhythms and astronomical truths. Political and legal reactions to nighttime resulted from more than just primal psychological fears of the unseen, social anxieties about the unknown, the danger of humanity's godlike pretentions in illuminating the darkness, or the ancient demonology of night. They are essentially political formations in that they are symptoms of the power dynamics of urban governance and the contest for power between certain social groups. The night as a legal and cultural concept has developed independently from the physical property of darkness and humans' diminished visual perception after sunset.[33]

In the history of the Atlantic world, sight, as an ability and a disability, has stoked the imagination with ways of thinking about the abstraction of justice and its pragmatic application. As Martin Jay points out, the portrayal of justice as a blindfolded woman alludes not only to fairness in carrying out the law but also to its opposite: blind justice performs its own sort of violence in subsuming unlike cases under a single rubric and in denying the female judge her sense of visual perception.[34] Municipal laws gave police who were visually limited by the darkness the latitude to arrest those who appeared—to the extent their appearance could be discerned at all—to endanger society. The social and legal construction of nighttime has been a crucial and an insufficiently studied factor in the historical processes through which state violence has enforced social hierarchies and forms of political exclusion.

Notes

1. *Light*, no. XIV, ano II, vol. II (March 1929); *Light*, no. 62, ano VI, vol. VI (March 1933).
2. Deborah T. Levenson, *Adiós Niño: The Gangs of Guatemala City and the Politics of Death* (Durham, NC: Duke University Press, 2013), 149, n. 7.
3. Sílvia Hunold Lara, *Campos de violência: Escravos e senhores na Capitania do Rio de Janeiro, 1750–1808* (Rio de Janeiro: Paz e Terra, 1988).
4. Centro Cultural da Light, "A iluminação no Rio de Janeiro," unpublished manuscript in the archive of the Centro Cultural da Light, Rio de Janeiro.

5. Arquivo Geral da Cidade do Rio de Janeiro (hereafter AGCRJ), códice 8.4.58, folha 49.

6. *Revista Trimestral do Instituto Histórico, Geográfico, e Etnográfico do Brasil* 33, Parte 1 (1870): 137; Mary Karasch, *Slave Life in Rio, 1808–1850* (Princeton, NJ: Princeton University Press, 1987), 60.

7. Manolo Garcia Florentino, *Em costas negras: Uma história do tráfico atlântico de escravos entre a África e o Rio de Janeiro (séculos XVIII e XIX)* (Rio de Janeiro: Arquivo Nacional, 1995), 38, 52.

8. Thomas H. Holloway, *Policing Rio de Janeiro: Repression and Resistance in a Nineteenth-Century City* (Stanford, CA: Stanford University Press, 1993), 58–59.

9. According to the census taken in 1849, Rio had 205,906 inhabitants in its urban zone, of which 78,855 were enslaved and 10,732 were freed former slaves; Luiz Carlos Soares, *O "Povo de Cam" na Capital do Brasil: A Escravidão Urbana no Rio de Janeiro do Século XIX* (Rio de Janeiro: Editora FAPERJ—7 Letras, 2007), 29.

10. Holloway, *Policing Rio,* 61.

11. Arquivo Nacional (hereafter AN), Seção de Guarda SDE 001, códice 325, vol. 4; AN, GIFI, caixa 6J 80.

12. In a long document dated November 1825, Aragão reorganized Rio's police force, created posts immediately under the *intendente,* and affirmed the twenty-four-hour-a-day professional policing of the city; AN, Fundo: Polícia da Côrte, códice 332, folhas 2–3.

13. AN, Polícia da Côrte, códice 323, vol. 8; AN, Polícia da Côrte, códice 327, vols. 1–2; AGCRJ, 6.1.25, f. 14.

14. *Império do Brasil: Diário Fluminense* 1, no. 5 (January 3, 1825), 2–3; João Paulo de Mello Barreto Filho and Hermeto Lima, *História da polícia do Rio de Janeiro: Aspectos da cidade e da vida carioca* (Rio de Janeiro: Editora A Noite, 1939), 288–89; Holloway, *Policing Rio,* 46–47; Zoraia Saint'Claire Branco, "Estórias da Policia do Rio de Janeiro," *Cadernos de Segurança Pública* 1:0 (December 2009), 3.

15. *Imperio do Brasil: Diário Fluminense,* April 18, 1825, 336.

16. Poignantly demonstrating how selective this curfew was, the same newspaper that published Aragão's edict and similar official orders reinforcing the curfew also published announcements and advertisements for cultural events occurring late into the night; see, for example, *Imperio do Brasil: Diário Fluminense,* June 9, 1825, 26, and July 30, 1825, n.p.

17. Walter A. Shumaker and George Foster Longdorf, *The Cyclopedic Law Dictionary* (Chicago: Callahan and Co., 1922), 753.

18. Jean Verdon, *Night in the Middle Ages,* trans. George Holoch (Notre Dame, IN: University of Notre Dame Press, 2002), 100.

19. Even today in Brazil, nighttime is considered an aggravating circumstance in criminal legal practice. According to a contemporary legal dictionary, criminal law defines the night as the period just after dusk and just before dawn, "the period during which, by virtue of the darkness or people's period of rest, the execution of a crime is facilitated, and for that reason it constitutes an aggravating circumstance for the crimes of robbery and the violation of a domicile"; R. Limongi França, ed., *Enciclopédia Saraiva do Direito* (São Paulo: Saraiva, 1977), 232.

20. Sílvia Hunold Lara, "Customs and Costumes: Carlos Julião and the Image of Black Slaves in Late Eighteenth-Century Brazil," *Slavery and Abolition: A Journal of Slave and Post-Slave Studies* 23, no. 2 (2002): 132.

21. Mello Barreto Filho and Hermeto Lima, *História da polícia do Rio de Janeiro*, 289.

22. Holloway, *Policing Rio*, 46–47.

23. Emília Viotti da Costa, *The Brazilian Empire: Myths and Histories* (Chicago: University of Chicago Press, 1985), 140.

24. Holloway, *Policing Rio*, 47–48.

25. Sandra Lauderdale Graham, "Making the Private Public: A Brazilian Perspective," *Journal of Women's History* 15, no. 1 (2003): 28–42.

26. AN, Fundo Polícia da Côrte, códice 330, vol. 6.

27. AN, Fundo: Polícia da Côrte, códice 330, vol. 7.

28. Holloway, *Policing Rio*, 79, 161, 191.

29. Ibid., 257–58. Soon after the curfew was ended, however, the government declared a state of siege and reinstated it during a popular riot in 1880 protesting a streetcar surcharge.

30. AN, Gifi 8N 014; Marcos Luíz Bretas, *Guerra das ruas: Povo e polícia na cidade do Rio de Janeiro* (Rio de Janeiro: Arquivo Nacional, 1997), 54, 59 n. 17, 60, 84.

31. *A Vida Fluminense*, January 18, 1868, 40; and June 27, 1868, n.p.

32. Regina Horta Duarte, *Noites circenses: Espectáculos de circo e teatro em Minas Gerais no século XIX* (Campinas: Editora da Unicamp, 1995), chap. 1.

33. Verdon, *Night in the Middle Ages*, 1–2.

34. Martin Jay, *Refractions of Violence* (New York: Routledge, 2003), 87–102.

8 Rebels, Outlaws, and Enemies

The Criminalization of Dissent in Colombia and Mexico

Luis Herrán Ávila

Moving beyond conventional approaches, comparative and transnational histories have offered new ways of understanding the history and legacies of the Cold War in Latin America in terms of the region's political and cultural milieu.[1] In this bourgeoning literature, analyses of legal structures, discourses, and practices in contexts of political conflict have received less attention than has the phenomenology of political violence linked to popular mobilization, revolution, and state repression. A common approach is to portray law, legality, and the justice system as unmediated tools of arbitrary power, or as formal justifications for situations in which elites' agendas are furthered at the expense of common citizens.

Without dismissing this instrumental dimension, I examine how actors and institutions equate certain social phenomena with criminality and thereby construct political dissidents as punishable and often expendable "enemies." As Pablo Piccato (chapter 1), Gema Santamaría (chapter 2), and Daniel Núñez (chapter 9), show with regard to lynchings, extrajudicial executions, and social cleansings, respectively, the construction of dangerous subjectivities and the circulation of socially shared notions of legitimate punishment blur the distinction between legality and illegality. By emphasizing the role of criminal law in legitimizing violent punishment against enemies, I situate the notion of the "political criminal" at the intersection between the criminalization of dissent and the politicization of crime. In the Cold War context I describe processes by which the political criminal was cast as a form of dangerous subjectivity that rendered the threat, real or imagined, of communist subversion as both a criminal offense and a challenge to the established order. I thus pay special attention to the relation between legality and repression, and to the types of subjects, audiences, and publics produced and targeted by discourses about legality, criminality, and security.

Using the concept of enemy criminal law I analyze two instances where political actors and institutions produced, shaped, and acted upon a punitive authoritarian legality that extended into politics by treating certain subjects as rights-less enemies of both the state and society.[2] First, I address the expansion of criminal law as an instrument of political and social control during the period known as La Violencia (1946–58) in Colombia. I examine how the passing of emergency criminal legislation under a state of exception legitimized forms of legal and social punishment, from above and below, against "communist bandits" that authorities and other social actors perceived as enemies of order. Next, I analyze the characterization of the political criminal as an agent of social dissolution in 1960s Mexico in order to punish and demonize subjects considered dangerous due to their dissident activities or ideas. I also examine some of the debates surrounding the use of legal and extralegal instruments to repress such individuals.

For both cases, I analyze how enemy criminal law reflected, or indeed created, categories of criminality and social danger informed by contextual meanings of crime, subversion, and antisocial behavior. These two cases highlight how the production and circulation of enemy constructs amongst various publics informed the legal and extralegal repression of alleged political criminals, and both reflected and shaped broader social perceptions about the nexus between criminality and dissent. Building on this volume's explicit critique of crime as an objective and legal-rational notion, I suggest that these Cold War cases shed light on the legal and social production of dehumanized subjects, thereby challenging the punitive turn in contemporary discourses and policies that conceive security as a war against criminal enemies.

Colombia: Bandits, Rebels, and Criminals in La Violencia

For historians and historical sociologists, banditry appears as a social byproduct or symptom of unfinished processes of state formation, characterized by the chronic absence or weakness of the state vis-à-vis the residues of civil war or rural resistance.[3] For the Colombian case, the groundbreaking work by Gonzalo Sánchez and Donny Meertens countered the narrative that banditry was a "depoliticized" residue of the period of "classic" bipartisan violence during La Violencia. Their analysis stresses the importance of *bandolerismo* both as a concept and a social phenomenon that sheds light on the connections between factionalism, clientelism, agrarian conflict, criminality, insurrection, and rural displacement throughout and after this period. As these various forms of violence intersected, bandolerismo assumed multiple meanings in the state's efforts to delegitimize, prosecute, and overcome its internal enemies.[4]

Studies on the role of enemy criminal law in Colombia's longstanding conflict have shown that the conceptual overlap of banditry with insurgency and, later, with terrorism is not simply the product of government rhetoric but results from three interrelated and recurring historical processes.[5] The first is the use of executive power to impose a form of punitive authoritarian legality; the second is the substitution of the rule of law for a *derecho de guerra* in a context of irregular armed conflict; and the third is the legitimation of violence against those deemed enemies of the state and society.

The logic of politicized criminalization that informs the Colombian state's strategy against subversion has deep historical roots in the social-institutional legacy of La Violencia.[6] In both collective memory and the historiography of the period, the event that inaugurates Colombia's manifold *violencias* is the 1948 assassination of Jorge Eliécer Gaitán, a popular Liberal Party leader who positioned his movement as an alternative to the politics of oligarchical negotiation behind closed doors.[7] Known as *El 9 de abril* or *El bogotazo,* the reaction to Gaitán's assassination was composed of a series of destructive riots in Bogotá, a mutiny led by police officers, and a number of failed insurrections in other cities.[8] Fearing a major revolt, Conservative President Mariano Ospina declared a state of siege (*estado de sitio*), imposed full censorship of the press, authorized the army to fulfill law enforcement functions, shut down all legislative bodies, and suspended the right of assembly.[9] Under the state of siege, *gaitanista* and Liberal Party sympathizers formed rural self-defense groups to repel repression by security forces and bands of armed civilians loyal to Conservatism, as the government alleged the assassination was a plot orchestrated by local Soviet agents to foment revolution in the country.

The allegation that a communist–Liberal Party conspiracy was behind the disturbances reinforced the anti-Liberal animosity of the faction led by Laureano Gómez, a fierce Conservative opponent of the social-democratic reforms implemented by the Liberals during the 1930s. With his characteristically sharp rhetoric, Gómez denounced the Liberal Party as a proxy for communist infiltration and stressed the monstrous nature of the criminal violence waged by the *gaitanista* multitude during *el bogotazo*:

> In Colombia, we still speak of a Liberal Party to refer to an amorphous and contradictory mass . . . that can only be understood through the ancient image of the basilisk. . . . Our basilisk walks with feet of confusion and ingenuity, with legs of violence and abuse, and an immense oligarchical stomach; with a chest of fury, Masonic arms and a tiny little communist head—but a head nevertheless. This is the result of a mental elaboration, product of careful observation of the latest events in our nation. Thus we deem the 9th of April as a typically communist phenomenon carried out by the basilisk.[10]

Through the image of the basilisk, Gómez conflated the Liberal opposition with the external forces that allegedly plotted against Gaitán, and with urban mob violence and rural criminality. This assessment stemmed from a longstanding political tradition that understood liberalism, modern mass democracy, and communism as threats to Colombia's "orderly" republic, a view shared even by some Liberal intellectuals who distanced themselves from the behavior of the "reckless and brutish" *gaitanista* multitude.[11] This negative interpretation of *el bogotazo* was central for swaying public opinion in favor of repression against those social groups identified with the basilisk.

Gaitanismo and banditry were constructed as a single seditious and criminal mass seeking to destabilize the Conservative government and as symptoms of the social decay caused by factionalism and an unruly population. This ideological conflation of dissent, rebellion, and criminality was reflected in the expansion of criminal law to punish certain offenses that, in the context of the state of siege, were recast as threats to the security of the state. The most immediate effect of this political use of criminal law was the implementation of Consejos de Guerra Verbales (military tribunals) to prosecute the types of crime associated with *el bogotazo*: arson, robbery, destruction of property, rebellion, and sedition.[12]

By adopting the principles governing these Consejos (brief trials with severe sentences), the civil criminal justice system became militarized, placing regular law enforcement under a frame of exceptionality that justified the continuous use of emergency powers to combat an alleged state of general social rebelliousness. Moreover, as censorship against Liberal newspapers and radio broadcasters tightened, the government decreed harsher sentences for those who supported or expressed sympathy for the Liberal Party and communist bandoleros. Such expressions were considered endorsements for bandolerismo and thus, as offenses against "the security of the state," they too fell under the authority of the Consejos de Guerra. In these ways, the state of siege exacerbated the public perception of a pervasive and general social danger of bandolero-like violence, initiated by the Bogotá rioters, the Liberal guerrillas, and peasant self-defense groups, and continued through the alleged influence of foreign and homegrown communists. In the following years, these social meanings attached to bandolerismo were institutionalized to support the use of extralegal means to persecute Liberals and combat "subversion." Using police forces and armed civilians, national and local Conservative officials coerced, terrorized, and often violently eliminated or displaced their opponents.[13]

Elected in 1950 in a climate of violence and intimidation, Laureano Gómez began his "Revolution of Order," an attempt to restore the hegemony of the Conservative Party by waging a crusade against the forces his administration perceived as being part of the dreaded basilisk. Like his predecessors, Gómez framed the suppression of *focos de bandolerismo* (peasant guerrillas of the Eastern Plains and Tolima regions) as a matter of law enforcement and social cleansing, established harsher sentences for crimes against "the integrity of the constitutional regime," and targeted *maleantes,* defined as "those who, in seeking to inflict damage on property, exert violence against the physical integrity of individuals."[14] In this crusade, Gómez had the support of Conservative governors and local authorities, who defined all actions by Liberal bandoleros as crimes against the life and property of Conservatives. These actors also referred to the bandoleros as *alzados en armas* (armed opposition), reinforcing the notion that a bandolero was both a political criminal and an ordinary felon.[15]

Unable to defuse the opposition and weakened by illness, Gómez stepped down and appointed his minister of government, Roberto

Urdaneta, as interim president. Urdaneta sent mixed signals, maintaining the state of siege and tightening controls over the press while offering amnesty to political criminals who were willing to lay down their arms.[16] While Liberals expected a rapprochement under Urdaneta, the factional violence inherited from Gómez's administration persisted at the grassroots level, fed by the demonization of Liberals and other dissenters. This became clear in September 1952, when Conservative sympathizers and police officers set fire to the headquarters of the Liberal newspapers *El Tiempo* and *El Espectador* and to the homes of Liberal Party leaders to avenge the deaths of police officers at the hands of bandoleros. These arsons were reviled by the government (and less enthusiastically by the Conservative Party), yet Urdaneta justified them as a natural revulsion of popular opinion against the support that Liberals had lent to the bandoleros.[17]

In 1953 a pact between Liberals and anti-Gómez Conservatives enabled General Gustavo Rojas Pinilla to take power via a coup d'état. With the self-professed goal of rooting out violence, Rojas maintained the state of siege, placed all law enforcement and censorship functions under the supervision of the Ministry of War, and created the Colombian Intelligence Service and the Office of Aid and Rehabilitation.[18] His plan for the "economic rehabilitation" of the Eastern Plains relied on an aggressive policy of civilian-military "colonization" and the "cleansing" of bandoleros.[19] Simultaneously, Rojas decreed a general amnesty for all political crimes committed prior to 1954, with the exception of acts of "extreme moral insensibility."[20] Thus, Rojas sought to end the violence through a combination of repression, coercion, and cooptation with increased state presence in the affected regions. In all these initiatives, the figure of the bandolero was central: as a target for intelligence and surveillance, as a subject of amnesty and rehabilitation, and as an enemy in war.

Escalating military campaigns in the Eastern Plains signaled the transformation of the state's crusade against bandolerismo into a scenario of anticommunist irregular warfare. Inspired in part by the participation of an army battalion in the Korean War, these campaigns featured the use of civilian and military counter-guerrilla forces.[21] In that context, Rojas introduced legislation that explicitly defined communist activity as a criminal offense, including the distribution of propaganda, belonging to or financing a communist organization, and expressing support for communism in any form. The new legislation established sentences of up to five years of imprisonment or forced labor at an agricultural penal colony for civilians engaged in communist activity, while public officials and police or military officers could be sentenced to ten or twenty years, respectively. More importantly, the decree empowered Consejos de Guerra to investigate and prosecute political as well as common crimes linked to this wide-ranging definition of communist activity.[22]

Even after the signing, in 1958, of a pact between Liberals and Conservatives to restore democracy and pacify the country, the use of the justice system as an instrument of counterinsurgency continuously relied on the construction and treatment of dissidents as dangerous subjects. Fixated on solving the problems of factionalism and antisocial behavior, the new regime struggled to address the underlying structural causes of violence and rendered any "residual violence" as criminal, antidemocratic, and outright subversive. In the following decade, this "residual violence" gave way to Cold War revolutionary *guerrilleros,* prompting a combination of legal and military means to wage a more technical, rational, and punitive war against these enemies. The deep institutional and societal legacies of La Violencia produced a long-lasting legal and extralegal order in Colombia that treated dissent as criminally subversive, through the suspension of constitutional guarantees, the use of punitive violence by state and non-state agents, and the normalization of an enemy-centered *derecho de guerra.*[23]

Mexico: Social Dissolution and the Criminalization of Dissent

In contrast to the political climate that characterized La Violencia in Colombia, Mexico's Cold War authoritarian legality emerged from a "national-revolutionary" regime that enjoyed relative political and institutional stability, a remarkable continuity in its political class, and a monotonous predictability in elections. Although never clearly centralized—especially in instances of agrarian conflict—the monopoly on violence remained firmly in control of state agents and their local proxies. Also, the hegemonic party was fairly successful in integrating the military and large portions of the agrarian and labor movements into its machinery, leading to the consolidation of the postrevolutionary state and its elusive "myth of the *pax priista.*"[24] Within this institutional continuity, the Law of Social Dissolution and the disputes that arose from its enforcement provide a glimpse into the overlaps between enemy criminal law and the regime's efforts to control and neutralize radical dissidents.

In Mexico political crimes were historically limited to four offenses listed in the Federal Criminal Code: high treason, rebellion, sedition, and mutiny. In 1941, Mexico entered World War II in support of the Allies, prompting Manuel Ávila Camacho's administration to reform the Criminal Code to include espionage (punishable by up to forty years in prison) and the ill-defined crime of social dissolution (*disolución social*), punishable by a prison term of two to six years. As defined in Article 145 of the Criminal Code social dissolution involved the dissemination of political propaganda; specifically "spreading ideas, programs, or forms of action for any foreign government which disturb the public order or affect the sovereignty of the Mexican state." Explicitly defined in Article 145A as a political crime, social dissolution also encompassed any expression of ideas that threatened "the territorial integrity of the republic," obstructed "the functioning of its legitimate institutions," or spread "contempt on behalf of Mexican nationals toward their civic duties."[25]

The law remained dormant until the late 1940s, when the administration of Miguel Alemán (1946–52) revived it as an instrument for the promotion of the "social peace" necessary for modernization.[26] In addition, following the U.S.-led strategy of anticommunist "containment," the doctrine of *mexicanidad* established by Alemán and his Institutional Revolutionary Party (PRI) explicitly rejected communism and presented the PRI regime as an allegedly "democratic nationalist alternative" to left- and right-wing totalitarianisms.[27] In the PRI's efforts to secure its hegemony, labor became one of the main spheres of action against "communist influence," largely through the exclusion of left-leaning factions from the party's decision-making structures; the support for PRI-sponsored worker, peasant, and student federations; and a strong alliance with the private sector.

In 1950 Alemán amended Article 145 to include acts of sabotage or any acts that "tend[ed] to produce rebellion, sedition, riot, or mutiny," and to increase maximum prison sentences to twelve years. Alemán introduced two other key changes. First, he expanded the definition of social dissolution to include "induction or incitation" to commit sabotage and acts "of provocation with the intent to disturb public peace and order."

And second, a sentence of ten to twenty years in prison was instituted for acts that "prepare, materially or morally, for the invasion of the national territory or the subordination of the country to a foreign government."[28] In sum, this Cold War iteration of Article 145 codified certain acts (even common, nonpolitical crimes) as social dissolution based on their alleged intention to promote communist agitation. In that context, the creation of the Federal Security Directorate in 1947 constituted an effort to professionalize the Mexican intelligence apparatus and to centralize it by linking it directly to the president's office, establishing the means to surveil and prosecute the intent to commit political crimes.[29]

In the early 1950s, social dissolution was seldom invoked to prosecute political dissidents. The sentences were often lenient and subject to appeal, but press coverage of such cases emphasized the defendants' suspected communist allegiance and inclination for violence.[30] Framed by the mobilization of teachers and railroad workers, and later, by the advent of the Cuban Revolution, social dissolution became a way of labeling dissidents as communists and hence as dangerous and punishable subjects. Social dissolution turned into a recurring trope as PRI officials, the Church, and the private sector fomented anticommunist sentiment to combat the anti-imperialist and pacifist rhetoric of the Left and its appeal in the labor and student movements. The government suppression of the railroad workers' strike of 1958–59 was a paradigmatic example of the exploitation of official anticommunist rhetoric and the criminalization of Leftist activism under the Law of Social Dissolution to dismantle the movement and imprison its leaders, Demetrio Vallejo and Valentín Campa. Far from promoting social dissolution, the railroad workers were striking for fair wages, better working conditions, nationalization of certain industries, and reform of fiscal policies. Still, Vallejo and Campa were found guilty and given unprecedented prison sentences of sixteen and ten years, respectively. In 1960, painter David Alfaro Siqueiros and journalist Filomeno Mata Jr. were also charged with social dissolution for their involvement in a committee seeking the release of these political prisoners.[31]

The Law of Social Dissolution shaped public discourse about the Left as a constant source of disruption and allowed the judicial system to prosecute what were essentially crimes of conscience. In this regard, the press was a central vehicle for the dissemination of discourses about social dissolution that conflated Leftist activity with criminality.

Anticommunist groups capitalized on the prevailing sentiment, as did MURO (University Movement of Renovational Orientation), a right-wing student organization created by Catholic groups and funded by businessmen and noted members of the PRI. Indeed, in 1961, after the reinstatement of two MURO activists expelled from the National University for violent acts during an anti-Castro demonstration, an editorial in the daily *Excélsior* lauded the "civic courage of the students, [and] their brave determination in confronting the apostles of hatred and social dissolution," and deemed their acquittal as "a triumph of public opinion."[32] A similar portrayal of social dissolution as a threat that justified extralegal forms of punishment appeared in a public statement by former president Abelardo L. Rodríguez:

> The Mexican people lack an adequate organization to combat the acts of dissolution perpetrated by agents—foreigners and native traitors—at the service of enslaving governments. . . . There lies the urgency for the representatives of groups with the means to counter these subversive activities . . . to cooperate as much as they can—intellectually, materially, and economically—in creating an independent organization to propagate the principles of political and economic liberalism amongst workers, peasants, and youth. . . . This entity will work vehemently to create centers where well-organized groups of citizens will be trained as shock brigades . . . with the ability to repel the acts of vandalism, social subversion, and provocation perpetrated by the agents of Russian-Cuban-Chinese communism.[33]

In this extract, the meaning of social dissolution is displaced from its legal codification toward a notion of enmity against the criminal and subversive activities of domestic and foreign communist agents, providing a platform for civil society to take whatever violent action may be necessary to "repel" such enemies. From this perspective, the enemies' *acción disolvente* (incitement of rebellion at the service of a foreign power) indeed justified political vigilantism (shock brigades) as a means of social defense encouraged and legitimized by specific sectors of civil and political society.

Social dissolution remained not only a legal instrument for authoritarian repression, but also a source of contestation against the blatant use of the legal apparatus to persecute dissidents.[34] During the medical workers' strike of 1964 and more clearly in the months prior to the

1968 Tlatelolco massacre, the demands to repeal Articles 145 and 145A resonated more loudly, prompting the creation of a congressional commission to investigate the constitutionality of the law. The commission's hearings became a space for debate among the different constituencies concerned with the broader implications of the law, thereby revealing institutional and social perceptions on dissidence.

Opposition to the law came from leftist militants, student organizations, and legal scholars concerned with the subjective application of the code and its use to persecute individuals for their ideas rather than for actual crimes. Others emphasized the "technical" weakness of the articles, as well as the inappropriateness of incorporating a wartime measure into the Criminal Code without considering its abrogation of due process.[35] Those who favored the law, such as Román Lugo, former attorney general of the Federal District, argued (1) that "Article 145 had its origin in conditions that still exist today . . . espionage, subversion, infiltration, and other threats to social peace"; (2) that the Mexican state had the right to use legal means to preserve its integrity; and (3) that all that was needed were revisions to address weaknesses in the article.[36] In the same vein, Dr. Margarita Lomelí argued that in light of the Second Declaration of Havana and the danger of anti-imperialist revolutionary agitation coming from Cuba, Article 145 served its original purpose as an instrument for the "penal defense of democracy" beyond the circumstances created by World War II.[37]

Another common argument was that of Professor Gustavo Serrano, who denounced "communist demagoguery" for deceiving well-intentioned students into protesting a measure aimed at "defending the integrity of Mexican nationality" against the threat of a communist attack on individual liberties.[38] Serrano reasoned that, since students opposed a law that clearly and almost exclusively would affect communists, the students' position could only be explained as either manipulation by or conscious acquiescence to communists. Serrano's argument was indicative of a broader governmental attitude that deemed the actions of *disolventes* detrimental to liberty, democracy, and sovereignty, therefore justifying repressive use of the legal apparatus against them.

Ultimately, the general council of the student movement adopted the abolition of Article 145 as part of its famous list of demands, which also included the release of all political prisoners, the dismissal of police chiefs responsible for violent repression, and the elimination of riot squads (*granaderos*). In response, the government insisted Article 145 was constitutional, current, and necessary. The then president of the PRI, Alfonso Martínez, claimed that "the youth do not know dictatorship and have not seen the blood-spattered face of the Right" and further denounced "fake Leftism" and the use of students as "cannon fodder by the conspirators, the promoters of subversion and anarchy." Martínez's widely publicized speech defended the alleged moderation and benevolence of a regime that in fact had the legal and material capacity to exert violence on its citizens.[39]

After the violent repression of the student movement in Tlatelolco, hundreds of detainees charged with social dissolution saw the "benevolent" face of the state: the Mexican Congress passed a presidential initiative to grant *libertad bajo protesta* (liberty under oath) to all first-time offenders accused of "crimes against the integrity of the state or of conspiracy to commit [such crimes]," if they provided proof of their domicile and of "an honest way of life."[40] The press immediately celebrated the initiative as evidence of the "democratic magnanimity" of the government toward "its enemies"[41] and as a message of tolerance and reconciliation that was not to be confused with impunity or a "renunciation of the rule of law."[42] An editorial in *El Heraldo* was even more histrionic in its exaltation of the government's "benevolence": "the generous hand, the noble heart of the president and his confidence in the strength of our institutions have allowed him to give a new gesture of his deep humanism. . . . The initiative opens the prison doors for the perpetrators of riots and violence; but it also opens the windows of optimism for all Mexicans."[43]

In 1970, the regime's attempt to make amends with the student movement combined with increased public pressure led to the elimination of Articles 145 and 145A. However, the emergence of new, urban-based, armed revolutionary organizations (such as the Liga 23 de Septiembre) drove the codification of terrorism as a political crime and as a new means to prosecute dissent. Terrorism carried prison sentences of up to forty years, and a "complicity" clause mandated sentences of up to nine years for those who "despite knowing the activities and identity of the terrorist, hide information from the authorities."[44] More importantly, terrorism became a trope in governmental discourse about the illegitimacy of violent contestation against the regime. As President Luis Echeverría put it, "The people will not fall for the language of the terrorists. They know terrorists seek to undermine the unity of all Mexicans and to force the authorities to toughen their position. . . . Terrorism is reactionary [and] fascist. . . . It is an expression of the lack of popular support, of the fear of intelligence; it hides clandestinely, threatening human existence."[45] In this way, the social and institutional memory of social dissolution as a form of authoritarian enemy criminal law enabled the construction of the terrorist guerrillero as a disolvente; that is, a criminal with political motivations (often communist ones) that made him an enemy of national sovereignty and the PRI's democracy.

Conclusion

These two instances of enemy criminal law exemplify parallel yet strikingly similar responses to the alleged threat of communism in the Cold War context. Both in their politico-legal rationale and in their specific mechanisms they reveal the use of public and legal discourse to construct the dissident as a political-criminal subject, shedding light on the use of authoritarian legality to punish and demonize these "enemies." In short, they expose the links between legal structures and the social and political construction and circulation of notions of criminality, and of the different publics through which these notions become socially validated. In the Colombian case, the figure of the communist bandolero synthesized the coupling of social protest and dissidence with the longstanding and multifaceted phenomenon of rural "social banditry." Thus, bandolerismo after La Violencia was not an anachronistic or residual form of social violence. Rather, framed by Cold War fears and the labeling of rural peasant resistance as subversion, it codified the legal-political enemy (the bandit-communist) as a threat to the "natural" equilibrium of bipartisan politics and the social order established by landowners, coffee growers, and political bosses. In that sense, the designation of the bandit-communist as a political criminal with no legitimacy reflected the modern state's anxieties about threats to its integrity coming from agents of social dissolution. In the Mexican context the same notion appeared clearly codified as a political crime that compromised both national sovereignty and social peace and facilitated foreign intervention.

In both the Mexican and Colombian cases, however, the significance of these threats went beyond the abstract undermining of national sovereignty. The links among criminality, dissidence, and subversion also implied the breakdown of the institutions, values, and practices that these regimes presented to society as components of an orderly, law-abiding republic. To the extent that they typified ideas, behaviors, and "tendencies" that were potentially disruptive to the larger social and political order, these politico-legal artifacts were often successful and powerful ideological instruments to reproduce the legitimacy of the regime and preserve the integrity of the state. Presented as mechanisms to defend democratic societies against their internal enemies, they also permitted the erosion of basic liberties and granted specific agents the power to determine the identity and motivations of "the enemy," the appropriate punishment, and even the path to amnesty or absolution.

Notwithstanding the vast contextual differences between Colombia and Mexico, their instruments of Cold War authoritarian legality responded to the same logic of exceptionality. Whereas in Mexico it was incorporated into "normal" legislation (the Federal Criminal Code), in Colombia it was preserved through an ongoing state of siege and the gradual subordination of the justice system to the logic of the Consejos de Guerra. In both cases, criminal legislation was the instrument that codified specific social behaviors as dangerous by situating them in a broader horizon of violence, real or imagined, in which communism became a criminal agent identified with murder, theft, street violence, destruction of property, and other offenses.

Legal artifacts that reflect ideas about the threat that certain political behaviors pose to an established or ideal order lend palpable significance to the notion of criminalization. Beyond the Cold War context, the juridical systems of Colombia and Mexico still reproduce institutionally embedded discourses and categories of political criminality, revealing that the criminalization of dissent is not just an arbitrary decision instantiated by the exertion of punitive violence against an enemy. To criminalize an individual, group, or idea also means rendering it as a subject of just or legitimate punishment, through state and non-state mechanisms, for the actual or potential breach of a norm. For political crimes, this norm is often portrayed in terms of a social contract, or the matrix of values that bonds society together. And although legal codes may permit harsh sentences, the punishment can also be social demonization, intimidation, and persecution. In that sense, acts of state repression tend to operate under a legal framework that is simultaneously a discourse about the legitimacy of violence against those defined as dangerous subjects. This discourse too often resonates in civil society, reflecting and prioritizing concerns about security and the need to defend the social order from its enemies through legal or extralegal means.

Notes

1. Hal Brands, *Latin America's Cold War* (Cambridge, MA: Harvard University Press, 2012); Tanya Harmer, *Allende's Chile and the Inter-American Cold War* (Chapel Hill: University of North Carolina Press, 2011); Greg Grandin and Gilbert M. Joseph, eds., *A Century of Revolution: Insurgent and Counterinsurgent Violence during Latin America's Long Cold War* (Durham, NC: Duke University Press, 2010); and Gilbert M. Joseph and Daniela Spenser, eds., *In from the Cold: Latin America's New Encounter with the Cold War* (Durham, NC: Duke University Press, 2008).

2. As conceived by legal theorist Günther Jakobs, enemy criminal law designates a sphere of legality compatible with the rule of law in constitutional regimes. This sphere is characterized by the selective suspension of individual guarantees and due process only for certain types of "threatening" subjects, often dangerous criminals. See Jakobs, *Derecho penal de enemigo* (Madrid: Civitas, 2003). While debates surrounding enemy criminal law remain relatively rare in the Anglo-American academy, the concept has been a subject of critique and revision by scholars elsewhere. See Manuel Cancio Meliá and Carlos Gómez-Jara Díez, *Derecho penal del enemigo: el discurso penal de la exclusión* (Madrid: Edisofer, 2006).

3. Eric J. Hobsbawm, *Primitive Rebels: Studies in Archaic Forms of Social Movement in the Nineteenth and Twentieth Centuries* (New York: W. W. Norton, 1965); see also his later *Bandits* (New York: Delacorte Press, 1969). Gilbert M. Joseph, "On the Trail of Latin American Bandits: A Reexamination of Peasant Resistance," *Latin American Research Review* 25, no. 3 (1990): 7–53; and Richard J. Slatta, ed., *Bandidos: The Varieties of Latin American Bandits* (Westport, CT: Greenwood Press, 1987).

4. Gonzalo Sánchez and Donny Meertens, *Bandoleros, gamonales y campesinos: el caso de la violencia en Colombia* (Bogotá: El Áncora, 1983); Mary Roldán, *Blood and Fire: La Violencia in Antioquia, Colombia, 1946–1953* (Durham, NC: Duke University Press, 2002); Daniel Pécaut, *Orden y violencia: Colombia, 1930–1953* (Medellín: Siglo XXI, 1987); James D. Henderson, *When Colombia Bled: A History of the Violence in Tolima* (Tuscaloosa: University of Alabama Press, 1985).

5. Iván Orozco Abad and Alejandro Aponte Cardona, *Combatientes, rebeldes y terroristas: guerra y derecho en Colombia* (Bogotá: Temis, 1992); Alejandro Aponte Cardona, *Guerra y derecho penal del enemigo. Reflexión crítica sobre el eficientismo penal de enemigo* (Bogotá: Ibáñez, 2006).

6. Gustavo Emilio Cote Barco, *Derecho penal de enemigo en La Violencia (1948–1966)* (Bogotá: Pontificia Universidad Javeriana, 2010).

7. W. John Green, *Gaitanismo, Left Liberalism, and Popular Mobilization in Colombia* (Gainesville: University Press of Florida, 2003).

8. Herbert Braun, *The Assassination of Gaitán: Public Life and Urban Violence in Colombia* (Madison: University of Wisconsin Press, 1985), chap. 7.

9. *Decretos extraordinarios y decretos reglamentarios de leyes expedidos por la Rama Ejecutiva, en desarrollo del artículo 121 de la Constitución Nacional, durante el año de 1949* (Bogotá: Imprenta Nacional, 1950), 52–67.

10. "Discurso pronunciado por el doctor Laureano Gómez en la Plaza de Berrío de Medellín a su regreso de España en 1949," in Testis Fidelis [pseud.], *El basilisco en acción, o los crímenes del bandolerismo* (Medellín: Olympia, 1953), 5.

11. "El Seis de Septiembre. Carta de Luis Eduardo Nieto Caballero al Señor Presidente Urdaneta Arbeláez," October 1952. Germán Arciniegas Latin America Papers, New York Public Library; box 1, folder 1.

12. *Decretos extraordinarios*, 60–61.

13. Eduardo Umaña Luna, Orlando Fals Borda, and Germán Guzmán Campos, *La violencia en Colombia. Estudio de un proceso social* (Bogotá: Tercer Mundo, 1963); Pécaut, *Orden y violencia*; Roldán, *Blood and Fire*; Henderson, *When Colombia Bled*.

14. *Compilación de disposiciones sobre reformas civiles, penales, administrativas, del trabajo y sobre justicia penal militar expedidas por el Ejecutivo nacional en los años de 1948 a 1957* (Ibagué: Imprenta Departamental, 1956), 27–28.

15. "Oficio no. 0463." November 27, 1951, Archivo General de la Nación, Colombia (hereafter AGN-COL), Fondo Presidencia, Secretaria General, Gobernaciones Correspondencia 1951, caja 273, carpeta 17.

16. *Decretos extraordinarios y decretos reglamentarios de leyes, expedidos por el gobierno nacional del 1º de julio al 31 de diciembre de 1952* (Bogotá: Imprenta Nacional, 1953), 31–32; 103–5.

17. *Alocución del Excelentísimo Señor Doctor Roberto Urdaneta Arbeláez* (Bogotá: Dirección de Información y Propaganda de la Presidencia, 1953), 7–11.

18. *Decretos extraordinarios y decretos reglamentarios de leyes expedidos por el gobierno nacional del 1º de julio al 31 de diciembre de 1953* (Bogotá: Imprenta Nacional, 1954), 2:6–7, 10–11, 21, 327–31.

19. "Plan de reestablecimiento económico de los Llanos Orientales," December 12, 1953, AGN-COL, Fondo Presidencia, Secretaria General. Ministerio de Guerra Transf. 6, caja 268, carpeta 28, fols. 51–55.

20. *Decretos extraordinarios y decretos reglamentarios de leyes expedidos por el gobierno nacional del 1º de enero al 30 de junio de 1954* (Bogotá: Imprenta Nacional, 1955), 1: 586–87.

21. Gustavo Sierra Ochoa, *La guerrilla de los Llanos Orientales* (Manizales, Colombia: Imprenta Departamental, 1954); Alberto Ruiz Novoa, *Enseñanzas de la campaña de Corea, aplicables a Colombia* (Bogotá: Antares, 1956).

22. *Decretos extraordinarios y decretos reglamentarios de leyes expedidos por el gobierno nacional del 1º de enero al 30 de junio de 1956* (Bogotá: Imprenta Nacional, 1958), 76–77.

23. Alejandro Aponte Cardona, *Guerra y derecho penal de enemigo*, esp. chaps. 3 and 4.

24. For a critical take on the stability of the PRI regime as a myth reproduced by the historiography, see Tanalís Padilla, *Rural Resistance in the Land of Zapata: The Jara-*

millista Movement and the Myth of the Pax Priísta, 1940–1962 (Durham, NC: Duke University Press, 2008); Paul Gillingham and Benjamin T. Smith, eds., *Dictablanda: Politics, Work, and Culture in Mexico, 1938–1968* (Durham, NC: Duke University Press, 2014).

25. *Código penal para el distrito y territorios federales, en materia de fuero común, y para toda la república en materia de fuero federal* (Mexico City: Farrera, 1941).

26. Tzvi Medin, *El sexenio alemanista: ideología y praxis política de Miguel Alemán* (Mexico City: Ediciones Era, 1990), 30–33.

27. Luis Medina, *Del cardenismo al avilacamachismo. Historia de la revolución mexicana* (Mexico City: Colegio de México, 1978), 18:176–80.

28. Carlos Sánchez Cárdenas, *Disolución social y seguridad nacional* (Mexico City: Linterna, 1970), 182–84.

29. Together with the Dirección General de Investigaciones Políticas y Sociales of the Secretaría de Gobernación, the DFS became a mechanism of political control by concentrating its efforts on the surveillance and active disruption of political opposition. Aaron W. Navarro, *Political Intelligence and the Creation of Modern Mexico, 1938–1954* (University Park: Pennsylvania State University Press, 2010), 150.

30. Jaime M. Pensado, *Rebel Mexico: Student Unrest and Authoritarian Political Culture during the Long Sixties* (Stanford, CA: Stanford University Press, 2013), 111–12.

31. Olga Pellicer de Brody and José Luis Reyna. *El afianzamiento de la estabilidad política* (Mexico City: Colegio de México, 1978), 205–14.

32. "Triunfo de la opinión pública," *Excélsior,* November 29, 1961.

33. Abelardo L. Rodríguez, "Despierten, hombres de negocios de México" (Frente Popular Anticomunista de México, 1961) reprinted from *El Universal Gráfico,* June 2, 1961. Archivo General de la Nación, Mexico (hereafter AGN-MEX), IPS, caja 2895A, exp. 21: Jorge Prieto Laurens.

34. Evelyn Stevens, "Legality and Extralegality in Mexico," *Journal of Interamerican Studies and World Affairs* 12, no. 1 (1970): 62–75.

35. "Opinión de Héctor Ramírez Cuéllar sobre el artículo 145 y 145 bis del Código Penal," *El Día,* October 24, 1968, 4.

36. "Las circunstancias que crearon el 145 se han agravado: Román Lugo," *El Día,* September 26, 1968, 1.

37. Untitled document, AGN-MEX, IPS, caja 1468B, exp. 56, fols. 30–60.

38. Untitled document, AGN-MEX, IPS, caja 1469B, exp. 56, fols. 7–9.

39. "Los jóvenes no saben lo que es la dictadura ni conocen el rostro sangriento de la Derecha," *El Día,* September 23, 1968, 4.

40. "Podrá obtener libertad bajo protesta quien esté procesado por conspiración," *El Día,* December 20, 1968, 1.

41. "Magnanimidad del estado democrático," *La Prensa,* December 21, 1968, 8.

42. "Puente de entendimiento," *El Día,* December 21, 1968.

43. "Generosa iniciativa del ejecutivo," *El Heraldo de México,* December 21, 1968.

44. Sánchez Cárdenas, *Disolución social,* 187.

45. *Informes presidenciales. Luis Echeverría Álvarez* (México: Cámara de Diputados, 2006), 348–49.

PART III

The Politics of Making Violence Visible

In many ways, violence in Latin America could hardly be more visible. According to a 2014 report by Mexico's Citizens' Council for Public Security and Criminal Justice, murder is more common in Latin America than any other region of the world.[1] Considered the most dangerous non–war zone city in the world, San Pedro Sula (Honduras) had 187 homicides for every 100,000 inhabitants in 2013. Thirty-three other Latin American cities ranked among the fifty most dangerous cities in the world, including eight in Mexico and sixteen in Brazil.[2] As valuable as that snapshot is, the report sensationalizes violence in Latin America and attributes violent crime to the usual factors: drug trafficking, poverty, corruption, political instability, and gang activity. By invoking an interpretive approach based on fields of representation, such reports can be mined for the data they contain and for their revelations about how people represent and conceptualize violence and crime. The contributors in this section examine the politics and publics of the multiple actors that portray, publicize, and perpetuate violence and crime.

These essays contextualize the forces and actors that make such violent crimes as murder and drug trafficking visible enough to gain international attention while other forms of violent crime (such as police extrajudicial killings or vigilante acts) remain obscured. Thereby they reveal the material and psychological consequences of those processes for countries' political and social fabrics. Whether they obscure or illuminate, representations can perpetuate the very phenomena they represent.

Just as rising incidents of violent crime have contributed to the region's international reputation as a dangerous place, so too can representations of violence and crime within Latin American countries serve to criminalize certain populations or to render some areas—usually, marginalized or socially excluded areas—sites of danger or disorder. While murder and other violent acts shape the process of making violence visible, their very public (or invisible) nature also influences their perpetuation. Thus, the amplification of violence within specific publics may serve to legitimate repression and state-sanctioned violence in the name of security. In Mexico and Guatemala, for example, *juvencidio* is a phenomenon whereby authorities target gang members, some as young as thirteen, as criminals who engage in drug trafficking, murder, extortion, and theft. This practice opens a window into how tactics of state terror can gain popular support by making certain crimes (and hard-line responses to them) visible. In stark contrast, the invisibility of white-collar crimes, from money laundering to corruption and bribery, often encourages state inaction or neglect, with the consequence that economic and political elites and public officials such as police and military personnel are seldom punished for their transgressions. The invisibility of certain crimes may thus signal state complicity or inertia in those realms.

In exploring the levels of visibility or invisibility of different forms of extralegal violence, Daniel Núñez identifies the interplay between public perceptions of crime and the legitimation of violence against suspected criminals in Guastatoya, a small municipality in eastern Guatemala. Justified as a necessary corrective to police corruption, the killing or expulsion of alleged criminals is referred to using the name given to the state-sanctioned extrajudicial killings during the war years: *limpieza social* (social cleansing). Núñez contrasts the silence and secrecy surrounding these killings with the public and visible nature of lynchings. The town of Guastatoya "lives under a regime of silence," he says. Whereas community members and authorities recognize that acts of limpieza social occur in Guastatoya, lynchings are either denied or simply not recorded by the police. As Núñez suggests, the apparent absence of lynching in this town has less to do with its actual incidence than with the notion—shared by authorities and locals—that lynchings happen in indigenous communities, not in ladino towns such as Guastatoya.

By exploring how and for what purposes drug traffickers decide to conceal or expose their use of violence, Angélica Durán-Martínez shows how visibility may be crafted not only by state actors and individual communities, but also by criminals themselves. The degree of visibility is driven by criminal organizations' decisions to "expose and claim responsibility for their attacks," and by their violent methods. Comparing the strategies used by the Medellín cartel during the 1980s in Colombia to those deployed by the Arellano Félix Organization (AFO) during the 1990s and 2000s in Mexico, Durán-Martínez demonstrates how state-cartel relationships can help predict whether criminals expose their violence. Facing a fragmented state that was incapable of or unwilling to offer it protection, the Medellín cartel decided to expose violence in order to force such protection and further advance its interests. In contrast, the AFO benefited from a stable network of protection within Mexico's government that shielded traffickers from law enforcement and provided it with incentives to opt for more "invisible" methods of violence.

Through their analysis of crime and its representations in Rio de Janeiro and Kingston, Enrique Desmond Arias and Kayyonne Marston too reveal how power and politics shape visibility and invisibility. Demonstrating that violent crimes taking place in peripheral areas have consistently attracted less attention and fewer resources than those taking place at the urban core, the authors trace how the realm of representation has influenced the reproduction of certain forms of violence. As in Mexico and Colombia, in Brazil and Jamaica networks of complicity and corruption shield political and economic elites from prosecution while they continue to subject economically and socially excluded populations to police abuse and repression. Long-established alliances between sociopolitical elites and authorities render violence invisible but also reveal the level of dominance and control a criminal organization exercises over a given territory. Violence perpetrated by Rio de Janeiro militias and Kingston gangs express those organizations' strangleholds over communities and neighborhoods.

The essays in this final section provide a framework for exploring how the power of representation, or making things visible (or invisible), relates to crime and violence. Whether they are intended to occlude or expose, fields of representation shape not merely perceptions of violence and crime, but also the very acts themselves. Shaped by state actors, civil society, and criminals, the politics of visibility offers a productive analytical site to understand violence and its reproduction.

Notes

1. José A. Ortega, "Por tercer año consecutivo, San Pedro Sula es la ciudad más violenta del mundo," Consejo Ciudadano para la Seguridad Pública y la Justicia Penal, January 15, 2014, www.seguridadjusticiaypaz.org.mx/sala-de-prensa/941-por-tercer-ano-consecutivo-san-pedro-sula-es-la-ciudad-mas-violenta-del-mundo (accessed November 20, 2014).

2. Pamela Engel and Christina Sterbens, "The 50 Most Violent Cities in the World," *Business Insider,* November 10, 2014, www.businessinsider.com/the-most-violent-cities-in-the-world-2014-11 (accessed November 18, 2014).

9 "There Are No Lynchings Here"

The Invisibility of Crime and Extralegal Violence in an Eastern Guatemalan Town

Daniel Núñez

Studies on violence against suspected criminals in postwar Guatemala have focused almost exclusively on the indigenous communities of the western highlands, where a series of lynchings were documented during the mid-1990s and early 2000s.[1] With the exception of a few studies, very little is known about similar forms of violence in other parts of the country, and about the relationship between these kinds of practices.[2] Focusing on the ladino eastern town of Guastatoya, where some locals claim a series of secret killings they refer to as *limpieza social* (social cleansing) or disappearances have occurred during the last few years, I discuss how state and non-state actors understand and represent both crime and the actions they take against it.

Although locals have traditionally regarded the small town of Guastatoya as a peaceful place, their assessment has changed over the last decades because of increasing levels of crime, unemployment, and migration. As perceptions of insecurity have shifted, some locals affirm clandestine forms of deadly violence against alleged wrongdoers have become more common. I analyze how social dynamics and perceptions of crime and violence inform the visibility and sanctioning of deadly acts against suspected criminals in Guastatoya. I also demonstrate that, despite the end of the Civil War (1960–96), extrajudicial killings continue to haunt contemporary Guatemala.

Overview of Limpieza Social in Guatemala

Limpieza social, or "social cleansing," has a long history in Guatemala. The term has had different uses, but it usually refers to the "serial killings of people who have been economically pushed so far toward the fringes of misery that the more affluent members of society classify them as 'undesirable,' 'throwaway' human beings."[3] As in other Latin American countries, the perpetrators of these killings have often been state agents or individuals associated directly or indirectly with the state.[4] The "undesirables," on the other hand, have usually been people from the so-called dangerous classes, such as petty thieves, street children, members of street gangs (mareros), and individuals considered enemies of the political establishment.[5]

During Guatemala's civil war the military and the police used the term "limpieza social" to mask violent actions against civilians or individuals suspected of being left-wing activists. The Commission for Historical Clarification (CEH, in Spanish) established that, in 1965, the Guatemalan military—with the help of USAID—"disappeared" several individuals during one of its first counterinsurgent operations in Guatemala City.[6] The campaign, known as *operación limpieza*, "was carried out through raids that included a police and military siege of several blocks within a specific perimeter that blocked the entry and exit of persons," a pattern repeated in municipalities throughout the country.[7] By the end of the 1970s, Donaldo Álvarez Ruiz, then the feared chief of the Interior Ministry, conceded in an interview that "in the country there is a death squad operating, but it has no link to the security forces . . . that group could be linked to a 'cleansing of criminals.'"[8]

Following Guatemala's democratic transition in 1985, the military and the police were still using the term "limpieza" to refer to secret operations against alleged criminals and left-wing militants. In 1988, the government established the System of Citizen Protection (SIPROCI, in Spanish), an organization designed to address public security concerns that included members of the military and the National Police.[9] Under SIPROCI, the National Police carried out "cleansing operations" that involved the torturing and extrajudicial killing of presumed criminals and students.[10] The recent discovery of the archives of the National Police has revealed further evidence of police use of operaciones de limpieza against civilians and political enemies during the 1970s and 1980s, many of which resemble the operations carried out by the military at the beginning of the 1960s.[11]

As the CEH report documents, the military also used "limpieza" to refer to the killing of those members of the organization that they believed knew too much or could potentially harm them as an institution. The report notes, "Many death squad members were eliminated by the Intelligence, given that they had too much information about the clandestine activities of the Army, which transformed them into a serious threat for the institution, or because they began to act autonomously without the Intelligence's control. This situation was frequent in the West of the country and was known as 'la limpieza.'"[12]

Although usually a clandestine matter, limpieza was also carried out publicly during the war. In 1982, in San Andrés Sajcabajá, a municipality in the department of Quiché, the CEH documented that the military and members of the Civilian Self Defense Patrols randomly killed community members in front of others as part of a "community cleansing" of people that were "contaminant agents of the rest because of their communist ideas."[13]

In contemporary Guatemala, just as during the war years, limpieza social constitutes an extralegal form of violence carried out with the tacit or outward involvement of state agents. According to the Human Rights Ombudsman Office, in 2004–5, approximately 975 people were killed in acts that bear the hallmarks of limpieza social.[14] Based on interviews with victims and local informants, the Human Rights Special Rapporteur to the United Nations, Philip Alston, concluded that members of the police Criminal Investigation Division (DINC, in Spanish) had been involved in many of those killings.[15]

Guastatoya: The Capital of Friendship

Guastatoya is the head municipality of El Progreso, a small and arid department in the central-eastern region of Guatemala. Located just forty-five miles away from Guatemala City, it has a population of approximately twenty-two thousand people, most of whom self-identify as ladino.[16] The municipality's urban center is made up of six neighborhoods (Las Joyas, La Democracia, Minerva, El Golfo, El Porvenir, and El Calvario) that surround a central plaza. Each neighborhood is made up of small houses along one or two main streets, occupied by small shops (*tiendas*) that sell all kinds of knickknacks and household items. Around the central plaza, one can find the municipal building, a church, the Interior Ministry office, the local Peace Court, and a police station, along with a couple of diners and small hotels.

Like many ladinos in Guatemala, most people in Guastatoya live in better than average conditions for the country. Back in 2002, for example, 21 percent of Guastatoyans lived in poverty and 2 percent lived in extreme poverty, whereas the national averages were 60 and 18 percent, respectively.[17] Nonetheless, many Guastatoyans face serious economic hardship. Unemployment has been on the rise since at least the 1990s, when a series of floods on top of historic droughts damaged the department's agricultural infrastructure.[18] These tragic events forced young peasant men to migrate to Guatemala City and to the United States, and pushed women out of their traditional household roles into agriculture.[19]

Many Guastatoyans still migrate to the United States or work in Guatemala City. The round trip to *la capital,* as they refer to the city, takes around three hours, which makes it possible for some to commute on a weekly or even a daily basis. A few Guastatoyans work at the small shops and restaurants scattered throughout the town, while others work at the local government institutions. Many young men work driving moto-taxis (locally known as *tuctucs*). Tuctucs are small three-wheeled taxi-motorcycles that can fit up to four people and can take them anywhere within the municipality for Q2.00 to Q20.00 (around US $0.25 to $2.50). "The rest," as a small businessman said to me, "see what they can do."[20]

Unlike many of the other municipalities in eastern Guatemala, Guastatoya has the reputation of being a peaceful place. This reputation goes back at least to 1976, when a group of locals began to call the town *La capital de la amistad* (Capital of Friendship) as a tribute to the well-respected and affable families that died during Guatemala's earthquake that year.[21] One can feel the friendliness of Guastatoyans on a daily basis, as it is common to receive a "hello" or a "good morning" with a welcoming smile while walking down the streets. Locals seem to value this characteristic, as many of my interviewees proudly mentioned it along with the town's nickname. In fact, the nickname is even featured in the Mayor's Office official letterheads.[22]

Those who refer to the peacefulness of Guastatoya generally do so in relation to the freedoms that the town "still" offers, like being able to go out late at night or being able to leave the doors of one's house open until late in the evening. As two local women expressed, "You can still go outside at twelve or one o'clock in the morning, because nobody is going to come after you."[23] "We can walk calmly at night, have our doors open, go to the park without fear, with freedom."[24] Others compare the peacefulness of Guastatoya with Guatemala City. Their general view is that la capital is a violent place where people get robbed and killed on a daily basis. Indeed, over the last few years this Latin American city has become one of the most violent places on the planet.[25] "This is a peaceful place. You don't hear of burglars or deaths, like in other places, [like in] la capital," explained a local who had lived in Guatemala City for several years. "People here are very peaceful . . . which is something you don't see in la capital."[26]

Locals also compared Guastatoya with Sanarate, a municipality in the southeast of El Progreso. Sanarate, along with its neighboring municipality of San Agustín Acasaguastlán, has traditionally been El Progreso's social and economic center.[27] Closer to Guatemala City, with easy access to other departments directly through Jalapa, and with a relatively larger population, Sanarate has much more dynamic commercial activity. People from Guastatoya generally see Sanarate as a violent place, where "there are mareros"[28] and where they "assault or kill you in the street."[29] They see it as a "super populated"[30] place with many outsiders or "people from other places."[31] As a young man concluded about his town, "They say this is the most peaceful place there is. Here, thank God that [crime] hasn't arrived yet."[32]

Not everyone thinks of Guastatoya as a peaceful town, however. As the introduction to this volume highlights, perceptions of crime and violence are often in the eye of the beholder. Almost half of the people I interviewed believed security had deteriorated over the last few years. Hearsay and news about murders, burglaries, and rapes have become more common over the last decade, a trend that coincides with official statistics on crime during the same period.[33] Some Guastatoyans attribute sexual assaults against women to the young male tuctuc drivers, who have a bad reputation in town because of their reckless driving and dubious activities. A woman working at one of the local state agencies, for example, said, "I see the tuctuc driver's little face . . . most of them are even extorting people."[34] Another woman from the same institution expressed similar concerns: "Tuctucs take them [women] away to rape them."[35] Several other Guastatoyans attribute the rise in crime to people who have migrated to their town from other places, as a university student explained: "Before, it was peaceful; now, yes, people from outside come to commit crimes."[36] These Guastatoyans say that most of these individuals come from nearby places that have a reputation for being violent, like la capital, Sanarate, and El Rancho, another small town in El Progreso. They also claim that some come from neighboring countries, like Honduras and El Salvador. Because Guastatoya is small and its residents know each other well, strangers automatically generate suspicion. A local merchant, for example, explained, "Now we have seen people from outside, from la capital, and since we don't know them, we don't know what ideas they have."[37]

Like many Guatemalans, Guastatoyans hold a deep distrust against the police and local authorities. They consider that "the police do nothing" when a crime occurs, or that, at best they show up hours later, sometimes just "to collect cadavers."[38] Faced with challenges such as lack of resources, poor salaries, and inadequate training, police performance is also undermined, according to locals, by the fact that many police officers were born in Guastatoya. Indeed, most of the new recruits for the Fifth Promotion of the National Civil Police in 1999 came from Santa Rosa, Jutiapa, and El Progreso, a recruitment pattern that was also present under the old National Police.[39] Because they are from Guastatoya, so the argument goes, local police officers are unable to remain impartial when they find friends or family members in conflict with the law, and so they help them out. As a consequence, most Guastatoyans deeply distrust the police and claim that citizens sometimes need to take justice into their own hands. A similar phenomenon can be seen in countries like Peru and Mexico, where distrust of the police and of penal institutions in general serves to justify extrajudicial killings, as Pablo Piccato and Gema Santamaría show in chapters 1 and 2.

The Silence of Guastatoya

Echoing earlier reports of anthropologists working in war-stricken areas of Guatemala, when Guastatoyans talk about extrajudicial killings they lower their voices, as if someone were eavesdropping, and they stop talking when they think they have said too much. Their stories are often vague and short, told from a third-person point of view and in the passive voice. Whereas some people assured me that the town was as peaceful as everyone claimed, others talked about a very different reality underneath the friendly atmosphere. As a local worker explained, "Right now we have taken the law into our own hands, because if we don't take care of ourselves, who is going to take care of us? The people, if it is too much, well, just like in other places, they get rid of them [criminals], because if they go to jail, they come back, because they are used to it. They only go to jail for six months. . . . They are removed and then they stop because they know that here, they have to show respect."[40]

Some Guastatoyans refer to these killings as limpieza social or as limpieza, using the term known during the war years. Others say that people who commit crimes are "disappeared," or they simply don't have a word for the phenomenon. Even though war violence was less intense in the eastern regions of Guatemala than in the indigenous western highlands,[41] some of my interviewees do remember violent incidents from those years. For instance, two women remember two sicarios (hit men) paid by a local landowner who was also head of a local government institution. This man, they say, "wanted to do limpieza in the town" and his hit men ended up killing around sixty people. "They would kill someone just because they didn't like the person," one of them recalls, while the other adds that they also killed a group of traveling teenage artists, because they were allegedly "putting revolutionary ideas" in people's heads. During those days, "after seven o'clock at night people would not go out anymore," they told me. "Many young people back then went to the United States because, otherwise, they would have been killed."[42]

Currently, Guastatoyans reportedly use extrajudicial violence against so-called criminals only as a last resort. Before resorting to violent means, they keep a close eye on suspects and investigate them, as they generally do with any strangers. They may also decide to confront or threaten them before taking a more extreme measure. One of my informants recounted how a woman confronted a group of young men who had been drinking and littering the front of her house almost every night. After failing to solve the problem through the local police, the woman decided to call her son-in-law, who arrived at her house, armed, and with a bodyguard. The man asked the young men to respect the woman's property, "or else they were going to have problems."[43]

During my fieldwork, people also referred to outsiders or so-called criminals being "thrown out" whenever they came to be regarded as a serious threat. In fact, a city councilman from Guastatoya mentioned this practice during an interview with *El Periódico* in 2010, as he explained why the town was so peaceful, "Here people reject every group of strangers that comes in. They investigate where they come from and what they do, and the information is immediately transferred to the authorities through the people in charge of the Citizen Security Local Juntas. An ultimatum is then given to the group before it is expelled."[44]

I did not find any evidence of a local junta being active in Guastatoya. What I did find were several stories about mareros being expelled from the town over the past few years. A local merchant, for example, recounted how an organized group of neighbors had thrown out a street gang from Jalapa that had settled in a commercial neighborhood in Guastatoya.[45] A woman working for the local state justice system, in turn, mentioned that the authorities had expelled a *mara* from Guatemala City that had arrived in Guastatoya a few years ago, "to set up drug-sale spots."[46] Similarly, a local municipal official recounted how some people in a village had decided to throw out a gang member who had broken into someone's house.[47]

As one of my informants admitted, however, references to people being "thrown out" often masked extralegal killings.[48] Although the frequency of these killings is impossible to establish, most of my interviewees assured me these types of incidents are rare but certainly not new. Some cases seem to involve an organization or group connected to state officials or to organized crime. A young man, for example, attributed these killings to "heavy people, as we say here; people with money and power."[49] Others referred to "an organization"[50] or a "small group of people."[51] But in some cases local neighbors apparently acted alone, with explicit or implicit acquiescence of the police. As such, these groups seem to operate in that "gray zone" between political and criminal violence that, as the introduction to this volume points out, characterizes many Latin American countries.[52] In contrast to what some researchers have found in other municipalities of eastern Guatemala, the hiring of sicarios seems to be a rare practice in Guastatoya.[53] Still, the question of who is responsible for these killings remains ambiguous, as the events are surrounded by secrecy and suppressed by people's fear to reveal more than they should. As a university student explained to me, "Here, they see a thief and they disappear him. . . . Here, they don't get to know who did it, or, if they know, they don't say who did it."[54]

In keeping with this veil of mystery, some of my informants mentioned incidents during which mareros or *patojos* (young kids) had been killed and their bodies had just "appeared" somewhere, sometimes bearing signs of torture. In some cases, not even the body was found; they just "disappeared." Men and women, youngsters and the elderly, state officials as well as professionals and merchants, recounted similar stories. "Three years ago, three marero kids came and began to break into houses. They killed the three of them."[55] "One time they caught five or six young kids in the river. They cut their parts off and put them in their mouths."[56] "Someone killed members of a small gang because they were stealing, and eight others [young men] because they were selling drugs."[57] "More or less two years ago, they caught some of them and dumped their bodies in front of the fire station. According to rumors, they were gang members, but others say they were drug traffickers."[58] "Here there was a movement of gang members, but here they do kill them. They appear [dead] one by one."[59] "When strangers come they identify them quickly, and then it is managed more easily. But they disappear quickly, too, I don't know how."[60] "Lately, there have been robberies, but locals disappear them. They kill them or take them somewhere else."[61] "But one thing is for sure: a criminal might come in here, but people quickly disappear him. He turns up dead without being heard."[62] "They do it quietly. The person is simply not there anymore."[63] "One is the judge, one does the trial, because the police do nothing."[64]

Although street gangs do seem to have been present in Guastatoya, locals also seem to use "marero" loosely to refer to any young kid who deviates from local moral standards. Young tuctuc drivers, for example, are often associated with mareros because of their suspicious activities, careless driving, loud music, and the funky motifs decorating their mototaxis. As Gema Santamaría and David Carey Jr. argue in the introduction, public representations of criminals or wrongdoers contribute to shaping and justifying people's violent reactions against them. Anthropologists working in Guatemala have identified similar dynamics of representation in indigenous communities like Todos Santos, Huehuetenango,[65] and Nahualá, Sololá,[66] where elderly, well-established community members often refer to young kids as mareros out of fear and to justify control over them. These people's views may be grounded in real concerns, but they are also a sign of the changing sociopolitical dynamics and attitudes toward youth in Guatemala. As Deborah T. Levenson argues, urban youth has been vilified and portrayed as "an obstacle to the future instead of its herald."[67] In such a context, older generations in power can manipulate public representations of violence as a means of "achieving the moral high ground on a contested sociopolitical terrain."[68]

In addition to stereotypes and prejudices, fear of crime becoming uncontrollable also plays a role in justifying violence.[69] Many people in Guastatoya regard taking violent measures against suspected wrong-doers as a bad but necessary step to control crime. For example, when explaining why he approved of such "immoral" actions, a young man said, "Because they let that [crime] progress and afterwards it can't be controlled. Look at Guate [Guatemala City], look at Sanarate."[70] This man's concern about crime can be interpreted as fear of indiscriminate violence, which is a particular kind of fear. Whereas under targeted violence people believe they can remain unharmed as long as they avoid taking risks, under indiscriminate violence people believe there is no way to remain safe and either become paralyzed by fear or decide to defend themselves.[71] This is a small but important distinction between kinds of fear. People who experience indiscriminate violence are more likely to engage in acts of aggression, because they see them as necessary acts of self-defense. In fact, because of its overwhelming nature, indiscriminate violence "erases the relationship between crime and punishment, thus abolishing the concept of transgression."[72] Mareros, whether real or perceived, embody this kind of violence in Guatemala. People see them as merciless incarnations of evil who will kill anybody for no reason. Their views may be chillingly accurate in some cases; but in others, they may reflect sensationalized and distorted media representations.[73] In the context of a petty theft or a more serious crime, a simple tattoo, a hairstyle, or a genre of music can thus be taken as definitive evidence of gang membership where there is actually none.

In sharp contrast to the silence and secrecy surrounding these killings, an incident that took place in 2006 in Guastatoya was highly visible and resembled a lynching. In fact, a few of my informants regarded it as such. The victim was, according to one person, a "big-time thief [ladronazo]" who had been incarcerated many times for various crimes. "I knew him. They would put him in jail, he would get out, they would put him in jail again."[74] According to locals, the man had repeatedly been warned about the potential consequences of his actions and had even been offered a job if he would stop stealing. This time, however, a group of young men who caught him red-handed decided to take justice into their own hands. They beat him and dragged him for five blocks to a street not far from the local police station. Some people claim the police never arrived while others say they arrived too late. Others say the police did arrive on time but decided to turn a blind eye. A man recalled someone asking the police to "step back a couple of blocks" and said the police agreed to this and told everyone "to go ahead and trash the guy."[75] The killing allegedly took place in one of the town's main streets. "They were like fifteen people," who beat him with fists, sticks, and stones, while the rest of the neighbors, "when hearing the screams, came out to the streets."[76] The man, who, according to one person, "was the worst, the scummiest, the lowest,"[77] died after the beating. "They beat him up with sticks. They beat him up and killed him in a very public place," a woman recalled. "When people see that authorities don't act, they decide to do this. It is bad, but it is good. . . . People who did it got fed up and saw it as their only way out," she added.[78]

The Visibility and Invisibility of Violence in Guastatoya

Guastatoya lives under a regime of silence. Most of my informants, when mentioning deadly acts of violence, avoided giving any details for fear of reprisals. "Here there is a saying which says that walls have ears and that rocks talk," a state agent expressed to me with concern.[79] The secrecy surrounding Guastatoya's violence has been pointed out as a distinctive feature of violence against suspected criminals in eastern Guatemala, one that stands in sharp contrast to the publicity of lynchings taking place in other parts of the country.[80] Indeed, most of the killings my informants described occurred out of the public eye, with people disappearing and bodies turning up somewhere afterwards. As during the war period, these acts of limpieza social often either remain obscure for years or perpetrators end up getting away with murder.

The public incident described earlier, however, suggests that the apparent invisibility of Guastatoya's violence may be determined by factors that go beyond the perpetrators' methods. Although some of my informants labeled the incident a lynching, the police never reported it as such in their official statistics. "They regarded it as limpieza," one of my informants said.[81] In fact, according to police figures, no lynchings occurred in Guastatoya from 2001 to 2011.[82] The only reference to this kind of violence during that period appears in a 2011 report on local conflicts published by the Human Rights Ombudsman Office, which lists "limpieza social" as one of the town's main problems.[83] Although this may be an isolated case, recent ethnographic research suggests the police are not reporting lynchings in some other municipalities of eastern Guatemala either. Regina Bateson, for example, found strong evidence of violent incidents similar to lynchings in Agua Blanca, Jutiapa, a municipality close to El Salvador. However, as in Guastatoya, police official statistics report no lynchings in that municipality from 2001 to 2011.[84] Similarly, a study reported that in 2007 a group of angry neighbors publicly killed a woman accused of stealing children in Camotán, another town in eastern Guatemala.[85] That year, however, the police reported only two cases of people being injured—not killed—by lynching in that community. In fact, the police did not report any deaths by lynching in Camotán in 2001–11.[86] In 2007, an attempted lynching took place in Jocotán, a municipality close to Camotán.[87] As in the previous cases, police statistics did not report any deaths or injuries by lynching in Jocotán in that year.[88]

The reasons why police do not report certain killings may vary from case to case, and they quite likely follow from weak police investigative capacities. Nonetheless, there are two other possible reasons why the police did not register these incidents as lynchings. First, police officers in Guatemala have often been involved in extrajudicial killings. Some of my informants suggested that this is particularly true in Guastatoya. The direct or indirect involvement of police officers in these violent acts might partly explain the gaps in official statistics. As Angélica Durán-Martínez argues in chapter 10, the visibility of violence can be shaped by the relationship between state officials and criminal organizations.

A second possible reason has to do with the racialization of lynchings in Guatemala. Several of my informants assured me that "there are no lynchings in Guastatoya," associating those practices with indigenous communities. For example, a young ladino man in his twenties stated lynchings did not occur there because, "In Guastatoya there are no indigenous people. . . . There are no Maya rites here."[89] Similarly, other informants argued that lynchings did not occur there because Guastatoyans were more educated,[90] or simply because they "think before [they] act."[91] In other words, in a town where most people self-identify as non-indigenous, acts of deadly violence against suspected criminals are not regarded as lynchings because lynchings are associated with the "savage," "barbaric," "ignorant," and "backward" world of the underclass and indigenous people. As Gema Santamaría demonstrates in chapter 2, this was commonly how newspapers represented lynchings in Mexico during the 1930s. In the context of Guatemala, to interpret lynchings in class and racial terms reveals a way of seeing violence through an ideology that, as David Carey Jr. argues in chapter 6, tends to criminalize indigenous people. This ideology permeates even the smallest town and can affect the way in which newspapers and other media outlets represent acts of violence. It can also affect how police officers and other state agents construct their official reports and statistics.[92]

As the essays in this volume emphasize, in many Latin American regions actions are considered criminal and become public, or vice versa depending on local power dynamics and representations of victims and perpetrators. Even within cities portrayed as plagued by criminal violence, the extreme publicity of some acts can make other similar acts less visible, depending on social, political and geographic factors (compare Enrique Desmond Arias and Kayyonne Marston in chapter 11). In Guatemala, an appraisal that accounts for not only the characteristics of violence but also the ways in which ethnic and state-society relations shape the meanings and representations of violence would provide a more complete view of the phenomenon.

Notes

This chapter is based on ethnographic research I carried out in Guastatoya during the fall of 2011 and spring of 2012. To protect participants' anonymity, all the interviews are coded with a letter and number. The letter "B" refers to a state agent, whereas "C" denotes a local resident.

I would like to thank John Markoff and the editors of this volume, Gema Santamaría and David Carey Jr., for their detailed and valuable comments and suggestions on previous versions of this chapter. I presented some of these findings at the 30th International Congress of the Latin American Studies Association in San Francisco in May 2012.

1. Misión de Verificación de las Naciones Unidas en Guatemala (MINUGUA), *Los linchamientos: un flagelo contra la dignidad humana* (Guatemala: MINUGUA, 2000); MINUGUA, *Los linchamientos: un flagelo que persiste* (Guatemala: MINUGUA, 2002); Angelina Snodgrass Godoy, *Popular Injustice, Violence, Community, and Law in Latin America* (Stanford, CA: Stanford University Press, 2006); Jim Handy, "Chicken Thieves, Witches, and Judges: Vigilante Justice and Customary Law in

Guatemala," *Journal of Latin American Studies* 36 (2004): 553; Marta Estela Gutiérrez and Paul Hans Kobrak, *Los linchamientos pos conflicto y violencia colectiva en Huehuetenango* (Guatemala, Huehuetenango: CEDFOG, 2001).

2. Brent Metz, Lorenzo Mariano, and Julián López García, "The Violence after 'La Violencia' in the Ch'orti' Region of Eastern Guatemala," *Journal of Latin American and Caribbean Anthropology* 15 (2010): 16–41; Regina Bateson, "Lynchings in Guatemala: A Legacy of Civil War?" (paper presented at the 30th LASA Congress, San Francisco, CA, May 25, 2012).

3. Leslie Wirpsa, "Deadly 'Social Cleansing' Hits Latino Poor: Police Are Killing Kids in Colombia, Brazil—Cover Story," *National Catholic Reporter,* December 17, 1993, 12, quoted incompletely in Elizabeth F. Schwartz, "Getting Away with Murder: Social Cleansing in Colombia and the Role of the United States," *University of Miami Inter-American Law Review* 27, no. 2 (1995–96): 384.

4. Schwartz, "Getting away with Murder," 384.

5. The term *marero* comes from the word *mara*, which is commonly used in Central America to refer to street gangs.

6. Comisión para el Esclarecimiento Histórico (CEH), *Guatemala, memoria del silencio* (Guatemala City: CEH, 1999), vol. 2, paragraphs 1059–60.

7. Ibid., paragraph 1060. My translation from Spanish. From here on, all translations from Spanish are my own.

8. *El Imparcial,* August 2, 1978, quoted in CEH, *Guatemala, memoria del silencio,* vol. 2, paragraph 1108.

9. Jennifer Schirmer, *The Guatemalan Military Project: A Violence Called Democracy* (Philadelphia: University of Pennsylvania Press, 1998), 186–205.

10. Ibid., 199.

11. Archivo Histórico de la Policía Nacional (AHPN), *Del silencio a la memoria. Revelaciones del Archivo Histórico de la Policía Nacional* (Guatemala: AHPN, 2011), 293–303.

12. CEH, *Guatemala, memoria del silencio,* vol. 2, paragraphs 1110, 1111. See paragraph 1131 for a related use of the term.

13. Ibid., paragraph 1844.

14. The Human Rights Ombudsman Office used signs of torture and the location of bodies described in newspaper reports as indicators of deaths by *limpieza social*. It reported that 327 bodies had signs of torture and 648 were found in places away from where they were killed. See Procurador de los Derechos Humanos, *Las características de las muertes violentas en el país,* 10–16, www.pdh.org.gt/archivos/descargas/Documentos/Informes%20Especiales/carácterísticas_de_las_muertes_violentas_pdh.pdf.

15. United Nations Human Rights Council, *Civil and political rights, including the questions of disappearances and summary executions: Report of the special rapporteur on extrajudicial, summary or arbitrary executions,* www.extrajudicialexecutions.org/application/media/A_HRC_4_20_Add_2.pdf.

16. Ladinos are Guatemalans of mixed ancestry who usually accentuate their Spanish and European heritage and play down or completely deny their indigenous roots.

They usually speak Spanish and live in relatively better conditions than indigenous people do.

17. Programa de las Naciones Unidas para el Desarrollo (PNUD), *Informe nacional de desarrollo humano: anexo estadístico* (Guatemala City: PNUD, 2005).

18. For droughts, see Claudia Dary, *Entre el hogar y la vega: estudio sobre la participación femenina en la agricultura de El Progreso* (Guatemala: FLACSO, 1994).

19. Ibid., 87–150.

20. Interview C21.

21. Interview C64.

22. Consejo Municipal de Desarrollo del Municipio de Guastatoya y SEGEPLAN, DPT, *Plan de desarrollo, Guastatoya, El Progreso* (Guatemala: SEGEPLAN/DPT, 2010), 1.

23. Interview C66.

24. Interview C40.

25. United Nations Office on Drugs and Crime (UNODC), *Global Study on Homicide, 2013: Trends, Contexts, Data,* www.unodc.org/documents/gsh/pdfs/2014_GLOBAL_HOMICIDE_BOOK_web.pdf.

26. Interview C49.

27. Dary, *Entre el hogar y la vega,* 60.

28. Interview B19.

29. Interview B22.

30. Interview B41.

31. Interview B16.

32. Interview C63.

33. Policía Nacional Civil, "Estadísticas de hechos delictivos registrados por departamento y municipio, 2001–2011" (unpublished dataset).

34. Interview B21.

35. Interview B14.

36. Interview C42.

37. Interview C44.

38. Interview C54.

39. Marie-Louise Glebbeek, "Police Reform and the Peace Process in Guatemala: The Fifth Promotion of the National Civil Police," *Bulletin of Latin American Research* 20 (2001): 443. See also Francisco Martínez, "En cada retén hay uno," *Revista D, Semanario de Prensa Libre,* September 19, 2004.

40. Interview C45.

41. CEH, *Guatemala, memoria del silencio;* Patrick Ball, "AAAS/CIIDH database of human rights violations in Guatemala (ATV20.1)," Human Rights Data Analysis Group, 1999, https://hrdag.org/guatemala-ciidh-data/. The data are published with this disclaimer: "These are convenience sample data, and as such they are not a statistically representative sample of events in this conflict. These data do not support conclusions about patterns, trends, or other substantive comparisons (such as over time, space, ethnicity, age, etc.)."

42. Interview C64.

43. Interview B6.

44. Rosmery González, "Estudio revela departamentos con problemas mínimos de violencia," *El Periódico,* February 20, 2010, 6.

45. Interview C42.

46. Interview B32.

47. Interview B8.

48. Interview B6.

49. Interview C63.

50. Interview B16.

51. Interview C34; Interview C40.

52. Javier Auyero, *Routine Politics and Violence in Argentina: The Gray Zone of State Power* (New York: Cambridge University Press, 2007).

53. Regina Bateson found this practice to be common in Agua Blanca, Jutiapa, while Debra Rodman found it to be common in San Pedro Pinula, Jalapa. See Bateson, "Lynchings in Guatemala"; Debra Rodman, "Forgotten Guatemala: Genocide, Truth, and Denial in Guatemala's Oriente," in *Genocide: Truth, Memory, and Representation,* ed. Alexander Laban Hinton and Kevin Lewis O'Neill (Durham, NC: Duke University Press, 2009), 207.

54. Interview B19.

55. Interview B27.

56. Interview B28.

57. Interview B29.

58. Interview B6.

59. Interview C30.

60. Interview C40.

61. Interview C56.

62. Interview C48.

63. Interview C31.

64. Interview C10.

65. Jennifer Burrell, *Maya after War: Conflict, Power, and Politics in Guatemala* (Austin: University of Texas Press, 2013).

66. Tristan P. Call, John P. Hawkins, James H. McDonald, and Walter Randolph Adams, "'There Is No Respect Now': Youth Power in Nahualá," in *Crisis of Governance in Maya Guatemala: Indigenous Responses to a Failing State,* ed. John P. Hawkins, James H. McDonald, and Walter Randolph Adams (Norman: University of Oklahoma Press, 2013), 218–42.

67. Deborah T. Levenson, *Adiós Niño: The Gangs of Guatemala City and the Politics of Death* (Durham, NC: Duke University Press, 2013), 2.

68. Peter Benson, Edward Fischer, and Kedron Thomas, "Resocializing Suffering: Neoliberalism, Accusation, and the Sociopolitical Context of Guatemala's New Violence," *Latin American Perspectives* 35 (2008): 42.

69. Mitchell A. Seligson, "Public Support for Due Process Rights: The Case of Guatemala," *Journal of the Southwest* 45, no. 4 (2003): 557–94; Krystin Krause, "Supporting the Iron Fist: Crime News, Public Opinion, and Authoritarian Crime Control in Guatemala," *Latin American Politics and Society* 56, no. 1 (2014): 98–119.

70. Interview C60.

71. Stathis N. Kalyvas, "The Paradox of Terrorism in Civil War," *Journal of Ethics* 8 (2004): 101–10.

72. Ibid., 104.

73. Levenson, *Adiós Niño*; Krause, "Supporting the Iron Fist."

74. Interview B24.

75. Interview C8.

76. Interview C60.

77. Interview C64.

78. Interview B24.

79. Interview B11.

80. Bateson, "Lynchings in Guatemala," 2. To contrast, see Regina Bateson, "Vigilantism in Postwar Guatemala" (paper presented at the Harvard-MIT-Yale Graduate Student Conference on Political Violence, April 23, 2011).

81. Interview C60.

82. Policía Nacional Civil, "Estadísticas de hechos delictivos."

83. Procuraduría de los Derechos Humanos, "Mapeo de conflictividad departamental de El Progreso correspondiente al año 2011" (El Progreso, Guatemala: Procuraduría de los Derechos Humanos, 2011).

84. See Bateson, "Lynchings in Guatemala"; Policía Nacional Civil, "Estadísticas de hechos delictivos."

85. Metz, Mariano, and López, "The Violence after 'La Violencia,'" 32–33.

86. Policía Nacional Civil, "Estadísticas de hechos delictivos."

87. Metz, Mariano, and López, "The Violence after 'La Violencia,'" 33.

88. Policía Nacional Civil, "Estadísticas de hechos delictivos."

89. Interview B40.

90. Interview B52; Interview B34.

91. Interview C52. Other informants claimed Guastatoyans simply did not have the "courage" to do something like that.

92. For an early study of how social dynamics can influence official crime reports, see Donald J. Black, "Production of Crime Rates," *American Sociological Review* 35 (1970): 733–48.

10 Silent Traffickers or Brutal Criminals

How State Power Shapes Criminals' Incentives to Expose Violence

Angélica Durán-Martínez

On November 6, 1986, Los Extraditables, a group founded by the Medellín Drug Trafficking Organization (DTO), officially made itself known to the Colombian public when it released a document calling for the end of extradition "in the name of national sovereignty, family rights, and human rights."[1] Over the following five years, the organization was responsible for a deadly period that claimed hundreds of lives. The evolution of Los Extraditables was marked by its willingness to claim responsibility for attacks, usually through communiqués that conveyed its rationale for the use of violence.

Los Extraditables's interest in publicity stands in sharp contrast to the efforts of the Arellano Félix Organization (AFO) in Tijuana, Mexico, to hide its violent acts in the 1990s and 2000s, exemplified by the use of acid to render unidentifiable the corpses of people killed by traffickers. The remains would be dumped in sewage systems or buried on the outskirts of the city. Such techniques of hiding attacks only became public in 2009, when Mexican authorities captured AFO member Santiago Meza, known as "El Pozolero del Teo."[2] Meza admitted that he and his associates had worked for the AFO and its enforcers, El Efra and El Teo, for more than ten years, and had disintegrated more than three hundred bodies.[3] Rather than publicly claiming responsibility, as Los Extraditables did, the AFO hid its attacks. Since the mid-1990s a few human rights organizations had been denouncing the disappearances of people thought to have been victims of drug traffickers in Baja California, and perhaps some of them were victims of the AFO.[4]

These contrasting cases highlight a crucial puzzle: Why would some criminal organizations, like Los Extraditables, perform visible violence that attracts attention from law enforcement and the media when this could be detrimental to their criminal interests? To answer this question I systematically explore the visibility of lethal violence. "Visibility" refers to instances where criminals claim responsibility for or publicly expose their attacks. I argue that interactions between state and criminal agents determine the visibility of lethal violence. Criminals may refrain from using visible violence when they receive stable state protection they fear to lose, or when they fear that the state could mount effective actions against them, and therefore prefer to lower their profile to avoid law enforcement. This argument questions the concept that violence is a simple reflection of a weak state; instead, active state involvement, whether aimed at protecting or confronting criminals, can shape how public criminal violence is. This chapter thus resonates with Arias and Marston's argument in chapter 11 that the nature of political-criminal alliances influence which forms of crime various publics recognize or ignore. It also shows, as the editors emphasize in the introduction, how relations between different social actors, in this case between criminals and state, shape crime in Latin America.

Other contributions to this volume focus on how audiences represent, normalize, reproduce, or react to violence. I focus instead on criminals' motivations to conceal, or alternatively, reveal, violence. Of course, public representations are key to understanding why visible violence effectively attracts attention: both civilians and states react differently to hierarchies of violence, as many contributors to this volume highlight. Representations alone, however, cannot explain the complex and contradictory incentives that drive traffickers' violent behavior and that make them active creators of categories of violence. The judicial testimony of El Pozolero precisely illustrates that traffickers' violent strategies can change over time: for almost a decade his job was to eliminate the evidence of violence; later, in 2008, he was specifically instructed that instead of burying the victims' remains, he should place them in the middle of well-transited streets, along with a note.

Though drug violence can also vary along the dimension of frequency, I focus on visibility because it is both the product of and a contributor to imaginaries of violence, reflects power relations between states and criminals, and shapes responses to violence, all key topics in this volume.[5] This does not mean that criminals can foresee how people create imaginaries about victims or perpetrators, but rather that their violent tactics can contribute to creating such imaginaries.

In the first section of the chapter I discuss the relevance of assessing visibility and operationalize the concept. Next I explain how traffickers' decision to expose violence results from their interaction with the state, using the cases of Los Extraditables in Medellín and the AFO in Tijuana. Finally, I explain how visibility is distinct from related concepts like brutality or symbolic violence, and from dynamics of media coverage. I conclude with implications of the analysis.

Visibility: Understanding the Content of Drug Violence

Literature on violence by non-state actors and during civil wars provides the crucial insight that variation in levels and types of violence is not purely irrational but rather purposeful.[6] Criminals' apparently irrational use of excessive violence that attracts enforcement attention can thus be seen as a strategic decision. Of course, violence is not always rational, and not all perpetrators are strategic thinkers, but many behaviors that appear gratuitous do, in fact, have clear motivations. The literature on illicit markets explores why violence can change and reach extreme levels, but it rarely considers that particular forms of violence can meet different strategic needs.[7]

Visibility refers to whether criminals expose or claim responsibility for their attacks in order to scare away enemies, retaliate against government action, or attempt to modify government behavior. Visible violence is similar to signaling in civil wars and terrorist actions. In civil wars, armed actors may deploy violence strategically to signal power and strength, infuse fear, and serve as a coercive tool that elicits civilian collaboration. Yet not all forms of physical violence generate the same reaction, and thus insurgents may choose to manipulate violent images to mobilize the population.[8] Similarly, terrorism can be a signaling tactic that emerges when rebels are weak and lack the power to extract concessions or impose their will on rivals, but want nevertheless to show power and resolve to attack, or to provoke state reactions that help them expand their support base.[9]

Unlike insurgents and terrorist organizations, drug trafficking organizations may benefit from, but do not depend on, civilian support for their survival. Rather, traffickers often require direct or indirect collaboration of state actors to operate. In consequence, a trafficker's violent act that signals power not only increases the risk of detention, as terrorist actions do,[10] but may also jeopardize state protection. A characterization of violence in criminal markets thus should account for its effects on the relationship between criminals and the state. It should also explain the repertoire of violent strategies criminals can use.

Different forms of violence elicit different state reactions and also reach different publics.[11] In turn, traffickers use violence that is functional in solving disputes and showing power, but simultaneously may choose to avoid violence that may attract enforcement attention and thus be detrimental.[12] In Colombia in the 1990s, the government persecuted Pablo Escobar and the Medellín DTO more severely than their rival Cali DTO. As a former minister of defense acknowledged, the government focused on Escobar in response to his extremely violent techniques because "a group placing bombs generates more social rejection"; unlike individual murders committed in marginalized areas, bombs are likely to affect the public at large and generate opposition even among those who are not directly victimized.[13] Similarly, since the Mexican government's declaration of war against trafficking organizations and its deployment of federal and army troops to cities in 2006, certain forms of violence have influenced decisions about where to mobilize federal troops. A high-level official described, for instance, that when masked gunmen stopped traffic on a busy highway in the state of Veracruz and dumped thirty-five bodies in broad daylight in September 2011, the federal government resolved to deploy troops to the area. This was not the first violent event in the region, but it was particularly visible: "[before that event] Veracruz did not report kidnappings and kept the statistics secret. People didn't know [about violence], but then, to make people aware, traffickers dumped thirty-five corpses. Those are clear images that say 'I'm the boss.' Of course, we hurried and we had to react to that. That's how we operate."[14]

Visibility affects not only the state's reaction, but also people's perceptions: before violence skyrocketed in 2006 Mexicans tended to see drug violence as respectful of honor codes and limited to "them" (criminal elements), in sharp contrast to the violence that ensued after that time, perceived as generalized, random, and dishonorable because it was thought to affect innocent people "outside" the criminal world. As other chapters in this volume discuss, social constructions of class, gender, and ethnicity can influence representations of violence, the application of the law, and state and civilian reactions. In the cases of ley fuga Pablo Piccato describes in chapter 1, or the lynchings Gema Santamaría describes in chapter 2, such constructions affect whether the general public believes in the guilt of the victim, which in turn determines whether these practices are legitimized or rejected. Similarly, the material characteristics of violence can also shape imaginaries about perpetrators and victims: less visible violence can easily be ignored or dismissed as limited to the criminal underworld. By contrast, when criminals commit visible violence, ignoring or legitimizing it becomes more difficult.[15]

The concept of visibility reveals potential tradeoffs in criminals' use of violence. Visibility enables traffickers to show power or infuse fear, but has the disadvantage of generating state attention and potential civilian outrage. Visibility thus captures instrumental changes in the use of violence.

Operationalizing Visibility

More than body counts are needed to characterize visibility; indicators should also reflect the various ways violence can be enacted.[16] I operationalize visibility using four indicators: the type of victims; the number of victims per attack; whether criminals claim responsibility for attacks; and whether the methods used to perform violence are designed to draw publicity.

The type of victims affects visibility because when criminals target public officials or public personalities like journalists, they are exposing themselves. Criminals may not necessarily target public figures to seek state or media attention, yet killing a rival clearly does not expose violence in the same way that killing a public official does.[17] In terms of the number of victims, the more victims there are, the more likely an event is going to be noticed by the public. A claim of responsibility signals criminals' interest in gaining the violent reputation associated with a particular attack. Finally, the methods used to carry out violence expose attacks in different ways; a corpse bearing gruesome evidence of torture and mutilation is far more visible than one with a single bullet to the head.

To illustrate the analytical value of operationalizing visibility, I briefly present results of a dataset created for a larger research project examining variation in drug violence across five cities in Colombia (Cali and Medellín) and Mexico (Ciudad Juárez, Culiacán, and Tijuana). The dataset contains at least three years of reports from the main newspapers in each of these five cities, documenting 6,497 events disaggregated along sixty variables.[18] It includes violent events that were directly attributed to drug traffickers or could reasonably be linked to them given the methods used, the victim, or the background provided. I do not assume that all victims of drug violence are either criminals or law enforcement, even though this method may overestimate drug-related crimes.

Table 10.1 summarizes the number of occurrences of each indicator in each city for the years studied. Visibility increases in a given city in correspondence with direct claims of responsibility, exposure of violence, number of victims per attack, and number of public figures (politicians, law enforcement, journalists) targeted.

Table 10.2 shows that the most common method of killing, the simple use of firearms, is not very visible, and that the most visible methods, such as mutilated corpses with notes attached, represent only a small proportion of total violent events. This can explain why most acts of drug violence can be ignored and why just a few attacks can create an image of extreme brutality. In addition, the media and the public stigmatize victims of drug violence as criminals who deserved to die, increasing the invisibility of many victims. The key point, however, is that the visibility of victims is a function not only of their class, race, gender, and criminal background, but also of how criminals purposefully perpetrate violence against them. Of course, how a killing is portrayed can also sway public opinion, as Piccato notes in chapter 1, creating an emotional context in newspaper reports was essential to legitimizing ley fuga cases. Manipulation was also evident in how reports about lynchings differed depending on who the victims or perpetrators were, as Santamaría points out. The point is that visible violence is more amenable to manipulation in the media, which is why it becomes effective: it is in itself a representation. Even if they are not representative of most murders, visible acts are crucial because a small number of such cases can affect public responses

		Events with high-visibility methods	Collective attacks (3+ victims)	Number of public targets*	Events with direct claim of responsibility†	Total Events
City	Year					
Cali	1984	4	2	2	0	41
Cali	1989	23	10	8	1	199
Cali	2009	8	3	4	0	79
Cd. Juárez	1984	7	0	1	0	131
Cd. Juárez	2010	86	101	61	4	689
Culiacán	1984	8	4	3	0	66
Culiacán	1986	15	4	12	0	140
Culiacán	1992	13	3	4	0	85
Culiacán	1996	9	1	2	0	120
Culiacán	2002	11	1	3	0	99
Culiacán	2009	71	11	8	13	252
Culiacán	2010	136	19	22	14	558
Medellín	1984	21	2	16	0	257
Medellín	1989	110	26	27	3	1,281
Medellín	2009	6	11	2	0	73
Tijuana	1984	3	0	2	0	33
Tijuana	1992	5	3	1	0	127
Tijuana	2002	52	1	5	0	189
Tijuana	2010	93	20	9	9	405

Table 10.1

Acts of visible violence in Colombian and Mexican cities

* Public targets include politicians, police, and journalists.

† A note or message left at a crime scene does not necessarily entail a claim of responsibility. Here I include only events where a specific organization made a direct claim of responsibility.

and perceptions more directly than a large number of nonvisible acts do. For example, the Colombian government enforced extradition treaties for traffickers after the assassination of Minister of Justice Rodrigo Lara Bonilla in 1984. Similarly, Mexican President Felipe Calderón deployed troops in his home state of Michoacán soon after the Familia Michoacana DTO threw five severed heads on the floor of a dance club in 2006.[19]

Table 10.2.
Violent acts by method in Colombian and Mexican cities

Method or key feature of event	Incidents (in order of frequency)	Percentage of total
Simple use of firearms	2,926	49.87
Drive-by shooting (*sicariato*)	1,206	20.56
Torture	379	6.46
Simple use of knives	374	6.37
Forced disappearance (*paseo* or *levantón*)	260	4.43
Combat with firearms	186	3.17
Wrapped in blanket	104	1.77
Corpse with note	98	1.67
Simple use of explosives	78	1.33
Mutilation or incineration without note	72	1.23
Mutilation or incineration with note	40	0.68
Fire	30	0.51
Strangulation	28	0.48
Car bomb	21	0.36
Dismembered head placed in cooler	17	0.29
Sexual violence	17	0.29
Grenade	13	0.22
Combat with explosives	9	0.15
Combat with explosives and firearms	6	0.1
Combat with knives	1	0.02
Frozen corpse	1	0.02
Poisoning	1	0.02
Total	5,867	100

Author's dataset, Cali and Medellín, Colombia, and Ciudad Juárez, Culiacán, and Tijuana, Mexico n = 5,867. Events with missing information not included.

Decisions to Expose or Hide Violence:
The Tradeoff of State Protection

Visibility depends on the interaction between a state and a criminal organization. Criminals may refrain from using visible violence if the state is cohesive. Cohesion refers to whether there is coordination among levels of government and across enforcement agencies, and whether public officials have relatively long time horizons (there is low rotation of appointed or elected officials). A cohesive state is effective at attacking, or alternatively protecting, a criminal organization, and in such a context criminals may refrain from using violence that could force an effective, or otherwise friendly state to act against them. By contrast, criminals may expose violence when the state is fragmented because protection and enforcement become more unpredictable. In a fragmented state coordination across agencies is difficult and hence some actors may protect criminals while others pursue them. When criminals have little fear of state action and little benefit of predictable state protection, they gain incentives to expose—or simply lose incentives to make the extra effort to hide—violence. Visible violence is not directed exclusively against the state: once the incentive to hide disappears, criminals may decide, depending on their interests, to use visible violence against their rivals, the state, or even civilians. One could argue that competition in the criminal market, or the relations between criminals and citizens, could also create incentives for visibility, because criminals benefit from a violent reputation when they need to eliminate rivals, fight for leadership, or defend turf and territory from competitors. Yet, in a cohesive state, the fear of state enforcement, or fear of losing state protection, may often outweigh this incentive.

The confessions of paramilitary leaders after a demobilization process conducted in 2003 in Colombia illustrate the tradeoff between hiding and exposing violence, as well as how relationships with the state determine the calculus of how to use violence.[20] The confession of paramilitary commander Jorge Laverde before a judge captures the tradeoffs of exposing violence:

> *Laverde:* Sir, In Villa del Rosario, where the sugar mill used to be, near the river, we built an oven where approximately forty or fifty people could be cremated after they were killed. . . .

Judge: Aside from that oven, those ovens used to dispose of bodies or the remains of people that the paramilitary assassinated, did you use any other method to dispose of the bodies?

Laverde: Yes sir. They were thrown in the river.

Judge: Which river?

Laverde: The Zulia River.

Judge: Who made the decision to get rid of the people? Why get rid of the people? Why not simply kill them?

Laverde: That began a long time ago in Urabá. The commanders in Urabá ordered [us] to disappear those who had been killed. Salvatore Mancuso said, "There's a reason they're killed. Let the community see who was killed and that we are cleaning up the area." But Commander Castaño disagreed. He said, "If dead bodies start piling up, it would make the authorities look bad. And it could be detrimental to us as well."

Referring to a similar effort to bury bodies in mass graves, paramilitary commander Ever Veloza described how hiding violence might be essential when criminals collaborate with state authorities:

Judge: When did you stop leaving bodies in plain sight and start digging mass graves?

Veloza: The commanders were responsible for that. More and more people were killed in Urabá every day. The homicide rate was going through the roof.

Judge: Under which commanders?

Veloza: Police or army commanders. The homicide rate kept rising. They started being pressured by their superiors or the media or various government organizations or NGOs because violence was happening right under their noses. So they asked us to please get rid of the dead bodies, to bury them to keep the statistics from rising. That's when the mass grave system began to be implemented and used. They authorized killings but only with the understanding that the bodies would disappear.[21]

This relation between the state's ability to protect or prosecute criminals and the visibility of violence is also evident in the examples that open this chapter. The Medellín DTO, led by infamous trafficker Pablo Escobar, created Los Extraditables in the 1980s. Its violent acts are painfully imprinted in the memories of Colombians during a period known as narcoterrorism (1984–93), when criminals used visible attacks like car bombs; assassinated public officials, presidential candidates, and police officers; and claimed many civilian lives. This violence was particularly acute in Medellín, which in 1989 had an extremely high homicide rate of 258 per 100,000 residents and highly visible murders.

The actions of Los Extraditables and Pablo Escobar have been analyzed extensively and have often been attributed to Escobar's megalomania and his fight against extradition. Yet they also illustrate how visibility of violence surges when criminals operate within a fragmented state unable to provide credible protection and use violence to force changes in enforcement policies, in this case, extradition laws. Los Extraditables often claimed "not to be scared of deaths, press scandals, or repression."[22] In a death threat sent to a Supreme Court justice, they claimed "to have used all possible means, legal and democratic, to end the extradition treaty. But it looks like our fight is pointless when facing the pro-Yankee government supporters like you. . . . What will follow is total war and lead [bullets]."[23] The note illustrates how Los Extraditables could not entirely rely on the collaboration of state authorities and thus they threatened to use extreme violence until the extradition treaty was declared unconstitutional. Indeed, after a new Constitutional Assembly declared extradition unconstitutional in 1991, Los Extraditables released a communiqué announcing the dismantling of their military machinery and the end of all actions against their pro-extradition enemies.[24]

The Medellín DTO certainly had strong national and local networks of protection, but it also faced opposition from some political and law enforcement sectors. The organization emerged precisely when Colombia was undergoing a decentralization and democratization process that created opportunities for criminals to access the political system but also increased the possibilities for politicians to denounce corruption, thus augmenting the risk associated with colluding with traffickers. In this context, Pablo Escobar attempted to run for political office but met with strong opposition from many politicians, including Justice Minister Lara Bonilla, whose assassination prompted the government to enforce extradition treaties, which in turn motivated the creation of Los Extraditables.

In the 1980s the Colombian state was also fragmented because its law enforcement was unprepared to deal with the security threat posed by narcoterrorism. The government tried many strategies to combat the problem, such as massive military deployments in Medellín, which were unsuccessful and often generated tensions between local police and government forces, further undermining the state's ability to dismantle the Medellín DTO. Eventually, after Escobar died in 1993, visible violence receded and although by 2009 Medellín still had very high homicide rate (94 per 100,000), the violence was less visible. Traffickers learned that visibility could be detrimental to their interests, as they expressed in a 2011 proposal presented to Colombian authorities to negotiate another group's dismantlement: "nowadays, because of the legal measures that exist around the world, drug trafficking is still a highly profitable but risky business."[25]

Unlike the Medellín DTO, the AFO—operating in Tijuana in the 1980s—consolidated within a tight network of protection that linked local, state, and federal authorities in Mexico. This protection shielded traffickers from law enforcement and motivated them to closely regulate violence. When turf wars between the AFO and other cartels emerged, traffickers did not eschew violence, but they did hide it. This strategic interest in hiding violence was evident in the judicial testimony of El Pozolero. He claimed that the aim of placing corpses in acid was to disappear bodies. He did not kill the victims, he stated, and he received the corpses after they had been killed but did not not know their identity. His only function was instrumental, to hide the murders; he alleged he did not know the reasons for the killings. As a result of these strategies, indicators of visibility were very low in Tijuana in the 1980s and 1990s. — So perceptions of crime/violence low

The stable protection the AFO received resulted from a cohesive state grounded in the political control of the Institutional Revolutionary Party (PRI), which facilitated coordination across multiple enforcement agencies. State cohesion was further facilitated by the centralization of enforcement responsibilities in the Attorney General's Office, which meant the AFO received more predictable protection than the Medellín DTO did. I do not mean to imply that state corruption was greater in Tijuana than in Medellín, but merely that corruption networks were more stable and predictable in the Mexican city.

As political transition and changes in enforcement responsibilities fragmented Tijuana's corruption networks, protection became less predictable and traffickers started to lose incentives to hide violence. By the time confrontations between different factions of the AFO and other criminal organizations, like the Sinaloa DTO, exploded in 2008, there were few incentives for criminals to hide. In this context El Pozolero was instructed to expose the corpses instead of burying the remains, to send a message to a rival faction. By the time El Pozolero was captured in 2010, violence had become significantly more visible and use of methods such as notes claiming responsibility for attacks were recurrent.

In sum, states contribute to the reproduction of violence by shaping perpetrators' incentives, by normalizing or legitimizing less-visible violence, and by responding more forcefully to visible violence. When criminals expose violence as a result of changes in their relationship with the state, the government reacts more strongly, and both sides constantly re-create a cycle that produces hierarchies of violence. In the next section I explore how visibility relates to but is different from other classifications of violence, in dialogue with the findings of other chapters.

Visibility, Symbolic Violence, Brutality, and Media Coverage

The concept of visibility is connected to ideas about semantic and symbolic violence, which analyze violence as a communicating tool.[26] María Uribe, for example, analyzed the symbolism in massacres and mutilations in Colombia during the period of civil war known as La Violencia (1948–64).[27] She described how parts of the body were separated and sometimes relocated (for example, the legs would be placed where the head should be) to desecrate the victims and how notes were left at massacre scenes to advertise who the perpetrators were. Recent analyses of violence in Mexico have similarly focused on understanding why certain methods, especially beheadings, became prevalent after 2005, emphasizing the combination of cultural and technological factors (such as the spread of communication technologies) and the varied meanings and symbols associated with different methods of assassination.[28]

Unlike concepts of symbolic violence, visibility emphasizes not unique cultural manifestations but rather the instrumental character of violence. For example, Uribe explains recurrent massacres and mutilations among peasants as a result of a latent aggressiveness, an honor code that mandates revenge, and superstitions about the adversary ingrained in the foundations of peasant loyalties and culture.[29] Uribe clarifies that these practices were not simply pathological, but occurred under particular political circumstances, motivated by revenge and other instrumental objectives such as the elimination of opposing political parties. Yet she does not elaborate systematically on why a cultural propulsion to kill in barbaric ways was activated only under certain conditions.

Ideas about culturally based manifestations of symbolic violence may simplify the motivations for violence and stigmatize certain cultures. For example, Mexicans' familiarity with death, as Claudio Lomnitz points out, has led to the characterization of Mexican lower classes as potentially barbaric.[30] Such familiarity has also been used to explain brutality as the product of cultural influences, such as Aztec indigenous practices or, in recent years, the cult of the Santa Muerte (Holy Death) among the proletariat and criminals.[31] Cultural influences may inform brutal practices such as beheadings, but they cannot explain why such practices are only employed at certain times, or why the same criminal organization both uses and refrains from using these methods. The concept of visibility advanced here focuses on when and why visibility increases, rather than on disentangling the meanings, rituals, and cultural practices attached to forms of killing.

Media Representations

Visibility is also connected to research on media representations, which emphasizes how different performances of violence can shape perceptions of security among those who are not the direct victims of violence.[32] This research also explores how media representations of both victims and perpetrators affect the coverage of violent events, as other contributors to this volume have discussed. Visibility reveals the other side of the equation; that is, how perpetrators' choices about how to carry out violence shape media coverage and public reactions.

Media coverage may indeed manipulate the visibility, or invisibility, of violence. For example, in Tijuana after 2010, government authorities and business leaders have actively shaped perceptions of the city by manipulating media coverage of violence. Indeed, a businessman in Tijuana explained to me that a leading objective of the business sector's active engagement in security policies was to change perceptions of the city as a dangerous place: "We started to monitor TV stations, we looked at each newspaper to see how many beheadings and deaths appeared in the headlines, and then we identified who was the main advertiser in each of them. We sat with the newspaper owners and told them, 'If you continue publishing violence your advertisers will stop buying publicity.'"[33] Media coverage is thus not neutral, and media outlets can be coerced or corrupted into reporting violence by certain criminal groups and not their rivals, or can be pressured to downplay reports of violence when it is in the government's or business sector's interest to reduce perceptions of insecurity.

Criminals' changing strategies for conducting violence, however, can also affect media coverage. Some forms of violence are more likely to be covered than others (for example, the dumping of a beheaded body in a public place versus someone being shot on the outskirts of the city). A freelance journalist in Tijuana explained to me how her priorities in covering violence shifted as the criminals' violent techniques changed. In 2008–9 "high-impact" violence (shootouts, beheadings) was frequent, but by 2010 it had declined. Even though less visible violence still occurred, especially in poor neighborhoods, she could not hope to sell stories about "low-impact" violence while her colleagues in other parts of the country could offer far more lurid stories of beheaded bodies or terrorist acts. Her decision not to report less-visible violence was thus a response to media interests and priorities, but such interests did not cause the change in violent techniques that motivated her decision in the first place.

Table 10.3 illustrates how visibility influences media coverage by analyzing what events are covered on the front page or in the first section of newspapers by visibility index. The visibility index corresponds to the sum of four indicators of visibility (number of victims, type of victim, claim of responsibility, and method of killing). For each violent event, each indicator was given a value of 1 (low visibility), 2 (medium), or 3 (high) that then was summed to create an index of visibility ranging from 0 to 9 (0 means no information was available for a variable; no event scored 3 on all four indicators, thus the maximum value is 9). Higher numbers reflect higher visibility scores. The results show that even though a small fraction of events were covered on the front page, visible events were more likely to receive prime coverage.

Table 10.3
Prominence of newspaper coverage of murders by visibility index

Visibility Index	Reported on front page			Reported in first section		
	No	Yes	Total events	No	Yes	Total events
0	372 (100%)	0	372	327 (87.90%)	45 (21.10%)	372
1	617 (99.84%)	1 (0.16%)	618	543 (87.86%)	75 (12.4%)	618
2	1,933 (99.64%)	7 (0.36%)	1,940	1,778 (91.65%)	162 (8.35%)	1,940
3	770 (98.72%)	10 (1.28%)	780	697 (89.36%)	83 (10.64%)	780
4	935 (99.36%)	6 (0.64%)	941	828 (87.99%)	113 (12.01%)	941
5	403 (97.11%)	12 (2.89)	415	365 (87.95%)	50 (12.05%)	415
6	170 (96.59%)	6 (3.41%)	176	148 (84.09%)	28 (15.91%)	176
7	25 (96.15%)	1 (3.85%)	26	22 (84.62%)	4 (15.38%)	26
8	1 (50%)	1 (50%)	2	1 (50%)	1 (50%)	2
9	1 (100%)	0	1	1 (100%)	0	1
Total	5,227 (99.17%)	44 (0.83%)	5,271	4,710 (89.36%)	561 (10.64%)	5,271

All differences are statistically significant at p < .005.

Brutality

Visibility is also related to but different from brutality. Brutality is a category often used in academic and nonacademic analyses, but it is never clearly defined and is often used synonymously with irrationality, cruelty, sadism, barbarism, or savagery. A systematic analysis of the concept of brutality is thus difficult. Here, I identify brutality as instances of violence where the corpses are manipulated or desecrated (without any assumption as to why the bodies are treated in such ways).[34] Research on traditional mafia organizations illustrates the difference between brutality and visibility. Mafiosi used brutal methods to impose sanctions, retaliate against offenses, gain prestige, and overpower rivals.[35] Yet the "honor dimension of murder" led Mafiosi to show brutality only to direct victims, group members, or rivals. According to Arlacchi, the change from the traditional to an entrepreneurial mafia was marked precisely by an increase in the scope of violence, which was no longer held in check by traditional honor codes and which became visible to a wider public.

El Pozolero exemplifies the distinction between brutality and visibility. Traffickers' decision to dissolve bodies in acid or to disappear people may have been brutal but it was performed in order to hide violence. The idea of brutality therefore does not capture these strategic decisions. Visible violence can be and usually is brutal, but low visibility violence can be very brutal too. Violence is always evident to direct victims, but visibility implies that brutality transcends direct victims and is communicated to the general public.

Conclusion: Visibility, Criminal Behavior, and Public Representations of Violence

The concept of visibility captures intricate interactions between the politics and publics of violence. The politics of the interactions between a state and criminal organizations shapes criminals' violent behavior. Such violent behavior, in turn, shapes public representations of and reactions to violence. Governments and civilians tend to react differently to visible versus invisible violence, and their reactions, by shaping law enforcement and citizen responses, can contribute to the reproduction of violence. A systematic analysis of visibility has several implications for the analysis of violent criminal behavior and the audiences of violence, as well as for methodologies and policies.

First, visibility shows that low violence statistics may mask situations where criminals have not abandoned violence altogether, but rather have engaged in less-visible forms, as occurred in Tijuana at the height of AFO control. Low visibility should not be equated with the absence of violent criminality, because peaceful situations may result instead from the dominance of strong criminal powers or from symbiotic relations between states and criminals. Even if it is very frequent, low-visibility violence may not generate strong reactions from the government or the general public because it may not instill a sense of insecurity and fear in the population, or a sense of threat in the government. Low-visibility violence can thus become normalized. For example, between 2008 and 2012 Medellín experienced high levels of violence that affected many people, but they remained less visible than in the years of Los Extraditables among wealthier sectors of the population, the media, and the national government. This fact underscores the role that public representations play in the reproduction of crime and violence (see the introduction).

Second, states and citizens typically react more strongly to visible violence, thus perpetuating hierarchies of violence and victims; as the editors of this volume contend, illegality alone, or even violence alone, does not determine what acts civil society and the state deem reprehensible. The emphasis on visibility may contribute to escalating violence because some government reactions, especially militarized responses to criminality, often generate more violence. Specifically, violence did not diminish following militarized responses in Colombia or in Mexico. Visibility, however, can have a positive effect that should be analyzed more carefully in future research: the public outrage generated by visible violence can motivate civilians to mobilize and demand state action, and can mitigate the stigma against those who die by criminal violence. This has occurred in Mexico with the creation of the Movement for Peace and Dignity. Thus, perhaps under some circumstances citizen and public reactions can contribute to deterring violence.

Third, a recognition of visibility requires that evaluations of criminal violence do more than analyze homicide trends. It calls for a diversification of information sources and an attention to how violence is performed. If criminals successfully eliminate all evidence of a criminal act, it may never be recorded. Sources such as human rights reports are essential to document crimes with very low visibility, but these may emerge long after the violence occurs. The characterization of violence may become more time-consuming if it entails collecting and analyzing information from multiple sources, but doing so is critical for understanding the dynamics and impacts of violence.

Fourth, visibility has implications for policies aimed at reducing or targeting violence. Any policy effort has to start from broad analyses that encompass varied manifestations of violence. If law enforcement resources must be allocated to the most violent consequences of drug trafficking,[36] the assessment needs to be broad enough to capture instances that authorities may overlook because they are not visible. Another important policy implication is that enforcement targeting may focus enforcement on the most violent organizations while leaving untouched powerful organizations that hide violence.

Finally, the concept of visibility can help us understand changing patterns in other forms of organized violence. For example, vigilantism can take highly visible forms such as lynching or less visible forms, such as disappearances or social cleansing (see chapter 9). Similarly governments can also overtly display violence to reassert their power, as when they mobilize the military into territories that are considered lawless, but they can also hide it, as in extrajudicial killings. A systematic analysis of such patterns can yield a deeper comprehension of how different perpetrators understand, reproduce, and represent their own production of violence.

Notes

I thank Gema Santamaría and David Carey Jr. for their comments on this chapter.

1. "El Fin de Los Extraditables," *El Tiempo*, July 4, 1991.
2. *Pozolero* can be translated as "stewmaker." Pozole is a traditional Mexican soup.
3. Procuraduría General de la República de Mexico, Declaración ministerial MESA III AP/PGR/BC/TIJ/217/09-M-III.
4. Relative of a victim of disappearance, interview by the author, Tijuana, October 21, 2011.
5. Angélica Durán-Martínez, "Criminals, Cops, and Politicians: Dynamics of Drug Violence in Colombia and Mexico" (PhD diss., Brown University, 2013).
6. Stathis Kalyvas, *The Logic of Violence in Civil War* (New York: Cambridge University Press, 2006).
7. For changes in violence see Peter Andreas and Joel Wallman, "Illicit Markets and Violence: What Is the Relationship?" *Crime, Law and Social Change* 52, no. 3 (2009), 225–29; Richard Snyder and Angélica Durán-Martínez, "Does Illegality Breed Violence? Drug Trafficking and State-Sponsored Protection Rackets," *Crime, Law and Social Change* 52, no. 3 (2009): 253–73. On extreme increases in violence see Luis Astorga and David Shirk, "Drug Trafficking Organizations and Counter-Drug Strategies in the U.S.-Mexican Context," Working Paper Series on U.S.-Mexico Security Cooperation (Woodrow Wilson International Center for Scholars and Transborder Institute, University of San Diego: San Diego, CA, 2010); Benjamin Lessing, "The Logic of Violence in Criminal War: Cartel-State Conflict in Mexico, Colombia, and Brazil" (PhD diss., University of California, Berkeley, 2012); Javier Osorio, "Hobbes on Drugs: Understanding Drug Violence in Mexico" (PhD diss., University of Notre Dame, 2012); Viridiana Rios, "How Government Structure Encourages Criminal Violence: The Causes of Mexico's Drug War" (PhD diss., Harvard University, 2012). One of the few sources to consider strategic forms of violence is Phil Williams, "Cooperation among Criminal Organizations," in *Transnational Organized Crime and International Security: Business as Usual?*, ed. Mats Berdal and Monica Serrano (Boulder, CO: Lynne Rienner, 2002), 67–80.
8. Gordon McCormick and Frank Giordano, "Things Come Together: Symbolic Violence and Guerrilla Mobilization," *Third World Quarterly* 28, no. 2 (2007): 295–320.
9. Andrew Kydd and Barbara Walter, "The Strategies of Terrorism," *International Security* 31, no. 1 (2006): 49–80; Bruce Hoffman and Gordon H. McCormick, "Terrorism, Signaling, and Suicide Attack," *Studies in Conflict and Terrorism* 27, no. 4 (2004): 243–81.

10. Ibid.

11. Attracting media and law enforcement attention may not be the intended objective of using visible violence. Criminals may intend to get rivals' attention, but alerting law enforcement may be a side effect of exposing violence.

12. Michael Kenney, *From Pablo to Osama: Trafficking and Terrorist Networks, Government Bureaucracies, and Competitive Adaptation* (University Park: Pennsylvania State University, 2007).

13. Former Defense Minister, interview by the author, Bogotá, January 13, 2011.

14. Official from the Federal Secretariat of Public Security, interview by the author, Mexico City, September 27, 2011.

15. For a discussion about solidarity of bystanders in criminal wars see Andreas Schedler, "The Collapse of Solidarity in Criminal War: Citizen Indifference Towards the Victims of Organized Violence in Mexico" (paper presented at the 110th Annual Meeting of the American Political Science Association, Washington, DC, August 28–31, 2014).

16. Giovanni Sartori, "Concept Misformation in Comparative Politics," *American Political Science Review* 64, no. 4 (1970): 1033–53.

17. Some murders of public officials may generate little attention, as, for example, the isolated murder of street cops. Yet when police officers are systematically targeted, violence is certainly more visible, especially to urban and middle-class publics.

18. I thank Rocio Durán, Mundo Ramírez, and Ernesto Cañas for valuable assistance in constructing this dataset. News reports do present issues of reporting biases, incomplete information, or over-reporting. But they can provide a level of detail absent from official homicide statistics.

19. William Finnegan, "The Kingpins: The Fight for Guadalajara," *New Yorker,* July 12, 2012, www.newyorker.com/magazine/2012/07/02/the-kingpins (accessed November 3, 2014).

20. Paramilitary groups in Colombia straddle a thin line between political and criminal violence as they have had a political agenda and have consolidated their control on international drug trafficking since the late 1990s. By discussing them here, I do not intend to demonstrate either a criminal or political motivation to their actions but rather to show that visibility captures changes in the strategic use of violence, especially when state complicity is possible.

21. Confession hearings of commanders Jorge Laverde "El Iguano" and Ever Veloza "HH." Footage contained in documentary film *Impunity*, dir. Juan Jose Lozano and Hollman Morris (2011, DVD). Emphasis is mine.

22. Undated Los Extraditables communiqué, author's personal files.

23. Los Extraditables, undated letter threatening Supreme Court Justice Fernando Uribe, author's personal files.

24. Los Extraditables, comuniqué, Medellín, July 4, 1991, author's personal files.

25. Juan David Laverde Palma, "Oferta secreta de los narcos para entregarse," *El Espectador,* May 4, 2014, www.elespectador.com/noticias/judicial/oferta-secreta-de -los-narcos-entregarse-articulo-490272 (accessed July 30, 2015).

26. On symbolic violence see Anton Blok, "Mafia and Blood Symbolism" in *Risky Transactions: Trust, Kinship, and Ethnicity,* ed. F. Salter (New York: Berghahn

Books, 2002), 109–29; María V. Uribe, "Dismembering and Expelling: Semantics of Political Terror in Colombia," *Public Culture* 16, no. 1 (2004): 79–95. For the use of symbolic violence as a communication tool see Diego Gambetta, *Codes of the Underworld: How Criminals Communicate* (Princeton, NJ: Princeton University Press, 2008).

27. María V. Uribe, *Matar, rematar y contramatar: las masacres de la violencia en el Tolima, 1948–1964* (Bogotá: Cinep, 1990), 159–60.

28. See, for example, Howard Campbell, "Narco-Propaganda in the Mexican Drug War: An Anthropological Perspective," *Latin American Perspectives* 41, no. 2 (2014): 60–77; Robert Bunker and John Sullivan, "Extreme Barbarism, a Death Cult, and Holy Warriors in Mexico: Societal Warfare South of the Border?" *Small Wars Journal*, May 22, 2011, 1–10; Rossana Reguillo, "De las violencias: caligrafías y gramáticas del horror," *Desacatos* 40 (September–December 2012): 33–46.

29. Uribe, *Matar, Rematar y contramatar,* 34; María V. Uribe and Teófilo Vásquez, *Enterrar y callar: las masacres en Colombia, 1980–1993* (Bogotá: Comité Permanente por la Defensa de los Derechos Humanos, 1995).

30. Claudio Lomnitz, *Death and the Idea of Mexico* (New York: Zone Books, 2005).

31. Bunker and Sullivan, "Extreme Barbarism."

32. Michelle Slone, "Responses to Media Coverage of Terrorism," *Journal of Conflict Resolution* 44, no. 4 (2000): 508–22.

33. Businessman, interview by the author, Tijuana, October 18, 2011.

34. For a discussion on the related concept of extra-lethal violence see Lee Ann Fujii, "The Puzzle of Extra-Lethal Violence," *Perspectives on Politics* 11, no. 2 (2013): 410–26.

35. Pietro Arlacchi, *Mafia Business: The Mafia Ethic and the Spirit of Capitalism* (London: Verso, 1986), 14; Blok, "Mafia and Blood Symbolism," 28.

36. Mark Kleiman, "Surgical Strikes in the Drug Wars: Smarter Policies for Both Sides of the Border," *Foreign Policy* 90, no. 5 (2011): 89–101.

11 Selective Blindness

*Criminal Visibility and Violence in
Rio de Janeiro and Kingston*

Enrique Desmond Arias and Kayyonne Marston

Across Latin America and the Caribbean, crime has drawn immense attention over the past thirty years as governments seek to respond to citizens' increasing concerns about violent crime. Although the region suffers from a diverse array of criminal activities, some are more visible than others. While this is not surprising, we know little about the effects that the differential visibility of crime has on politics, society, and policy in the region. This chapter examines the more and less visible forms of crime in two historically crime-prone cities in the region: Rio de Janeiro, Brazil, and Kingston, Jamaica.

We argue that in both Rio and Kingston there exists a distinct texture to the discussions of criminal activity that privileges addressing some violent crimes over others. In Rio over the past thirty years, enormous interest has focused on the problems of drug gangs and responses to that problem, such as the Unidades de Policia Pacificadora (UPP, Police Pacification Units) program. Less attention, however, has been paid to extortion rackets and politically connected death squads. Similarly, many of the narratives on Jamaica's crime problem focus on partisan gangs in Kingston's inner-city communities, while much less attention has been paid to intra-elite corruption and drug trafficking rings on other parts of the island, often led by established members of the local business community. These particular foci of violence have affected criminal justice policy and illegal practices. We contend that the visibility of crime depends on the centrality of these activities to powerful groups and their potential impact on privileged spaces. This is consistent with the notion presented in the introduction to this volume that political and ideological processes as well as power dynamics significantly influence public views of crime. Understanding these perceptual limitations can help broaden our view of security in Rio and Kingston as well as in other violent spaces across the Americas.

Perceiving Violence

In recent years conflict scholars have stressed the logic of armed control in understanding violence. Armed actors and violence are not spread evenly across territory. Rather, they concentrate in pockets that Guillermo O'Donnell referred to as brown areas, but which are often referred to today as gray areas.[1] These zones are generally locales where there is an apparent absence of state power. Usually these spaces correlate strongly with poverty and exclusion and often become the focus of intensive, punitive criminal justice policy, especially when they are in close proximity to seats of wealth and power.[2] This view leads to the redoubling of state policy against long-oppressed populations while, at the same time, reducing state focus on other areas or activities that may merit serious criminal justice attention.

Comparatively neglected in the public discourse are violent activities in peri-urban and rural areas, and crimes such as extortion rackets that generate less visible patterns of violence. In many cases, elites engage in illicit activities and corruption with impunity, and, if the state reacts, its responses are usually more measured than when it targets marginalized communities. Differential perceptions of criminality within societies, as discussed in the introduction, reinforce existing political and power dynamics contributing to failed crime control policies. Through a discussion of crime in the Rio metropolitan area and in Kingston and Jamaica more broadly, we will offer a nuanced vision of violence and a framework for understanding how the visibility of violence is both informed and impacted by the politics and policies of crime in Latin America and the Caribbean.

The Politics of the Invisible

Scholarly literature has explored the ways in which different types of violence are made to be more or less visible in a given context, and with what consequences. Loïc Wacquant, for instance, has shown how states can

control disadvantaged populations through technologies of criminalization and mass incarceration, which are often normalized or rendered
invisible.[3] By the same token, studies in a variety of Latin American and
Caribbean contexts have shown how violence against socially excluded
populations is often obscured, and how those populations may resort to
violence both to control crime in their communities and to assert their
legitimate place in the political system by maintaining the type of order
the ruling classes accuse them of collectively disregarding.[4] Similarly, in
an effort to restore a perceived social order, police resort to extrajudicial
executions.[5] Even though extralegal violence does not reduce crime,
public support for both state and non-state forms of vigilantism helps
to legitimize this practice. Finally, work on civil conflicts and organized
crime has shown how armed organizations can make violence less visible by silencing or exerting control over given communities.[6]

These writings reflect the different dynamics behind patterns of
visibility and invisibility of violence. While there are many ways to
understand perceptions of violence, data we will examine in the coming
sections point to three axes that condition how scholars and public opinion collectively understand crime and violence.

First, the relationship between urban center and periphery contrib-
utes to textured perceptions of violence. In major cities, violence in the
urban core draws enormous attention. If there is a wave of robberies or a
gunfight in the central areas of a metropolis, large numbers of individuals either have personal knowledge of the event or see reports in the press.
The media, government, and non-governmental organizations all have
dense presences in these areas, as do some of the most well-connected
individuals and businesses. In outlying areas or suburbs, however, individuals have much less voice and presence in the news, policy, and even
academic discussions. This generates different levels and types of attention that help to reinforce varied patterns of violence and power.

The second axis of visibility is the violence associated with dominance
as opposed to contestation. Much attention is focused on public disorder
such as gunfights, riots, and roadblocks, which tend to appear in press
and government accounts and drive debate over and perceptions of the
problem of violence. As conflict scholars have made clear, however, areas
under the strong domination of armed groups tend to have fewer public
clashes. In these places violence may take the form of disappearances
and threats that silence people and thus these types of violence play a

much smaller role in defining debates and popular narratives on violence. In this way violence undertaken by powerful criminal or political actors receives little attention as compared to public clashes in locales where groups compete for power. This phenomenon is closely related to politically connected crime groups that, as Angélica Durán-Martínez discusses in chapter 10, may prefer to conceal or utilize less visible forms of violence in order to maintain state protection. In contemporary Latin America, the result of this is that public attention tends to focus on places where, as a result of the state's confrontation with armed actors, violence becomes more visible, rather than on areas where the state has ceded control to armed actors or is collaborating with those actors.

In this sense visibility and media attention are deeply intertwined with dominance and contestation. Where the state builds close relationships with armed actors, police confrontations and gang clashes decrease and criminals engage in surreptitious violence as they silence opponents and extort money from business leaders. Facing criminal domination, often in alliance with the state, reporters encounter material risks. This results in lesser media coverage and lower visibility.

The final axis of perception, consistent with the introduction to this volume, is related to the economic and social position of so-called perpetrators of crime and violence. Ordinary citizens are likely to be more interested in violent activities that affect their personal security than in nonviolent activities, like elite corruption, to which they have become accustomed and which they perceive as being only marginally connected to their own safety. Indeed, the experience of crime victimization has significant effects on individuals' participation in and perception of politics.[7] As we will discuss in this chapter, a great deal of attention is often paid to the socially excluded young men who populate the most violent communities while nonviolent crimes committed by elites tend to be ignored. Furthermore, police abuse and violence against these populations draw markedly less attention even as these actions tend to promote more violence and greater ties between the target community and illicit armed actors. Beyond police actions, high-level government decisions that tend to reinforce marginalization and violence, such as cuts to social services and inadequate pay and training of police, receive little attention. Finally, the voices of the poor, excluded, and marginal are collectively less visible than the voices of the well-off and powerful. Thus, narratives of violence are focused heavily on the broader interests and narrative of state actors or economic elites.[8]

In the following sections we examine the ways that each of these axes of perception operates in Rio de Janeiro and Kingston. The evidence in each section will show that the visibility and invisibility of violence operates in consistent ways across each city but also in ways that reflect the unique circumstances of each place.

Rio de Janeiro

The city of Rio de Janeiro, with a population of around six million, is the capital of the state of Rio de Janeiro and the center of a metropolitan area that includes twenty-one municipalities with nearly twelve million inhabitants.[9] The region is marked with stunning inequality: portions of metropolitan Rio have a human development index (HDI) higher than Norway's and others have one equivalent to Lebanon or Azerbaijan.[10]

The Rio de Janeiro metropolitan region has suffered historically from serious issues of violence and police abuse that date at least to the early twentieth century. These problems dramatically worsened in the mid-1980s with Rio's emergence as a transshipment hub in the international cocaine trade. Violence nearly tripled between 1980 and 1994 as gangs, both in conflict and in collaboration with the police, took control of many of the region's poor areas.[11] Ultimately *favelas,* shantytowns that provide housing for about a quarter of the population, became the public face of the city's violence problems. Gangs controlling these areas battled with one another and police over control of the rapidly growing retail drug trade.

After years of failed efforts to suppress gang violence, the Rio state government implemented the UPP program in 2008, which maintained an ongoing police presence in gang-dominated communities in order to strengthen the rule of law. The program began in the Zona Sul favela of Santa Marta and has slowly expanded to thirty-six sites concentrated in the wealthy seaside South Zone and portions of the industrial North Zone closely connected to downtown Rio. While the program encountered some serious problems throughout 2014, it also attracted an immense amount of international attention as a strategy to reclaim urban areas from gangs. Indeed, the UPP became highly ritualized, with police announcing their entry into favelas and raising the Brazilian flag over the community to signify the reclaiming of territories the state had lost. A focus on these police units and the particular problems they confront, however, has served to deviate public attention from other concrete problems the city is facing. These include continuing conflict in more peripheral areas, violence associated with collusive as opposed to competitive criminal actors operating in poor neighborhoods, and the role of the region's elite in perpetuating these tensions.

Central and Peripheral Violence

Criminal conflict has long attracted a great deal of attention in Rio de Janeiro. Attention to violence, however, focuses on the regions most central to the wealthy Zona Sul and, to a lesser extent, downtown Rio and the Zona Norte.

In 2013, one of the safest years in more than a generation, the Rio metropolitan area had a homicide rate of 31 per 100,000 inhabitants. This number, however, obscured marked differences within the region. The neighborhoods that comprise the South Zone had a homicide rate of only 5 per 100,000 inhabitants. Downtown and the North Zone reported a rate of 10.6 per 100,000, a level comparable to a city like Dallas. The West Zone of Rio and the eastern suburbs had homicide rates of 34 per 100,000. The western suburbs meanwhile recorded homicides of 46 per 100,000, a rate similar to that of Colombia in 2009 and a bit higher than Guatemala had in the same year.[12]

Basic indicators of police activity confirm the marginalization of peripheral areas. The North and South Zones host thirty-four of the thirty-six UPPs and have disproportionately benefited from the program's actions. The police, whose more positive crime-control activities tend to concentrate in the North and South Zones, show higher rates of arrest in these areas than in other parts of the city. With the lowest homicide rates in 2013, the South Zone had 264 arrests per 100,000 inhabitants against 178 per 100,000 in the North Zone and 152 per 100,000 in the West Zone. Throughout Rio, however, lower arrest rates generally correlate with greater police violence. In the highly policed South Zone there were 0.62 killings by police per 100,000 inhabitants. In the North Zone the rate was 2.36 per 100,000. In the West Zone, the region with the fewest arrests, there were 5.7 police killings per 100,000, double the metropolitan average and nine times the average in the South Zone.

Crime and criminal justice vary significantly across this large and complex metropolitan area. Crime-control strategies tend to focus on

Table 11.1

Homicides, arrests, and killings by police in the Rio metropolitan area

Area	Population (Total)	Homicides (per 100,000)	Arrests (per 100,000)	Killings by police (per 100,000)
North and South Zones and downtown combined	3,705,718	10.60	193.21	2.08
South Zone	638,050	5.49	264.55	0.62
North Zone and downtown	3,067,668	11.67	178.37	2.36
West Zone	2,614,728	35.60	152.29	5.70
Western suburbs	3,718,369	46.44	164.78	2.90
Eastern suburbs	2,050,276	31.57	199.24	3.45
Metro Rio total	12,089,091	30.54	173.88	3.35

Sources: Rio de Janeiro city population by Região Administrative from Instituto Perreira Passos; Fundação CEPERJ, *Anuario Estatistico do Estado do Rio de Janeiro, 2013*; Instituto de Segurança Pública, Monthly Crime Data Reports for 2013.

areas with the least mortal violence and the highest concentrations of wealth and power. The more central a neighborhood, the more attention it gets in terms of formal government assistance and strategies to combat crime. More peripheral areas are less often the sites of effective policies and receive relatively less assistance, while they experience police and criminal impunity.

Domination Versus Contestation

Rio's drug trade is centered on the core areas of the North and South Zones, close to wealthy retail markets and major transit facilities. On a retail level, the drug trade is based around a large number of open-air drug markets that are predominantly located in favelas and, in some cases, are only a few steps away from a compliant police post. Rio's highest homicide rates in the 1990s were associated with periods of intense gang competition and moments when the state government adopted particularly aggressive antigang tactics. This included the implementation of a "bravery bonus" for police who fired on civilians.[13] The expansion of the UPPs has markedly improved conditions in parts of the North and

South Zones where these units have been able to displace some gang activities and establish a regularized police presence.

Conditions in outlying portions of the city, where there is virtually no UPP presence, are markedly different. The West Zone hosts a variety of criminal activities, including gangs of powerful drug dealers and paramilitary groups connected to the police, known as *milícias*. In general, smaller retail markets and less access to major transport facilities limit drug gangs' operational scope. By providing security and imposing taxes on the local economy, milícias have established control over many neighborhoods.

The West Zone has long operated by its own rules. Until late in the twentieth century the region was composed of a set of small suburbs largely cut off from the city. Some portions of it were referred to as the Sertão Carioca (Rio's Backlands), in reference to the impoverished and famously unruly interior of Brazil's northeast.[14] Geographically, socially, and economically most of the region has much more in common with the suburban municipalities than it does with Rio's urban core in the North and South Zones.[15] The region has, on average, the lowest levels of human development and the highest levels of poverty.[16]

In this context, milícias mediate between expanding unregulated neighborhoods and a complex bureaucratic and economic system that does not serve the area. Lacking state-supported infrastructure, local populations often develop their own. Milícias help drive these efforts by using armed power to overcome local collective action problems. They may force businesses to pay for upgrades to a water or sanitation system, for example. On the bureaucratic side, milícias mediate negotiations among police, growing illegal settlements, and informal service providers such as unlicensed minibus services. Given their close connections to the police, milícias are positioned to negotiate ongoing payoffs between informal service providers and the relevant authorities.[17]

The West Zone is the most violent region of the Rio metropolitan area, but most violence differs from popular images of conflicts over gang-controlled favelas. While these types of gang rivalries certainly exist, neighborhoods under milícia control encounter more subtle violence. Violence is more targeted and guns less visible, which can lead to greater feelings of security. This type of selective violence is possible in areas dominated by one group, as opposed to the city's urban core, where competing criminal groups are constantly contesting the control of given territories.

The celebrated UPP program would not make as much sense in a milícia-ridden context. Regular police presence on the ground can contribute to preventing gang confrontations but is less useful in stopping the extortions and targeted killings that are common in this region. Indeed, as we will discuss in the next section, the only UPP in a formerly milícia-run favela is in Batan, where a milícia made the mistake of kidnapping a group of journalists, generating unprecedented attention to their activities.

Elite and Popular Crime

The involvement in and perpetuation of crime by elites is also generally overlooked in discussions on public safety in Rio. In the core areas of the South and North Zones the most common elite-criminal exchanges are payments and other arrangements politicians make with gang leaders to gain access to the communities they control. Often these exchanges go through standard clientelist channels, with politicians simply making arrangements with formal association leaders who have semiclandestine ties to local gang leaders. In one case in the North Zone, for example, a politician built a gymnasium and dancehall for a community that came under the control of the local association leader, who was also the father of the area's gang leader.[18]

In the West Zone, and to a lesser extent in the North and South Zones, armed groups have managed to elect their own members and close allies to political office at the city and state levels. Whereas gangs have had only limited success with political activities, milícias have achieved significant electoral success. At one point in the last decade these groups controlled multiple seats in the Rio state assembly and city council. Other politicians associated with these groups have won elections at the municipal, state, and federal levels. State and local leaders have also given milícia members positions in their administrations.

Milícia members and their political contacts have gone to great lengths to maintain public silence regarding their activities. In 2008, for example, a group of reporters from a major Rio de Janeiro daily were engaged in undercover reporting of a small and inexperienced police-run milícia in the Batan favela. Milícia members kidnapped and tortured the reporters, seeking to intimidate them and destroy data about their activities stored in an e-mail account. Eventually, the reporters were released amid threats. After the journalists had gone into hiding in other cities, the newspaper published reports on the events.[19] The milícia abuses backfired on a grand scale. Groups that normally drew only limited journalistic and political interest briefly became the focus of intense international attention. This led these milícias to change some of their criminal and political practices to decrease public visibility of their activities.[20] With new strategies and many old political alliances in place, attention waned.

Finally, armed groups have had a marked impact on suburban political life. These areas have a strong history of politicians running death squads that serve their political and economic interests. In the wake of the lootings that took place in the early 1960s, the Brazilian military dictatorship supported the development of police death squads that later engaged in targeted political killings and "social cleansing" operations.[21] In the 1990s these death squads provided support for politicians seeking public positions by serving as conduits between political patrons and their electoral clientele.[22] The drug trade in this region is integrally linked to the systems of clientelist power that death squads enable.[23]

Despite its clear impact on the perpetuation of violence, elite crime has long been overlooked in Brazil as the wealthy have held disproportionate power in society and have been largely protected by the state. Contemporary violence and perceptions of it are rooted in a long history of patrimonial power and violence that goes back to the foundation of the colony by Portugal and to the ensuing centuries of slavery established by local elites. In more recent years powerful economic and political elites have engaged in extensive corrupt exchanges that have led to mutual enrichment at the expense of other social sectors. However, all of this is largely tolerated because of the relative power of these groups and their history of impunity.

Kingston

The narrative on violence in Jamaica normally emphasizes the criminal activities of socially excluded populations in certain areas of Kingston, the country's capital and largest city. Rapid urbanization, poverty, high unemployment, clientelist relationships, the city's history of political conflict, and cultural norms among the poor populations seeking to reclaim dignity in the context of political exploitations, what Obika Gray has called "badness-honour,"[24] have influenced the dynamics of crime in this city.[25] Studies on violence have usually focused on political conflicts taking place within the politically homogenous communities known as garrisons and on the criminal gangs that entered the drug trade during the 1980s.[26] In particular, they explain that the zero-sum nature of garrison politics was the main cause of violence from the 1960s through the early 1980s, and that the boom in the narcotics trade in the 1980s drove crime issues for another decade.[27] The city's homicide rate consistently remained above the national rate between 2006 and 2011,[28] which further contributed to placing Kingston at the center of political and academic discussions on crime in the country.

Although warranted, the attention that Kingston has received from scholars and public officials alike has drawn attention away from other parishes where crime is also problematic. It also has served to obscure the diverse manifestations of crime on the island and the elite networks that often underlie criminal activities. To create a more nuanced portrait of criminality in the country, we examine the nature, distribution, and evolution of different types of criminal activities in diverse areas, contexts, and populations in Jamaica.

Central and Peripheral Violence

Between 2008 and 2011, 84 percent of the murders in Jamaica were attributed to organized crime, gang-related activities, robberies, and similar criminal acts.[29] Most of this violence took place in Kingston. In 2013, the police division of Kingston Western, which includes the garrisons of Denham Town and Tivoli Gardens, recorded the highest number of murders, shootings, and seizures of firearms in the capital.[30] These communities have attracted extensive media and scholarly attention as a result of ongoing gang dominance and the controversy that erupted around the 2010 extradition of Christopher "Dudus" Coke, a notorious gang leader who controlled these areas and was involved in illicit trades between Kingston, Miami, and New York.[31] Several gangs are now competing to fill the vacuum left after Coke's arrest in 2010.[32] Nearby regions also show high levels of violence and have experienced greater levels of murders, breaks-ins, larceny, and cocaine seizures.[33]

Beyond Kingston's environs, violence is entrenched in major urban centers such as Spanish Town and Portmore, in St. Catherine, a parish located next to Kingston that has drawn markedly less scholarly attention. St. Catherine's increasing prominence as a crime hotspot is reflected in figure 11.1, which shows that the majority of Jamaica's murders in 2013 took place in that jurisdiction. One gang in Spanish Town with strong political affiliations reportedly had a yearly income of approximately J$448 million, based on extortion and contract killing businesses.[34] Rising violence in Portmore coincides with the municipality's explosive population growth in recent years, as well as with the development of highway infrastructure connecting the city to other areas. Like in Spanish Town, extortion rackets and turf wars are the norm in Portmore's volatile communities.[35] Little is known, however, about the criminal dynamics and political-criminal connections in the municipality.

Another key area of criminal activity on the island is Montego Bay, the capital of the parish of St. James and Jamaica's second largest city. Illicit economic activities thrive in the area alongside important industries such as tourism and telecommunications. The island's police force (Jamaica Constabulary Force, or JCF), estimates that up to 50 percent of the violence in the city is related to lottery scams. The U.S. Federal Bureau of Investigations has suggested that seventeen of the twenty-one gangs operating in Montego Bay are involved in this type of criminal activity.[36] One newspaper reports the Stone Crusher gang provided protection for scammers in exchange for cash, firearms, and cars, and was also linked to the guns-for-drugs trade in Haiti.[37] Reports suggest that these organized criminal activities in Montego Bay are linked to other parishes, particularly those with high homicide rates such as Clarendon, Hanover, and Westmoreland.[38]

The limited attention paid to these manifold expressions of violence and crime taking place outside of Kingston restricts our understanding of the diversity and changing nature of organized crime in Jamaica and undermines the government's capacity to balance and optimize the allocation of crime-control resources throughout the country.

Domination versus Contestation

The 2010 extradition of Christopher Coke, who received government contracts and political protection, revealed the power drug traffickers can wield in garrison communities and the nature of political-criminal ties in Jamaica.[39] Political leaders from the two major parties allowed criminals like Coke to dominate these neighborhoods in exchange for securing votes, providing social welfare, and maintaining neighborhood stability.[40]

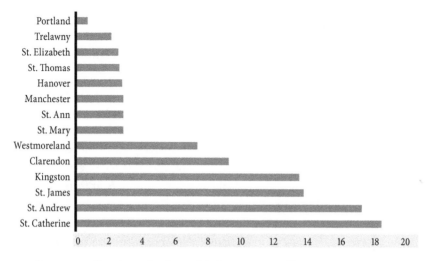

11.1. Percentage of total murders by parish, Jamaica, 2013. The percentages were calculated using 2013 homicide data from the Jamaica Constabulary Force.

Consistent with Angélica Durán-Martínez's findings in chapter 10, criminal elites who have consolidated control over garrisons tend to shy away from public performances of violence that would increase state intervention and threaten the profitability of their illicit activities. In 2006, a Jamaican newspaper reported Coke's displeasure with an attack on Denham Town's police station that was allegedly carried out by one of his soldiers.[41] Coke's attempt to "discipline" the individual for the incident resulted in a temporary escalation of violence in West Kingston. Coke made no comments on the incident. Such silence and quick reaction to violations of informal norms is typical of the criminal elite's behavior and may have contributed to Coke's ability to dominate a large region of the city for nearly fifteen years.

Domination also includes consolidation over illicit markets. Many gangs control lucrative extortion rackets, and competition over these markets is a major cause of violence in many parts of Jamaica.[42] Coke's extradition, for instance, led to competition amongst smaller gangs that once operated under his orders but are now attempting to gain control of criminal activities in the area, contributing significantly to an increase in crime in downtown Kingston.[43] This suggests that powerful party-connected criminal leaders do more than generate violence and crime. Rather, their control of certain areas also creates a semblance of safety and stability in some poor communities. This helps to explain why community members continue to support these criminals, despite their brutality.

Although the drug trade has allowed gang leaders to become patrons in their own right, which increases their power vis-à-vis state officials in inner-city communities, political-criminal networks have remained strong. These networks usually remain relatively invisible until they experience periods of contestation or instability due to external factors like extradition requests, as the Coke example shows, or internal factors such as the inability of politicians to control the behavior of criminal actors. For instance, a prominent politician in Kingston reportedly turned over the names of criminals in his constituency to the police because he claimed that they were creating problems in the community.[44]

In addition to gaining authority through their connections with politicians, many criminals have maintained control over garrisons by implementing their own justice systems and operating within the frameworks of tacit agreements with law enforcement officials.[45] Some police officers, however, interpret these informal agreements as direct challenges to their authority and use violence as a means to curtail the criminals' power.[46] With 21 deaths per 100,000, the parish of Westmoreland recorded the highest rate of police-related fatalities in Jamaica, followed by other high-crime areas such as St. James and St. Catherine (see figure 11.2). High levels of official homicides have earned the JCF a reputation for being one of the deadliest police units in the world.[47] These abuses increase tensions between community members and the police and may, in turn, strengthen ties between gang leaders and the poor. Despite efforts to improve the JCF's reputation through community policing and other strategies of social engagement, pervasive violence continues to mar police-citizen relations.

Elite and Popular Crime

Increasing allegations of corruption with respect to government contracts and electoral financing suggests that political leaders in Jamaica are diversifying the types of illicit activities in which they engage. The decline in party membership and the loopholes in campaign finance laws, which make it hard to detect electoral and political crimes, mean that grand corruption may become the new norm in Jamaica.[48] The

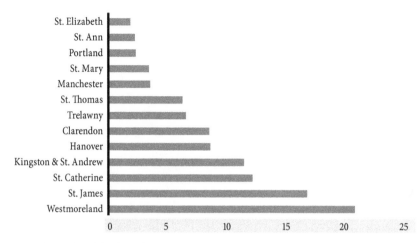

11.2. Police-related fatalities by parish, Jamaica, 2013, expressed as rate per 100,000. The rate was calculated using 2013 data from the Independent Commission of Investigations and 2011 population data for each parish taken from the national census as reported by the Statistical Institute of Jamaica.

Trafigura scandal illustrates well how government contracts can be used in order to gain political contributions. Allegedly, Trafigura Beheer, a Dutch multinational, donated J$31 million to the People's National Party in 2006 in order to obtain the contract to trade crude oil on behalf of Jamaica.[49] Political leaders have taken advantage of the lack of clarity in domestic and international laws to support the claim that the donation was a gift. Politicians also benefit from citizens' tendency to overlook acts of corruption that do not have a direct impact on their personal security.

Prominent business leaders in wealthier communities have also been involved in the narcotics trade but have received less attention than their counterparts from marginalized neighborhoods. For example, until his extradition in 2007 Leebert Ramcharan owned and operated several businesses in Montego Bay, as well as a major narcotics distribution network between Colombia, Jamaica, and the United States. His businesses and drug trafficking operations allegedly supported members of local communities, who after his extradition became involved in illegal lottery schemes as an alternative source of income.[50] Although Ramcharan was linked to one of the major political parties, limited scholarly and media attention has prevented a deeper understanding of the nature of his and other business leaders' alliances with politicians.[51]

Other types of political-business networks exist outside of the drug trafficking industry but these have attracted very limited attention. One of the more blatant examples is Olint, a failed Ponzi scheme organized and promoted by former banker David Smith. The Olint scheme targeted mostly middle- and upper-income individuals in Jamaica, but the company was linked to similar investment schemes in the Caribbean and the United States.[52] Smith reportedly made financial contributions to Jamaica's two major political parties during their 2007 general election campaigns.[53] Although Smith was never prosecuted in Jamaica, he was charged in Turks and Caicos and the United States for money laundering and wire fraud. Public attention to Smith and the larger problem of fraudulent investment schemes declined after his incarceration.

Conclusion

The three axes of crime examined in this chapter point to important issues regarding illegal practices and their different degrees of visibility in Brazil and Jamaica. Kingston and Rio offer stark evidence that greater attention is paid to armed activities in centrally located neighborhoods than in outlying areas even when peripheral areas face serious, and in some cases greater, problems than central areas do. The key difference between the two cases is that Rio's large territory and population density generates a more nuanced pattern of armed activity across different parts of the metropolitan area. In Kingston, on the other hand, the smaller population and more isolated nature of the different components of the urban landscape lead to distinct, though poorly understood, patterns of armed activity emerging in key areas of dense population growth.

Similarly, there is substantial evidence that more attention is paid to conflicts in contested areas than to different, but often equally violent areas strongly under the domination of a single armed group. In both Rio and Kingston armed groups have established high levels of dominance over certain neighborhoods. Thus, the areas Christopher Coke controlled in western Kingston existed in a system of total state-sanctioned criminal control. Similarly in Rio, milícias, which for years have existed with strong support from state actors, maintain armed control over local markets, security, politics, and dispute resolution. This dominance only becomes the focus of attention once it is threatened by shifting relationships between state and criminal actors or by external factors such as extradition requests. From a policy perspective this means that these groups can perpetrate violence in areas they dominate with little risk of external attention and, as a result, can operate with a high degree of impunity.

The dissimilar levels of attention given to elite and popular crime also highlight the different publics of violence in Latin America and the Caribbean. While immense attention has focused on crimes committed by the poor and working classes, less is understood about elite criminal networks. Jamaica has a long history of involvement between criminal actors and elected representatives, but this issue receives relatively scant attention in the contemporary press even though these relationships have clear impacts on crime in the city. The media regularly document gunfights in downtown Kingston, but the broader and often equally destructive elite networks receive little attention except when occasional events conspire to bring these activities to public light. Similarly, in Rio it took years for the press to pay serious attention to contacts between elite politicians and the West Zone's milícias, and death squad politics in the suburbs continues to receive little attention. Ultimately, we know little about the nature and implications of these connections. As a result, policy responses address only the most publicly violent outcomes of these activities.

Lastly, a great deal of attention is paid to gangs of drug dealers operating in poor neighborhoods. These groups are often treated as outsiders to the political system rather than as actors empowered by that system. This leads to a textured understanding of the situation that obscures many other dimensions of violence and that does not fully contemplate the influence of elite circles in supporting and perpetuating ongoing criminal activities. Ultimately, this selective blindness results in a limited and biased basis for developing sophisticated social and political responses to the manifold interconnected problems of violence affecting these and other metropolitan areas.

Notes

1. Guillermo O'Donnell, "On the State, Democratization, and Some Conceptual Problems: A Latin American View with Glances at some Postcommunist Countries," *World Development* 21, no. 8 (1993): 1355–69.
2. On the negative impacts of heavy-handed policing policies in Central America see José Miguel Cruz, "Criminal Violence and Democracy in Central America: The Survival of the Violent State," *Latin American Politics and Society* 53, no. 4 (2011): 1–33.

3. Loïc Wacquant, *Punishing the Poor: The Neoliberal Government of Social Insecurity* (Durham, NC: Duke University Press, 2009).

4. Daniel Goldstein, *The Spectacular City: Violence and Performance in Urban Bolivia* (Durham, NC: Duke University Press, 2004); Mark Ungar, "The Privatization of Citizen Security in Latin America: From Elite Guards to Neighborhood Vigilante," *Social Justice* 34, nos. 3–4 (2007–8); G. Frederick Allen, "Vigilante Justice in Jamaica: The Community against Crime," *International Journal of Comparative and Applied Criminal Justice* 21, no. 1 (1997): 1–12; Javier Auyero, *Routine Politics and Violence in Argentina: The Gray Zone of State Power* (New York : Cambridge University Press, 2007).

5. Paul G. Chevigny, "Police Deadly Force as Social Control: Jamaica, Argentina, and Brazil," *Criminal Law Forum* 1, no. 3 (1990): 389–425; Anthony Harriott, *Police and Crime Control in Jamaica: Problems Reforming Ex-Colonial Constabularies* (Kingston: University of the West Indies Press, 2000).

6. Stathis N. Kalyvas, *The Logic of Violence in Civil War* (New York: Cambridge University Press, 2006); Mary Roldán, *Blood and Fire: La Violencia in Antioquia, Colombia, 1946–1953* (Durham, NC: Duke University Press, 2002), 21; Enrique Desmond Arias, "The Impacts of Differential Armed Dominance on Politics in Rio de Janeiro, Brazil," *Studies in Comparative International Development* 48, no. 3 (2013): 263–84; Federico Varese, *The Russian Mafia: Private Protection in a New Market Economy* (New York: Oxford University Press, 2001).

7. Regina Anne Bateson, "Crime Victimization and Political Participation," *American Political Science Review* 106, no. 3 (2012): 571.

8. Statement by Marcos Alvito, "Debate 3: Criminalidade e Violência," in Gilberto Velho and Marcos Alvito, eds., *Cidadania e Violência* (Rio de Janeiro: Editora FGV, 1996), 175–78.

9. Agenda 21 COMPERJ, "Região Metropolitana ganha 2 municípios: Rio Bonito e Cachoeiras de Macacu," January 3, 2014, www.agenda21comperj.com.br/noticias/ regiao-metropolitana-ganha-2-municipios-rio-bonito-e-cachoeiras-de-macacu (accessed June 23, 2014).

10. Geo-Rio, "Tabela 1172: Desenvolvimento Humano e Condições de Vida na Cidade do Rio de Janeiro" (Estudo No. 1347)," www.camara.rj.gov.br/planodiretor/pd2009/ saudepd/Anexo3_IDH.pdf (accessed June 23, 2014).

11. Jacobo Waiselfisz, *Mapa da Violência: Os Jovens do Brasil* (Rio de Janeiro: Editora Garamond, 1998), 107.

12. Homicide, arrest, and police killing counts reported by Instituto de Segurança Pública, Monthly Crime Data Reports for 2013, www.isp.rj.gov.br/ (accessed June 23, 2014); Rio de Janeiro city population by Região Administrativa from Instituto Perreira Passos, "Tabela 484: População residente, segundo as Áreas de Planejamento e Regiões Administrativas–1991/2010," http://portalgeo.rio.rj.gov.br/ (accessed November 26, 2014). Populations of Rio suburbs for 2011 are from Fundação CEPERJ, "Anuario Estatistico do Estado do Rio de Janeiro–2013," www.ceperj.rj.gov.br/ceep/Anuario2013/ ApresentacaoDemografiaPopulacao.html (accessed June 24, 2014); International Comparisons from Julio Jacobo Waiselfisz, *Homícidios e Juventude no Brasil* (Brasilia:

Secretaria-Geral da Presidência da República, 2013), 68. Aggregation of data by region and rate computations are by the authors.

13. Enrique Desmond Arias, *Drugs and Democracy in Rio de Janeiro: Trafficking, Networks, and Public Security* (Chapel Hill: University of North Carolina Press, 2006).

14. Brodwyn Fischer, *A Poverty of Rights: Citizenship and Inequality in Twentieth-Century Rio de Janeiro* (Stanford, CA: Stanford University Press, 2008), 214–15.

15. Notable exceptions are the wealthy beachfront neighborhoods of Barra da Tijuca and Recreio dos Bandeirantes.

16. The lowest HDI numbers in Rio actually come from large and politically powerful favelas in the Zona Norte and Zona Sul that have succeeded in being recognized by the city as independent from their surrounding neighborhoods, thus statistically setting off those areas from neighboring regions.

17. On this see Enrique Desmond Arias, "Dispatches from the Field: Milícias and Police Corruption in Rio de Janeiro," *Americas Quarterly* 3, no. 2 (2009): 90–93.

18. Arias, *Drugs and Democracy in Rio de Janeiro*, 115.

19. Arias, "Dispatches from the Field."

20. Ignacio Cano and Thais Duarte, *No Sapatinho: A Evolução das Milícias no Rio de Janeiro [2008-2011]* (Rio de Janeiro: Laboratório de Análise da Violência [LAV-UERJ] and Fundação Heinrich Böll, 2012).

21. Henrique Rodrigues de Andrade Goulart and Leandro Pereira Gonçalves, "O Regime de Extermínio: A Concretização da Violência Ilegal enquanto Ferramenta Político no Brasil Pós-Golpe em 1964," *CES Revista* 25 (2011): 159–72; José Claudio Souza Alves, "Violência e Política na Baixada: O Caso dos Grupos de Extermínio," in *Impunidade na Baixada Fluminense* (Parceria: CESeC, Fase, Justiça Global, Laboratório de Análises da Violência da UERJ, SOS Queimados e Viva Rio, 2005), 26–36.

22. José Claudio Souza Alves, "Relgião, Violência e Poder Político na Baizada Fluiminense (Rio de Janeiro, Brasil)," *Ciencias Sociais y Religião* 6, no. 6 (2004): 153–78.

23. FASE–Educação e Solidariedade, "Dilemas e Desafios para a Cidadania na Baixada Fluminense," in *Impunidade na Baixada Fluminense,* September 2005, 35.

24. Gray defines badness-honour as "the oral-kinetic practice in Jamaica that enables claimants, usually from the disadvantaged groups, to secure a modicum of power and respect by intimidation." This cultural practice is usually encouraged and sometimes adopted by politicians as a means to gain political support in urban areas, particularly in Kingston. See Obika Gray, *Demeaned but Empowered: The Social Power of the Urban Poor in Jamaica* (Kingston: University of the West Indies Press, 2004), 122–23.

25. Colin Clarke, "Politics, Violence, and Drugs in Kingston, Jamaica," *Bulletin of Latin American Research* 25, no. 3 (2006): 420–40; Mark Figueroa and Amanda Sives, "Homogeneous Voting, Electoral Manipulation, and the 'Garrison' Process in Post-Independence Jamaica," *Commonwealth and Caribbean Politics* 40, no. 1 (2002): 81–108; Laurie Gunst, *Born Fi' Dead: A Journey through the Jamaican Posse Underworld* (New York: Henry Holt and Co., 1996); Anthony Harriott, *Organized Crime and Politics in Jamaica: Breaking the Nexus* (Kingston: University of the West

Indies Press, 2008); Amanda Sives, *Elections, Violence, and the Democratic Process in Jamaica, 1944–2007* (Kingston: Ian Randle Press, 2010); Carl Stone, *Democracy and Clientelism in Jamaica in Jamaica* (New Brunswick, NJ: Transaction Books, 1980).

26. See, for example, Sives, *Elections, Violence, and the Democratic Process*; Clarke, "Politics, Violence and Drugs in Kingston"; Harriott, *Organized Crime and Politics in Jamaica.*

27. Sives, *Elections, Violence, and the Democratic Process.*

28. United Nations Office on Drugs and Crime (UNODC), *Global Study on Homicide, 2013: Trends, Contexts, Data* (Vienna: UNODC, 2014), 125, 148, www.unodc.org/ documents/gsh/pdfs/2014_GLOBAL_HOMICIDE_BOOK_web.pdf (accessed June 5, 2014).

29. Ibid., 41, 140.

30. Jamaica Constabulary Force (JCF), *Jamaica Constabulary Force Annual Report, 2013* (Kingston: JCF, 2014), www.jcf.gov.jm/article/2014-06-02/jamaica-constabulary-force -annual-report-2013 (accessed June 10, 2014).

31. See, for example, Amanda Sives, "A Calculated Assault on the Authority of the State: Crime, Politics, and Extradition in 21st-Century Jamaica," *Crime, Law, and Social Change* 58, no. 4 (2012): 415–35; David Kilcullen, *Out of the Mountains: The Coming Age of the Urban Guerrilla* (New York: Oxford University Press, 2013); Mattathias Schwartz, "A Massacre in Jamaica," *New Yorker,* December 12, 2011, www.newyorker .com/reporting/2011/12/12/111212fa_fact_schwartz (accessed January 15, 2013).

32. "Gang Feuds Put Tivoli Gardens on Edge," *Jamaica Observer,* January 11, 2013, www .jamaicaobserver.com/news/Gang-feud-puts-Tivoli-Gardens-on-edge_13346079 (accessed June 23, 2014); "Police Say 9 'High Ranking' Gang Members Held in West Kingston," *Jamaica Observer,* September 15, 2013, www.jamaicaobserver.com /News/Police-say-9-high-ranking-gang-members-held-in-West-Kgn_15074311 (accessed June 23, 2014).

33. *Jamaica Constabulary Force Annual Report, 2013.*

34. Karyl Walker, "Bulbie's Ruthless Reign Shielded by Politicians," *Jamaica Observer,* February 10, 2008, www.jamaicaobserver.com/news/132366_Bulbie-s-ruthless-reign -shielded-by-politicians (accessed May 10, 2014); Livern Barrett, "Spanish Town Turmoil—$400m-a-Year Racket; Gangsters Use Church as Cover; Brazen Attack on Police Station and Hospital," *Jamaica Gleaner,* March 13, 2011, http://jamaica-gleaner.com/gleaner/20110313/lead/lead1.html (accessed June 16, 2014).

35. Kimmo Matthews, "Police Reacts as Portmore Gang Feud Heats Up," *Jamaica Observer,* September 2, 2009, www.jamaicaobserver.com/news/158698_Police-react -as-Portmore-gang-feud-heats-up (accessed June 21, 2014).

36. "Jamaica and U.S. Authorities Work Towards Ending Lottery Scam," *Jamaica Gleaner,* March 10, 2013, http://jamaica-gleaner.com/latest/article.php?id=43354.

37. Adrian Frater, "Montego Bay: Breeding Ground for Crime," April 8, 2010, http:// jamaica-gleaner.com/gleaner/20100408/lead/lead3.html; Frater, "A City under Siege—12 Killed as New Wave of Criminality Rocks MoBay," *Jamaica Gleaner,* December 15, 2013, http://jamaica-gleaner.com/gleaner/20131215/lead/lead1.html.

38. Oshane Tobias, "Clarendon Police Happy with Year's Work . . . Despite High Mur-

der Rate," *Jamaica Observer,* January 1, 2010, www.jamaicaobserver.com/news/ Clarendon-police-happy-Fri-Jan-1_7292623; "Multiple Arrests in Anti-Lottery Scam Operation," *Jamaica Observer,* July 11, 2014, www.jamaicaobserver.com/ news/Multiple-arrests-in-anti-lottery-scam-operation.

39. See Kilcullen, *Out of the Mountains;* Schwartz, "Massacre in Jamaica."

40. Harriott, *Organized Crime and Politics in Jamaica;* Sives, *Elections, Violence, and the Democratic Process.*

41. "West Dons at Odds," *Jamaica Star Online,* August 18, 2006, http://jamaica-star.com /thestar/20060818/news/news1.html.

42. Frater, "Montego B ay"; Tobias "Clarendon Police Happy with Year's Work"; Matthews, "Police Reacts as Portmore Gang Feud Heats Up"; Corey Robinson, "Extortion: Culture of Silence," *Jamaica Gleaner,* April 10, 2014, http://jamaica-gleaner .com/gleaner/20140410/lead/lead1.html.

43. "Gang Feuds Put Tivoli Gardens on Edge"; "Police Say 9 'High Ranking' Gang Members Held"; Robinson, "Extortion: Culture of Silence."

44. Amanda Sives, "Changing Patrons, from Politician to Drug Don: Clientelism in Downtown Kingston, Jamaica, *Latin America Perspectives* 29, no. 5 (2002): 66–89.

45. John Rapley, "Jamaica: Negotiating Law and Order with the Dons," *NACLA Report on the Americas* 37, no. 2 (2003): 25–29.

46. Chevigny, "Police Deadly Force as Social Control"; Harriott, *Police and Crime Control in Jamaica.*

47. Amnesty International, *Killings and Violence by Police: How Many More Victims?* www.amnesty.org/download/Documents/124000/amr380072001en.pdf.

48. For a more detailed discussion of this problem in Jamaica, see Trevor Munroe, *Voice, Participation, and Governance in a Changing Environment: The Case of Jamaica* (Kingston: University of the West Indies, 2000).

49. "Trafigura Haunts PNP: Contractor General Recommends Colin Campbell Be Charged for Obstruction in Probe," *Jamaica Observer,* August 24, 2010, www .jamaicaobserver.com/news/ Trafigura-haunts-PNP.

50. Paul Bourne et al., "Lottery Scam in a Third World Nation: The Economics of a Financial Crime and Its Breadth," *Asian Journal of Business Management* 5, no. 1 (2013): 19–51.

51. Wikileaks, Jamaica, "Former National Security Minister and Key Opposition Figure Slams PM as 'Indecisive in 'Dudus' Extradition Request," September 17, 2009, www.wikileaks.org/plusd/cables/09KINGSTON695_a.html (accessed April 2, 2014).

52. Robert Di Pano, "Olint: A Caribbean Ponzi Scheme Prosecuted in the U.S.," *Caribbean Law Yearbook,* inaugural edition, 2011, http://commonsenseja.files.wordpress .com/2011/05/ponzi_paper-may_draft-2.pdf (accessed October 6, 2013).

53. "Parties See No Reason to Return Olint Funds," *Jamaica Gleaner,* July 18, 2013, http://jamaica-gleaner.com/gleaner/20130718/lead/lead6.html (accessed October 17, 2013).

Conclusion

The Politics of Violence Control in Latin America

Jenny Pearce

One of the connecting tissues among the chapters in this volume is that nearly all deal with varied forms of violence control in past and present Latin America. This might seem an odd conclusion, in that so many of the chapters narrate multiple acts of violence by multiple actors. Yet these acts of violence are frequently also responses to violence or perceived threats of violence from within society as well as between armed non-state and state actors. The publics of these acts of violence and crime are far from passive audiences; they actively sanction violent responses at times and may directly participate in them. The sanctioning can often be attributed to the "invisible hand" of cultural ideas and meanings attached to violence and crime and those deemed responsible—what the editors call "representations of violence." These meanings justify violent responses to violent acts.

The outcome of these dynamics is reproduction of violence in the name of violence control. Another outcome is a form of citizenship that remains deeply imbued with the authoritarian implications that arise variously from the daily insecurities of the poor, from the middle-class anxieties about social disorder, and from the impulse to protect wealth and power at whatever cost amongst the few who possess such goods in abundance. I call this form of citizenship in Latin America authoritarian because it justifies and actively engages in the denial of rights to others. I argue that the most disturbing findings about these chapters are the implications for citizenship and democracy in Latin America, as these two appear to be shaped by and in turn to shape the politics around violence and crime. The creative criminal also emerges as a significant actor, partly from within society but often linked in mutually beneficial ways to political actors and the state. Sometimes this actor is a victim of, and sometimes a perpetrator of, lawless violence, sanctioned partly from below and partly from above. Thus, while repressive states clearly play a significant role in these chapters, I wish to emphasize the way the politics of violence control constitutes and then perpetuates authoritarian citizenship.

Repressive states and authoritarian citizens are not counterposed; the repressive state merely stands out in the history of Latin America, while the idea of citizenship is a relatively recent concept in the region that lacks foundations in an effective and egalitarian rule of law.[1] Authoritarian citizens with no experience of a rule of law have *demanded* states underpinned by violence and violence-protection mechanisms. And they have often sought to deny rights to certain groups, particularly those deemed responsible for acts of violence and crime. Thus, the editors highlight how these social constructions and representations of the violent and the criminal reflect a rupture between what might be formally considered illegal and what is considered criminal and violent in the everyday. This, in turn, links to the process of perverse state formation in Latin America, which as these chapters demonstrate has complex historical antecedents in a range of countries in the region.[2] These antecedents are deeply embedded in socialization spaces from the intimate to the community and to the construction of the nation-state itself. As David Carey Jr. and Gema Santamaría have underlined in their introduction, what matters is the *process through which* shared meanings and understandings of what is considered violent or criminal have evolved, because this process shapes and is shaped by the politics of violence control.

With its historical sweep from the nineteenth to the twenty-first centuries, and its geographical breadth that includes countries such as Chile and Argentina not usually considered to be among the most violent in Latin America, this collection of essays poses new questions about how violence and crime in the region are constructed and understood. Despite the many differences between and within Latin American countries and the nuances and variations over time, there are threads that interweave through the chapters in this volume. One thread is the representations of violence and criminality and the power dynamics behind them; another is the patterns of violence control. Both themes bring into focus the question of the body as the subject of representations and that of a politics of violence control. In this conclusion I will use the body in the body politic of Latin America as a lens for analyzing the conditions in which authoritarian citizenship emerges. I use this transversal theme to symbolize and reinforce the volume editors' analytical framework and their emphasis on the way violence derives its potency and meanings from various social, cultural, and symbolic dimensions.

Violence and the Body Politic

While the medieval concept of the body politic suggests a biological analogy to the political system, in the twenty-first century it serves to recall the bodies that make up the political community and are deeply impacted by violence and fear. By focusing on the body in the body politic, I suggest that authoritarian citizenship gestates historically in contexts where elites lack incentives to build a rule of law, preferring instead to use and promote violence for their personal and political goals, and to condone or collude at times with popular violence. In other words, they reproduce violence through the politics of violence control, by portraying certain members of society as dangerous and implicitly or directly encouraging state and non-state actors, and citizens themselves, to enact violence toward them. In this way they contribute to a form of citizenship where many are willing to deny rights to certain categories of people and sanction the use of violence against them.

Controlling the Body

Controlling violence is also about controlling bodies. The chapters in this volume tell us a great deal about efforts to control bodies and the violence that surrounds those efforts. Notions of citizenship, of who does and does not belong to the political community, are deeply embodied. One of the recurrent themes in these chapters is the political importance of efforts to differentiate between those bodies that matter and those considered inferior and even dangerous—and thus excluded from the political community and potentially subjected to violence. This is an aspect of Carey and Santamaría's distinction between a top-down understanding of violence and one rooted in long-term dynamics of state-society relations.

Race, ethnicity, and gender are notable markers of bodily differences. Thus Guatemala, a majority indigenous nation, features strongly in this volume. In the early twentieth century, positivist criminology, argues David Carey Jr., gave Latin American elites a pseudo-scientific framework for maintaining racial stratifications. In Guatemala, President Ubico deployed this framework in the 1930s and early 1940s to control indigenous peasants and workers in the name of violence containment and a project of national modernity in which cheap indigenous labor was a vital component. Even though those responsible for drunken and murderous behavior were statistically more likely to be ladinos, the construction of indigenous customs as degenerate and violent and the promulgation of a law against vagrancy were ways of controlling the indigenous population.

The indigenous body has been a continuous source of fear for ladino elites in Guatemala, and was the focus of extreme counterinsurgent state violence under President José Efraín Ríos Montt in the early 1980s. Evangelical Christianity and the dominating, all-powerful, and militarized male body (the iron fist) were offered to the "Guatemalan mother" as the source of security for her children while the military launched a campaign of genocidal violence against indigenous communities. As Gabriela Torres discusses, this justification for violence worked particularly well in a context where fathers and husbands legally controlled the bodies of their women and children.

In nineteenth-century Rio de Janeiro, the bodies of slaves were legal property and were under competing demands from a city in search of labor for its infrastructural expansion and urban modernization. Slaves and the growing corpus of freed persons were also a source of fear that required a special regime of control, particularly after dark. Curfews selectively restricted their movements at night just when the installation of lanterns made it possible to illuminate the city after dark. Thus, as Amy Chazkel demonstrates, the nighttime curfew emphasized the danger that slaves and the freed poor represented, controlled their labor power, and created a state of exception that gave the police the right to subject them to harassment and violence.

In contemporary Rio, it is less light and dark than territory and space which subject the poor to varied regimes of body control that justify the use of violence, particularly away from the gaze of the city and a potentially inquisitive press or NGO. Enrique Desmond Arias and Kayyonne

Marston discuss how the police pacification program managed to control homicides in some of the slums closest to the city center through physical police presence. In these areas, characterized by frequent homicides associated with gang fights and police violence, arrest rates are very high. Incarceration has become one of the favored regimes of body control in Brazil, resulting in severe overcrowding and high levels of prison violence.[3] However, regimes differ in the poor outer suburbs of Rio. Arias and Marston show how the more peripheral areas of the city are left to the selective assassination and harassment of militias, which often work closely with the police and offer various services to a local population lacking government infrastructure. The bodies of suspected gang members in these areas are subject less to arrests and more to selective assassination. Fewer arrests correlate with greater police violence.

In Latin American cities, regimes of control are often implemented by criminal or state actors, and sometimes by the two actors in tacit collaboration or through implicit arrangements or understandings. In Medellín, Colombia, homicide rates have declined to their lowest point since the early 1990s.[4] However, in the poorest *comunas* of the city armed criminal groups have developed new forms of violent protection and extortion rackets. In 2012, comuna residents of Medellín explained to me that when there is a knock on the door and they are shown a bag, it is not to collect money but rather for their dead bodies should they not pay for protection. Since compliance is internalized into the collective psyche of citizens, murder is less common. Armed actors embody the terrors of citizens who know they have nowhere else to go and who also learn that they are not in fact citizens whose rights are actively upheld by the state. This creates orders of control and security in poor areas that attract little attention because they do not impinge on middle-class areas. In the process, the politics of representation distinguishes "ungoverned" neighborhoods inhabited by "dangerous" individuals from safe areas populated by law-abiding citizens.

Two other themes in this volume pertain to the discussion on violence and the politics of representation and regimes of body control. The first is the selective use of the law and the exceptionality invoked to abandon the law. In Latin America, laws have been designed very specifically for purposes of violence control but in practice they have acted as justifications for violence against targeted groups. The Guatemalan vagrancy laws discussed previously are an early example of how the law and policing were invoked to subject the indigenous and poor population to a particular legal regime, just as the slaves and freed poor of nineteenth-century Rio de Janeiro came under a specially designed curfew law.

The tortuous challenges of Latin America's legal approaches to violence and crime are exemplified in the chapter on early twentieth-century sodomitic violence. As Robert Alegre demonstrates, Chilean courts dealt with the lack of distinction in the country's nineteenth-century penal code between consensual sodomy, pedophilia, and rape. Doctors came to arbitrate these boundaries in Chile, which goes to the heart of strategies of body control and representation in intimate as well as public spaces and to the enforcement regimes that emerge to address sexuality, violence, and crime. Latin America's ongoing failure to construct effective legal mechanisms to address violence is exemplified in the efforts since the early 2000s to frame the crime of femicide. In 2010, for instance, Chile amended its national penal code to include femicide as an "aggravated circumstance of homicide"; however, it also defined the crime as a form of parricide, limiting prosecution to cases where a woman is murdered by someone with whom she has had an intimate relationship.[5] This obscures the public context of normalized misogyny and indifference to violence against women's bodies; many murders of women in Latin America are preceded by violent rape and sexual torture.[6] From sodomitic violence in the early twentieth century to femicide in the early twenty-first century, Chile illustrates the slow pace and complexity surrounding understandings of sexualized violence and what they reveal about public and legal perceptions of sex and representations of the bodies of particular subjects.

The second theme that emerges in this volume related to regimes of body control is the evolution of law enforcement, the role of policing in Latin America, and its selective ethos of control and containment of violence. In her account of policing in early twentieth-century Buenos Aires, Lila Caimari reminds us that police are interpreters of laws that lack enforcement capacity—there are never enough police to enforce all laws, or even enough appropriate laws. Therefore, police officers make decisions about which laws to apply and to whom. She argues, "This modest guardian of order must decide every day which incidents or social groups merit intervention." The Buenos Aires police force attempted to construct its own esprit de corps in the 1920s and 1930s, at a time when they were trapped between their preferred role of protecting neighborhoods from the violence of the modern city and their own unwillingness to see themselves as defenders of the wealthy elites.

As social conflicts intensified in Latin America in the course of the twentieth century and elites sought to protect their interests, the many ambiguities around violence, law, and law enforcement mounted. The politics of violence control took on particular dimensions in the Cold War as social protest and armed rebellions grew in Latin America. Elaborate codifications and states of exception were drawn up and, as Luis Herrán Ávila discusses with respect to Colombia and Mexico, "enemy penologies" expanded the reach of punitive criminal law into politics and denoted a particular sphere of legality reserved for enemies. In the 1960s and 1970s Colombia came to be ruled almost permanently under state of siege legislation, which effectively criminalized dissent. Mexico embraced the strategy of containment against communism articulated by the Truman Doctrine on the eve of the Cold War. In the 1950s and especially after the Cuban Revolution, the use of the law grew to punish teachers, railroad workers, and later the student movement. It became a particular tool for shaping attitudes toward dissent, which encouraged private vigilante violence as well as state repression leading up to the violent repression of the student movement in 1968.

Gabriela Torres discusses how Guatemalan President Ríos Montt normalized legal exception in three law-decrees in 1982 that served to concentrate power in a military executive and facilitated the onslaught against armed insurgents with mass torture, executions, and disappearance of indigenous people. Amnesty and special exemption tribunal laws placed counterinsurgency violence within a legal framework justified by the moral authority of the Guatemalan army as protector of the nation.

Legal maneuvers to justify the total subjugation of the bodies of suspected dissidents as well as insurgents became part of a highly bureaucratized military project in the Southern Cone in the 1970s and 1980s. Torture was both a punishment and a method of control in Chile, Argentina, and Uruguay when the military intervened in the name of national security to target leftists who articulated demands for radical reform. Water and electricity were used systematically on captured militants before many of them were executed and then, in the case of Argentina, thrown out of planes and dropped into the Río Plata. This is surely the no-man's land Giorgio Agamben discusses, between "public law and political fact, and between the juridical order and life."[7] States of exception in Latin America have exposed the moral ambiguities of law when it appears as the "legal form to what cannot have legal form" and subjects bodies to the cruel whim of the state and its punishments.[8]

Punishing the Body

Through vagrancy, curfew, and social dissolution laws along with states of siege and exception, the bodies of significant groups of Latin American citizens—indigenous people, slaves, trade unionists, student militants, poor urban youth—have been singled out, accused of posing a danger to the state, controlled, contained, and savagely punished. The accusation provides the grounds for winning support from those considered part of the order that violence is protecting. As this volume demonstrates, however, some citizens also mete out their own punishments, such as lynchings that involve public torture and horrific public executions of victims who are accused of crimes or violent acts. Who should be punished for what acts, how, and by whom are questions that underlie the politics of violence control in Latin America and indeed, give permission for citizens as well as the state to act violently on the representations of "dangerousness" the state promotes.

For Pablo Piccato, an underlying tension exists between popular moral codes and the written law in post-independence Mexico, with the former taking precedence. Since these moral codes expressed collective sentiments toward criminals, lynchings and the ley fuga, despite being illegal, were rarely punished. These forms of extralegal punishment serve political orders where violence control is managed not by a functioning and impartial rule of law but by a range of semilegal, extrajudicial, and exceptional mechanisms. Public punishments by the masses, or decisions by prison officers to mete out a harsher punishment than the penal code would permit, allow authorities to send messages of deterrence to the population, despite the growing impetus to embrace a civilizing modernity that requires at least a nod toward the rule of law.

The potency of violence lies precisely in its being an instrumental and expressive means of communicating messages across cultures, as David Riches has argued.[9] Though they invest different meanings in violence, all cultures recognize bodily pain. The ambivalence of state and society toward the legal and harsher extralegal punishments and the meanings attached to them is brought into focus in Gema Santamaría's chapter on 1930s Puebla, where lynchings were represented in the press as either justice or barbarism. Given that state officials often organized extrajudicial punishments as part of private vendettas, widespread sanctioning of these practices came from above and below. What was clearly missing was the political will from state and other elites to assert the rule of law and make it work fairly; they preferred a mixture of public and private methods for controlling and deterring violence and crime, and it did not matter how much violence was used in the deterrence. Lynchings often are semipublicly endorsed executions, through public authorities' omission or failure to act, if not their direct participation. This is clear from Daniel Núñez's account of contemporary lynchings in the town of Guastatoya in Eastern Guatemala. Mirroring the situation Lila Caimari discusses in the context of Buenos Aires, in Guatemala the police decide which vigilante killings they will report, depending on relationships with victims and perpetrators and their own perceptions of class, race, and gender.

The persistent ambiguities around public, private, popular, and state forms of violence in Latin America link the discussion of punishments to the histories of systematic state torture and police brutality in the region. Cruel punishment is part of the historic repertoire of violence control by state and non-state armed actors. The degree to which violence is publicly performed varies. Foucault explores precisely when violent punishment as spectacle began to diminish and enter the hidden chambers of the penal process in Europe. He argues this shift "leaves the domain of more or less everyday perception and enters that of abstract consciousness; its effectiveness is seen as resulting from its inevitability, not from its visible intensity."[10] It is worth asking whether, where, and how this transition has taken place in Latin America. The rise of the prison population in Brazil and elsewhere in Latin America suggests emerging preferences to use the penal process to discourage crime and violence. However, the prison is also about punishment of the body.[11] The extreme violence that takes place in many Latin American prisons suggests that prison populations are another category of "noncitizens," their bodies subject to an undeclared state of exception in which they can be deprived of basic human dignity because of their "dangerousness," both past and present. While they are incarcerated in infrahuman conditions, others who are considered undesirables have literally been cleansed from the body politic, a euphemism for violent death.

Cleansing the Body Politic

Limpieza social (social cleansing) has multiple histories and manifestations in Latin America. Núñez discusses its history in Guatemala, where state security agencies, notably the army and the police, consciously used the term as they purged the polity of those considered enemies of the order they were defending. In 1965, one of the first systematic counterinsurgency operations was called Operación Limpieza (cleansing operation).

In other countries of Latin America, this form of violence control has been directed against categories of people deemed unfit for or of no use to society. They are often people who have ended up living on the streets. Medellín, Colombia, has had a particularly long history of social cleansing. In a 1998 study of victims of social cleansing in Antioquia, Colombia, the authors listed the victims as indigents, beggars, street sellers, drug addicts, prostitutes, rubbish recyclers, ex-prisoners, drug sellers, displaced people, street children, and the mentally ill. They documented 947 cases of social cleansing between 1988 and 1997, with a sharp rise in 1997.[12] The authors also identified particular categories of victims who were socially cleansed in busy commercial and financial districts, including muggers and car thieves.[13] Reminding us that popular forms of justice and punishment are not just perpetrated by the poor (though they are primary victims), traders, businessmen, and property owners, as well as sectors of the state, were involved in social cleansing in Medellín.

Social cleansing uses extreme violence to rid society of very vulnerable people who often have no family to record or question their manner of death. Street children are another category of victim. In Brazil, for instance, notorious death squads made up of former and current police officers have killed street children to address a perceived social problem and source of disorder deemed to have no other solution. Social cleansing is about controlling potential sources of crime and violence, but also serves to proclaim the right to establish certain kinds of social order and behaviors. They are normalizing operations that project a sense of defending communities from troublesome deviants. Núñez's chapter demonstrates how loosely the locals in present-day Guastatoya, a mostly ladino town, use the term "marero" to refer to any young person who deviates from local moral standards.

At the height of their territorial occupations from the late 1990s to the mid-2000s, Colombian paramilitary groups executed anyone departing from the norms of behavior they claimed to defend. This included those suspected or accused of theft, drug abuse, drunkenness, domestic violence, or rape. In the small town of Concordia in southeast Antioquia, the paramilitary began their rule in the 1990s with the social cleansing of youth, some of whom had turned to crime at a time of economic crisis. Locals' approval and appreciation of this intervention is palpable more than a decade later, even though most residents gradually turned against the paramilitary.[14]

The publics of social cleansing are fearful citizens, who are mostly colluding bystanders, convinced that no legal process or security force can deal with real and imagined threats and satisfy their yearning for stability in a world of multiple uncertainties. Social cleansing—like lynchings, violent incarcerations, and extrajudicial killings—gains a complex kind of acceptance by appearing to offer swift solutions to violence and crime. What is the precise nature of this acceptance? The answers to this question take us to the heart of the politics of violence control, which I will discuss in the final section. First, however, we need to discuss what happens to the bodies.

Displaying, Disappearing, and Disposing of Bodies

The visibility and invisibility of violent acts is a strong theme in these chapters. The spectacle of violence and punishment plays a significant role in many of the contexts discussed. The degree of visibility of violence conveys to various publics messages that are difficult to interpret without deep ethnography. Violence often is kept out of the world's gaze. At times the violence is the absence of a body and at times it is its presence. How might we account for these differences and the effects they have?

Angélica Durán-Martínez sets out to analyze these questions in relationship to drug-trafficking violence in Colombia and Mexico, and the motivations of criminals when they decide to conceal or reveal their violence. We might call these decisions tactics of group self-control around the desired impacts of violence. There is a tradeoff between showing power and infusing fear, argues Durán-Martínez, either of which can trigger state reprisals or citizen outrage. She finds that by responding more forcefully to visible violence, the state shapes incentives around concealing or revealing acts of violence. The media too plays a role through its responses to pressures of many kinds to either report or not report violent acts. Drug cartels and organized criminals also have particular commercial, security, and tactical motivations for how they deal with the bodies of their victims and what messages they want to send to different publics (including rival cartels).

Other perpetrators of violence have different and more mixed incentives. In Colombia, the false positive scandal, as it was known, involved the armed forces. In order to display bodies of dead guerrillas to the public as a message that they were winning the war, they killed thousands of civilians, notably young men from poor neighborhoods, and dressed them up as guerrillas. This practice took place particularly in the 2000s, reaching a peak in 2007, with 5,763 named victims.[15]

In this case, a perverse form of body reappearance and reidentification was used to communicate army success in controlling guerrilla violence. Latin America has a much longer history of disappearing victims' bodies. Here a range of implicit messages are communicated, by punishing not only the victim but also the living, as families are left without a body and with a strange mixture of hope and hopelessness. For Gabriel Gatti, the practice of disappearance in Uruguay and Argentina in the 1970s is a catastrophe for identity and meaning that cannot be overcome because there are no elements of culture, language, or identity left with which to overcome it: "The language, the identity, the meaning that forced disappearance shatters are the language, identity, and meaning of modernity, of those beauties of rationality and order that we around here, in the Americas, project ourselves as being: individuals, citizens, lettered people."[16]

Disappearances continue in Latin America, in cities, for example, that otherwise continue to proclaim their modernity. In La Escombrera, a rubbish dump in the upper reaches of Comuna 13, Medellín, an unknown number of bodies of young men (some estimate up to three hundred) lie seventy meters beneath the rubbish. They were disappeared following Operation Orion in 2002, when President Álvaro Uribe launched a counterinsurgency operation in the comuna, which had become a bastion of the FARC guerrillas. The paramilitary were involved in this operation and subsequently "cleaned up" the area, killing suspected guerrilla collaborators.[17] Despite this, the city continued to pile more rubbish on the site until 2015, when mothers of the disappeared finally won a decade-long campaign to have the bodies of their children exhumed.

Disposing of the bodies of victims evokes aspects of the politics of violence control that are not normally taken into account. At one level, there are practical questions about what to do with the bodies; on another level, there are concerns regarding the public or private intent of the violence and issues of evidence. Disappearance means there is no body and no evidence unless the body surfaces. In Concordia, bodies were thrown into the local river, to float away. When the corpses clogged up and contaminated the river, residents asked the paramilitary to stop the practice. The paramilitary were then forced to dig clandestine mass graves.[18]

In September 2014 in Mexico, the search for the bodies of the forty-three disappeared student protestors in Iguala, Guerrero, generated a complex and painful discussion about whether the bodies had been or could have been incinerated. The families continued to claim their loved ones were still alive through the months of uncertainty.

Counting the Bodies and New Forms of Violence Control

Varied approaches to the bodies of victims reflect the nuances around violence control methods and when violence should and should not be displayed. Bodies become cards to play in messages to survivors and families, to states, to rival criminal organizations, and to wider publics. Or they become cards to conceal in accordance with other calculations, such as obscuring an evidence trail. However, global attention to homicide data has begun to influence the politics of violence control. The high levels of homicides in Latin America compared to other regions of the world embarrass governments in the region and statistics are becoming more nuanced.[19] The United Nations Office on Drugs and Crime has done a lot of work on consolidating their homicide statistics to reveal the "many faces of homicide" and the subregional and subnational patterns of violence.[20]

Comparative homicide data speak to global publics, including investors, and encourage new thinking on the politics of violence control. They have activated efforts by city leaders and businessmen to market their cities' success in addressing violence. This has a considerable impact on the visibility and form of violence. As seen in the case of Rio, the reduction in homicides conceals the selective murders and extortion rackets that take place with police collusion in the outer suburbs. In Medellín, a number of commentators have attributed the decline in homicides to pacts over territory between gangs. As the official murder rate has gone down, however, the number of people who disappear and whose bodies are never found has increased.[21] In this case, the disappearance of the body serves both city officials and criminal organizations. The absence of a body allows investors and data gatherers to claim statistical evidence of successful violence control.

Political Violence and Violence as Politics

The previous sections have discussed various forms of violence control in Latin America through a focus on the body in a body politic. The bodies of participants in and victims of multiple acts of violence bear the imprint of historical patterns of violence control and, as the editors of this volume argue, of social and cultural representations around criminality and violence. These are transmitted to future generations through memory, stories, and values. This transmission has a profound effect on the nature of politics and the ongoing but evolving forms of violence control in the region. The idea that some human beings do not merit rights of any kind and can be subjected to violence remains strongly embedded in the political culture of Latin America, albeit differentially across the region and within countries. The conclusion Piccato draws in regards to the ley fuga in Mexico remains pertinent throughout Latin America: there is a need for a "reconsideration of the relationship between violence and politics . . . [and] violence [is] not an irrational byproduct of inequality or culture but an integral part of politics."

These essays are about violence that is rooted in a general understanding of politics that constructs enemies, dissidents, undesirables, and noncitizens in order to mobilize common interests and fears around which the state can be built. In the name of controlling the forms of violence that elites associate with these categories, the wealthy and powerful directly and indirectly condone and often promote horrific violence. By establishing categories of citizens and noncitizens, encouraging cruel violence against social and political activists, collaborating with private armed groups when necessary, and using popular violence as a substitute for an effective legal system, political and economic elites have shaped the politics of violence control. The failure to build the rule of law has been at the core of their role in relation to historical and contemporary violence and insecurity, and it has favored the perpetuation of extreme inequality in the region.

The politics of fear lies behind the form of citizenship in Latin America I have called authoritarian. Violence reproduction as violence control is justified under this form of citizenship and becomes a tool for candidates to pursue political careers and appeal to insecure publics. But what is the nature of acceptance by these publics? Do they, through their support and sometimes active participation in violence, legitimize the violent acts described in this volume? Hannah Arendt has argued that violence can be justifiable but is never legitimate.[22] That distinction is crucial to analyzing the nature of communities' consent to extralegal violence. This volume locates this consent in long-term processes around the manufacture of such violence. The editors have brought together a collection of essays which show that explanations for violence reproduction cannot be reduced to either state failure or neoliberal economics. We can only appreciate the dynamics of violence reproduction if we locate them in the way social, cultural, and symbolic components have been mobilized to give violence its multiple, deeply embodied meanings in the public sphere.

Many organizations and individuals in Latin America have attempted to desanction violence in the region; it can be argued that in so doing they both challenge authoritarian citizenship and build legitimate power. Emboldened by evolving global human rights norms and global exposure of the high levels of regional violence, many societal actors and movements in Latin America have sought to defy the logics that draw them into violence control mechanisms. This is not a new phenomenon. Human rights movements and families of the disappeared played an important role in exposing the violence of military regimes in the 1970s and 1980s. Citizens' groups have made vital contributions to exposing gender-based violence in the Guatemalan and Colombia civil wars; to tracing kidnapped children in El Salvador and Argentina; and to campaigning against violence against members of the lesbian, gay, bisexual, and transgender communities and the everyday forms of violence that women and children experience at home. Mexican families led protests against the disappearance of their sons at the end of 2014. These citizens' actions reflect the critical current in social agency throughout Latin American history and are a potential source of new meanings surrounding violence. We might call them the dissident publics and critical citizens of violence politics.

Notes

1. Although it existed previously, this concept only gained traction in the decade after the so-called democratic transition of the 1980s; it entered the political lexicon with the 2004 UN report on democracy in Latin America. See Programa de Naciones Unidas para el Desarrollo, *La Democracia en América Latina: hacia una democracia de ciudadanas y ciudadanos* (Buenos Aires: Aguilar, Altea, Taurus, Alfaguara, 2004)

2. Jenny Pearce, "Perverse State Formation and Securitized Democracy in Latin America," *Democratization* 17, no. 2 (2010): 286–306.

3. "Prison in Brazil: Welcome to the Middle Ages," *The Economist*, January 18, 2014.

4. Alcaldía de Medellín, "29% disminuyeron los homicidios en 2014 en Medellín, 62% durante lo que va de la administración del Alcalde Anibal Gaviria Correa," January 14, 2015, www.medellin.gov.co.

5. Evidence and Lessons from Latin America (ELLA), "Building Legal Frameworks to Address Femicide in Latin America," policy brief, 2014, p. 4, http://fundar.org .mx/mexico/pdf/Brief-BuildingLegalFrameworkstoAddressFemicide.pdf (accessed January 13, 2015).

6. Ibid., 2. The same report found that fourteen of the twenty-five countries with the highest rates of femicide in the world are located in Latin America and the Caribbean.

7. Giorgio Agamben, *State of Exception* (Chicago, IL: University of Chicago Press, 2005), 1.

8. Ibid., 1.

9. David Riches, "The Phenomenon of Violence," in *The Anthropology of Violence*, ed. David Riches (Oxford: Blackwell, 1986), 1–28.

10. Michel Foucault, *Discipline and Punish: The Birth of the Prison* (London: Penguin, 1991), 9.

11. Ibid., 16.

12. Instituto Popular de Capacitación (IPC), *Guerra, paz y derechos humanos en Antioquia* (Medellín: IPC, 1998), 146.

13. "Reapareció el Grupo Maja," *El Tiempo*, May 9, 1995.

14. Jenny Pearce fieldwork notes, Concordia, Colombia, November 2014.

15. Fellowship of Reconciliation and Colombia-Europe-U.S. Human Rights Observatory, "The Rise and Fall of 'False Positive' Killings in Colombia," 2014, http://forusa .org/sites/default/files/uploads/false-positives-2014-colombia-report.pdf (accessed January 6, 2015).

16. Gabriel Gatti, *Surviving Forced Disappearance in Argentina and Uruguay. Identity and Meaning* (Basingstoke: Palgrave Macmillan, 2014), 16

17. Verdad Abierta, "La tenebrosa máquina de guerra que dirigió 'Don Berna,'" March 22, 2014, www.verdadabierta.com/imputaciones/5289-la-tenebrosa-maquina-de-guerra -que-dirigio-don-berna (accessed January 7, 2015).

18. Jenny Pearce, fieldwork notes, November 2014.

19. See, for example, World Health Organization, "Global Status Report on Violence Prevention, 2014," www.who.int/violence_injury_prevention/violence/status_report/ 2014/en/ (accessed January 6, 2015).

20. United Nations Office on Drugs and Crime (UNODC), "Global Study on Homicide, 2013" (Vienna: UNODC, 2014), 26, www.unodc.org/documents/gsh/pdfs/2014_GLOBAL_HOMICIDE_BOOK_web.pdf.

21. Liliana Bernal Franco and Claudia Navas Caputo, "Urban Violence and Humanitarian Action in Medellin," HASOW Discussion Paper 5, June 2013, http://reliefweb.int/sites/reliefweb.int/files/resources/Hasow_5_Urban%20violence%20and%20humanitarian%20action%20in%20Medellin_(8jun).pdf (accessed January 6, 2015).

22. Hannah Arendt, *On Violence* (London: Harvest, 1970), 52.

Epilogue

Apocalypse Now?

Diane E. Davis

The powerful essays in this edited volume paint a stark and depressing picture of the ways that violence has persisted in Latin America over much of the twentieth century, owing not just to the hegemonic powers of repressive state actors, but also to the normalization of its occurrence within everyday life. With a focus on how social constructions of violence and crime inform cultural practices, the persistence of impunity, and identity formation in Latin America, we have learned that violence seeps into just about every institution and experience, thus justifying and at times helping to recast predominant categorizations of what constitutes criminal activity and state responses to it. As we have also learned, far from lurking in the shadows of state–civil society relations, violence is always visible and at times even celebrated. As it bursts into view, violence and pervasive criminality inform collective understandings of how social and political power is wielded through coercive actions from above and below, by state and non-state actors. In so doing, these violent practices have not only ravaged the distinction between legal and illegal, civilized and barbaric, state and non-state, they have prioritized the everyday management of fear as a defining ethos of Latin American society, even while imposing ever newer forms of establishing social and political order outside the rule of law.

As most readers of this volume are probably aware, Latin America today is suffering intensely from the weight of this tragic history. As a region, it hosts three times the world average rate for death by firearms and among the highest homicide rates.[1] In some of the most violence-prone countries, unprecedented levels of police corruption and impunity have contributed to rising public insecurity,[2] thus producing entrenched ecosystems of violence marked by accelerating levels of robbery, assault, and kidnapping.[3] In certain locales, most notorious among them several cities in Mexico, Brazil, and Colombia, organized gangs equipped with a sophisticated cache of arms and advanced technologies for protection and detection against law enforcement raids have blatantly attacked police and military as well as the citizens who report them to the authorities.[4] With trust in the coercive apparatus of the state and its justice system in steep decline, citizens take matters into their own hands—either through vigilante acts or, more commonly, through the standard route of hiring private security guards who act on behalf of individuals and communities but not the larger public.[5]

This volume has shown that in Latin America these conditions have existed for decades, and life goes on. Even so, it is tempting to say that this sorry state of affairs has now reached apocalyptic levels, even in comparison with the past, owing to the long-term fragmentation of the modern state and the near-breakdown of collective norms about what types of violence will and will not be tolerated. All of this could be considered to be the path-dependent consequence of the structures and processes outlined in the preceding chapters. To bring this point home, a recent article published in the UK-based *Guardian* identified "rampant violence in Latin America" as the region's "worst epidemic" ever, with other news outlets labeling Latin America's scourge of urban violence as more deadly than Ebola.[6] Among the countries called out for concern in just the last several years are Venezuela, Bolivia, the Dominican Republic, El Salvador, Guatemala, and Honduras. They join the ranks of Brazil, Colombia, and Mexico as countries being pulled into the orbit of extraordinary and spiraling everyday violence. But more important than the expanding number of countries that now face these tragic developments is the growing concern with the spillover impacts of violence on the cultural, social, and political infrastructures of Latin America. A recent special issue of *Environment and Urbanization* entitled "Conflict and Violence in Twenty-First-Century Cities" highlighted such problems as large-scale population displacement, accelerating regional and transnational migration, youth alienation, intensifying gender violence (now more likely to be termed "femicide"), and conflicts over land and property rights as among the newest challenges to public order in Latin America.[7] Likewise, citizens themselves have begun to identify the role that media distortions of violence and new forms of cultural expression (e.g., *narcocorridos*) play in reinforcing this deadly and vicious cycle of violence and impunity. Together these trends suggest that twenty-first-century Latin American cities are saddled with new forms of inequality, fear, and terror that do not map easily to conventional class or income metrics, and that in their entirety are producing distorted citizenship patterns and a hollowing out of democratic institutions and practices.

Seeing these concerns through the lens of recent tragic developments in Mexico, where the carnage has been mind-boggling, one can only continue to register disbelief. As if criminals who built their reputations on heaving their adversaries into boiling cauldrons of oil were not enough (that perpetrator came to be known as El Pozolero), not to mention an estimated national total of close to sixty thousand killed by the drug wars in the past decade, the tragic 2015 massacre of forty-three young students from Ayotzinapa, Guerrero, who were training to be teachers, showed just how sad and desperate conditions have become. The students were captured and tortured by local police from the nearby city of Iguala, who subsequently turned them over to a criminal gang for assassination. In the search for the disappeared victims, scores of other unidentified bodies showing signs of torture were discovered in mass graves, further fueling citizen outrage and a sense that abusive actions against the poor and powerless had become routine, leaving untold scores of nameless victims in their wake. Adding insult to injury, the Ayotzinapa students' kidnapping and presumed murder had occurred under orders from Iguala's mayor, whose motivations were first reported as resting in a desire to thwart student attendance at a public meeting where his wife was giving a speech, but which later evidence suggested to have been drug cartel–related. That the mayor identified as responsible for these conscience-numbing acts of impunity was affiliated with the ostensibly progressive Partido de la Revolución Democrática (PRD, or Democratic Revolutionary Party), which built its political reputation around a mission to move Mexico into more accountable democratic terrain after years of one-party rule, made clear that the politics of violence have transcended political party bounds to become part of the social and political landscape. This trend was further confirmed by an independent investigation carried out by an international group of experts, initially invited by Mexico's federal government and then denied permission to extend their mandate. The group's findings suggested the presence—and plausible negligence—of military elements and federal officials on the night of the events.

To be sure, in Mexico and elsewhere, there is huge local and regional variation in violence levels, and only certain urban and regional locations host higher than average homicide rates. The larger point here is that violence has not unfolded equally across the spaces of Latin American cities, regions, and nations. One thing that the most violent locations have in common is that state and non-state coercive actors are less motivated by political ideals linked to democratic governance, or even by monopolization of the means of coercion, and more oriented toward totalitarian control over the everyday lives of those who happen to populate their particular territorial orbit in some way. Anyone familiar with contemporary Latin America is aware that this is by no means a problem only in Mexico. There exist many no-man's-lands across localities and neighborhoods of Rio de Janeiro, Caracas, San Salvador, Guatemala City, Kingston, and São Paulo. In these sites, mafia organizations, local gangs, or drug traffickers hold sway over large swaths of the population, often in complicity with local authorities—as Graham Denyer Willis demonstrates in his study of police behavior in São Paulo.[8] Whether working together or in opposition, police and criminal efforts to monopolize extortion rackets and supply chains of illicit activities are manifest in ongoing struggles over physical space, from streets to neighborhoods or entire cities. It also is evident in the strategies of smuggling organizations and pirating forces that operate in both urban economies and through transnational networks of trade structured around clandestine networks of capital accumulation.

Such developments have not only laid the groundwork for challenging the traditional functions, legitimacy, coercive capacities, and territorial logic of democratic nation-states. They also signal the rise of new networks of loyalties that fragment the state apparatus and link non-state armed actors to a variety of communities or constituencies with varying economic and social agendas that direct their attention locally and transnationally more than nationally. At times, their subnational and transnational activities form the basis for alternative networks of commitment or coercion that territorially cross-cut or undermine old allegiances to a sovereign national state. While this characterization may well describe conditions in Mexico, it is clearly a larger regional problem. Several observers have suggested that such developments have overtaken Peru, where the 2014 elections were considered the most violent in more than a decade, where gubernatorial and local mayoral candidates have been identified as intricately involved in drug trafficking, and where gangs assassinated several political candidates in 2015.[9]

The question that emerges is whether the history detailed in the chapters of this volume can help us understand these more contemporary forms of violence and the fragmentation of national state authority. Could we look back at the cities and countries examined here and find a direct trajectory from the past to the present—or, if not direct, then path-dependent? If so, what foundational roots and subsequent developments produced this historical trajectory? If there indeed were some connection, it would be rather paradoxical given that many of the chapters in this volume show that the imposition and internalization of state violence and police abuse of power was undertaken in the service of political projects intended to strengthen the state's hegemony and its capacities to monopolize the means of coercion in the first place. This was certainly true in most of the cases where the police or the state were the main protagonists in the perpetration of violence. Giving some plausibility to this supposition, we can see that among the most troubled countries in the region today are those where police abuse of power began early in the century, such as in Brazil, Mexico, Colombia, Guatemala, and El Salvador. Many of these countries have long suffered from a democracy deficit due to having never consolidated a democratic regime out of the hands of agrarian oligarchs, having had a single party dominate the state, or having alternated between dictatorship and democracy.

Such explanations do not account for everything. Of the countries analyzed historically in this volume, Chile seems to have avoided the brunt of these problems, and it too has a nondemocratic and militarized past. And although violence exists in Santiago, it pales in regional comparison. The question is why? The nature of violence in early to mid-twentieth-century Chile described in this volume comes in the form of sodomy, a set of practices that might be understood as working on the margins of the main organizational and institutionalized interests that sustained the state–civil society governance pact. One is tempted to speculate that when the state directs its repressive arm against populations that are not formally or collectively organized to assert their interests, impunity and repression may fail to become politically institutionalized within the practices of the state. Conversely, when relationships of repression are strategically formulated to intimidate formally recognized groups that can potentially threaten monopolized state power (such as working-class, peasant or indigenous, and even middle-class organizations), and when those groups bargain or negotiate with state actors, or perhaps fight back, such actions may succeed in bringing these potentially oppositional actors into a tangled web of complicity, thus reinforcing the institutionalized cultures and practices of terror as part of the state–civil society nexus.

Any argument about why Chile has not suffered more violence must, of course, be grounded in serious historical and contemporary analysis. In the context of regional variations in violence we might frame the origins of violence as less linked to democracy and its absence, and more linked to patterns of citizen mobilization and state formation, or even sovereignty. Elsewhere I have argued that the proliferation of a wide range of non-state armed actors organized around overlapping and territorially diverse networks of commitment and coercion can be considered both product and producer of the changing nature of states and sovereignty in the developing world.[10] Recent events further suggest that the form of sovereign power emerging in Latin America advances a destructive fragmentation of legitimate authority that reinforces rather than resolves problems of violence. Rather than seeing the "all-encompassing structural and centralized modality of control" that is the standard form of sovereignty associated with the modern nation-state, we are seeing the proliferation of "multiple, localized, and relatively autonomous cores of power," a phenomenon described by Nir Gazit in his study of the Arab-Israeli context.[11] In countries like Mexico, Colombia, and Brazil this fragmented sovereignty is evident in the incapacity of the state or even its nationally organized political elites to discipline both state and non-state actors whose claim to authority derives from their formal and informal association with these essential building blocks of modern sovereignty. In such a context, we see a return to a situation where localized bands of thieves with a commitment to private gain through use of personalistic authority and unrestrained impunity are undermining national state authority while foreclosing citizens' attempts to challenge them.

While the analogy to the Israeli-Palestinian conflict might seem like a problematic analytical leap, not to mention inappropriate in the Latin American context where most violence stems from claims other than denied national statehood, there may indeed be some parallels worth reflecting upon. For one, as in the Middle East, the escalating violence in Latin America has eluded local, regional, and international efforts at resolution. For another, in Mexico, Brazil, Colombia, Guatemala, Honduras, El Salvador, and elsewhere in the region, the state has failed to win the war against accelerating violence despite resorting to militaristic tactics that sometimes incentivize human rights violations. This outcome not only echoes the Israeli-Palestinian situation; it also undermines the legitimacy of Latin American states, driving citizens away from national political leadership in ways that limit leaders' capacity to defeat criminal enemies, further fueling the vicious cycle of violence. With the state weakened in the face of declining legitimacy, criminal networks of allegiance may start to provide new forms of welfare, employment, and perceived security, operating as the functional equivalents of states. Thus they encourage new forms of non-state sovereignty that contrast to the real or imagined communities that sustained modern nationalism and traditional patterns of national state sovereignty along the lines articulated by Benedict Anderson.[12] All this suggests a potentially dystopian future for Latin American nations, particularly if the fragmented or competing sovereigns within their national spaces are not brought under control, a lesson that haunts other nations in the developing world.[13]

One cannot help but note the tragedy of this situation in which the state's incapacity to reverse or eliminate the root causes of violence leads not to full state collapse but to a situation of fragmented sovereignty. The latter outcome may actually be worse if it enables the pretense of state authority or democracy to coexist in an environment where criminality and unrestricted violence flower.[14] Much of our theoretical knowledge of how and why sovereignty becomes either hegemonic or failed is informed by the work of anthropologists, political scientists,[15] and sociologists like Charles Tilly.[16] Tilly argued that in order to defend or establish national sovereignty, state actors engaged in armed warfare, with *interstate* violence fueling both domestic monopolization of the means of coercion and modern state formation. To successfully wage and win wars, the state created new institutions (government bureaucracies), new revenue sources (taxes), and new avenues for securing legitimacy (citizenship rights) that then allowed it to extract funds and moral support from the citizenry to employ armed actors in the process of building stronger state-society connections. But in Latin America, this process was distorted by the state's use and abuse of violence against its own peoples. This form of *intrastate* warfare socially and institutionally empowered the state's coercive forces while undermining the rule of law, further entrenching violence and coercion as the currency of political and economic power. Today, the state's control of the means of violence is far from monopolized in most of Latin America, as state actors at a variety of scales work with criminals or non-state armed actors as much as against them, thereby splintering national state authority in destructive ways. Elected officials may still attempt to assert their Agambenian "state of exception,"[17] but when they do so they are often in conflict with or undermined by other state and non-state actors.

So, what is to be done? Is there any scope for optimism? In an updating of his original ideas, Tilly underscored the importance of trust relations in cementing the dynamics of cooperation between citizens and state authorities in order to strengthen the former's allegiance to the rule of law and the enlightenment ideals of the modern state.[18] Trust is in short supply in Latin America, given the histories of violence with impunity. But it is not entirely absent, at least not at the local level and for some citizens. One of the upsides of fragmented sovereignty is that it has helped shift the locus of political claim-making away from national state authorities and toward the city, other subnational scales of determination, and even individual citizens. It is at the level of the neighborhood and street, as well as in public spaces both real and virtual, that citizens are most vigorously lashing back at the debilitated state and its connection to criminals. In the wake of student massacres in Guerrero, massive protests in the capital cities of both that state (Chilpancingo) and the nation (Mexico City) unleashed a geographically distributed energy not seen in Mexico in decades, since the Chiapas revolts. Through petitions, ongoing demonstrations, and nonstop media coverage, a new political culture of opposition is being constructed, inspired by the sense that Mexico is in crisis and facing an emergency that must not be allowed to pass without seizing the moment. Perhaps such mobilizations are on the ascent in Mexico because so many regions in that country have hit rock bottom, and few citizens have faith in nationally elected officials to extract themselves from decades of impunity and complicity so as to counter local strongmen and other perpetrators of violence. Yet elsewhere across Latin America, we are also starting to see organized social movements taking up the anticrime banner, although this trend has been limited primarily to middle-class groups and has not incorporated large swaths of society in most countries.[19]

Perhaps a return to the case of Michoacán, noted in David Carey Jr. and Gema Santamaría's introduction, will help explain when hope materializes and why it still exists within an environment of fragmented sovereignty, even as it helps us see how the representation, sanctioning, and resisting of certain forms of violence remains central to our understanding of contemporary patterns of violence. With conditions in Michoacán spiraling downward owing to clandestine and highly contested relations between the Mexican military and regional drug traffickers throughout 2015, local militias organized at the community level have continued to push back against both these state and non-state armed actors. Their assertions of autonomy and self-defense (*autodefensa*) have raised vexing questions about the rule of law and who has the right to bear arms in an environment where the state and its purported mafia enemies are both suspect. Drawing on references to their indigenous past and to the Zapatista legacies of the Mexican Revolution, Michoacán's armed community militias have generated larger visibility across Mexico. But their capacities to generate sympathy in the larger national sphere were catapulted to new heights when Mexico's most notorious drug trafficker, Joaquín "El Chapo" Guzmán, made a daring escape from a maximum-security prison. (This was, in fact, the second such incident, itself a telling indicator of the symbolic and actual power embodied in this particular persona.) In both press coverage and citizen responses to the "escape," the discovery of a deep tunnel constructed from within El Chapo's prison cell was collectively understood to be the product of a range of complicities that most likely involved actors ranging from prison guards and officials all the way up to national cabinet ministries and possibly even the president.

The representational meaning and larger symbolism of this event was soon translated into a sign of the corruption and failure of the rule of law that persists within the Mexican political system. And with the inner workings of impunity revealed so resoundingly through El Chapo's escape, community groups in Michoacán had further reason to reinvigorate their ongoing struggles for local autonomy and to call for a reassessment of a militarization strategy that harms poor citizens while letting drug traffickers go free. Not surprisingly, such efforts were met by forceful repression from Mexican military forces, one of which ended in a shootout in the town of Santa María Ostula, where four local residents were massacred and several community leaders arrested.[20] Even so, there was an upside to this display of state violence: in the larger national environment of ridicule, in which newspapers and blogs called for investigations into high-level networks of complicity between armed drug gangs and multiple branches of the state, local peasant communities from Ostula, Michoacán, and their sympathizers were emboldened to take their struggle to the streets, marching in the capital city and targeting national offices of government.[21] As this book goes to press, it is unclear whether such mobilizations will continue to accelerate and whether they can do anything to reverse the impunity and violence that haunts Michoacán and other locations in Mexico. El Chapo was ultimately recaptured and is now facing extradition to the United States. Whether or not this development will have much impact on the drug trade and conditions of violence and impunity, these events do reveal the political processes and power relations that have emerged from—and will structure—debate about what forms of violence are justifiable, for whom, and for what purposes.

Thinking about the Ostula mobilizations in Mexico in light of the information presented in this book should, however, raise the question of why so few chapters have identified collective action and oppositional uses of culture to undermine (rather than sustain) the forces and conditions that have perpetuated violence, impunity, and corruption over the decades. Indeed, complicity and internalization of norms that sustain debilitating conditions of violence appear to have been the rule, with vigilantism against criminals being one of the few forms of pushback. Did no larger social movements or proactive responses ever materialize in reality, or do scholars just not know where or how to find them? If we were to use Albert Hirschman's famous dictum, we might ask whether citizens opted for voice or exit rather than loyalty as they faced an increasingly repressive state, and why.[22] Although the answers to such questions remain beyond the scope of this volume, to answer them it would be important to return to the histories reported here and to ferret out alternative narratives. Perhaps doing so would uncover hidden ways that Latin American citizens may indeed have fought back against the legacies that now haunt them, even if only in fits and starts. Revealing such histories may not be the only way to sustain a hope that the future can be better, but it surely could help inspire the sense that agency is always possible, even in the direst of circumstances.

Notes

1. Kees Koonings and Dirk Kruijt, *Fractured Cities: Social Exclusion, Urban Violence, and Contested Spaces in Latin America* (London: Zed Books, 2007); Mark Cohen and Mauricio Rubio, "Violence and Crime in Latin America" (paper prepared for the Consulta de San José and presented at the 2007 Copenhagen Consensus Conference), www.copenhagenconsensus.com/publication/copenhagen-consensus-latin -america-violence-and-crime (accessed December 16, 2014).

2. Diane E. Davis, "The Political and Economic Origins of Violence and Insecurity in Contemporary Latin America: Past Trajectories and Future Prospects," in *Violent Democracies in Latin America,* ed. Enrique Desmond Arias and Daniel Goldstein (Durham, NC: Duke University Press, 2010), 35–62; Mercedes Hinton and Timothy Newburn, *Policing Developing Democracies* (New York: Routledge, 2009).

3. Cathy McIlwaine and Caroline Moser, "Violence and Social Capital in Urban Poor Communities," *Journal of International Development* 13, no. 7 (2001): 965–84; Caroline Moser, "Urban Violence and Insecurity: An Introductory Roadmap," *Environment and Urbanization* 16, no. 2 (2004): 1–16.

4. John Bailey and Roy Godson, *Organized Crime and Democratic Governability: Mexico and the U.S.-Mexican Borderlands* (Pittsburgh, PA: University of Pittsburgh Press, 2000).

5. Daniel Goldstein, *The Spectacular City: Violence and Performance in Urban Bolivia.* (Durham, NC: Duke University Press, 2004).

6. Rory Carroll, "Rampant Violence Is Latin America's 'Worst Epidemic,'" *The Guardian,* October 8, 2014, www.theguardian.com/world/2008/oct/09/mexico.human rights?CMP=share_btn_link.

7. Caroline Moser and Cathy McIlwaine, eds., "New Frontiers in 21st-Century Urban Conflict and Violence," *Environment and Urbanization* 26, no. 2 (2014): 331–44; see also Rosa-Linda Fregoso and Cynthia Bejarano, eds., *Terrorizing Women: Femicide in the Americas* (Duke, NC: Duke University Press, 2010).

8. Graham Denyer Willis, *The Killing Consensus: Police, Organized Crime, and the Regulation of Life and Death in Urban Brazil* (Los Angeles and Berkeley: University of California Press, 2015).

9. Associated Press, "Peru Vote Marred by Violence, Drugs," *AP/The Big Story,* October 5, 2014, http://bigstory.ap.org/article/f3e513b45a394e55b63e167a3209718d/peru -vote-marred-violence-drugs.

10. Diane E. Davis, "Irregular Armed Forces, Shifting Patterns of Commitment, and Fragmented Sovereignty in the Developing World," *Theory and Society* 39, no. 3

(2010): 397–413; Diane E. Davis and Anthony Pereira, *Irregular Armed Forces and Their Role in Politics and State Formation* (Cambridge: Cambridge University Press, 2004).

11. Nir Gazit, "Social Agency, Spatial Practices, and Power: the Micro-foundations of Fragmented Sovereignty in the Occupied Territories," *International Journal of Politics, Culture, and Society* 22 (March 2009): 83–103.

12. Benedict Anderson, *Imagined Communities: Reflections on the Origins and Spread of Nationalism* (London: Verso, 1983).

13. Robert Jackson, *Quasi-States: Sovereignty, International Relations, and the Third World* (Cambridge: Cambridge University Press, 1990).

14. Ralph A. Litzinger, "Contested Sovereignties and the Critical Ecosystem Partnership Fund," *PoLAR: Political and Legal Anthropology Review* 29, no. 1 (2006): 66–87.

15. John Agnew, "Sovereignty Regimes: Territoriality and State Authority in Contemporary World Politics," *Annals of the Association of American Geographers* 95, no. 2 (2008): 437–61; Arjun Appadurai, "Sovereignty without Territoriality: Notes for a Postnational Geography," in *The Anthropology of Space and Place: Locating Culture,* ed. Setha Low and Denise Lawrence-Zuniga (Boston: Blackwell, 2003), 337–49.

16. Charles Tilly, *Capital, Coercion, and European States, AD 990–1992* (Cambridge: Basil Blackwell, 1990).

17. Giorgio Agamben, *State of Exception,* trans. Kevin Attell (Chicago: University of Chicago Press, 2005).

18. Charles Tilly, "Cities, States, and Trust Networks," in *Contention and Trust in Cities and States,* ed. Michael Hanagan and Chris Tilly, 1–16 (Springer ebooks, 2011), www.springer.com/us/book/9789400707559 (accessed November 24, 2015).

19. Diane E. Davis and Graham Denyer Willis, "Anticrime Movements in Latin America," in *The Wiley-Blackwell Encyclopedia of Social and Political Movements,* ed. David A. Snow et al. (Hoboken, NJ: Wiley-Blackwell, 2013).

20. Santa María Ostula has a long tradition of struggling for community autonomy. For more on this history and how it has been mobilized in the context of the current drug war, see John Gledhill, "Violence and Reconstitution in Indigenous Communities," in *Violence, Coercion, and State-Making in Twentieth-Century Mexico: The Other Half of the Centaur,* ed. Wil G. Pansters (Stanford, CA: Stanford University Press, 2012).

21. See "DF: Xochicuautla and Ostula Solidarity March," www.elenemigocomun .net/2015/07/df-xochicuautla-and-ostula-solidarity-march/ (accessed August 1, 2015).

22. Albert O. Hirschman, *Exit, Voice, and Loyalty Responses to Decline in Firms, Organizations, and States* (Cambridge, MA: Harvard University Press, 1970).

Works Cited

PRIMARY SOURCES

Newspapers, Periodicals, and Media
A Vida Fluminense
Alarma!
Associated Press
Atlantic
Business Insider
Diario de Centro América
Diario de Puebla
Don Roque
The Economist
El Águila
El Día
El Diario de Puebla
El Heraldo de México
El Imparcial
El Periódico
El Sol del Pacífico
El Tiempo
El Universal
Excélsior
Foreign Policy
Gaceta Policial
Gallup.com

The Guardian
Império do Brasil: Diário Fluminense
Jamaica Gleaner
Jamaica Observer
Jamaica Star
La Gaceta: Revista de Policía y Variedades
La Opinión
La Prensa
La Voz de México
Light
Magazine Policial
National Catholic Reporter
NBC News
New Yorker
New York Times
Prensa Libre
Proceso
Revista D, Semanario de Prensa Libre
Revista Trimestral do Instituto Histórico, Geográfico, e Etnográfico do Brasil
Últimas Noticias de Excélsior
Wall Street Journal
Washington Post
Wikileaks

Archives
Archivo General de Centro América, Guatemala (AGCA)
Archivo General de la Nación, Chile (AGN-CHI)
Archivo General de la Nación, Colombia (AGN-COL)
Archivo General de la Nación, Mexico (AGN-MEX)
Archivo Histórico del Distrito Federal, Mexico (AHDF)
Archivo Histórico de la Policía Nacional, Guatemala (AHPN)
Archivo Municipal de Sololá, Guatemala (AMS)
Archivo Nacional de Chile
Arquivo Geral da Cidade do Rio de Janeiro, Brazil (AGCRJ)
Arquivo Nacional, Brazil (AN)
Biblioteca del Congreso de la República de Guatemala
Dirección General de Estadística, Guatemala (DGE)
Dirección de Información y Propaganda de la Presidencia, Colombia
New York Public Library, New York, NY
Procuraduría General de la República de México, Mexico City

Interviews

Carey, David Jr. Oral history interview with Ix'aj. San Juan Comalapa, Guatemala. February 9, 1998.

Durán-Martínez, Angélica. Interview with former Colombian defense minister. January 13, 2011.

———. Interview with anonymous businessman. Tijuana, Mexico, October 18, 2011.

———. Interview with anonymous official from the Federal Secretariat of Public Security. Mexico City, September 27, 2011.

———. Interview with anonymous relative of a victim of disappearance. Tijuana, Mexico, October 21, 2011.

Núñez, Daniel. Interviews with anonymous residents of Guastatoya. Fall 2011.

Torres, M. Gabriela. Interview with Marcela Aguilar, Quetzal Edzna. Campeche, Mexico, April 23, 1995.

Government Documents

Alcaldía de Medellín. "29% disminuyeron los homicidios en 2014 en Medellín, 62% durante lo que va de la administración del Alcalde Anibal Gaviria Correa." January 14, 2015. www.medellin.gov.co.

Alocución del Excelentísimo Señor Doctor Roberto Urdaneta Arbeláez. Bogotá: Dirección de Información y Propaganda de la Presidencia, 1953.

Archivo Histórico de la Policía Nacional (AHPN). *Del silencio a la memoria. Revelaciones del Archivo Histórico de la Policía Nacional.* Vol. 1. Guatemala City: AHPN.

Biblioteca del Congreso de la República de Guatemala. Law-Decree 24-82. Estatuto Fundamental de Gobierno.

———. Law-Decree 27-83. Ley de Amnistía.

———. Law-Decree 33-82. Ley de Amnistía.

———. Law-Decree 46-82. Ley de Tribunales Fuero Especial.

Código penal para el distrito y territorios federales, en materia de fuero común, y para toda la república en materia de fuero federal. Mexico City: Farrera, 1941.

Compilación de disposiciones sobre reformas civiles, penales, administrativas, del trabajo y sobre justicia penal militar expedidas por el Ejecutivo nacional en los años de 1948 a 1957. Ibagué: Imprenta Departamental, 1956.

Consejo Municipal de Desarrollo del Municipio de Guastatoya y SEGEPLAN, DPT. *Plan de desarrollo, Guastatoya, El Progreso.* Guatemala City: SEGEPLAN/DPT, 2010.

Constituição Política do Império do Brasil. March 25, 1824. www.planalto.gov.br/ccivil_03/constituicao/constituicao24.htm. Accessed November 17, 2014.

Decretos extraordinarios y decretos reglamentarios de leyes, expedidos por el gobierno nacional [July 1, 1952–June 30, 1956]. Bogotá: Imprenta Nacional, 1953–58.

Decretos extraordinarios y decretos reglamentarios de leyes expedidos por la Rama Ejecutiva, en desarrollo del artículo 121 de la Constitución Nacional, durante el año de 1949. Bogotá: Imprenta Nacional, 1950.

Dirección General de Estadística (DGE). *Censo de la república levantado el 28 de agosto de 1921. 40 censo, parte II.* Guatemala City: Talleres Gutenburg, 1926.

———. *Quinto censo general de población levantado el 7 de abril de 1940.* Guatemala City: Tipografía Nacional, 1942.

Fundação CEPERJ, "Anuario Estatistico do Estado do Rio de Janeiro—2013." www.ceperj.rj.gov.br/ceep/Anuario2013/ApresentacaoDemografiaPopulacao.html. Accessed June 24, 2014.

Geo-Rio, "Tabela 1172: Desenvolvimento Humano e Condições de Vida na Cidade do Rio de Janeiro" (Estudo No. 1347), January 2004. www.camara.rj.gov.br/planodiretor/pd2009/saudepd/Anexo3_IDH.pdf. Accessed June 23, 2014.

Human Rights Watch, "World Report 2015: Mexico." www.hrw.org/world-report/2015/country-chapters/mexico#899ef4. Accessed April 25, 2016.

INDECOM's Statistics on Security Force Related Fatalities—2013. Kingston: Independent Commission of Investigations, 2014. www.indecom.gov.jm/2013%20Statistics%20Press%20Release.pdf.

Informes presidenciales. Luis Echeverría Álvarez. Mexico City: Cámara de Diputados, 2006.

Instituto de Segurança Pública. Monthly Crime Data Reports for 2013. www.isp.rj.gov.br/. Accessed June 23, 2014.

Instituto Nacional de Estadística y Geografía (INEGI). Censo de Población y Vivienda 1940. www.inegi.org.mx/est/contenidos/proyectos/ccpv/cpv1940/. Accessed December 14, 2014.

Instituto Perreira Passos, "Tabela 484: População residente, segundo as Áreas de Planejamento e Regiões Administrativas—1991/2010." http://portalgeo.rio.rj.gov.br/. Accessed November 26, 2014.

Jamaica Constabulary Force. "Jamaica Constabulary Force Annual Report, 2013." Kingston: JCF, 2014. www.jcf.gov.jm/article/2014-06-02/jamaica-constabulary-force-annual-report-2013. Accessed June 10, 2014.

Memoria del cuerpo de policía de la república rendida al ministerio de gobernación y justicia, correspondiente a los años 1922 y 1923. Guatemala City: Tipografía Nacional, 1924.

Memoria de la Dirección General de la Policía Nacional, presentada al Ministro de Gobernación y Justicia. Guatemala City: Tipografía Nacional, 1899–1943.

Memoria de los trabajos realizados por la dirección general de la Policía Nacional. Guatemala City: Tipografía Nacional, 1930–45.

Procurador de los Derechos Humanos. *Las características de las muertes violentas en el país.* Guatemala City: Procurador de los Derechos Humanos, 2006.

www.pdh.org.gt/archivos/descargas/Documentos/Informes%20Especiales/ carácterticas_de_las_muertes_violentas_pdh.pdf. Accesed November 15, 2014.

Procuraduría de los Derechos Humanos. "Mapeo de conflictividad departamental de El Progreso correspondiente al año 2011." El Progreso, Guatemala: Procuraduría de los Derechos Humanos, 2011.

Statistical Institute of Jamaica. "2011 Census of Population and Housing— Jamaica." Kingston: Statistical Institute of Jamaica, 2012, http://statinja.gov .jm/Census/Census2011/Census%202011%20data%20from%20website.pdf. Accessed June 10, 2014.

Secondary Sources

Agamben, Giorgio. *Homo Sacer: Sovereign Power and Bare Life.* Translated by Daniel Heller-Roazen. Stanford, CA: Stanford University Press, 1998.

———. *State of Exception.* Translated by Kevin Attell. Chicago: University of Chicago Press, 2005.

Agenda 21 COMPERJ. "Região Metropolitana ganha 2 municípios: Rio Bonito e Cachoeiras de Macacu," January 3, 2014. www.agenda21comperj.com.br/ noticias/regiao-metropolitana-ganha-2-municipios-rio-bonito-e-cachoeiras -de-macacu. Accessed June 23, 2014.

Agnew, John. "Sovereignty Regimes: Territoriality and State Authority in Contemporary World Politics." *Annals of the Association of American Geographers* 95, no. 2 (2008): 437–61.

Aguirre, Carlos. *The Criminals of Lima and Their Worlds: The Prison Experience, 1850–1935.* Durham, NC: Duke University Press, 2005.

Aguirre, Carlos A., and Robert Buffington, eds. *Reconstructing Criminality in Latin America.* Wilmington, DE: Scholarly Resources, 2000.

Alexander, Claire. "Rethinking 'Gangs': Gangs, Youth Violence and Public Policy." In *Runnymede Report.* London: Runnymede Trust, 2008.

Allen, G. Frederick. "Vigilante Justice in Jamaica: The Community against Crime." *International Journal of Comparative and Applied Criminal Justice* 21, no. 1 (1997): 1–12.

Amnesty International. "Killings and Violence by Police: How Many More Victims?" www.amnesty.org/en/library/asset/AMR38/003/2001/%20en/dd481313- dc2d-11dd-9f41-2fdde0484b9c/amr380032001en.html. Accessed October 29, 2015.

Anderson, Benedict. *Imagined Communities: Reflections on the Origins and Spread of Nationalism.* London: Verso, 1983.

Andreas, Peter. "The Politics of Measuring Illicit Flows and Policy Effectiveness." In *Sex, Drugs, and Body Counts: The Politics of Numbers in Global Crime and Conflict,* 23–45. Ithaca, NY: Cornell University Press, 2010.

Andreas, Peter, and Kelly M. Greenhill. *Sex, Drugs, and Body Counts the Politics of Numbers in Global Crime and Conflict*. Ithaca, NY: Cornell University Press, 2010.

Andreas, Peter, and Joel Wallman, "Illicit Markets and Violence: What Is the Relationship?" *Crime, Law and Social Change* 52, no. 3 (2009): 225–29.

Anfuso, Joseph, and David Sczepanski. *Efraín Ríos Montt: Servant or Dictator? The Real Story of Guatemala's Controversial Born-Again President*. Ventura, CA: Vision House, 1984.

Aponte Cardona, Alejandro. *Guerra y derecho penal del enemigo. Reflexión crítica sobre el eficientísimo penal de enemigo*. Bogotá: Ibáñez, 2006.

Appadurai, Arjun. "Sovereignty without Territoriality: Notes for a Postnational Geography." In *The Anthropology of Space and Place: Locating Culture*, edited by Setha Low and Denise Lawrence-Zuniga, 337–49. Boston: Blackwell, 2003.

Arendt, Hannah. *On Violence*. New York: Harcourt, Brace, 1969; London: Harvest, 1970.

Arias, Enrique Desmond. "Dispatches from the Field: Milícias and Police Corruption in Rio de Janeiro." *Americas Quarterly* 3, no. 2 (2009): 90–93.

——. *Drugs and Democracy in Rio de Janeiro: Trafficking, Networks, and Public Security*. Chapel Hill: University of North Carolina Press, 2006.

——. "The Impacts of Differential Armed Dominance on Politics in Rio de Janeiro, Brazil." *Studies in Comparative International Development* 48, no. 3 (2013): 263–84.

Arias, Enrique Desmond, and Daniel M. Goldstein, eds. *Violent Democracies in Latin America*. Durham, NC: Duke University Press, 2010.

Arlacchi, Pietro. *Mafia Business: The Mafia Ethic and the Spirit of Capitalism*. London: Verso, 1986.

Astorga, Luis, and David Shirk. "Drug Trafficking Organizations and Counter-Drug Strategies in the U.S.-Mexican Context." Working Paper Series on U.S.-Mexico Security Cooperation. University of San Diego and Woodrow Wilson International Center for Scholars and Transborder Institute, San Diego, CA, 2010. www.wilsoncenter.org/sites/default/files/Chapter%201-Drug%20Trafficking%20Organizations%20and%20Counter-Drug%20Strategies%20in%20the%20U.S.-Mexico%20Context.pdf.

Auyero, Javier. *Routine Politics and Violence in Argentina: The Gray Zone of State Power*. New York: Cambridge University Press, 2007.

Auyero, Javier, and María Fernanda Berti. *La violencia en los márgenes. Una maestra y un sociólogo en el conurbano bonaerense*. Buenos Aires: Katz, 2013.

Azaola, Elena, and Marcelo Bergman. *Delincuencia, marginalidad y desempeño institucional principales resultados de la encuesta a población en reclusión en tres entidades de la República Mexicana, Distrito Federal, Morelos y estado de*

México. Mexico City: Centro de Investigación y Docencia Económica, División de Estudios Jurídicos, 2003.

Bailey, John, and Roy Godson. *Organized Crime and Democratic Governability: Mexico and the U.S.-Mexican Borderlands*. Pittsburgh, PA: University of Pittsburgh Press, 2000.

Ball, Patrick, Paul Kobrak, and Herbert F. Spirer. *Violencia institucional en Guatemala, 1960 a 1996: una reflexión cuantitativa*. Washington, DC: American Association for the Advancement of Science, 1999.

Baratta, Alessandro. *Criminología crítica y crítica del derecho penal*. Mexico City: Siglo XXI, 1991.

Barrera Bassols, Jacinto. *El caso Villavicencio: violencia y poder en el porfiriato*. Mexico City: Alfaguara, 1997.

Bateson, Regina. "Crime Victimization and Political Participation." *American Political Science Review* 106, no. 3 (2012): 570–87.

———. "Lynchings in Guatemala: A Legacy of Civil War?" Paper presented at the 30th Latin American Studies Association Congress, San Francisco, CA, May 25, 2012.

———. "Vigilantism in Postwar Guatemala." Paper presented at the Harvard-MIT-Yale Graduate Student Conference on Political Violence, April 23, 2011.

Batres Jáuregui, Antonio. *Los indios, su historia y su civilización*. Guatemala City: Tipografía La Unión, 1894.

Beezley, William H., Cheryl E. Martin, and William E. French, eds. *Rituals of Rule, Rituals of Resistance: Public Celebrations and Popular Culture in Mexico*. Wilmington, DE: Scholarly Resources, 1994.

Benson, Peter, Edward Fischer, and Kedron Thomas. "Resocializing Suffering: Neoliberalism, Accusation, and the Sociopolitical Context of Guatemala's New Violence." *Latin American Perspectives* 35 (2008): 38–58. DOI: 10.1177/0094582X08321955.

Berco, Cristian. "Silencing the Unmentionable: Non-Reproductive Sex and the Creation of a Civilized Argentina." *Americas* 58, no. 3 (2002): 419–41.

Berger, Susan A. *Guatemaltecas: The Women's Movement, 1986–2003*. Austin: University of Texas Press, 2006.

Bergman, Marcelo, and Laurence Whitehead, eds. *Criminality, Public Security, and the Challenge to Democracy in Latin America*. Notre Dame, IN: University of Notre Dame Press, 2009.

Bergquist, Charles. *Labor in Latin America: Comparative Essays on Chile, Argentina, Venezuela, and Colombia*. Stanford, CA: Stanford University Press, 1986.

Bernal Franco, Liliana, and Claudia Navas Caputo. "Urban Violence and Humanitarian Action in Medellin." HASOW Discussion Paper 5, June 2013.

http://reliefweb.int/sites/reliefweb.int/files/resources/Hasow_5_Urban%20
violence%20and%20humanitarian%20action%20in%20Medellin_(8jun).pdf.
Accessed January 6, 2015.

Black, Donald J. "Production of Crime Rates." *American Sociological Review* 35
(1970): 733–48.

Blacklock, Cathy. "Democratization and Popular Women's Organizations." In
Journeys of Fear: Refugee Return and National Transformation, edited by
Liisa L. North and Alan Simmons, 196–212. Montreal: McGill-Queen's Press,
1999.

Blakemore, Harold. "From the War of the Pacific to 1930." In *Chile since Independence*, edited by Leslie Bethell, 33–85. New York: Cambridge University Press,
1993.

Blok, Anton. "Mafia and Blood Symbolism." In *Risky Transactions: Trust, Kinship, and Ethnicity*, edited by Frank K. Salter. New York: Berghahn Books,
2002.

Bourne, Paul, Andrew Bourne, Chad Chambers, Damian K. Blake, Charlene
Sharpe-Price, and Ikhalfani Solan. "Lottery Scam in a Third World Nation:
The Economics of a Financial Crime and Its Breadth." *Asian Journal of Busi-
ness Management* 5, no. 1 (2013): 19–51.

Brands, Hal. *Latin America's Cold War.* Cambridge, MA: Harvard University
Press, 2012.

Branco, Zoraia Saint'Claire. "Estórias da Policia do Rio de Janeiro," *Cadernos de
Segurança Pública* 1 (December 2009): 2–9.

Braun, Herbert. *The Assassination of Gaitán: Public Life and Urban Violence in
Colombia.* Madison: University of Wisconsin Press, 1985.

Bretas, Marcos Luíz. *Guerra das ruas: Povo e polícia na cidade do Rio de Janeiro.*
Rio de Janeiro: Arquivo Nacional, 1997.

Brooks, Peter. *The Melodramatic Imagination: Balzac, Henry James, Melodrama,
and the Mode of Excess.* 2nd ed. New Haven, CT: Yale University Press, 1995.

Buffington, Robert M. *Criminal and Citizen in Modern Mexico.* Lincoln: University of Nebraska Press, 2000.

———. "*Los Jotos*: Contested Visions of Homosexuality in Modern Mexico." In
Sex and Sexuality in Latin America, edited by Daniel Balderston and Donna
J. Guy. New York: New York University Press, 1997.

Buffington, Robert, and Pablo Piccato, comps. *True Stories of Crime in Modern
Mexico.* Albuquerque: University of New Mexico Press, 2009.

Bulnes, Francisco. *El verdadero Díaz y la revolución.* 2nd ed. Mexico City: Editora Nacional, 1960.

Bunker, Robert, and John Sullivan. "Extreme Barbarism, a Death Cult, and
Holy Warriors in Mexico: Societal Warfare South of the Border?" *Small Wars
Journal*, May 22, 2011, 1–10.

Burrell, Jennifer. *Maya after War: Conflict, Power, and Politics in Guatemala.* Austin: University of Texas Press, 2013.

Caimari, Lila. *Apenas un delincuente. Crimen, castigo y cultura en la Argentina, 1880–1955.* Buenos Aires: Siglo XXI, 2004.

———. *Mientras la ciudad duerme. Pistoleros, policías y periodistas en Buenos Aires, 1920–1945.* Buenos Aires: Siglo XXI, 2012.

———. "Remembering Freedom: Life as Seen from the Prison Cell." In *Crime and Punishment in Latin America: Law and Society since Late Colonial Times,* edited by Ricardo D. Salvatore, Carlos Aguirre, and Gilbert M. Joseph, 391–414. Durham, NC: Duke University Press, 2001.

Caldeira, Teresa Pires Do Rio. *City of Walls: Crime, Segregation, and Citizenship in São Paulo.* Berkeley: University of California Press, 2001.

Caldeira, Teresa Pires Do Rio, and James Holston, "Democracy and Violence in Brazil." *Comparative Studies in Society and History* 41, no. 4 (1999): 691–729.

Call, Tristan P., John P. Hawkins, James H. McDonald, and Walter Randolph Adams. "'There Is No Respect Now': Youth Power in Nahualá." In *Crisis of Governance in Maya Guatemala: Indigenous Responses to a Failing State,* edited by John P. Hawkins, James H. McDonald, and Walter Randolph Adams, 218–42. Norman: University of Oklahoma Press, 2013.

Campbell, Howard. "Narco-Propaganda in the Mexican Drug War: An Anthropological Perspective." *Latin American Perspectives* 41, no. 2 (2014): 60–77.

Cancio Meliá, Manuel, and Carlos Gómez-Jara Díez. *Derecho penal del enemigo: el discurso penal de la exclusión.* Madrid: Edisofer, 2006.

Cano, Ignacio, and Thais Duarte. *No Sapatinho: A Evolução das Milícias no Rio de Janeiro [2008–2011].* Rio de Janeiro: Laboratório de Análise da Violência (LAV-UERJ) and Fundação Heinrich Böll, 2012.

Carey, David Jr. "Drunks and Dictators: Inebriation's Gendered, Ethnic, and Class Components in Guatemala, 1898–1944." In *Alcohol in Latin America: A Social and Cultural History,* edited by Gretchen Pierce and Áurea Toxqui, 131–57. Tucson: University of Arizona Press, 2014.

———. *I Ask for Justice: Maya Women, Dictators, and Crime in Guatemala, 1898–1944.* Austin: University of Texas Press, 2013.

———. *Our Elders Teach Us: Maya-Kaqchikel Historical Perspectives. Xkib'ij kan qate' qatata'.* Tuscaloosa: University of Alabama Press, 2001.

Carey, David Jr., and M. Gabriela Torres. "Precursors to Femicide: Guatemalan Women in a Vortex of Violence." *Latin American Research Review* 45, no. 3 (2010): 142–64.

Carrigan, William D., and Christopher Waldrep, eds. *Swift to Wrath: Lynching in Global Historical Perspective.* Charlottesville and London: University of Virginia Press, 2013.

Centeno, Miguel Angel. "Centre Did Not Hold: War in Latin America and the Monopolisation of Violence." In *Studies on the Formation of the Nation-State in Latin America*, edited by James Dunkerley, 54–76. London: Institute of Latin American Studies, 2002.

Chevigny, Paul G. "Police Deadly Force as Social Control: Jamaica, Argentina, and Brazil." *Criminal Law Forum* 1, no. 3 (1990): 389–425.

Christiansen, Tanja. *Disobedience, Slander, Seduction, and Assault: Women and Men in Cajamarca, Peru, 1862–1900*. Austin: University of Texas Press 2004.

Clarke, Colin. "Politics, Violence and Drugs in Kingston, Jamaica." *Bulletin of Latin American Research* 25, no. 3 (2006): 420–40.

Cockcroft, Tom. *Police Culture: Themes and Concepts*. New York: Routledge, 2013.

Cohen, Mark, and Mauricio Rubio. "Violence and Crime in Latin America." Paper prepared for the Consulta de San José and presented at the 2007 Copenhagen Consensus Conference. www.copenhagenconsensus.com/publication/copenhagen-consensus-latin-america-violence-and-crime. Accessed December 16, 2014.

Comaroff, Jean, and John Comaroff. "Criminal Obsessions, after Foucault: Postcoloniality, Policing, and the Metaphysics of Disorder." *Critical Inquiry* 30, no. 4 (2004): 800–824.

Comisión para el Esclarecimiento Histórico (CEH). *Guatemala, memoria del silencio*. 12 vols. Guatemala City: UNOPS, 1999.

Cote Barco, Gustavo. *Derecho penal de enemigo en La Violencia (1948–1966)*. Bogotá: Pontificia Universidad Javeriana, 2010.

Cruz, José Miguel. "Criminal Violence and Democracy in Central America: The Survival of the Violent State." *Latin American Politics and Society* 53, no. 4 (2011): 1–33.

Da Costa, Emília Viotti. *The Brazilian Empire: Myths and Histories*. Chicago: University of Chicago Press, 1985.

Dammert, Lucía. *Fear and Crime in Latin America: Redefining State-Society Relations*. New York: Routledge, 2012.

———. ed. *Seguridad ciudadana: experiencias y desafíos*. Valparaíso, Chile: Municipalidad de Valparaíso, 2004.

Dary, Claudia. *Entre el hogar y la vega: estudio sobre la participación femenina en la agricultura de El Progreso*. Guatemala City: FLACSO, 1994.

Davis, Diane E. "Irregular Armed Forces, Shifting Patterns of Commitment, and Fragmented Sovereignty in the Developing World." *Theory and Society* 39, no. 3 (2010): 397–413.

———. "Policing and Regime Transition: From Postauthoritarianism to Populism to Neoliberalism." In *Violence, Coercion, and State-Making in Twentieth-*

Century Mexico: The Other Half of the Centaur, edited by Wil G. Pansters, 68–90. Stanford, CA: Stanford University Press, 2012.

———. "The Political and Economic Origins of Violence and Insecurity in Contemporary Latin America: Past Trajectories and Future Prospects. In *Violent Democracies in Latin America,* edited by Enrique Desmond Arias and Daniel Goldstein, 35–62. Durham, NC: Duke University Press, 2010.

———. "Undermining the Rule of Law: Democratization and the Dark Side of Police Reform in Mexico." *Latin American Politics and Society* 48, no. 1 (2006): 55–86.

Davis, Diane E., and Graham Denyer Willis. "Anticrime Movements in Latin America." In *The Wiley-Blackwell Encyclopedia of Social and Political Movements,* edited by David A. Snow, Donatella della Porta, Bert Klandermans, and Doug McAdam. Hoboken, NJ: Wiley-Blackwell, 2013.

Davis, Diane E., and Anthony Pereira. *Irregular Armed Forces and Their Role in Politics and State Formation.* Cambridge: Cambridge University Press, 2004.

Del Olmo, Rosa. *América Latina y su criminología.* Mexico City: Siglo XXI, 1981.

Denyer Willis, Graham. *The Killing Consensus: Police, Organized Crime, and the Regulation of Life and Death in Urban Brazil.* Los Angeles and Berkeley: University of California Press, 2015.

Desrosieres, Alain. *The Politics of Large Numbers: A History of Statistical Reasoning.* Cambridge, MA: Harvard University Press, 1998.

Durán-Martínez, Angélica. "Criminals, Cops, and Politicians: Dynamics of Drug Violence in Colombia and Mexico." PhD diss., Brown University, 2013.

Elias, Norbert. *El proceso de la civilización: investigaciones sociogenéticas y psicogenéticas.* Mexico City: Fondo de Cultura Económica, 2009.

Evans, Ivan. *Cultures of Violence: Racial Violence and the Origins of Segregation in South Africa and the American South.* Manchester, UK: Manchester University Press, 2011.

Evidence and Lessons from Latin America (ELLA). "Building Legal Frameworks to Address Femicide in Latin America." Policy brief, 2014. http://fundar.org .mx/mexico/pdf/Brief-BuildingLegalFrameworkstoAddressFemicide.pdf. Accessed January 13, 2015.

Fallaw, Ben. *Religion and State Formation in Postrevolutionary Mexico.* Durham, NC: Duke University Press, 2013.

FASE-Educação e Solidariedade. "Dilemas e Desafios para a Cidadania na Baixada Fluminense." In *Impunidade na Baixada Fluminense,* September 2005, Observatório de Segurança Pública. www.observatoriodeseguranca .org/. Accessed November 18, 2014.

Fellowship of Reconciliation and Colombia-Europe-US. Human Rights Observatory. "The Rise and Fall of 'False Positive' Killings in Colombia." 2014.

http://forusa.org/sites/default/files/uploads/false-positives-2014-colom-bia-report.pdf. Accessed January 6, 2015.

Figueroa, Mark, and Amanda Sives, "Homogeneous Voting, Electoral Manipu-lation, and the 'Garrison' Process in Post-Independence Jamaica." *Common-wealth and Caribbean Politics* 40, no. 1 (2002): 81–108.

Fischer, Brodwyn. *A Poverty of Rights: Citizenship and Inequality in Twenti-eth-Century Rio de Janeiro*. Stanford, CA: Stanford University Press, 2008.

Florentino, Manolo Garcia, *Em costas negras: Uma história do tráfico atlântico de escravos entre a África e o Rio de Janeiro (séculos XVIII e XIX)*. Rio de Janeiro: Arquivo Nacional, 1995.

Fornaro, Carlo de. *Díaz, Czar of Mexico: An Arraignment by Carlos de Fornaro: With an Open Letter to Theodore Roosevelt*. 2nd ed. New York: Carlo de Forn-aro, 1909.

Foucault, Michel. *Discipline and Punish: The Birth of the Prison*. 2nd ed. Lon-don: Penguin, 1991; New York: Vintage Books, 1995.

———. *The History of Sexuality*. 3 vols. Translated by Robert Hurley. New York: Vintage Books, 1988–90.

———. "'Omnes et singulatim': vers une critique de la raison politique." In *Dits et écrits II, 1976–1988*, 953–80. Paris: Quarto Gallimard, 2001.

França, R. Limongi, ed., *Enciclopédia Saraiva do Direito*. São Paulo: Saraiva, 1977.

Frederic, Sabina. "Oficio policial y usos de la fuerza pública: aproximaciones al estudio de la policía de la Provincia de Buenos Aires." In *Un estado con rostro humano. Funcionarios e instituciones estatales en la Argentina desde 1880*, edited by Ernesto Bohoslavsky and Germán Soprano, 281–307. Buenos Aires: Prometeo, 2010.

Fregoso, Rosa-Linda, and Cynthia Bejarano, eds. *Terrorizing Women: Femicide in the Americas*. Durham, NC: Duke University Press, 2010.

Fruhling, Hugo. *Violencia y policía en América Latina*. Quito: FLACSO, 2009.

Fuentes Díaz, Antonio. *Linchamientos, fragmentación y respuesta en el México neoliberal*. Puebla, Mexico: Benemérita Universidad Autónoma de Puebla, 2006.

Fujii, Lee Ann. "The Puzzle of Extra-Lethal Violence." Paper presented at the Institute for Global and International Studies, George Washington Univer-sity, April 12, 2012.

———. "The Puzzle of Extra-Lethal Violence." *Perspectives on Politics* 11, no. 2 (2013): 410–26.

Gambetta, Diego. *Codes of the Underworld: How Criminals Communicate*. Princeton, NJ: Princeton University Press, 2008.

Gandin, Greg, and Gilbert M. Joseph, eds. *A Century of Revolution: Insurgent and Counterinsurgent Violence during Latin America's Long Cold War*. Durham, NC: Duke University Press, 2010.

Garay Salamanca, Luis Jorge, and Eduardo Salcedo-Albarán, eds. *Narcotráfico, corrupción y estados: cómo las redes ilícitas han reconfigurado las instituciones en Colombia, Guatemala y México.* Mexico City: Debate, 2012.

García Ferrari, Mercedes. *Ladrones conocidos/sospechosos reservados. Identificación policial en Buenos Aires, 1880–1905.* Buenos Aires: Prometeo, 2010.

Garland, David. *The Culture of Control: Crime and Social Order in Contemporary Society.* Chicago: University of Chicago Press, 2001.

———. "Of Crimes and Criminals: The Development of Criminology in Britain." In *The Oxford Handbook of Criminology,* edited by Mike Maguire, Rod Morgan, and Robert Reiner, 17–68. New York: Clarendon Press, 1994.

———. "Penal Excess and Surplus Meaning: Public Torture Lynchings in Twentieth-Century America." *Law and Society Review* 39, no. 4 (2005): 793–833.

Garrard-Burnett, Virginia. "Indians Are Drunks, Drunks Are Indians: Alcohol and Indigenismo in Guatemala, 1890–1940." *Bulletin of Latin American Research* 19, no. 3 (2000): 341–56.

———. *Terror in the Land of the Holy Spirit: Guatemala under General Efraín Ríos Montt, 1982–1983.* New York: Oxford University Press, 2010.

Gatti, Gabriel. *Surviving Forced Disappearance in Argentina and Uruguay: Identity and Meaning.* Basingstoke, UK: Palgrave Macmillan, 2014.

Gazit, Nir. "Social Agency, Spatial Practices, and Power: The Micro-foundations of Fragmented Sovereignty in the Occupied Territories." *International Journal of Politics, Culture, and Society* 22 (March 2009): 83–103.

Ghassem-Fachandi, Parvis. *Pogrom in Gujarat: Hindu Nationalism and Anti-Muslim Violence in India.* Princeton, NJ: Princeton University Press, 2012.

Gillingham, Paul, and Benjamin T. Smith, eds. *Dictablanda: Politics, Work, and Culture in Mexico, 1938–1968.* Durham, NC: Duke University Press, 2014.

Glebbeek, Marie-Louise. "Police Reform and the Peace Process in Guatemala: The Fifth Promotion of the National Civil Police." *Bulletin of Latin American Research* 20 (2001): 431–53. DOI: 10.1111/1470-9856.00024.

Gledhill, John. "Violence and Reconstitution in Indigenous Communities." In *Violence, Coercion, and State-Making in Twentieth-Century Mexico: The Other Half of the Centaur,* edited by Wil G. Pansters. Stanford, CA: Stanford University Press, 2012.

Godio, Julio, *La semana trágica de enero 1919.* Buenos Aires, Hyspamérica, 1985.

Goldstein, Daniel M. *Outlawed: Between Security and Rights in a Bolivian City.* Durham, NC: Duke University Press, 2012.

———. *The Spectacular City: Violence and Performance in Urban Bolivia.* Durham, NC: Duke University Press, 2004.

González Mello, Renato, and Ana Laura Cué. "El asesinato de Arnulfo Arroyo." In *Posada y la prensa ilustrada: signos de modernización y resistencias,* 103–19. Mexico City: Instituto Nacional de Bellas Artes–Museo Nacional de Arte, 1996.

González Undurraga, Carolina. "Entre 'sodomitas' y 'hombres dignos, trabajadores y honrados.' Masculinidades y sexualidades en causas criminales por sodomía (Chile a fines del siglo XIX)," MA thesis, Universidad de Chile, 2004.

———. "La sexualidad como representación y las representaciones de la sexualidad: la construcción del sodomita en Chile, 1880–1910." In *Del nuevo al viejo mundo: mentalidades y representaciones desde América*, edited by Alejandra Araya Espinoza, Azun Candina Polomer, and Celia Cussen, 184–99. Santiago, Chile: Fondo de Publicaciones Americanistas–Facultad de Filosofía y Humanidades de la Universidad de Chile, 2007.

Goulart, Henrique Rodrigues de Andrade, and Leandro Pereira Gonçalves. "O Regime de Extermínio: A Concretização da Violência Ilegal enquanto Ferrementa Político no Brasil Pós-Golpe em 1964." *CES Revista* 25 (2011): 159–72. www.cesjf.br/revistas/cesrevista/edicoes/2011/09_HISTORIA_ORegime .pdf.

Gramajo Morales, Héctor Alejandro. *De la guerra a la guerra: la difícil transición política en Guatemala*. Guatemala City: Fondo de Cultura Editorial, 1995.

Grandin, Greg. *The Blood of Guatemala: A History of Race and Nation*. Durham, NC: Duke University Press, 2000.

Grandin, Greg, and Gilbert Joseph, eds. *A Century of Revolution: Insurgent and Counterinsurgent Violence during Latin America's Long Cold War*. Durham, NC: Duke University Press, 2010.

Gray, Obika. *Demeaned but Empowered: The Social Power of the Urban Poor in Jamaica*. Kingston: University of the West Indies Press, 2004.

Green, James N. *Beyond Carnival: Male Homosexuality in Twentieth-Century Brazil*. Chicago: University of Chicago Press, 1999.

Green, Linda. *Fear as a Way of Life: Mayan Widows in Rural Guatemala*. New York: Columbia University Press, 1999.

Green, W. John. *Gaitanismo, Left Liberalism, and Popular Mobilization in Colombia*. Gainesville: University Press of Florida, 2003.

Grieb, Kenneth. "El gobierno de Jorge Ubico." In *Historia general de Guatemala*, edited by Jorge Luján Muñoz. Vol. 5: *Época contemporánea: 1898–1944*, edited by J. Daniel Contreras R., 43–60. Guatemala City: Asociación de Amigos del País, Fundación para la Cultura y el Desarrollo, 1996.

Guerra, Elisa Speckman. "'I Was a Man of Pleasure, I Can't Deny It': Histories of José de Jesús Negrete, aka 'The Tiger of Santa Julia.'" In *True Stories of Crime in Modern Mexico*, edited by Robert Buffington and Pablo Piccato, 57–105. Albuquerque: University of New Mexico Press, 2009.

Guerrero, Julio. *La génesis del crimen en México: estudio de psiquiatría social*. Mexico City: Porrúa, 1977.

Gunst, Laurie. *Born Fi' Dead: A Journey through the Jamaican Posse Underworld*. New York: Henry Holt and Co., 1996.

Gutiérrez, Marta Estela, and Paul Hans Kobrak. *Los linchamientos pos conflicto y violencia colectiva en Huehuetenango, Guatemala*. Huehuetenango: CEDFOG, 2001.

Guy, Donna J. *Sex and Danger in Buenos Aires: Prostitution, Family, and Nation in Argentina*. Lincoln: University of Nebraska Press, 1991.

Guzmán, Martín Luis. "El águila y la serpiente." In *Obras completas*, 1: 329–38 (Mexico City: Fondo de Cultura Económica, 1984).

Hagedorn, John M. "The Global Impact of Gangs." *Journal of Contemporary Criminal Justice* 21 (2005): 153–69.

Handy, Jim. "Chicken Thieves, Witches, and Judges: Vigilante Justice and Customary Law in Guatemala." *Journal of Latin American Studies* 36 (2004).

Harmer, Tanya. *Allende's Chile and the Inter-American Cold War*. Chapel Hill: University of North Carolina Press, 2011.

Harriott, Anthony. *Organized Crime and Politics in Jamaica: Breaking the Nexus*. Kingston: University of the West Indies Press, 2008.

———. *Police and Crime Control in Jamaica: Problems Reforming Ex-Colonial Constabularies*. Kingston: University of West Indies Press, 2000.

Henderson, James D. *When Colombia Bled: A History of the Violence in Tolima*. Tuscaloosa: University of Alabama Press, 1985.

Hinton, Mercedes, and Timothy Newburn. *Policing Developing Democracies*. New York: Routledge, 2009.

Hirschman, Albert O. *Exit, Voice, and Loyalty Responses to Decline in Firms, Organizations, and States*. Cambridge, MA: Harvard University Press, 1970.

Hobsbawm, Eric J. *Bandits*. New York: Delacorte Press, 1969.

———. *Primitive Rebels: Studies in Archaic Forms of Social Movement in the Nineteenth and Twentieth Centuries*. New York: W.W. Norton, 1965.

Hoffman, Bruce, and Gordon H. McCormick. "Terrorism, Signaling, and Suicide Attack." *Studies in Conflict and Terrorism* 27, no. 4 (2004): 243–81.

Holloway, Thomas. *Policing Rio de Janeiro: Repression and Resistance in a Nineteenth-Century City*. Stanford, CA: Stanford University Press, 1993.

Horta Duarte, Regina. *Noites circenses: Espetáculos de circo e teatro em Minas Gerais no século XIX*. Campinas: Editora da Unicamp, 1995.

Huggins, Martha K. *Vigilantism and the State in Modern Latin America: Essays on Extralegal Violence*. New York: Praeger, 1991.

Human Rights Watch, "Informe mundial, 2014: Mexico." http://www.hrw.org/es/world-report/2014/country-chapters/121995. Accessed March 25, 2014.

Impunity. Directed by Juan José Lozano and Hollman Morris. Switzerland: Arte/Dolce Vita Films/Intermezzo Films S.A./Radio Télévision Suisse (RTS), 2010. DVD.

Instituto Popular de Capacitación. *Guerra, paz y derechos humanos en Antioquia*. Medellín: IPC, 1998.

Isla, Alejandro. "La calle, la cárcel y otras rutinas de los ladrones. Tradición y cambio en el mundo del delito." In *Seguridad ciudadana: experiencias y desafíos*, ed. Lucía Dammert, 59–101. Valparaíso, Chile: Municipalidad de Valparaíso, 2004.

Isla, Carlos. *El mejor caso de Valente Quintana. Los "Corta Mechas."* Mexico City: Fontamara, 2004.

Jackson, Robert. *Quasi-States: Sovereignty, International Relations, and the Third World*. Cambridge: Cambridge University Press, 1990.

Jakobs, Günther. *Derecho penal del enemigo*. Madrid: Civitas, 2003.

Jay, Martin. *Refractions of Violence*. New York: Routledge, 2003.

Johnson, Lyman L., ed. *The Problem of Order in Changing Societies: Essays in Crime and Policing in Argentina and Uruguay, 1750–1919*. Albuquerque: University of New Mexico Press, 1990.

Joseph, Gilbert M. "On the Trail of Latin American Bandits: A Reexamination of Peasant Resistance." *Latin American Research Review* 25, no. 3 (1990): 7–53.

Joseph, Gilbert M., and Daniel Nugent, eds. *Everyday Forms of State Formation: Revolution and the Negotiation of Rule in Modern Mexico*. Durham, NC: Duke University Press, 1994.

Joseph, Gilbert M., and Daniela Spenser, eds. *In from the Cold: Latin America's New Encounter with the Cold War*. Durham, NC: Duke University Press, 2008.

Kalyvas, Stathis N. *The Logic of Violence in Civil War*. New York: Cambridge University Press, 2006.

———. "The Paradox of Terrorism in Civil War." *Journal of Ethics* 8 (2004): 101–10. DOI: 10.1023/B:JOET.0000012254.69088.41.

Karasch, Mary. *Slave Life in Rio, 1808–1850*. Princeton, NJ: Princeton University Press, 1987.

Kenney, Michael. *From Pablo to Osama: Trafficking and Terrorist Networks, Government Bureaucracies, and Competitive Adaptation*. University Park: Pennsylvania State University, 2007.

Kessler, Gabriel. *El sentimiento de inseguridad. Sociología del temor al delito*. Buenos Aires: Siglo XXI, 2009.

Kilcullen, David. *Out of the Mountains: The Coming Age of the Urban Guerrilla*. New York: Oxford University Press, 2013.

Kleiman, Mark. "Surgical Strikes in the Drug Wars: Smarter Policies for Both Sides of the Border." *Foreign Policy* 90, no. 5 (2011): 89–101.

Knight, Alan. "Habitus and Homicide: Political Culture in Revolutionary Mexico." In *Citizens of the Pyramid: Essays on Mexican Political Culture*, edited by Wil G. Pansters, 107–29. Amsterdam: Thela, 1997.

———. "Narco-Violence and the State in Modern Mexico." In *Violence, Coercion, and State-Making in Twentieth-Century Mexico: The Other Half of the Centaur*, edited by Wil G. Pansters, 115–34. Stanford, CA: Stanford University Press, 2012.

Koonings, Kees, and Dirk Kruijt, eds. *Armed Actors: Organised Violence and State Failure in Latin America*. London: Zed Books, 2004.

———. *Fractured Cities: Social Exclusion, Urban Violence, and Contested Spaces in Latin America*. London: Zed Books, 2007.

———. *Societies of Fear. The Legacy of Civil War, Violence, and Terror in Latin America*. New York: Zed Books, 1999.

Krause, Krystin. "Supporting the Iron Fist: Crime News, Public Opinion, and Authoritarian Crime Control in Guatemala." *Latin American Politics and Society* 56, no. 1 (2014): 98–119. DOI: 10.1111/j.1548-2456.2014.00224.x.

Krupa, Christopher. "Histories in Red: Ways of Seeing Lynching in Ecuador." *American Ethnologist* 36, no. 1 (2009): 20–39.

———. "State by Proxy: Privatized Government in the Andes." *Comparative Studies in Society and History* 52, no. 2 (2010): 319–50.

Kydd, Andrew, and Barbara Walter. "The Strategies of Terrorism." *International Security* 31, no. 1 (2006): 49–80.

La France, David. *La revolución mexicana en el estado de Puebla, 1910–1935*. Puebla, Mexico: Ediciones de Educación y Cultura, 2010.

Lara, Sílvia Hunold. *Campos de violência: Escravos e senhores na Capitania do Rio de Janeiro, 1750–1808*. Rio de Janeiro: Paz e Terra, 1988.

———. "Customs and Costumes: Carlos Julião and the Image of Black Slaves in Late Eighteenth-Century Brazil." *Slavery and Abolition: A Journal of Slave and Post-Slave Studies* 23, no. 2 (2002): 123–46.

Larson, Brooke. *Trials of Nation Making: Liberalism, Race, and Ethnicity in the Andes, 1810–1910*. Cambridge: Cambridge University Press, 2004.

Lauderdale Graham, Sandra. "Making the Private Public: A Brazilian Perspective." *Journal of Women's History* 15, no. 1 (2003): 28–42.

Lerner, Jesse. *El impacto de la modernidad: fotografía criminalística en la ciudad de México*. Mexico City: Turner-CNCA, INAH–Editorial Océano, 2007.

Lessing, Benjamin. "The Logic of Violence in Criminal War: Cartel-State Conflict in Mexico, Colombia, and Brazil." PhD diss., University of California, Berkeley, 2012.

Levenson, Deborah. *Adiós Niño: The Gangs of Guatemala City and the Politics of Death*. Durham, NC: Duke University Press, 2013.

Little, Walter E. "A Visual Political Economy of Maya Representations in Guatemala, 1931–1944." *Ethnohistory* 55, no. 4 (2008): 633–63.

Litzinger, Ralph A. "Contested Sovereignties and the Critical Ecosystem Partnership Fund." *PoLAR: Political and Legal Anthropology Review* 29, no. 1 (2006): 66–87.

Lomnitz, Claudio. *Death and the Idea of Mexico*. New York: Zone Books, 2005.

———. "Mexico's First Lynching: Sovereignty, Criminality, Moral Panic." *Critical Historical Studies* 1, no. 1 (2014): 85–123.

Lucchi, Elena. "Humanitarian Interventions in Situations of Urban Violence." *ALNAP Lessons Paper*. London: ALNAP/ODI, 2013.

Mallon, Florencia E. *Peasant and Nation: The Making of Postcolonial Mexico and Peru*. Berkeley: University of California Press, 1995.

Marchak, Patricia. *God's Assassins: State Terrorism in Argentina in the 1970s*. Montreal: McGill-Queen's University Press, 1999.

Márquez, Jesús. "Oposición contrarrevolucionaria de derecha en Puebla, 1932–1940." In *Religión, política y sociedad: el sinarquismo y la iglesia en México (nueve ensayos)*, edited by Rubén Aguilar V. and Guillermo Zermeño P., 31–54. Mexico City: Universidad Iberoamericana, Departamento de Historia, 1992.

Marroquín Rojas, Clemente. *Crónicas de la Constituyente del 1945*. Guatemala City: Tipografía Nacional, 1970.

McCormick, Gordon, and Frank Giordano. "Things Come Together: Symbolic Violence and Guerrilla Mobilization." *Third World Quarterly* 28, no. 2 (2007): 295–320.

McCreery, David. *Rural Guatemala, 1760–1940*. Stanford, CA: Stanford University Press, 1994.

McIlwaine, Cathy, and Caroline Moser. "Violence and Social Capital in Urban Poor Communities." *Journal of International Development* 13, no. 7 (2001): 965–84.

Meade, Everard Kidder. "Anatomies of Justice and Chaos: Capital Punishment and the Public in Mexico, 1917–1945." PhD diss., University of Chicago, 2005.

———. "La ley fuga y la tribuna improvisada: Extrajudicial Execution and Public Opinion in Mexico City, 1929–1940." Paper presented at the Kayden Colloquium on Crime and Punishment in Latin America: Practices and Representations, University of Colorado, Boulder, October 7–8, 2011.

Medin, Tzvi. *El sexenio alemanista: ideología y praxis política de Miguel Alemán*. Mexico City: Ediciones Era, 1990.

Medina, Luis. *Del cardenismo al avilacamachismo*. *Historia de la revolución mexicana*. Vol. 18. Mexico City: Colegio de México, 1978.

Mello Barreto Filho, João Paulo de, and Hermeto Lima. *História da polícia do Rio de Janeiro: Aspectos da cidade e da vida carioca*. Rio de Janeiro: Editora A Noite, 1939.

Méndez, Juan, Guillermo O'Donnell, and Paulo Sergio Pinheiro, eds. *The (Un) Rule of Law and the Underprivileged in Latin America*. Notre Dame, IN: University of Notre Dame Press, 1999.

Metz, Brent E. *Chorti-Maya Survival in Eastern Guatemala: Indigeneity in Transition*. Albuquerque: University of New Mexico Press, 2006.

Metz, Brent, E. Lorenzo Mariano, and Julián López García. "The Violence after 'La Violencia' in the Ch'orti' Region of Eastern Guatemala." *Journal of Latin American and Caribbean Anthropology* 15 (2010): 16–41. DOI: 10.1111/j.1935-4940.2010.01061.x

Meyer, Jean. "An Idea of Mexico: Catholics in the Revolution." In *The Eagle and the Virgin: Nation and Cultural Revolution in Mexico, 1910–1940*, edited by Mary Kay Vaughan and Stephen E. Lewis, 281–96. London: Duke University Press, 2006.

Misión de Verificación de las Naciones Unidas en Guatemala (MINUGUA). *Los linchamientos: un flagelo contra la dignidad humana.* Guatemala City: MINUGUA, 2000.

———. *Los linchamientos: un flagelo que persiste.* Guatemala City: MINUGUA, 2002.

Moheno, Querido. *Procesos Célebres. Rubin: discurso en defensa de la acusada.* Mexico City: Botas, 1925.

Monjardet, Dominique. *Ce que fait la police. Sociologie de la force publique.* Paris: La Découverte, 1996.

Monsiváis, Carlos. *Los mil y un velorios: crónica de la nota roja en México.* 2nd ed. Mexico City: Asociación Nacional del Libro, 2009.

Moser, Caroline. "Urban Violence and Insecurity: An Introductory Roadmap." *Environment and Urbanization* 16, no. 2 (2004): 1–16.

Moser, Caroline, and Cathy McIlwaine. *Encounters with Violence in Latin America: Urban Poor Perceptions from Colombia and Guatemala.* New York: Routledge, 2004.

———. "New Frontiers in 21st-Century Urban Conflict and Violence." *Environment and Urbanization* 26, no. 2 (2014): 331–44.

Müller, Markus-Mikael, "Assessing an Ambivalent Relationship: Policing and the Urban Poor in Mexico City." *Journal of Latin American Studies* 44, no. 2 (2012): 319–45.

Munroe, Trevor. *Voice, Participation, and Governance in a Changing Environment: The Case of Jamaica.* Kingston: University of the West Indies, 2000.

Navarro, Aaron W. *Political Intelligence and the Creation of Modern Mexico, 1938–1954.* University Park: Pennsylvania State University Press, 2010.

Nelson, Diane. *Reckoning: The Ends of War in Guatemala.* Durham, NC: Duke University Press, 2009.

Nesvig, Martin A. "The Complicated Terrain of Latin American Homosexuality." *Hispanic American Historical Review* 81, nos. 3–4 (2001): 689–729.

Núñez Cetina, Saydi. "El Caso de el 'Tigre del Pedregal': homicidio y justicia en la ciudad de México durante la posrevolución." In *Crimen y justicia en la historia de México: nuevas miradas,* edited by Elisa Speckman Guerra and

Salvador Cárdenas Gutiérrez, 315–53. Mexico City: Suprema Corte de Justicia de la Nación, 2011.

O'Donnell, Guillermo. "On the State, Democratization, and Some Conceptual Problems: A Latin American View with Glances at Some Postcommunist Countries." *World Development* 21, no. 8 (1993): 1355–69.

Oliver-Smith, Anthony. "The Pishtaco: Institutionalized Fear in Highland Peru." *Journal of American Folklore* 82, no. 326 (1969): 363–68.

Orlove, Benjamin. "The Dead Policemen Speak: Power, Fear, and Narrative in the 1931 Molloccahua Killings (Cusco)." In *Unruly Order: Violence, Power, and Cultural Identity in the High Provinces of Southern Peru*, edited by Deborah Poole, 63–95. Boulder, CO: Westview Press, 1994.

Orozco Abad, Iván, and Alejandro David Aponte Cardona. *Combatientes, rebeldes y terroristas: guerra y derecho en Colombia*. Bogotá: Temis, 1992.

Ortega, José A. "Por tercer año consecutivo, San Pedro Sula es la ciudad más violenta del mundo." Consejo Ciudadano para la Seguridad Pública y la Justicia Penal, January 15, 2014. www.seguridadjusticiaypaz.org.mx/sala-de -prensa/941-por-tercer-ano-consecutivo-san-pedro-sula-es-la-ciudad-mas -violenta-del-mundo. Accessed November 20, 2014.

Osorio, Javier. "Hobbes on Drugs: Understanding Drug Violence in Mexico." PhD diss., University of Notre Dame, 2012.

Padilla, Tanalís. *Rural Resistance in the Land of Zapata: The Jaramillista Movement and the Myth of the Pax Priísta, 1940–1962*. Durham, NC: Duke University Press, 2008.

Pansters, Wil G. *Política y poder en Puebla. Formación y ocaso del cacicazgo avilacamachistas, 1927–1987*. Mexico City: Fondo de Cultura Económica, 1998.

———, ed. *Violence, Coercion, and State-Making in Twentieth-Century Mexico: The Other Half of the Centaur*. Stanford, CA: Stanford University Press, 2012.

Pearce, Jenny. "Bringing Violence Back Home." In *Global Civil Society 2006/7*, edited by Marlies Glasius, Mary Kaldor, and Helmut Anheier, 62–79. London: Sage, 2006.

———. "Perverse State Formation and Securitized Democracy in Latin America." *Democratization* 17, no. 2 (2010): 286–306.

Pécaut, Daniel. *Orden y violencia: Colombia, 1930–1953*. Medellín: Siglo XXI, 1987.

Pellicer de Brody, Olga, and José Luis Reyna. *El afianzamiento de la estabilidad política*. Mexico City: Colegio de México, 1978.

Pensado, Jaime M. *Rebel Mexico: Student Unrest and Authoritarian Political Culture during the Long Sixties*. Stanford, CA: Stanford University Press, 2013.

Perera, Victor. *Unfinished Conquest: The Guatemalan Tragedy*. Berkeley: University of California Press, 1993.

Pettit, Becky, and Bruce Western. "Mass Imprisonment and the Life Course: Race and Class Inequality in U.S. Incarceration." *American Sociological Review* 69 (2004): 151–69.

Pfeifer, Michael. *The Roots of Rough Justice: Origins of American Lynching.* Urbana: University of Illinois Press, 2011.

———. *Rough Justice: Lynching and American Society, 1874–1947.* Urbana: University of Illinois Press, 2004.

Piccato, Pablo. *City of Suspects: Crime in Mexico City, 1900–1931.* Durham, NC: Duke University Press, 2001.

———. "The Girl Who Killed a Senator: Femininity and the Public Sphere in Post-Revolutionary Mexico." In *True Stories of Crime in Modern Mexico,* edited by Robert Buffington and Pablo Piccato, 128–53. Albuquerque: University of New Mexico Press, 2009.

———. "Murders of Nota Roja: Truth and Justice in Mexican Crime News." *Past and Present,* 223, no. 1 (2014): 195–231.

———. "'Such a Strong Need': Sexuality and Violence in Belem Prison." In *Gender, Sexuality, and Power in Latin America since Independence,* edited by William E. French and Katherine Elaine Bliss, 163–86. Lanham, MD: Rowman and Littlefield, 2007.

Piñero, Octavio A. *Los orígenes y la trágica semana de enero de 1919.* Buenos Aires: Bellsolá, 1956.

Pinto V., Julio. *Desgarros y utopías en la pampa salitrera. La consolidación de la identidad obrera en tiempos de la cuestión social (1890–1923).* Santiago, Chile: LOM Ediciones, 2007.

Polit Dueñas, Gabriela, and María Helena Rueda, eds. *Meanings of Violence in Latin America.* New York: Palgrave Macmillan, 2011.

Poole, Deborah. "Introduction: Anthropological Perspectives on Violence and Culture: A View from the Peruvian High Provinces." In *Unruly Order: Violence, Power, and Cultural Identity in the High Provinces of Southern Peru,* ed. Deborah Poole, 1–30. Boulder, CO: Westview Press, 1994.

Presunto culpable. Directed by Roberto Hernández and Geoffrey Smith. Mexico: Abogados con Cámara/Instituto Mexicano de Cinematografía CONACULTA/ Fondo para la producción cinematográfica, 2010. DVD.

Programa de las Naciones Unidas para el Desarrollo (PNUD). *Informe nacional de desarrollo humano: anexo estadístico.* Guatemala City: PNUD, 2005.

———. *La democracia en América Latina: hacia una democracia de ciudadanas y ciudadanos.* Buenos Aires: Aguilar, 2004.

Rangel, Salomón H. *Forjando mi destino: apuntes de mi vida.* Mexico City: EPESSA, 1989.

Rapley, John, "Jamaica: Negotiating Law and Order with the Dons." *NACLA Report on the Americas* 37, no. 2 (2003): 25–29.

Reguillo, Rossana. "De las violencias: caligrafías y gramáticas del horror." *Desacatos* 40 (September–December 2012): 33–46.

———. "Sociabilidad, inseguridad y miedos: una trilogía para pensar la ciudad contemporánea." *Alteridades* (Mexico City: UAM) 18 (2008): 63–74.

Reiner, Robert. *The Politics of the Police.* Oxford: Oxford University Press, 2000.

Rendon, Catherine. "El Gobierno de Manuel Estrada Cabrera." In *Historia general de Guatemala,* edited by Jorge Luján Muñoz. Vol. 5, *Época contemporánea: 1898–1944,* edited by J. Daniel Contreras R., 15–36. Guatemala City: Asociación de Amigos del País, Fundación para la Cultura y el Desarrollo, 1996.

Riches, David. "The Phenomenon of Violence." In *The Anthropology of Violence,* edited by David Riches, 1–28. Oxford: Blackwell, 1986.

Rios, Viridiana. "How Government Structure Encourages Criminal Violence: The Causes of Mexico's Drug War." PhD diss., Harvard University, 2012.

Rodman, Debra. "Forgotten Guatemala: Genocide, Truth, and Denial in Guatemala's Oriente." In *Genocide: Truth, Memory, and Representation,* edited by Alexander Laban Hinton and Kevin Lewis O'Neill, 192–215. Durham, NC: Duke University Press, 2009.

Rodríguez Guillén, Raúl. "Crisis de autoridad y violencia social: los linchamientos en México." *Polis. Investigación y Análisis Sociopolítico y Psicosocial* 8, no. 2 (2012): 43–74.

Roldán, Mary. *Blood and Fire: La Violencia in Antioquia, Colombia, 1946–1953.* Durham, NC: Duke University Press, 2002.

Romariz, José Ramón. *La semana trágica. Antecedentes sociales, económicos y políticos: episodios y relatos históricos de los sucesos sangrientos de enero del año 1919.* Buenos Aires: Hemisferio, 1952.

Rotker, Susana. *Citizens of Fear: Urban Violence in Latin America.* New Brunswick, NJ: Rutgers University Press, 2002.

Ruiz Novoa, Alberto. *Enseñanzas de la campaña de Corea, aplicables a Colombia.* Bogotá: Antares, 1956.

Salamanca, Luis Jorge, and Eduardo Salcedo-Albarán, eds. *Narcotráfico, corrupción y estados: cómo las redes ilícitas han reconfigurado las instituciones en Colombia, Guatemala y México.* Mexico City: Debate, 2012.

Salessi, Jorge. *Médicos, maleantes y maricas: higiene, criminología y homosexualidad de la construcción de la nación argentina, Buenos Aires, 1871–1914.* Rosario, Argentina: B. Viterbo, 1995.

Salvatore, Ricardo D., Carlos Aguirre, and Gilbert M. Joseph, eds. *Crime and Punishment in Latin America: Law and Society since Late Colonial Times.* Durham, NC: Duke University Press, 2001.

Sánchez, Gonzalo, and Donny Meertens. *Bandoleros, gamonales y campesinos: el caso de la violencia en Colombia.* Bogotá: El Áncora, 1983.

Sánchez Cárdenas, Carlos. *Disolución social y seguridad nacional.* Mexico City: Linterna, 1970.

Santamaría, Gema. "Lynching in Twentieth-Century Mexico: Violence, State Formation, and Local Communities in Puebla." PhD diss., New School for Social Research, 2015.

Sartori, Giovanni. "Concept Misformation in Comparative Politics." *American Political Science Review* 64, no. 4 (1970): 1033–53.

Sawyer, Susana. *Crude Chronicles: Indigenous Politics, Multinational Oil, and Neoliberalism in Ecuador.* Durham, NC: Duke University Press, 2004.

Scarry, Elaine. *The Body in Pain: The Making and Unmaking of the World.* New York: Oxford University Press, 1985.

Schedler, Andreas. "The Collapse of Solidarity in Criminal War: Citizen Indifference Towards the Victims of Organized Violence in Mexico." Paper presented at the 110th Annual Meeting of the American Political Science Association, Washington, DC, August 28–31, 2014.

Scheper-Hughes, Nancy, and Philippe Bourgois, eds. *Violence in War and Peace: An Anthology.* Oxford: Blackwell, 2004.

Schirmer, Jennifer. "Enfoque militar de ley y seguridad." In *Las intimidades del proyecto político militar en Guatemala.* Guatemala City: FLACSO, 1999.

———. *The Guatemalan Military Project: A Violence Called Democracy.* Philadelphia: University of Pennsylvania Press, 1998.

Schwartz, Elizabeth. "Getting Away with Murder: Social Cleansing in Colombia and the Role of the United States." *University of Miami Inter-American Law Review* 27, no. 2 (1995–96).

Scott, James C. *Domination and the Arts of Resistance: Hidden Transcripts.* New Haven, CT: Yale University Press, 1990.

———. *Seeing Like a State: How Certain Schemes to Improve the Human Condition Have Failed.* New Haven, CT: Yale University Press, 1998.

Seligson, Mitchell A. "Public Support for Due Process Rights: The Case of Guatemala." *Journal of the Southwest* 45, no. 4 (2003): 557–94.

Seri, Guillermina. *Seguridad: Crime, Police Power, and Democracy in Argentina.* New York: Continuum, 2012.

Shirk, David. *Drug Violence in Mexico: Data and Analysis through 2013.* San Diego, CA: Justice in Mexico Project, 2014.

Shumaker, Walter A., and George Foster Longdorf. *The Cyclopedic Law Dictionary.* Chicago: Callahan and Co., 1922.

Sieder, Rachel. "'Paz, progreso, justicia y honradez': Law and Citizenship in Alta Verapaz during the Regime of Jorge Ubico." *Bulletin of Latin American Research* 19 (2000): 283–302.

Sigal, Peter. "Queer Nahuatl: Sahagún's Faggots and Sodomites, Lesbians and Hermaphrodites." *Ethnohistory* 54, no. 1 (2007): 9–34.

Sierra Ochoa, Gustavo. *La guerrilla de los Llanos Orientales*. Manizales, Colombia: Imprenta Departamental, 1954.

Sives, Amanda. "A Calculated Assault on the Authority of the State: Crime, Politics, and Extradition in Twenty-First-Century Jamaica." *Crime, Law and Social Change* 58, no. 4 (2012): 415–35.

———. "Changing Patrons, from Politician to Drug Don: Clientelism in Downtown Kingston, Jamaica," *Latin America Perspectives* 29, no. 5 (2002): 66–89.

———. *Elections, Violence, and the Democratic Process in Jamaica, 1944–2007*. Kingston: Ian Randle Press, 2010.

Slatta, Richard J., ed. *Bandidos: The Varieties of Latin American Bandits*. Westport, CT: Greenwood Press, 1987.

Slone, Michelle. "Responses to Media Coverage of Terrorism." *Journal of Conflict Resolution* 44, no. 4 (2000): 508–22.

Snodgrass Godoy, Angelina. *Popular Injustice, Violence, Community, and Law in Latin America*. Stanford, CA: Stanford University Press, 2006.

———. "When 'Justice' Is Criminal: Lynchings in Contemporary Latin America." *Theory and Society* 33, no. 6 (2004): 621–51.

Snyder, Richard, and Angélica Durán-Martínez. "Does Illegality Breed Violence? Drug Trafficking and State-Sponsored Protection Rackets." *Crime, Law, and Social Change* 52, no. 3 (2009): 253–73.

Soares, Luiz Carlos. *O "Povo de Cam" na Capital do Brasil: A Escravidão Urbana no Rio de Janeiro do Século XIX*. Rio de Janeiro: Editora FAPERJ-7 Letras, 2007.

Souza Alves, José Claudio. "Relgião, Violência e Poder Político na Baizada Fluiminense (Rio de Janeiro, Brasil)." *Ciencias Sociais y Religião* 6, no. 6 (2004): 153–78.

———. "Violência e Política na Baixada: O Caso dos Grupos de Extermínio." In *Impunidade na Baixada Fluminense*, 26–36. Parceria: CESeC, Fase, Justiça Global, Laboratório de Análises da Violência da UERJ, SOS Queimados e Viva Rio, 2005.

Souza Martins, José. "Lynching—Life by a Thread: Street Justice in Brazil." In *Vigilantism and the State in Modern Latin America: Essays on Extralegal Violence*, edited by Martha K. Huggins. New York: Praeger, 1991.

Spierenburg, Pieter. *The Spectacle of Suffering. Executions and the Evolution of Repression from a Preindustrial Metropolis to the European Experience*. Cambridge: Cambridge University Press, 1984.

Stanley, Ruth. "Conversaciones con policías en Buenos Aires: en busca de la 'cultura policial' como variable explicativa de abusos policiales." In *Estado, violencia y ciudadanía en América Latina*, edited by Ruth Stanley, 77–105. Madrid: Entinema, 2009.

Stephan, Nancy. *"The Hour of Eugenics": Race, Gender, and Nation in Latin America.* Ithaca, NY: Cornell University Press, 1991.

Stevens, Evelyn. "Legality and Extralegality in Mexico." *Journal of Interamerican Studies and World Affairs* 12, no. 1 (1970): 62–75.

Stone, Carl. *Democracy and Clientelism in Jamaica.* New Brunswick, NJ: Transaction Books, 1980.

Téllez Vargas, Eduardo, and José Ramón Garmabella. *¡Reportero de policía!: El Güero Téllez.* Mexico City: Ediciones Océano, 1982.

Testis Fidelis [pseud. Juan Manuel Saldarriaga Betancur]. *El basilisco en acción, o los crímenes del bandolerismo.* Medellín: Olympia, 1953.

Tilly, Charles. *Capital, Coercion, and European States, AD 990–1992.* Cambridge: Basil Blackwell, 1990.

———. "Cities, States, and Trust Networks." In *Contention and Trust in Cities and States,* edited by Michael Hanagan and Chris Tilly, 1–16. New York: Springer ebooks, 2011. www.springer.com/us/book/9789400707559. Accessed November 24, 2015.

———. *The Politics of Collective Violence.* Cambridge: Cambridge University Press, 2003.

Torres, M. Gabriela. "Art and Labor in the Framing of Guatemala's Dead." *Anthropology of Work Review* 35, no. 1 (2014): 14–24.

Torres-Rivas, Edelberto. "Prólogo: la metáfora de una sociedad que se castiga a sí misma." In *Guatemala: causas y orígenes del enfrentamiento armado interno,* edited by Comisión para el Esclarecimiento Histórico. Guatemala City: F and G Editores, 2000.

Tortorici, Zeb. "'Heran todos putos': Sodomitical Subcultures and Disordered Desire in Early Colonial Mexico." *Ethnohistory* 54, no. 1 (2007): 35–67.

Twinam, Ann. *Public Lives, Private Secrets: Gender, Honor, Sexuality, and Illegitimacy in Colonial Spanish America.* Stanford, CA: Stanford University Press, 1999.

Umaña Luna, Eduardo, Orlando Fals Borda, and Germán Guzmán Campos. *La violencia en Colombia. Estudio de un proceso social.* Bogotá: Tercer Mundo, 1963.

Ungar, Mark. *Policing Democracy: Overcoming Obstacles to Citizen Security in Latin America.* Washington, DC: Woodrow Wilson Center Press; Baltimore, MD: Johns Hopkins University Press, 2011.

———. "The Privatization of Citizen Security in Latin America: From Elite Guards to Neighborhood Vigilante." *Social Justice* 34, nos. 3–4 (2007–8).

United Nations Development Program (UNDP). "Regional Human Development Report: Citizen Security with a Human Face, Evidence and Proposals for Latin America." 2013–14. www.undp.org/content/undp/en/home/library

-page/hdr/human-development-report-for-latin-america-2013-2014.html. Accessed January 14, 2015.

United Nations Human Rights Council. *Civil and political rights, including the questions of disappearances and summary executions: Report of the special rapporteur on extrajudicial, summary or arbitrary executions, Philip Alston* (Addendum); Mission to Guatemala, August 21–25, 2006. www .extrajudicialexecutions.org/application/media/A_HRC_4_20_Add_2.pdf. Accessed November 13, 2014.

United Nations Office on Drugs and Crime (UNODC). "Global Study on Homicide, 2013: Trends, Contexts, Data." Vienna: UNODC, 2014. www.unodc.org/ documents/gsh/pdfs/2014_GLOBAL_HOMICIDE_BOOK_web.pdf. Accessed October 15, 2015.

Uribe, María V. "Dismembering and Expelling: Semantics of Political Terror in Colombia." *Public Culture* 16, no. 1 (2004): 79–95.

———. *Matar, rematar y contramatar: las masacres de la violencia en el Tolima, 1948–1964*. Bogotá: Cinep, 1990.

Uribe, María V., and Teófilo Vásquez. *Enterrar y callar: las masacres en Colombia, 1980–1993*. Bogotá: Comité Permanente por la Defensa de los Derechos Humanos, 1995.

Vanderwood, Paul J. *Disorder and Progress: Bandits, Police, and Mexican Development*. Wilmington, DE: Scholarly Resources, 1992.

———. *Juan Soldado: Rapist, Murderer, Martyr, Saint*. Durham, NC: Duke University Press, 2004.

Varese, Federico. *The Russian Mafia: Private Protection in a New Market Economy*. New York: Oxford University Press, 2001.

Vaughan, Mary K. *Cultural Politics in Revolution: Teachers, Peasants, and Schools in Mexico. 1930–1940*. Tucson: University of Arizona Press, 1997.

———. "El papel político del magisterio socialista de México, 1934–1940: un estudio comparativo de los casos de Puebla y Sonora." In *Memoria del XII Simposio de Historia y Antropología*, 175–97. Hermosillo, Mexico: Universidad de Sonora, Departamento de Historia y Antropología, 1988.

Velho, Gilberto, and Marcos Alvito, eds. *Cidadania e Violência*. Rio de Janeiro: Editora FGV, 1996.

Venkatesh, Sudhir Alladi, and Ronald Kassimir. *Youth, Globalization, and the Law*. Stanford, CA: Stanford University Press, 2006.

Verdad Abierta. "La tenebrosa máquina de guerra que dirigió 'Don Berna,'" March 22, 2014. www.verdadabierta.com/imputaciones/5289-la-tenebrosa -maquina-de-guerra-que-dirigio-don-berna. Accessed January 7, 2015.

Verdon, Jean. *Night in the Middle Ages*. Translated by George Holoch. Notre Dame, IN: University of Notre Dame Press, 2002.

Vicuña, Manuel. *La belle époque chilena: alta sociedad y mujeres de elite en el cambio de siglo.* Santiago: Editorial Sudamericana, 2001.

Villarreal Palo, Arturo. "Ministerio público y policía de investigación en México: una reforma incompleta." *Letras Jurídicas* 5 (Fall 2007).

Wacquant, Loïc. "From Slavery to Mass Incarceration: Rethinking the 'Race Question' in the U.S." *New Left Review* 13 (2002): 41–60.

———. *Punishing the Poor: The Neoliberal Government of Social Insecurity.* Durham, NC: Duke University Press, 2009.

Waddington, P. A. J. *Policing Citizens: Authority and Rights.* New York: Routledge, 1999.

Waiselfisz, Jacobo. *Homicídios e Juventude no Brasil.* Brasilia: Secretaria-Geral da Presidência da República, 2013.

———. *Mapa da Violência: Os Jovens do Brasil.* Rio de Janeiro: Editora Garamond, 1998.

Weld, Kirsten. *Paper Cadavers: The Archives of Dictatorship in Guatemala.* Durham, NC: Duke University Press, 2014.

Williams, Phil. "Cooperation among Criminal Organizations." In *Transnational Organized Crime and International Security: Business as Usual?,* edited by Mats Berdal and Monica Serrano, 67–80. Boulder, CO: Lynne Rienner, 2002.

Woodward, Ralph Lee Jr. *Rafael Carrera and the Emergence of the Republic of Guatemala, 1821–1871.* Athens: University of Georgia Press, 1993.

World Health Organization. "Global Status Report on Violence Prevention, 2014." www.who.int/violence_injury_prevention/violence/status_report/2014/en/. Accessed January 6, 2015.

Zechmeister, Elizabeth J., ed. *The Political Culture of Democracy in the Americas, 2014: Democratic Governance across 10 Years of the Americas Barometer.* Washington, DC: USAID, 2014.

Contributors

Robert F. Alegre is a Chilean American historian of Latin America who has a particular interest in the history of gender and sexuality and its intersection with wage and coerced labor. His book *Railroad Radicals in Cold War Mexico: Gender, Class, and Memory* (University of Nebraska Press, 2013) analyzes how a patriarchal culture specific to the railway industry informed everyday life and political organizing during a critical juncture in Mexican politics. He is Associate Professor of History and an affiliated member of the Women's and Gender Studies Program at the University of New England.

Enrique Desmond Arias is Associate Professor of Public Policy in the School of Policy, Government, and International Affairs at George Mason University. He is the author of *Drugs and Democracy in Rio de Janeiro: Trafficking, Social Networks, and Public Security* (University of North Carolina Press, 2006) and is coeditor of *Violent Democracies in Latin America* (Duke University Press, 2010). His writing has appeared in *Comparative Politics, Perspectives on Politics, Journal of Latin American Studies, Policing and Society, Qualitative Sociology, Latin American Politics and Society, Studies in Comparative International Development*, and *Revista de Estudios Socio-Juridicos*.

Lila Caimari is an independent researcher at CONICET and Director of the Post-Graduate Program in History at San Andrés University (Buenos Aires). Her work on issues of criminality has been published in four books, including *Apenas un delincuente. Crimen, castigo y cultura en la Argentina, 1880–1949* (Siglo XXI, 2004); *La ciudad y el crimen. Delito y vida cotidiana en Buenos Aires, 1880–1940* (Sudamericana, 2009); and *Mientras la ciudad duerme. Pistoleros, policías y periodistas en Buenos Aires (1920–1945)* (Siglo XXI, 2012). The author of numerous articles and book chapters about the social and cultural history of Argentina, she is currently researching the history of news in Latin America.

David Carey Jr. is the Doehler Chair in History at Loyola University. He received his PhD in Latin American studies from Tulane University and his BA in political science from the University of Notre Dame. In addition to writing some two dozen peer-reviewed articles and essays and editing two books, he is the author of *I Ask for Justice: Maya Women, Dictators, and Crime in Guatemala, 1898–1944* (University of Texas Press, 2013), which was the co-recipient of the Latin American Studies Association Bryce Wood Book Award; *Engendering Mayan History: Kaqchikel Women as Agents and Conduits of the Past, 1875–1970* (Routledge, 2006); *Ojer taq tzijob'äl kichin ri Kaqchikela' Winaqi'* (A History of the Kaqchikel People) (Q'anilsa Ediciones, 2004); *Our Elders Teach Us: Maya-Kaqchikel Historical Perspectives* (University of Alabama Press, 2001); and the forthcoming *Unlocking the Spoken Archive: A Guide to Oral History in Latin America.*

Amy Chazkel is Associate Professor of History at Queens College and the Graduate Center, City University of New York and Cochair of the *Radical History Review* Editorial Collective. She is the author of *Laws of Chance: Brazil's Clandestine Lottery and the Making of Urban Public Life in Brazil* (Duke University Press, 2011; Brazilian edition by Editora da Unicamp, 2014) and articles on Brazilian sociolegal and urban history and a coeditor of *The Rio Reader: History, Culture, Politics* (Duke University Press, 2015). Her projects in progress include a study of the social, cultural, and legal history of nighttime in nineteenth-century urban Brazil.

Diane E. Davis is the Charles Dyer Norton Professor of Regional Planning and Urbanism at the Harvard University Graduate School of Design. Trained as a historical sociologist, Davis focuses her research on relations between urbanization and national development, politics of urban policy, socio-spatial practice in conflict cities, and transformation of cities of the global south in response to globalization and violence. Her books include *Urban Leviathan: Mexico City in the Twentieth Century* (Temple University Press, 1994); *Discipline and Development: Middle Classes and Prosperity in East Asia and Latin America* (Cambridge University Press, 2004); *Irregular Armed Forces and Their Role in Politics and State Formation* (Cambridge University Press, 2002); and *Cities and Sovereignty: Identity Politics in Urban Spaces* (Indiana University Press, 2011).

Angélica Durán-Martínez is Assistant Professor of Political Science at the University of Massachusetts–Lowell. She received her PhD in political science from Brown University and her MA in Latin American and Caribbean Studies from New York University. Her research on organized crime, violence, and the state in Latin America has received funding from the United States Institute of Peace (USIP), the Social Science Research Council (IDRF-SSRC), and the Open Society Foundation through the Drugs, Security, and Democracy Fellowship. She has published articles in the *Journal of Conflict Resolution*, *Comparative Political Studies*, *Latin American Politics and Society*, the *Journal of Peace Research*, and *Crime, Law, and Social Change*.

Luis Herrán Ávila is a PhD candidate in history and politics at the New School for Social Research. He also holds a BA in Latin American studies from UNAM and an MA in politics from the New School, and is an occasional contributor to the Mexican dailies *El Norte* and *Reforma*. His research focuses on the history of the extreme right and the transnational dimension of Cold War anticommunism in Latin America, particularly in Argentina, Colombia, and Mexico.

Kayyonne Marston is a doctoral candidate in the School of Policy, Government, and International Affairs at George Mason University. Her research focuses on organized crime, governance, and socioeconomic development in Latin America and the Caribbean. She recently received a dissertation fellowship from the Social Science Research Council's Drugs, Security and Democracy Program to conduct research on the dynamics of political-criminal networks in Jamaica. In addition to her research, Marston has worked professionally on security projects in the Caribbean and Central America and on community development programs in fragile and conflict-affected states.

Cecilia Menjívar is Foundation Distinguished Professor in the Sociology Department at Kansas University. Her research on violence has focused on technologies of state terror; political violence; and gender, symbolic, and structural violence in Latin America, especially Central America. She is the author of *Fragmented Ties: Salvadoran Immigrant Networks in America* (University of California Press, 2000) and *Enduring Violence: Ladina Women's Lives in Guatemala* (University of California Press 2011). In addition, she is editor of *Through the Eyes of Women: Gender, Social Networks, Family, and Structural Change in Latin America and the Caribbean* (De Sitter, 2003) and coeditor of *When States Kill: Latin America, the U.S., and Technologies of Terror* (University of Texas Press, 2005).

Daniel Núñez is a sociologist interested in the study of culture and violence in Latin America. He was a Visiting Lecturer during the 2015–16 academic year in the Department of Sociology at the University of Pittsburgh, where he had received his PhD in 2015. His doctoral dissertation is an ethnographic study of lynching and other forms of extralegal violence in postwar Guatemala. Before pursuing his graduate studies in the United States, Núñez worked in Guatemala doing research on political parties, street-gang violence, and conflict resolution mechanisms in Maya Q'eqchi' communities.

Jenny Pearce is Professor of Latin American Politics in Peace Studies at the University of Bradford. She works on violence, participation, agency, and social change in Latin America. Her books include *Promised Land: Peasant Rebellion in Chalatenango* (Latin American Bureau, 1985); *Colombia: Inside the Labyrinth* (Latin American Bureau, 1990); and (with Jude Howell) *Civil Society and Development: A Critical Exploration* (L. Rienner, 2001). She was principal investigator on research into democracy and participation in three cities in Latin America and three in the United Kingdom and was editor of *Participation and Democracy in the Twenty-First Century City* (Palgrave Macmillan, 2010). She has a particular interest in methodologies for researching violence. She is currently conducting a study of elites and violence in Latin America and writing a book on politics and violence.

Pablo Piccato is Professor in the Department of History at Columbia University. His research and teaching focus on modern Mexico, particularly on crime, politics, and culture. His work includes *City of Suspects: Crime in Mexico City, 1900–1931* (Duke University Press, 2001); *Actores, espacios y debates en la historia de la esfera pública en la ciudad de México* (Instituto Mora/IIH-UNAM, 2005, coedited with Cristina Sacristán); *True Stories of Crime in Modern Mexico* (University of New Mexico Press, 2009, coedited with Robert Buffington); and *The Tyranny of Opinion: Honor in the Construction of the Mexican Public Sphere* (Duke University Press, 2010). Among his articles he has published "Murders of Nota Roja: Truth and Justice in Mexican Crime News," in *Past and Present* (2014).

Gema Santamaría is Assistant Professor in the Department of International Studies at the Instituto Tecnológico Autónomo de México. She holds a PhD in History and Sociology from the New School for Social Research and an MA in Gender and Social Policy from the London School of Economics. Her doctoral dissertation, on lynching and vigilante violence in twentieth-century Mexico, was awarded the Charles A. Hale Fellowship in Mexican History by the Latin American Studies Association (LASA) and the Albert Salomon Memorial

Award in Sociology by the New School. Santamaría specializes in violence, crime, and state-building in Latin America. She has been a Chevening Fellow, a Fulbright Scholar, and a Visiting Fellow at the Center for U.S.-Mexican Studies at the University of California, San Diego.

M. Gabriela Torres, Associate Professor of Anthropology at Wheaton College, Massachusetts, is a Guatemalan-born anthropologist specializing in the study of violence and state formation. Her work has been published in numerous journals and edited collections, including *Anthropologica, Anthropology of Work Review, Studies in Social Justice, Journal of Poverty,* and *Latin American Research Review.* Her book, coedited with Kersti Yllö, is entitled *Marital Rape: Consent, Marriage, and Social Change in Global Context* (Oxford University Press, 2016). An American Anthropological Association Leadership Fellow, M. Gabriela Torres has been funded by the Wenner Gren Foundation and the Social Sciences and Humanities Research Council of Canada.

Index

Page references ending in *f* indicate figures,
and those ending in *t* indicate tables.